Tony Eggleton AO CVO was intimately involved in the advent of Australian television; the loss of HMAS *Voyager*; the drowning death of Harold Holt; the hugely successful 1970 Royal Tour; the end of John Gorton's tumultuous prime ministership; the reconfiguration of the British Commonwealth; the dismissal of the Whitlam Government; re-electing the Fraser Government; the Coalition's 'wilderness years'; international humanitarian crisis intervention; commemorating Australian nationhood; and, the nurture of Asia-Pacific democratic institutions.

This biography reveals his private thoughts as press secretary to four Australian prime ministers, Federal Director of the Liberal Party, Secretary-General of CARE International and CEO of the National Council for the Centenary of Federation. It explores the management of public opinion, the design of election strategies and the influence of political journalism on government policy.

A very proper man: the life of Tony Eggleton | Tom Frame

ISBN: 9781922815156

Published in 2022 by Connor Court Publishing Pty Ltd

Connor Court Publishing Pty Ltd
PO Box 7257
Redland Bay QLD 4165

sales@connorcourt.com
www.connorcourtpublishing.com.au

Printed in Australia

Cover and page layout by Graham Lindsay

Cover images: Liberal Party of Australia and Auspic.

Connor Court Publishing

A VERY PROPER MAN

THE LIFE OF TONY EGGLETON

TOM FRAME

2022

In memory of

John 'J R' Nethercote

1 March 1948 – 3 May 2022

Mentor, colleague, friend

CONTENTS

INTRODUCTION

When Tony Eggleton was born there were no hints he would become one of Australia's most astute political operators. He was raised in an English provincial town that was struggling with the lingering depravations of the Great Depression. His middle-class family was without any interest in politics. After a conventional childhood and an unremarkable adolescence shaped by the rise of totalitarianism and the onset of another European war, Tony resolved to become a journalist. Making the most of wider employment opportunities and better remuneration in the antipodes, he came to Australia and made it his home.

It was not until his 30th birthday that Tony was drawn into political life. Until then he had applied for jobs that attracted his professional interest and fulfilled his personal ambition. He was not a man-on-a-mission nor driven to transform human society. He was a small cog in the large machinery of national government. It was not long before federal parliamentarians noticed his unique skills. He had an ability to discern the popular mood and an aptitude for selling public policy. After two decades on the political stage, Tony became secretary-general of an international aid organisation and then chief executive of a Commonwealth agency. In 'retirement', he contributed to public and private organisations dedicated to good corporate governance and social progress. His full and productive working life offers a series of lessons worthy of close consideration.

I met Tony in February 1989. I was then undertaking part-time research for my doctoral thesis on the loss of the destroyer HMAS *Voyager* after a collision with the aircraft carrier HMAS *Melbourne* on 10 February 1964. It was a terrible tragedy with enduring human consequences. I was a young naval officer working as speechwriter to the Chief of Naval Staff and Tony was the long-standing Federal Director of the Liberal Party. We met at the Secretariat's headquarters, Menzies House, in the Canberra suburb of Barton and established an immediate rapport. I was particularly interested in how the Navy conducted its relations with the parliament, the press and the public after the sinking of *Voyager*, and how the Naval Staff managed the damaging fallout from the first of two royal commissions into the causes of the collision. Tony's answers to my questions were clear and concise. He responded with facts and, only with my prompting, his own opinions. From our conversations I gained a good sense of the political terrain between 1959, when the Navy was beset by a series of mishaps and accidents at sea, and 1968, when the report of the second *Voyager* royal commission was finally released. Tony's vivid recollections and insightful observations were crucial to the story.

After publishing *Where Fate Calls: the HMAS Voyager Tragedy* in February 1992, I decided to write a biography of Harold Holt because his handling of the controversy tarnished his reputation and damaged his government's standing. As Tony had been the Prime Minister's Press Secretary in 1966–67, and was very close to Holt and his family, we were in contact again. I asked Tony hundreds of questions about Holt's attitudes, habits and foibles. After being distracted by several other writing projects, *The Life and Death of Harold Holt* eventually appeared in August 2005.

Tony and I stayed in touch after his retirement in 2002. I became a more frequent visitor to his home in 2017 when I was appointed inaugural director of the John Howard Prime Ministerial Library established by UNSW Canberra in the former ministerial wing at Old Parliament House. As the 'keeper' of John Howard's legacy, I wanted Tony's recollections of Howard's time as Federal Treasurer (1977–83), deputy leader of the Liberal Party (1982–1985), Leader of the Opposition (1985–89) and Prime Minister (1996–2007). He was able to explain debates and decisions that were previously inexplicable, at least to me. Tony was reticent in offering assessments of people and appraisals of their performance. Any criticisms were veiled. I was left to make my own judgements of character and conduct.

Over lunch at the Commonwealth Club in 2018, Tony mentioned he had drafted a personal 'chronicle' that was intended primarily for his family. He also had a substantial collection of well-ordered personal papers, comprising 13 archive boxes, relating to the main chapters in his life. As someone fascinated with Australian politics between 1960–90, I explored the possibility of producing a biography that would draw on both the chronicle and his papers. At a time when politics seemed to be dominated by controversy and confrontation,

I wanted to explore how he had achieved so much in public life when neither belligerence nor assertiveness were part of his persona. Tony gave me a copy of his chronicle. I then took possession of his archive which included thousands of documents, memoranda, letters, newspaper clippings and photographs. He set no limits on the use of these materials or impose any conditions on the book that would be produced from them. He trusted me to be responsible and restrained, given some of the papers contained confidential information and revealed his private views. Of greatest value were contemporaneous reflections usually headed, 'Note for File'.

Throughout his working life, Tony produced dozens of these notes on people, places and problems. He explained in his chronicle that they were

> written on my portable typewriter in the immediate wake of the episodes they describe. The writing often took place late at night, in hotel rooms and during aircraft flights. Literary merit was never the intention of the notes. But they are a faithful recording of events and my reactions to them. They are not reflections in retrospect; they were contemporary records.

These notes were kept private and never shown to researchers or interviewers. As someone who had previously sought his assistance on several occasions, I had no idea they were so comprehensive and detailed, documenting his thoughts and emotions.

Tony had been approached several times over the years to write an 'insider's account' of Holt's short prime ministership and Gorton's unexpected ascension to national leadership. Political reporter David Solomon thought that few observers had a better vantage point from which to assess the prime ministerships of Menzies, Holt and Gorton than Tony Eggleton. Writing in November 1969, Solomon told readers of the *Australian*:

> Eggleton's intentions are strictly honourable. He says he won't be writing a book for a long, long time (though from time to time he jots down notes of his recollections of important events) and when the book does appear it will be more about people than politics.

Solomon explained Tony's rationale:

> [Eggleton] believes that if the people he dealt with were ever convinced that he was planning a book in the immediate future, his ability to do his job would

immediately suffer. He needs inside information to put himself in the best position to advise the prime minister on what the press should be told.

After leaving the prime minister's office in March 1971, Sun Books invited Tony to produce a candid account of Australian politics during the previous five years. After arriving in London the following month he was offered an advance on royalties of $50,000 by another publisher who wanted the 'real story' behind Liberal party intrigue. A London newspaper offered him a hefty sum to write on Gorton's time in office. He steadfastly declined these offers, explaining: 'I have extensive notes of what occurred, and may eventually put them down in book form. But it would be a long time in the future, and purely as a matter of record. They would then have no commercial value'. In an interview with Robert Milliken for *The Eye* magazine in 2000, Tony was asked about retirement plans and a possible autobiography. Given he 'is a meticulous writer of minutes and reports', Milliken thought 'his personal records of public life since Menzies would make a fascinating addition to Australian history'. When asked whether he 'is likely to commit them to a book', Eggleton replied: 'It's not the sort of thing I see myself doing'.

When all of these 'Notes for File' were assembled in 2002, Tony was concerned about the 'unintended hurt that these records might cause, and was tempted to destroy or sanitise them'. After contemplating self-censorship, he decided 'in the interests of a candid account' that it was 'best to leave the records in the form in which they were originally written'. Tony told former *Weekly Times* columnist, Vincent Matthews, that he was not intending to 'capitalise on my experiences and insights' with the publication of a memoir 'in his lifetime'. The book that Solomon and others hoped he would write never eventuated. I have drawn sparingly on Tony's unpublished chronicle but made extensive use of his contemporaneous notes. They detail the personality clashes that shaped Australian public life and reveal Eggleton's role as mediator, conciliator and counsellor. In these notes I encountered a man who struggled with the demands of conscience and whether he would continue to be demeaned by those with whom he worked.

Tony is a reserved man whose emotions are rarely on display. He is controlled and measured. While this was a personal strength in the discharge of his professional duties, it made my task of isolating his motivations and interpreting his actions more difficult. In many ways, Tony would prefer to be known by his deeds rather than whatever deep feelings might have prompted them. He would rather be judged by a balanced appraisal of his contribution to the public interest – however indirectly that contribution might have been. As someone who has known and admired Tony for more than 30 years, being candid about his life was not without risks. I did not want to damage our friendship. Thankfully, I was not obliged to be censorious or judgemental. But I have concluded in several instances that he might have taken a stronger stand against bad behaviour or adopted a different approach when confronted with institutional folly. I leave readers to decide whether I have been overly generous to Tony and whether he was too forgiving in his appraisal of several public figures.

Throughout this book I have endeavoured to explain how Tony managed to work constructively with difficult people, why he was such an effective public servant and what he did to retain the respect of political adversaries. I tried to find instances in which he emulated or imitated other people. This line of inquiry yielded nothing of substance. There was an Eggleton style but not a distinct method or set of practises. Tony brought his personality and principles to every aspect of his work. As there is much in his style to commend, aspiring politicians and campaign strategists might absorb elements of his outlook on public life. More broadly, I also hope this book might encourage other writers to consider the responsibilities of journalists in Australian political life and the place of character in national affairs.

Tom Frame
Canberra
June 2022

CHAPTER 1

From there to here   1932–46

Thomas Osman Eggleton and his wife, Winnifred Louise Eggleton (nee Bolter), lived on Gordon Road in Swindon, Wiltshire, in the south-west of England. Originally a stone age village and the site of a later Roman settlement, Swindon was a small market town until 1840 when the industrial revolution changed it forever. Located astride the railway linking London and Bristol, Swindon became an important transport hub. It hosted locomotive workshops, light manufacturing and extensive infrastructure supporting the inland canal system.

The Eggletons lived in Swindon 'New Town' which consisted of rows of small drab redbrick terraced houses. The larger and more genteel homes were located on the hill in Swindon 'Old Town'. Tom and Winnie had grown up in the country. They met in the village of Brinkworth, 15 kilometres west of Swindon and not far from the ancient town of Malmesbury. Both aged 20, they were married at the Swindon Registry Office on 23 November 1916. Tom was a private soldier in the Fourth Gloucester Regiment and saw active service in Mesopotamia (now Iraq), Egypt, India and Russia. After the war, Tom found work with the Great Western Railway (GWR) company. The young couple lived with Winnie's parents in Swindon Old Town before buying a house on Gordon Road.

Their first child was born in 1921 and named Stanley. Three years later they welcomed a daughter, Ruby. Their third child, Tony, was born in the family home on 30 April 1932. He was named Tony although most people presumed his legal name was Anthony until corrected. Winnie was unwell following the birth of her 'fragile' baby boy. Also living in the Gordon Road terrace was 'Uncle Jack' (Jack Brown), a family friend whose wife had recently died. Jack was a temporary lodger but became part of the family. He worked in the workshops where the GWR locomotives were built and was a consistent contributor to the family finances.

From the parlour front window of the small terrace house, the young Tony could watch the passing blue and yellow Swindon Corporation buses, horse-drawn commercial vehicles, bicycles and pedestrians. In the early morning, a high-pitched siren summoned workers to the railway workshops. A little later, children made their way to the junior and senior schools in the adjoining road. With the men at work and their children at school, women armed with their baskets walked down to the main street shops. This was an ordered world of disciplined people who appreciated their jobs and were grateful for stable incomes. The previous few years had been disruptive of routines and distressing for those struggling to cope with the worst economic upheaval in modern times.

The Eggleton home was a place of warmth, security, happiness and love. A family of modest means, there was always food on the table and new clothes when needed. The neighbours owned a confectionary shop and generously shared a selection of sweets. The children enjoyed holiday outings and a succession of toys. Tony had a tricycle and a pedal car. He would accompany his mother on shopping trips. He also enjoyed the weekly 'bath night' with hot water running directly into a tub that his father had installed in the terrace's small scullery. The toilet remained outside.

The 'fragile' child rarely felt ill but his family were concerned that he was not as strong or as healthy as they would have wished. He appeared to have no appetite and ate little. There were visits to doctors who devised various regimes to 'put meat on his bones' and build up his constitution. For reasons that were never disclosed in any great detail, one doctor prescribed the consumption of clotted cream. Only the bribe of a penny from Uncle Jack could induce the boy to eat the dreaded dairy product. To the surprise of his family, Tony loved Heinz baked beans. They became his staple diet. The little boy's previously stable world was fractured by the announcement that he would start school at the age of four. He sobbed and threw tantrums. They were to no avail. Although the College Street school was not far from his home on Gordon Road, he hated the harsh surroundings, the bleak buildings, the bare playgrounds and the strong smell of disinfectant. Tony's mother took him to school every day for weeks. She waited at the corner of College Street and Gordon Road to make sure he arrived safely.

Overcoming his initial anxieties, Tony settled into school and enjoyed the lessons, especially history. He learned about England's glories and Britain's special place in the world. The annual celebration of 'Empire Day' was a major occasion in Swindon. Children dressed up in their make-believe outfits and headed off to the town's parks and gardens for public events. There were bands and flags and demonstrations of national pride. The young Eggleton wore a policeman's outfit, including a sturdy wooden truncheon and a helmet made from reinforced cardboard. The outfit had been acquired for the tap-dancing classes he had started with his sister Ruby and a concert routine being prepared for their parents entitled 'The Policeman's Holiday'. By this time, Tony was old enough to go to the local barber for haircuts. The barbershop situated across the road and close to the school did not satisfy his mother. She took him to a hairdresser near the Swindon markets who made a decision that was to last a lifetime. The hairdresser decided that his hair would sit better if parted on the right side of his head, rather than on the customary left side. The right side part became permanent.

At the end of the school year in early August, Swindon became a ghost town. During the designated holiday shutdown, the railway workers and their families headed off for their annual summer vacation which was heavily subsidised by GWR. The Eggletons went to Paignton and Goodrington in Devon. They stayed in private homes where the householders let out several rooms to capitalise on the holiday season. Ample meals were provided by the host families with a pervasive smell of gas from the lamps in each room. At the seaside, the Eggletons rented their own beach hut where they would spend most of the day after breakfast, playing with the sand and venturing into the water. Winnie prepared the daily lunch with the help of a spirit cooker. The day was abbreviated by '99s', ice-cream featuring spears of chocolate flakes, and sticks of confectionary 'rock'. There were various entertainment parks nearby. At the close of day, the family packed up their possessions, locked the hut and walked back to their accommodation for dinner. The pattern was followed every day until it was time to return to Swindon and their familiar routine. Tom Eggleton would head off to the railway track and Uncle Jack would cycle to the workshops.

With continuing concerns about Tony's health, the family decided in 1937 to move away from the air pollutants of industrial Swindon for the nearby country-side. The Eggletons move to Chisledon, a small village on the edge of the Wiltshire Downs, some eight kilometres from Swindon on the road to Marlborough. The physical distance may not have been great but the cultural change was immense. The rows of terraced houses and the sound of factories were replaced by open spaces and the chirping of birds. In their new home at 24 Hodson Road, the makeshift furniture consisted of card tables with fruit boxes serving as chairs.

It was a relatively new street consisting mainly of free-standing 'bungalows' – the English term for single storey homes. The brick, tiled roof houses were on one side of the road facing trees and open fields. Hodson Road linked the original village with the equally old hamlet of Hodson which lay on the route to Swindon. Number 24 looked out across a small valley to the village church on the opposite ridge. In the distance was Liddington Castle. It was not a castle in the literal sense but the earthworks of an Iron Age fort. The 'castle' took the form of a moat encircling a grassy hill, topped by a small stand of prominent trees. The recently vacated home, with the dampness of the rainy day, had a disturbing 'empty house' feel. As they awaited the furniture truck, Uncle Jack took Tony for a walk down the country lane opposite their new home. There were fields on each side of the laneway which made its way past a couple of older houses sheltered behind established gardens. The laneway then went down under the railway bridge to a stream. The narrow path beside the stream led to a larger group of cottages near the Chiseldon railway station.

The new Eggleton family home was modern and spacious in comparison to the Gordon Road terrace. There was an entrance hall giving access to three bedrooms and the front sitting room. There was a combined dining-living room and a kitchen. The biggest improvement was a fully equipped bathroom with tiled floors and a floor-to-ceiling airing cupboard. The main rooms had open fireplaces. The Eggletons were now enjoying all the pleasures of English village life. Their kitchen garden adjoined green fields and lush farms. For a child, Chiseldon was an endless playground. The two-teacher school was another dramatic change for the better. There was little local traffic and walking to school was a daily adventure. The classrooms were surrounded by thatched cottages. Across the road was the village pub, known as the Patriot's Arms. Almost everything was home-delivered: bread, milk and vegetables. The grocer operated a thriving corner store and made deliveries in his impressive black Jaguar car.

With another major European conflict looming and military recruitment on the rise, Stan Eggleton applied to join the Royal Air Force Apprentice (RAF) College. He left home in August 1937. Ruby passed the entry exams for Swindon College and was travelling to school each day on the train. Despite the transition, Tony's health was not improving. He spent weeks in bed with Winnie encouraging him to eat mashed potato that she fashioned into various shapes and patterns. Topped with tomato sauce and sometimes mixed with baked beans, he was at least willing to eat a little more. One doctor thought he would do much better without his tonsils and prepared to remove them at home. The doctor failed to return and the operation never occurred. Without further medical intervention, Tony's wellbeing appeared to improve by the time he was seven. He was eating better and seemed to be responding to the clean rural air and more physical exercise. Despite prolonged absences from school, he managed to keep up with the academic progress of other children.

The spectre of another world war was, however, casting a shadow over idyllic English rural life. When Tony asked the headmistress about rumours of conflict with Hitler's Germany and Mussolini's Italy, she made her displeasure plain. This was not a matter she would discuss or wanted the children to speak about among themselves. They knew that something awful was on the horizon. On 3 September 1939, which was a sunny autumn day in Chisledon, the Eggleton family gathered around the wireless to hear Prime Minister Neville Chamberlain announce that Britain had declared war on Germany which had persisted with its invasion of Poland. The reaction of adults was the source of worry for their children. Tony had little understanding of what was about to happen nor how his family would be affected. He was deeply troubled. His father had been in the Great War of 1914–18 and knew of its horrors. To lighten the mood, Uncle Jack took Tony for a bike ride to nearby Wroughton which would soon become the site of an RAF airfield and occasionally a target for German fighters and bombers.

The British Broadcasting Corporation (BBC) radio news was dominated by the outbreak of war. At school, the children talked about their parents' reactions. The reality of armed hostilities did not dawn on most of the children until they were assembled on a cold night in the Chisledon village hall for the issue of gas masks. The masks came in different sizes and in bright colours for the smaller children. There were masks for babies, more like cribs with a protective cover, junior masks, adult masks and military-style versions. Tony was issued with a black elastic mask that he struggled to wear with any comfort. It had an unpleasant, pungent smell of rubber. The children, unfamiliar as they were with the brutalities of indiscriminate warfare, returned home with their gas masks. They were carried in square cardboard boxes that were fitted with a string to hang over the shoulder. The local shops were soon selling customised respirator containers. Winnie acquired brown metal cases (resembling a lunch box) for her family. For the next few years, the metal box became a constant companion for every British man, woman and child after the authorities directed that gas masks should be carried at all times.

The issue of gas masks was followed by the imposition of blackout restrictions to prevent the pilots and navigators of German Luftwaffe aircraft from orientating themselves when flying over British soil. All houses had to be 'blacked out' at night. There was to be no external lighting and no internal lighting visible from the street or air. Most families devised various methods of covering their windows. Tony's father and Uncle Jack made portable timber shutters that could be pushed into the frames of the larger windows at night. This was not a workable solution for all the windows. Homemade blackout curtains were the preferred supplementary measure. A member of the Eggleton family went out every night to check there were no extrusions of light. Air Raid Wardens patrolled the village streets and were soon knocking on the doors of dwellings with inadequate measures. Motor vehicles had 'black out' hoods placed over their headlights, leaving only a weak, narrow beam of light directed onto the road. Not surprisingly, driving at night became increasingly hazardous.

Younger men and women were soon enlisting in the armed services. The older men, some veterans of the Great War of 1914–18 like Tom Eggleton, assembled in their civilian clothes each evening for Home Guard drill. The Home Guard initially paraded with garden forks and spades as a substitute for rifles and bayonets. It was not long before the Home Guard were turning out in their uniforms, equipped with lethal weapons. The village children were fascinated by this unprecedented activity. On Sundays, church bells were silent. While the war raged they would only ring as a warning of a German invasion and alert the local population to the possibility of enemy paratroopers. The once welcome bells now became a source of deep dread.

When German air raids threatened London and the other major population centres, the government devised plans for the evacuation of children to overseas destinations and the English countryside. The people of Chisledon were asked to advise the authorities of the size of their homes, the number of occupants and whether they had space for evacuee children. The Eggletons had no room for evacuees as their three bedroom home was already accommodating three adults and two children. The influx of city children was also a challenge for the village school which was full to overflowing with scared and bewildered young-sters, mainly from London. The local children were told their new classmates were adjusting to new families and life in the country and were asked to make them feel welcome. They were an intriguing assortment of children, many with cockney accents and strange city ways. Most settled down quickly and became part of village life.

The influence of the evacuee children added to the difficulties Tony was facing at school. It was apparent that his basic writing, reading and arithmetical skills were now lagging behind the other eight year-olds in his class. A family confer-ence discussed the possibility of enrolling him in a private school in Swindon Old Town. 'The High School' had a prestigious Bath Road address and was attended by the boys of the town's better-off families. The fees were substantial and this was a significant hurdle for the lower middle-class Eggleton family. A big metal moneybox was placed on the table. Uncle Jack kindly said he would contribute. Tony was offered a place at the school with a group of boys of similar age. He would need additional tutoring to catch-up with the rest of his class. Wearing his eye-catching red and black striped blazer, the young Eggleton started his daily commute on the 8.25am steam train from Chisledon to Swindon Old Town, initially accompanied by sister Ruby to ensure he was safe.

The school was a converted and extensively remodelled private home known as 'The Gables'. It had a dining room, a well-equipped gymnasium and a range of classrooms catering for students from eight year-olds through to matricula-tion students aged 16 years. As expected, the staff recommended that Tony have extra tuition and suggested the family consider private elocution classes whose principal aim seemed to be the elimination or, at least, the softening of the boy's pronounced Wiltshire accent. The daily disciplinary regime was harsh, if not draconian. Boys who misbehaved were caned at the school assembly or made to stand in a dark cupboard for 15 or 30 minutes. All boys were called by their surnames and the male teachers were addressed as 'sir'.

Each day began with the boys lining up in the schoolyard, class by class, in descending order of height. Politeness and good manners were highly esteemed with the boys being required to raise their caps whenever they were addressed in the street. They were also expected to offer their seats to adults on buses and trains. Those failing to observe these courtesies risked being punished. 'Team points' were given in recognition of superior academic work on a day-by-day and subject-by-subject basis. The 'points' were tokens handed to the student at the end of each day before being collected and tallied by the class teacher at the end of the week. The boy with the highest number of points was announced at morning assembly and received a special 'merit' badge worn the following week. It was not long before the determined Tony had scored the most points and received the merit badge which was worn with much pride.

The boys later became aware of where their teacher, Miss Scrivener, kept the tin box in which the tokens were stored. Several boys were so preoccupied with achieving success that they helped themselves to the team points. After winning the badge with the aid of furtively gained tokens, the young Eggleton learnt an important lesson. There was little satisfaction in ill-gotten gains. On the way home from school he buried the unearned tokens in a patch of neglected garden at a nearby garage. He did not win the coveted merit badge again that year. There were other challenges.

Tony faced hostilities from the village children who took a dim view of his departure from the primary school. They saw it as a snobbish act embodied in the eye-catching school uniform. Sometimes there were ambushes on the walk home. The bigger boys hit his legs with stinging nettles and showered stones from the railway bridge as he walked up the lane. This harassment persisted for months. It was disquieting and sometimes frightening. But he felt good about his new school, was making many new friends, and was determined not to be deterred by the bullies. It was a hard but valuable insight into human nature and essentially part of growing up. Sadly, but perhaps inevitably, relationships with the village children were never the same.

By the end of 1940, there was no sign of the war ending any time soon. Its influence on daily life widened and deepened. The availability of basic foodstuffs, such as meat, flour, sugar, butter and eggs, was restricted. Ration books were issued with coupons exchanged for victuals. Spam, powered potato and eggs were common as luxury items like chocolate and ice-cream became a rarity. Imported fruits, such as bananas and mangoes, disappeared entirely from view. People throughout Wiltshire grew their own vegetables and built chicken runs. An army camp was hurriedly built at Chisledon and soldiers appeared everywhere. They were conducting training in fields, marching down roads, and crowding into public transport. A search-light unit was deployed in fields behind the Eggleton home. A substantial airfield and military hospital were established a few kilometres away at Wroughton. Soldiers were willing to exchange ration coupons for home-grown produce as an unofficial local market flourished.

There were also air raids although they were less frequent in Swindon than in London and the big cities. Private air raid shelters were built in back gardens. The Eggletons were not persuaded one was needed at 24 Hodson Road. At the sound of a daytime warning siren, the family assembled under the dining room table, and at night they sought refuge under beds with the mattress springs inches from their noses. Children were soon able to distinguish the engines of enemy Luftwaffe bombers from friendly RAF aircraft. As the aircraft engine noises faded into the distance, the welcome sound of the 'all clear' siren followed. The human cost of the conflict was never far away. At the local railway station, wounded soldiers were unloaded from hospital trains and laid out on stretchers awaiting an ambulance journey to the fully functioning Wroughton Military Hospital. Occasionally, military police would be seen escorting captured German airmen whose aircraft had been shot down during the night.

Children were not spared the ravages of war. They walked to school each morning with a satchel of books over one shoulder and the ubiquitous gas mask case over the other. The school assembly began with gas mask drill, conducted on the count of one, two, three. One: the gas mask was removed from the case. Two: the mask was placed over the head and under the chin. Three: the mask was secured and an air-tight seal was established. The children became highly proficient and usually had the masks in place at the end of the count. They were kept on for a few minutes to familiarise the wearer with how they felt. When the air raid sirens sounded during class time, children with friends living nearby were allowed to rush to their homes. Tony took shelter in the substantial cellar of a house owned by the parents of his good friend, John Perry. During prolonged raids, they would play with a selection of toys including an extensive Hornby train set. Once the 'all clear' siren was sounded, the children were expected to hurry back to class. On one occasion, Tony was walking towards the Swindon Town Hall to catch the bus home when the air raid siren sounded. A concerned woman ran out of her house, grabbed the young Eggleton and rushed him inside to relative safety as a German plane flew overhead. The noise of machine gun and cannon fire could be heard in the surrounding streets. When the 'all clear' sounded, he conveyed his thanks and continued on his way. The possibility of being injured or killed was becoming an everyday reality and readily accepted, even by children. There was no alternative. Life went on with the least disruption possible.

Tony's parents took him on day trips to London. They visited Trafalgar Square where parts of German aircraft shot down over England were on display. Beach holidays had ended as the foreshores were now covered with barbed wire and other physical entanglements to hamper the possible landing of enemy troops. Pillboxes, machine-gun posts and concrete barriers were erected at strategic points along the beaches. Tony's mother still planned the occasional day outing to the seaside. They would take the train to Weston-Super-Mare on the Bristol Channel. Since the beginning of the war, the popular seaside resort had become a shadow of its joyous peacetime self. The pier was closed and there were no donkeys carrying children on the beach. The restaurants and coffee shops were mostly in wartime hibernation. On the way home one evening from such a trip, the train in which the young Eggleton was travelling halted outside Bristol. The sky was full of flashing lights and the carriages were reverberating to loud explosions as German bombers attacked the heart of the historic city in an attempt to destroy its industrial infrastructure. Reading in Berkshire was the location of his favourite toy shop. Fascinated by Monopoly, he persuaded his mother to buy the sequel, Totopoly, which was based on training and racehorses. Within days of what would be his final visit, Reading was the target of a massive air raid and much of the shopping centre was destroyed.

Like many English families, the Eggletons refused to let the war eclipse the spirit of Christmas. The living areas in their home were festooned with paper trimmings, stars and baubles, and the circular window in the lounge-room was decorated with miniatures of Santa Claus, glass Christmas symbols and colourful strings of beads. As a special treat, the fireplaces were kept alight throughout Christmas Day and Boxing Day. Fuel for fires was rationed and it was almost impossible to get coal. Tony's father and Uncle Jack had earlier set off with a snow sledge to collect wood from around the old golf links. The only other heating was provided by two-bar electric radiators. Until the fires began to generate their heat, the windows were often covered in frost. When melted, the scene across the valley to the church and to Liddington Castle was misty and grey, with touches of white on hedges and branches. All was quiet and all were calm. After church, the family enjoyed a special lunch of roast chicken and vegetables, and the traditional Christmas pudding. No ice cream, of course, but plenty of custard.

Late in 1942, the first American servicemen arrived at the Chisledon camp. They came with their own marching band and used the neighbourhood for training. Each Saturday a dance for the soldiers was held at the village memorial hall. Tony and sister Ruby helped sell and serve food, taking orders and distributing sandwiches and other snacks. The Americans liked the small local boy and were amused by his presence. Australian soldiers were the next to arrive at Chisledon. The local villagers remembered the Australians for their stature, slouch hats and strange customs. When trains pulled into Swindon Old Town Station, the Australians would jump from the carriages on the track side and dash across the lines, rather than stepping off at the platform and paying for their tickets. This was Tony's first contact with Australians. They were colourful, unconventional and he liked them.

Together with his closest friends John Perry and Keith Eyles from Swindon, Tony was an adventurous child whose character and temperament were formed by his home life and by the everyday challenges of wartime. He was a keen member of the Boy Scouts, became a patrol leader of the 'Peewee troop', and gained a number of special badges. As the son of Tom Eggleton, a popular figure with GWR workers, he was sometimes invited to ride in the train engine on the journey home, occasionally sounding the train's whistle as he watched the crew shovelling coal into the locomotive's furnace. He had opportunities to enter the signal boxes and pull the levers or travel home with the guard in his compartment at the rear of the train.

Imperceptibly, he was growing in strength and in confidence. Days missed from school because of ill health (for reasons that were still not clear) were much rarer. He was not as sturdy as many of the other boys and had difficulty with much of the school gymnasium equipment. The vaulting horse and rope climbing presented few problems and he did reasonably well with wrestling and boxing. The team sports were soccer in the winter and cricket in the summer, although he never excelled. His form of manly toughness was demonstrated in other ways. In mid-winter, when the snowplough could not keep the line open for the morning train, and snow and ice made the roads too dangerous for the buses, he resolutely walked to school. Wrapped in a heavy coat and scarf and clad with long Wellington boots, he began the five-mile trek to Swindon through the snow across the fields. There were unexpected snowdrifts and other hazards but he relished the challenge. At school he was treated as something of a hero for having trudged through the wintry landscape. He was usually sent home immediately after lunch to ensure he had time to retrace his steps through the fields and the woods before the early afternoon darkness descended. Tony was seen as defiant, determined and disciplined.

He discovered golf at the age of 11. One of his female teachers at the village primary school who continued a friendship with his mother, encouraged him to share her interest in the sport. The nearby Marlborough golf course had been neglected and was officially closed because of the war. Although the fairways were overgrown and the greens were untended, the public were still able to wander around the course. Having demonstrated an aptitude for the sport, Tony received a set of clubs for his birthday. With so many men overseas on active service, a lot of sporting gear was available at second-hand shops. His new clubs and carry bag were in first-class condition and he wanted a more satisfactory arrangement than the abandoned Marlborough course. Tony became a member of the Swindon Golf Club on the road between Chisledon and Marlborough. He was the club's first boy player and the rules were changed to allow his membership. His clubs could be left in the locker-room and he could cycle to the course. Many of his school friends were introduced to golf when they served as his caddie, followed by lemonade at the clubhouse.

The same teacher also recruited Ruby and Tony to serve as teachers in the Sunday School operated by the local parish church. He was regularly placed in charge of a dozen smaller children aged between 6–8 years. He was left to tell them Bible stories. The need to hold their attention refined his reading and writing skills. As a young Sunday school teacher he was invited to garden parties at the vicarage, a large house adjoining the church. Tony seemed at ease in adult company by the time his secondary schooling commenced. He was confounded by mathematics but was doing well in English literature, essay writing and religious studies, winning prizes for poetry and composition. The famed Victorian nature writer and children's novelist, Richard Jefferies (1848–87), had lived at Coate near Swindon. His work was closely studied. Sister Ruby, well-suited to being the schoolteacher she became, supervised his homework each evening.

Inclined to literature and having a facility with words, Tony began to think about becoming a journalist. His ambition was provoked by the war correspondents.

He listened to their reports on the radio and followed their exploits in cinema newsreels. As the war progressed, his bedroom was lined with maps, dotted with pins and markers to trace the course of the war. On going to bed each night he would listen to the news bulletins and the war correspondents to ensure his maps remained up-to-date. His mother was much keener on him becoming a clergyman but he was drawn to the world of newspapers.

As a Christmas gift in 1943, Ruby gave him a copy of *You Want to be a Journalist?* by Cecil Hunt, a prolific English journalist who rose to fame after publishing collections of the unintended errors made by British schoolchildren in essays and examinations. They included statements like 'Lourdes is a cricket ground in London' and 'parsimony is money left by your father'. They were commonly known as 'howlers' – a term that continues to have currency. Hunt counselled anyone considering journalism to determine whether they had a facility with words and enjoyed writing. In terms of temperament, Hunt suggested 'the phlegmatic, placid disposition is unlikely to possess many of the attributes essential to success in journalism. Those whose dispositions and temperament best suit them to the craft are naturally imaginative, sensitive, to some extent artistic'.

As a teenager, Tony was keenly interested in most modes of literature, not unlike Jefferies whose wide-ranging work spanned reports and essays, travel guides and fantasy novels. Tony was a regular visitor to the Swindon Library and was getting through several books a week, mainly schoolboy adventures, such as Biggles. His reading was augmented by increasingly frequent visits to the cinema. As a teenager he was allowed to go alone. Together with his friends they joined queues outside theatres and, if the programme had a rating that excluded unaccompanied children, they asked adults to 'take us in'. This usually worked as they soon slipped away from the obliging adults once inside the cinema.

The radio also played a central role in Tony's life. It was a constant source of entertainment including the comedies, adventure serials, evening plays and the all-important news bulletins. The voice of Prime Minister Winston Churchill brought comfort and encouragement. He collected knick-knacks bearing quotes from Churchill's speeches and there was a portrait of the prime minister on his bookshelf. Tony listened avidly to his radio talks, convinced by Churchill's oratory the Allies would eventually prevail. They were winning battles in North Africa and Italy, and there was talk of a 'Second Front' to invade Germany through France.

With the surrender of Mussolini's fascist forces in September 1943, Italian prisoners-of-war (POW) started to appear in Chisledon. With their distinctive POW uniforms, they could be seen working on local farms. They were regarded in a much friendlier light than the Germans and were allowed to wander around the village without an armed escort. As their labour was welcome, they were generally well accepted by the community. The following year brought a tangible increase in military preparations. There were more troops in the village, greater concentrations of army trucks and other military vehicles on the roads, and more activity at the surrounding airfields. The fear that England might be invaded had receded. Tony's horizons extended beyond life in Swindon and Chisledon.

He was now permitted to embark on railway day trips on his own. The family was able to secure 'free passes' because his father worked with GWR. He would head for various surrounding towns and villages, exploring new places, making sure to be home before dark. Tony could always seek assistance from the railway people when he mentioned his father's name. As well as trains, he was venturing further on his bicycle. In the summer, he normally rode the eight kilometres to school. This made travel to sports grounds much easier. But riding home along the country roads near Coate and Hodson was not without its hazards. The narrow, winding roads were cluttered with speeding American army trucks and jeeps leaving little room for a boy on a bike.

By mid-1944, adults and children across England were waiting for the Allied return to Europe and the advance on Germany. The skies around Chisledon were marked with aircraft towing gliders. In the hours leading to 'D-Day' – 6 June 1944 – aircraft and gliders filled the sky as far as the eye could see. It was a great aerial armada. It was evident the Normandy invasion was about to begin. Tony and all his young friends were excited, tuning into radio news bulletin for updates. Within days of the landings, the Chisledon railway station was the scene of hectic comings and goings as Red Cross trains shuttled the injured from France. The ambulances sped down Hodson Road past his home at Number 24 as they headed for the military hospital at Wroughton.

In less than a year, and soon after his thirteenth birthday, England and its people were celebrating the cessation of hostilities. Victory in Europe Day, known as 'VE Day', was a moment of relief and joy. On 8 May 1945, a huge bonfire was built on the ridge alongside the church in Chisledon. The villagers turned out in large numbers. They gathered around the fire and the church to sing songs and give thanks. On returning home, the Eggletons could see the fire still burning on the hill as the celebrations continued well into the night. The war in Europe was over and, three months later in the Pacific fighting also ended. It would, however, take time for 'hostilities only' servicemen and women to rejoin their families in the village, and for normality to return. The rationing of food and fuel would continue until officially ending in July 1954. The hardships of the war did not finish with the fighting.

Like most boys his age, the young Eggleton now looked for new forms of excitement. After reading books like *Tom Brown's School Days*, Tony was increasingly convinced he wanted to attend a traditional boarding school. His parents were not persuaded but, given their son's enthusiasm, they made enquiries about suitable establishments. The family decided to try the King Alfred School at Wantage which was then in Berkshire.[1] Located at the birthplace of King Alfred the Great on the railway line between Swindon and London, the school had a good reputation.[2] Tony was invited for an interview. He set off on the train with his mother to meet the headmaster, Canon WM Peacock, an Anglican cleric who also ministered at the local parish church. It was essentially a re-run of the interview for The High School at Swindon some years earlier. A few tests revealed his academic studies were still languishing. Nevertheless, the headmaster offered Tony a place on the understanding that he would begin in a lower year than was usual for his age. Overcoming their previous hesitation, his parents agreed and a flurry of activity followed.

New uniforms and other garments, consistent with the clothing list provided by the school, needed to be purchased. The school colours were black and gold, less striking than the bright red and black of The High School. Name tags had to be obtained and attached to all clothing. New schoolbooks were to be acquired. Tony's belongings were forwarded to the school in a trunk despatched in advance by rail. He commenced at King Alfred's on Thursday 20 September 1945 – less than three weeks after representatives of the Japanese Government signed the formal surrender document presented to them by the Allies on board USS *Missouri* in Tokyo Bay. Tony was 13 and leaving home. Winnie was upset by the departure of her youngest child. Tom delivered his son to Wantage on a wet and stormy day.

The school was relatively small with around 250 boys. 'Wantage House' was for local boys; 'Faringdon House' was for day boys from the town of Faringdon and outlying areas; and 'School House' was for the boarders who came from across England, many from London. The school was a five-minute walk from the centre of Wantage and looked out to the downs, running the whole length of the horizon. The main part of the school was a large grey stone building, with lawns at the front and a quadrangle at the side. The oldest part of the building had a Norman archway and door leading into the library. Extensive playing fields, including the cricket pitch and areas for ball games, were across the road from the main school buildings. It was an idyllic English scene.

Tony was personally welcomed by the headmaster, shown around the school, taken to the dormitory and introduced to his bed. The familiarisation was brief as classes began immediately after lunch. 'Fagging' duties, a system where the younger boys served the older boys, were assigned in the evening. These were not too arduous as the prefects were friendly and considerate. The younger boys often helped each other to complete their 'fag' duties. Days began with the rising bell at 7am. Bathrooms were conveniently located adjacent to the dormitories but were bitterly cold in the winter. Breakfast was at 8am followed by morning chapel at 8:45am. The chapel was central to school life. In addition to daily prayer, there was always a Sunday morning service at 10.45am and an evening service at 6.40pm. The Sunday morning service was held in the parish church when Canon Peacock was rostered to officiate. There were four instructional periods in the morning and three in the afternoon. Tea was served at 4pm. Supper was 7pm, and then 'prep' (preparation for the next day) from 8pm to 9pm, then prayers and bed at 9:15pm. There were tuition periods on Saturday mornings until lunchtime although Tuesday afternoon was left free for sport and Thursday afternoons were devoted to the Officer Training Corps (OTC) – elementary military training.

The school was generally run with military-like precision. Everything was implemented like clockwork. Discipline was firm but not severe. Boys were not abused or intimidated by staff or other students. In Tony's small boarding house, the housemaster, Mr Price, was always on hand and devoted to promoting the interests of his charges. Recently married, his wife was also considerate and willing to be help boarders with problems. There were also two matrons who closely observed the boarders and monitored their health. Being ordered to the sick room was considered welcome respite, especially in the winter months. The sick room was warm, the Matrons were motherly and food was delivered on a tray. Tony's health continued to improve and his visits to the sick room were for the usual illnesses and injuries that beset teenage boys.

King Alfred's provided a very different lifestyle to the one Tony had known at Chiseldon. Although he was initially troubled by academic work, after ten days he was promoted to Form 3A and confronted by new subjects, including Latin. Alongside classroom learning, programmed sport consisted of regular gym, nightly boxing, fencing and football with tennis in the summer. Weekly military drill with the OTC added to the demands imposed on the boys. The OTC was a world of its own, especially the maintenance of strict dress standards. The young Eggleton, who liked order but disliked regimentation, found it unappealing. He was nonetheless consoled by new friends. Most of the boys mixed easily and well. Like the other students, he had his own tuck box and greatly welcomed regular food parcels from home. Winnie's homemade cakes were popular with Tony and his immediate circle of friends. Despite continuing shortages and the mandatory surrender of each boy's ration card, the school food was better than adequate. The greatest disappointment was the long-awaited delivery of bananas. There was universal anticipation of peeling what had become a rare treat during the war. When an insufficient quantity was delivered for each of the boarders to enjoy his own banana, they were served portions of fried banana which neither looked nor tasted like banana.

Although the school was only 39 kilometres from his home (less in a straight line), Tony felt the absence from his parents keenly. He received letters every few days and wrote at least twice a week. All the new boys were homesick but usually put on a good front. They were made to feel at home by Canon and Mrs Peacock who would invite small groups of boys for afternoon tea in their elegant sitting room in the Headmaster's House. Parents could visit on weekends and take their sons to lunch at the historic 16th century Bear Hotel in the town market square. Tony accepted responsibility for the junior dormitory after developing close rapport with the younger boys and the housemaster. He had discovered a distinct talent for connecting with people, a facility that stood him in good stead with everyone at the school. As the boys were allowed 30 minutes for stories after lights out, the young Eggleton became the chief storyteller. He managed to make up yarns about menacing ghosts, ghastly crimes, dramatic adventures and wartime exploits. Not excelling on the sporting field and being a plodder in the classroom, storytelling brought him recognition and respect. Between homework sessions in the evenings, the boys were allowed to read in the library and listen to the radio. Tony had brought his cherished Monopoly game to the school. With all the money and playing cards carefully marked, he was confident they would not be souvenired. These were, he knew, difficult times.

During winter, chill winds swept across the school from the distant downs. The boarders, while coping with cool dormitories and freezing bathrooms, made the best of the situation. Before going to bed, they poured water over the quadrangle so that, after a severe frost, there would be extensive sheets of ice. These were soon turned into skating rinks in the morning. The boys would dash towards the ice, take a running jump and then skid across the quadrangle. The area remained a hazard for much of the day as hurrying masters found to their discomfort. Other boys would be preparing dumps of snowballs. When the Wantage day boys arrived on buses from outlying areas, they faced a barrage as the boarders had highly elevated, strategic positions overlooking the entrance to the school. The fortress, with its ready-made supply of snowballs, usually kept the day boys at bay until the masters demanded a truce.

Even in the bleak mid-winter, the boarders looked forward to getting away from the school on long walks. A special pass from a prefect was needed before a boy could visit the town. It was normally not difficult to get such a pass. The most compelling reason was to visit the local confectionary shop, armed with the necessary coupons, to collect the sweet ration. But there were no restrictions on country walks. At weekends the boys set off in groups to explore the surrounding villages. With the arrival of spring and then summer, many of the boys returned to the school with their bicycles. Tony's bike came by train in the guard's van. He and his friends were able to venture much further and covered considerable distances. The historic Ridge Way, dating from the Iron Age, was a popular expedition. It included Uffington Castle and White Horse Hill. Village churches were often on the itinerary with their names recorded in visitors' books. These outings were abbreviated by calls home from village telephone boxes. Boarders were permitted to return home for the occasional long weekend as well as for the term holidays. For Tony, it was a quick and easy train trip. There would be a large supply of recent newspapers when he arrived at Chiseldon and he would spend hours catching up on all the local news missed while away at Wantage.

Despite forming firm friendships and coping with the benign culture at King Alfred's, the environment and the schooling unsettled him. He struggled with advanced mathematics and science, and encountered difficulty with languages, especially Latin. He felt out of his depth and missed the concentration on English, literature and the associated subjects that had been his strength at The High School in Swindon. He was also missing the convenience and comfort of home, making the prospect of more years at King Alfred's a steadily more daunting proposition. In June 1946, he raised these concerns with his mother. She was sympathetic and readily agreed to speak with Dr Sam Bowring at The High School, raising the possibility that he might return at the start of the new school year in September. Bowring said he would be delighted to welcome Tony back after what would have been no more than a 12-month absence. Canon Peacock was not pleased. He felt Tony had settled well and was making reasonable progress. But the young man was adamant: he no longer wanted the institutional life of the boarding school. Not then apparent, this fateful decision set the scene for a series of events that would, over the course of the next three years, change the direction of his life. In making the most of the unanticipated challenges and opportunities that lay ahead, he nonetheless owed much to the confidence and maturity gained from the year spent at Wantage.

Tony said a goodbye to King Alfred's on 26 July 1946. The summer holidays did not leave much time for him to worry about whether he had made the right choice. Over the next few weeks the Eggletons enjoyed their last family holiday at Goodrington and Paignton, and there were train trips with his parents to London, Cheltenham and Cardiff. He returned to The High School in September as planned. Aside from some trepidation and awkwardness in admitting he might have made a mistake going to Wantage, Tony soon felt he had never been away. He was warmly greeted by the staff and reunited with his former classmates in Form 4A. The first six months after his return from Wantage were largely uneventful, other than a major examination in December.

The Preliminary Certificate granted by the College of Preceptors was a prelude to the Higher School Certificate and Matriculation. The High School took the exams very seriously, and all boys were under pressure to do well and contribute to the school's overall academic reputation. Tony was anxious about his performance after being inducted into a different education system at King Alfred's. Although he felt under-prepared, he was awarded the Certificate with passes in English language and literature, history, algebra, French, and drawing. He was awarded a distinction for Scripture. It was his only academic accolade and led to his promotion to the Upper Fifth Form.

The new year saw the start of the worst winter in living memory. Blizzards, ice and snow brought the country to a near standstill in February 1947. There were shortages of food and coal accompanied by extensive power blackouts. The press were calling it the 'Great Freeze', with three metre snowdrifts closing many roads. Chiseldon was cut off from the surrounding countryside with no access by road or rail. Candles were providing the only light in the evenings as Tony, his father and Uncle Jack fossicked for wood to burn. When the blizzard ended, huge mounds of snow gradually melted and flooded the valleys. The rivers, including the Thames, burst their banks, further dislocating life and work across southern England. By this time Tony's parents had decided to move back to Swindon. His health, the reason they had initially moved to Chiseldon, had consistently improved. The Eggletons bought a large three-storey house at 39 Lansdowne Road in Swindon Old Town, very close to The High School.

Tony's bedroom was at the top of the house, giving him a view across Swindon New Town to the distant suburbs and countryside. There was ample space for a desk, chairs and bookshelves. He also had a table for the gramophone and his record collection which included the famous Australian bass-baritone, Peter Dawson, singing 'Waltzing Matilda'. Shortly afterwards, Tom Eggleton was promoted to the post of Permanent Way Inspector at Bewdley in Worcestershire. Ruby had graduated from Hereford Teachers' College and was employed at the College Street School where each of her siblings had commenced their education. As Tony concentrated on his matriculation studies, his mother noticed an advertisement in the local newspaper. Swindon Press was seeking two 'cub' reporters. He applied instantly. Within a week he was invited to meet the chief reporter, Leslie Lister. The interview seemed to go well. A few days later he was given an appointment to see the general manager, Raymond Thompson. Things were now moving very quickly. On 30 May, he was offered a six-month trial in the sub-editors' room with a starting salary of 15 shillings a week. At the end of his probation, Thompson said: 'I will advise you if, in our opinion, it will be worth your while and ours for you to pursue a journalistic career'. If he accepted, Monday 9 June 1947 would be his first day in the workforce.

The need to make an instant decision caused great consternation at school and home. Should he complete his secondary education and improve his long-term prospects or join the workforce and gain practical experience? Tony's headmaster was firmly of the view that he should matriculate. His parents and sister knew he had been talking about journalism for several years. They were supportive and a decision was made. Two months after his 15th birthday and just three weeks after responding to the advertisement, Tony Eggleton joined the staff of Swindon Press Limited, publishers of the *Swindon Evening Advertiser*, the *North Wilts Herald* and the *Football Pink*.

His formal preparation for adult life was essentially at an end. He could draw three enduring lessons from his upbringing. The first was the importance of acknowledging strengths and shortcomings. The second was the centrality of family to an individual's sense of themselves and their place in the world. The third was learning the virtues of patience and persistence. At school he had been taught discipline and self-reliance; resilience and forbearance. He was a natural leader in certain circumstances. It was leadership conveyed through personal interaction, undergirded by empathy and understanding. The young Eggleton was neither assertive or aggressive but he could bring people together and elicit their cooperation.

He had also discovered a capacity for story-telling. By every other measure, however, his preparation for life as a journalist was minimal. He was leaving school before his peers. His experience of the world was limited to middle class life in the south of England. He had not travelled abroad nor seen how most other people lived. But he was eager for adventure and believed journalism would allow him to explore vistas that were presently unknown and, for such a young man, wholly unimaginable.

Endnotes

1   Wantage became part of Oxfordshire in 1974.
2   King Alfred ruled Wessex from 871–99.

CHAPTER 2

Adventure and advancement   1947–58

I t was much less rare during the 1940s for a very young man – one still considered a child under the law – to enter full-time employment and embark upon what he or she might have considered his or her life's work. Before the 1960s, many teenagers needed to get a job to relieve the financial burden they imposed on their families. Many trades and occupations accepted minors, some as young as 14, into their ranks in apprentice and noviciate roles while there was never any shortage of manual labouring jobs that did not require technical skills or specific qualifications. Few teenagers went to university partly because the expense of tertiary education was out of reach and partly because they were not seeking a professional vocation that required a degree. For many first-time job-seekers in the early post-war period, adolescence was brief as the adult world imposed demands that made no allowance for youth, other than lower pay. For most women, paid employment was still the principal precursor to marriage and motherhood. Many trades and professions actively discouraged women from joining their ranks.

The thought that a young person of average ability and ordinary aptitude would complete their secondary schooling to matriculation, give themselves 12 months to ponder life's possibilities in a 'gap year', complete a tertiary qualification (possibly in three to four years) and then, in the second half of their twenties, think about either a postgraduate qualification or finding employment, was simply unthinkable after the Second World War. Tony Eggleton's decision to leave school and become a journalist at 15 was unusual but not uncommon at that time. It was a defining moment that influenced the rest of his life.

On his first day at work with Swindon Press in the building known as 'Newspaper House', a Grade II heritage listed building completed in 1855, Eggleton met Ken Smith, the other successful cub reporter applicant. They joined an experienced team who believed that on-the-job training was the most effective way for young journalists to learn their profession. Among old school newspaper men, university graduates were regarded with cynicism and even a hint of prejudice. Graduates were, in any event, thin on the ground after 1945. Eggleton began at the bottom as a 'copy boy' in the sub-editors' room. It was a friendly atmosphere but an unhealthy environment. The five middle-aged sub-editors produced clouds of thick smoke from pipes and cigarettes. He was seated under the hatch through which the teleprinter operators passed the national and international news streaming off the clattering teletype machines. It was Eggleton's job to sort the endless sheets of copy and pass the pages to the relevant sub-editors, depending on whether the stories were national news, world news or sport. He also made frequent trips to the reporters' room to collect local copy for the sub-editors. Alongside his desk was a chute through which prepared material travelled to the linotype operators on the floor below. Eggleton learned every aspect of the newspaper business including supplying the sub-editors with coffee and tobacco.

In the evenings Eggleton attended shorthand and typing classes, and an advanced English course. He persisted with his old portable typewriter and soon became a proficient touch typist. Shorthand was more challenging. He eventually gained his 'Pitmans' 70 world-per-minute certificate. He was now working five and a half days each week. With the arrival of autumn, he was busy on Saturday afternoons helping with the production of the *Football Pink*. Eggleton would take telephone calls from football grounds around the country and prepare the list of final scores. Away from Newspaper House he learnt ballroom dancing and became a proficient road cyclist, selling his sturdy pre-Wantage bike for £7 and paying £19 for a top-of-the-line sports bike with racing handlebars. It became his pride and joy.

At the start of 1948, Eggleton was due to complete his first six month placement in the sub-editors' room and was eager to begin training as a reporter. After a brief stand-off that involved the general manager and his sister Ruby, it was agreed that he would continue with the sub-editors for the first part of the day before heading into the reporters' room for the afternoon and evening assignments. He soon went from accompanying experienced reporters to writing his own copy. Without supervision, he was covering weddings and funerals, community activities and flower shows, card tournaments and the reaction of lottery winners. With positive appraisals from the chief reporter, he was transferred permanently to the reporters' room after a few months and given his own district on the outskirts of Swindon to cover. He travelled by bus or by bicycle in search of stories. He spoke with parish clergy, community leaders, shopkeepers, teachers and policemen in a quest for reliable information and newsworthy material.

Every reporter at Newspaper House was allocated a small desk but each was expected to possess his own typewriter. As Eggleton's had seen better days, his parents offered to buy a new model for his 16th birthday. At a cost of £33–10, he became the proud owner of the latest Remington Rand portable typewriter. It was the envy of the other reporters as the staff at Swindon Press continued to expand. An Australian journalist, Roy Creswick, joined the reporting staff. He was tasked with travelling beyond Swindon on a motorbike to gather news stories. Another reporter, Maurice Trowbridge, arrived at Newspaper House after completing his Naval National Service. He later became a Fleet Street political correspondent and was closely involved with the Conservative Party, becoming press secretary to British Prime Minister, Ted Heath. Both Creswick and Trowbridge encouraged the young cubs to seek new challenges.

Eggleton was asked to write a column for young people, headed 'Juvenus'. This initiative connected him with a range of organisations including the Young Conservatives, who made him an honorary member (he joined the Swindon branch on 26 January 1949 and paid an annual subscription of three shillings), and the Young Communists who were active in the affairs of trade unions. Eggleton's column proved a popular innovation and was followed by reviews of the latest movies and theatre productions. The chief reporter explained that: 'It is the privilege of a press representative to enter any cinema or theatre as a guest'. All that was required was a visiting card. An avid cinema-goer, Eggleton arranged a ready supply of personal cards identifying him as a newspaper reporter. Impressed with his work, the editors of the *Evening Advertiser* and the *North Wilts Herald* recommended a pay rise. His starting weekly salary of 15 shillings was increased to £2. The adult wage for a senior provincial journalist was £7–17–6 when the five-day working week was introduced in mid-July 1948. Eggleton joined the Swindon Branch of the National Union of Journalists (NUJ) on 8 March 1948 and contributed three shillings in membership fees each month. The local branch of the NUJ made him the correspondent for its magazine, *Journalist*, which featured a short news item headed 'He's our baby'.

It read: 'At 16½, a Swindon junior, Tony Eggleton, is the branch's new *Journalist* correspondent. Have we any competition from other branches?'[1] He was a trade unionist *and* a Young Conservative.

Eggleton was also learning more about media culture. Among the older staff in Swindon were a number of former high-flying Fleet Street journalists who had been sacked from their London jobs, mainly because of alcohol problems. The consequence of their ill-discipline was not lost on the eager young man. His mother had already urged him to avoid intoxicants because of her own father's fondness for alcohol. Eggleton did not like the taste of either beer or spirits. Abstaining from alcohol would differentiate Eggleton from journalist colleagues for the rest of his working life. Exuding professionalism well beyond his years, he was noticed by the editor of the *North Wilts Herald*. Clearly impressed with his approach to journalism, he implored Eggleton to remain motivated and pursue his goals. The Westminster Press Group, which owned the Swindon papers, was identifying the company's most promising juniors for additional responsibility and accelerated promotion. The editor intended to nominate Eggleton.

The chief reporter at Newspaper House, Leslie Lister, suggested that Eggleton might take responsibility for the Cirencester Office of Swindon Press which had its premises in the centre of the old Roman town. The office was tucked away in a narrow street, close to the market square and the ancient church. Lister's preference was that Eggleton commute daily to Cirencester to ensure he was available for assignments in Swindon. Unable to rely on public transport, his father offered to buy him an Austin 8 motor car. After passing a driving test and gaining his licence, Eggleton accepted the job. He was now on his own in the Cotswolds district of neighbouring Gloucestershire. The most newsworthy stories were relayed by phone from the Cirencester Office to copytakers in Swindon. Feature articles were written when he returned to Swindon at the end of the day. His stories ranged from court cases and inquests to council decisions and charity events. Although petrol was still strictly rationed, Swindon Press was entitled to special coupons for its business vehicles. To obtain additional petrol, Eggleton delivered the *Football Pink* to newsagents in nearby villages on Saturday afternoons.

To assist his professional development, Swindon Press enrolled their promising young journalist in a course at Urchfont Manor, an Adult Education College run by the Wiltshire County Council. The course focussed on 'The Economic and

Social Development of Country Life' and was attended by a dozen people from different walks of life. As Eggleton had a car, he took the College's staff and his fellow students into the nearby town of Devizes. In a show of confidence, his duties were expanded from Cirencester to coverage of events around Swindon itself including the launch of television in 1949. Radio retained much of its popularity because most British families could not afford to buy a television. Eggelton's introduction to broadcasting was an invitation from the British Broadcasting Corporation (BBC) to take part in its popular 'Any Questions' radio programme which was recorded in Cirencester.

On an otherwise unremarkable day, a letter arrived that would change Eggleton's life. Roy Creswick, the Australian journalist who had worked briefly for Swindon Press, had returned home and was now editing the *Bendigo Advertiser* which, he proudly announced, was recently named the best provincial paper in the Commonwealth by the Australian Broadcasting Corporation (ABC). Creswick wanted to recruit two young English reporters because finding suitable local staff was proving difficult. Eggleton decided to apply. It was a rare opportunity to broaden his professional skills as well as being a personal adventure. In any event, if he did not consider employment in distant Australia he would soon be called up for National Service. All able-bodied men aged 18 years and over were required to spend two years in the Navy, Army or Air Force. After basic training, Eggleton would probably be sent to one of Britain's overseas colonies, such as Cyprus, Malaya or Kenya, where indigenous aspirations were challenging the continuation of imperial rule. The prospect of staying in journalism, avoiding military training and seeing Australia was far more appealing. As he was not yet aged 18, Eggleton secured the in-principle agreement of his parents to leave Britain. He would register his interest in the Bendigo job and seek more information. Christmas 1949 was only a few weeks away.

The chance to work in Australia was entirely unexpected. Cecil Hunt had told readers of *You Want to be a Journalist?* that 'in Australasia opportunities are rare. It might be imagined that Australia and New Zealand would welcome expert workers, but they have their own ways and they have had time to train their own products.'[2] Hunt drew a distinction between Canada, which was seeking aspiring journalists and Australia which 'presents a highly-organised journalistic profession' and New Zealand which presented even fewer opportunities. Hunt thought Australia was 'almost a closed profession, and while there is no active resentment of the imported labour, particularly from the Homeland, neverthe-less the local workers see no particular deficiencies in their source of supply'. Furthermore, Australian journalists 'should possess, or can easily acquire, their particular 'slant' on writing and editing'.

Early in 1950, Eggleton received a reply from Creswick. The *Bendigo Advertiser* wanted him and his cub reporter colleague, Ken Smith, who had applied for the other position, to be available at the end of February. Soon afterwards, the *Bendigo Advertiser*'s managing director, Bert Mundy, offered them each a three-year contract as 'D' grade journalists with a weekly salary of £8–5. Compared with the £2 that both Eggleton and Smith were receiving from Swindon Press, it seemed a princely sum. It even exceeded the £7–17–6 that senior journalists at Newspaper House were receiving. Creswick advised that with satisfactory performance they would soon be promoted to 'B' grade with a weekly salary of £12. This was an opportunity too good to refuse. Eggleton resigned from Swindon Press with effect from mid-February and prepared to sail for Australia in SS *Orcades* on 17 March 1950.

After 30 months with Swindon Press, Eggleton was leaving with mixed emotions. He was sad to be leaving men and women who had introduced him to journalism in a generous and genial setting. He was, however, anxious about what awaited on the other side of the world. Apart from Roy Creswick, whom he hardly knew, Eggleton had no friends or relatives in Australia. He knew little about the country or its culture. Australia was an integral part of the British Empire but he knew from passing encounters that Australians were different from the English; they spoke differently, had different social customs and the landscape was different. Eggleton would depart England's 'green and pleasant lands' for a 'sunburnt country with droughts and flooding rains'.

He made a final visit to his childhood haunts and farewelled his close friends John Perry and Keith Eyles. It was Eyles who purchased his beloved bicycle for £14. Eggleton's last day at Cirencester was Saturday 11 February 1950. Reflecting a keen sense of duty, he worked a full rather than half day. The editorial team arranged a send-off at which the editors of the *Evening Advertiser* and the *North Wilts Herald* were complimentary. The gift of a leather writing case was an invest-ment in his future. The chief reporter, Leslie Lister, provided a glowing reference:

Over the previous two years, Eggleton's progress had been most commendable, the result of constant application to duty and a desire to make headway in his profession. He is very reliable, a good news gatherer, and works well without supervision. Smart in appearance and with good manners and a polished approach, with a composure seldom found in one of his age, Tony Eggleton gives promise of doing exceptionally well in journalism.

After some confusion about who would fund his passage to Australia (his parents eventually offered to cover the cost), Eggleton spent the last few weeks in England with his family. He was not able to see his sister Ruby. She was working with the Royal Air Force as an educator in Egypt. He bought new clothes and an extra cabin trunk. With uncertainty over who was funding his travel, Eggleton missed the chance of sailing in the 28,164-ton SS *Orcades*, which had first and tourist class compartments, but was offered an alternative: the smaller 14,362-ton single class tourist vessel SS *Largs Bay* which was operated by the Aberdeen and Commonwealth Line. *Largs Bay* was due to sail from Southampton on 31 March. He could secure passage in a two-berth cabin on the promenade deck for £89. He was leaving England with two trunks, a suitcase and a typewriter. This was his first 'great adventure'. The question was: how long would the adventure last? His parents assured him of a warm welcome home if life in Australia did not meet his expectations.

The passage to Australia was made easier by the close camaraderie that developed among a small group of people in their late 20s who welcomed the younger Eggleton into their social circle. *Largs Bay* stopped at Malta and then Port Said in Egypt before the ship made its way through the Suez Canal. A night visit to Aden (a British protectorate that later became South Yemen) was followed by a stopover at Colombo in Ceylon (now Sri Lanka). In the absence of air-conditioning, many passengers slept on the upper decks to enjoy the cooling sea breeze. *Largs Bay* arrived in Fremantle on 30 April 1950 – Eggleton's 18th birthday. His shipboard companions took him to the Esplanade Hotel for a birthday celebration and showed him around King's Park. As they walked down St George's Terrace and passed the offices of the *West Australian* newspaper, he was sad that Perth was not his Australian destination. On the final leg from Fremantle to Melbourne, a local journalist suggested Eggleton should think about abandoning regional Bendigo for one of Australia's capital cities.

The ship's arrival in Melbourne coincided with a waterfront strike. *Largs Bay* lay at anchor in Port Phillip Bay for several frustrating days. The ship finally docked on Tuesday 9 May. As visitors streamed on board, a tall man in a scout's uniform named George Stafford bounded up the gangway. Among the badges on his shirt were 'Swindon' and the Wiltshire Scout Emblem, the White Horse. Eggleton had to shake his hand. Stafford responded with enthusiasm, explaining that his own mother in Swindon had told him that Eggleton was coming to Australia after she read about his new position in the *Evening Advertiser*. Stafford had checked incoming passenger lists and saw the name Eggleton. He wore his scout uniform in the hope of standing out. He administered the Melbourne Police Training Depot and was an Assistant Scout Commissioner. Stafford invited Eggleton to visit him in Melbourne once he was settled in Bendigo.

Eggleton received a telegram on arriving at Port Phillip. He was instructed to make his own way to Bendigo via Spencer Street Station and the 1.30pm train. The welcoming party consisted of Roy Creswick, Harry Thompson, the news-paper's chief-of-staff, and Geoffrey Wright, a reporter who had been assigned to look after Eggleton's luggage. They gave their new colleague a quick tour of the *Advertiser*'s office. The building had seen better days. The reporters' room was tatty and ramshackle. Eggleton was delivered to his lodgings, a five-minute drive from the office. His room was timber-lined, sparsely furnished, cold and uninviting. He felt alone for the first time since leaving Swindon and reflected on the wisdom of his decision. He began work the next day and any lingering regrets quickly faded. His first assignment was reporting the annual music competition being held at the Bendigo town hall.

Eggleton was impressed with his new home. The weather in early May was sunny and pleasant. He soon found autumn, and even winter, in Bendigo was better than an English summer. The town centre was graced with fine buildings that lined the wide main street, Pall Mall. The range and abundance of food was the greatest surprise. He went walking through shopping centres looking at items he had forgotten even existed. Bacon, eggs and milk were freely available and could be purchased without restriction or the need for a ration card.

The staff at the *Bendigo Advertiser* went out of their way to be friendly as Eggleton quickly adjusted to the new surroundings. He was encouraged to dress down a little and avoid referring to wealthy landholders as the 'country gentry'. After nearly four months away from a newsroom, Eggleton's confidence behind the typewriter was quickly restored in what proved to be an ideal introduction to Australia and its press. A provincial paper was a good place for an inexperienced reporter to develop skills and gain insights. It was also an opportune time for a journalist interested in public affairs. Eggleton had arrived in Australia within months of Robert Menzies beginning his record-breaking run as Prime Minister. Closer to home, the people of Bendigo were getting ready to celebrate their city's centenary in 1951, marking its role as one of the great gold mining centres of colonial Australia.

There were a few professional adjustments to negotiate as well. Eggleton needed to attune himself to the routine of a morning rather than an evening newspaper. His working day began in the late afternoon and ended in the early hours of the morning. He often returned to his lodgings after 2am. On a busy night it was 3am or later. The office adhered rigidly to union rules. There was overtime when specified and a firmly observed five-day working week. He tended to rise late morning, combine breakfast and lunch and devote the afternoons to exploring the city, its parks and the old gold diggings. The landlady, Mrs Heaphy, managed to cope with his odd hours and provided regular meals for £2–10 a week with laundry. Initially a taciturn host, she gradually became less reserved and more engaging. He never saw her as a surrogate mother. Eggleton was writing home at least once, and sometimes twice, every week. These letters eased his parents' fears and anxieties; he told them he liked Australia and was finding his work fulfilling. After three months in Bendigo he had sufficiently impressed his editors to be promoted. As a 'B' grade journalist he was now on a weekly salary of £10–10. With overtime, he was earning £13–12 a week. This was almost double the wages of a senior reporter in Swindon.

Eggleton quickly proved to be a valuable asset to the *Bendigo Advertiser*. He was writing stories attracting praise from the newspaper's chief-of-staff and editor. He was given important assignments and covering significant events. For Eggleton, the greatest encouragement was finding his stories were rarely altered by the sub-editors. A feature story about Britain which he had drafted while waiting for the voyage to Australia was given a prominent placement in the newspaper under the heading 'Spring brings hope to the land of John Bull'. His profile on the celebrated Australian author, Ion Idriess, was published in the Melbourne *Age*. Having heard Idriess was in a Bendigo bookshop signing books, Eggleton 'walked along the dusty streets in search of the shop [and] visualised a large, hulking man perspiring over a mountainous pile of books'. He was surprised to meet 'a rugged, mild-mannered man of advancing years who, seated behind a counter, was scrawling his name on the cover of countless books. Could this be the man who weaved stirring tales of bush and desert, of prospector and pioneer?' It was.

One particular assignment was to have enduring influence on his future. He was told to interview the former Kerang Shire President and newly elected Liberal Senator for Victoria, John Grey Gorton. The future prime minister warmed to the young reporter and liked his work. Eggleton had disclosed something of his political temperament in a series of opinion pieces. An article headed 'Korean Propaganda Spread in Bendigo' revealed his sympathy for Liberal Party policies. He began with a question: 'Did you have a Communist leaflet waved in your face or thrust into your hand while walking through the streets of Bendigo during the weekend?' After arguing that the 'Red Menace' was real and lamenting the exploitation of 'ill-informed political waverers' by Marxist ideologues, the ardent young journalist warned the *Bendigo Advertiser*'s readers not to pretend 'that the local branch of the Communist Party is a joke, for it is an active tentacle of the Kremlin octopus ... the solution to this menace lies in our hands, the citizens of Australia'. Notably, Eggelton was not an Australian citizen. He concluded: 'we must ensure that the Reds are prevented from infiltrating further into the Commonwealth, and support the Federal Government's plans to ban Communism in this country'. After considerable controversy, the *Communist Party Dissolution Act* was enacted but later ruled unconstitutional by the High Court of Australia.

By the time that Eggleton's former Swindon colleague, Ken Smith, arrived in Australia, Eggleton was already thinking about his next career move. He had in mind a large metropolitan newspaper. His advocate, Roy Creswick, had secured a position with the ABC in Melbourne and suggested Eggleton follow. Creswick arranged for him to be interviewed by the manager and news editor of the ABC in Melbourne. The interview went well but could have been a disaster. Without Eggleton's knowledge, the application that Creswick submitted on his protege's behalf embellished his experience and lifted his age to 20. As he waited to hear from the ABC, Eggleton spent his first Christmas Day in Australia writing feature stories for the *Bendigo Advertiser*. His diary note for 1 January 1951 read: 'Well, here I am 12,000 miles away from home, setting out on a new year. Despite the everyday challenges and problems, I am very happy. I would not change things for the world'. After eight months in Australia, he had no intention of returning to Britain.

Early in the New Year, Eggleton spent a weekend with Roy Creswick and his family in Melbourne. Before returning to Bendigo, Creswick arranged for him to have another informal meeting with the ABC News Editor, Jack Taylor, who intimated that Eggleton was almost certain to be given a job in Melbourne. On 9 February, he received a letter from the ABC offering him appointment to a Metropolitan 'D' grade vacancy with a starting salary of £10–18. Accepting the position meant a two-grade demotion and a 30 percent pay cut. Taking the longer view, Eggleton was still keen to be Melbourne-based and accepted the offer. Although ABC management wanted him to start immediately, he was not released from the *Bendigo Advertiser* until mid-March. No-one wanted to see the energetic young Englishman leave but the mercurial Creswick had presented Eggleton with another ideal opportunity. Creswick found a place for Eggleton to live in an up-market boarding house in East Hawthorn. But as Eggleton arrived in Melbourne, Creswick moved to Brisbane and disappeared entirely from Eggleton's life. He later wrote features for *Country Life* magazine in Sydney.

The ABC was then in the historic Olderfleet Building in Collins Street. The newsroom was located at the end of a long, gloomy and musty corridor at the unfashionable rear of the building. The newsroom windows looked out over railway yards and a drab industrial area. There was a reasonably spacious report-ers' room, a typists' pool, a sub-editors' area, a couple of partitioned areas for the chief-of-staff and his deputy, and a private office for Jack Taylor. These were still early days for the independent ABC News Service which began after the Second World War. The Chifley Labor Government had concluded the time had come for the ABC to have its own reporters who would gather and present the news. The previous practice was for ABC announcers to read lead stories from the daily newspapers to its listeners.

Eggleton found his new reporting role with the ABC slightly daunting. He was assigned to the early morning shift, starting work an hour or so before the 6am news bulletin. The 'dawn patrol' shift meant getting out of bed at 4am and being conveyed by taxi to the newsroom. The shift finished around 2pm. His job was to check overnight developments with the police, the weather bureau, the port authorities (for ship arrivals), the railways for news of train delays and anything else deemed newsworthy. The harvest of his pre-dawn enquiries was fed to the early morning sub-editor for inclusion in the radio bulletins. His colleagues among the young journalists at the ABC included Alan Trengove who became the doyen of tennis reporting in Australia and John Gorton's first biographer.

Eggleton soon graduated from the 'dawn patrol' to a variety of daytime assignments, ranging from Anzac Day at the Shrine to meetings of the Melbourne City Council. After the 'city round' he assisted the state parliamentary roundsman. Occasionally he went further afield. He was asked to produce a feature story on the Royal Australian Air Force (RAAF) in northern Victoria and southern New South Wales. He travelled to Tocumwal in a Douglas DC-3 Dakota transport plane. This was his first experience of flying and an introduction to a lifetime of air travel. When the chief sub-editor unexpectedly found himself short of staff, Eggleton was asked to deputise and quickly displayed the attributes of a good sub-editor. He made the most of the opportunity and continued to be given sub-editorial duties. Jack Taylor encouraged him with fresh challenges and was impressed with his progress and diligence. He was rewarded with a weekly £1 'loading'. Before long, Eggleton was again thinking about career advancement, applying for positions with the ABC News Service in Sydney, Brisbane and Adelaide.

While he considered a range of new positions at the end of 1951, he was conscious of being romantically drawn to a kindergarten teacher, Mary Stuart Walker. In early 1952, Eggleton consulted her father about a potential engagement. There were certain concerns. He was a practising Anglican and Mary was a committed Roman Catholic; her family were well settled in Melbourne and, they presumed, Eggleton would eventually return to England and take their daughter with him. Mary's parents were, however, impressed with the young journalist and indicated they would not oppose an engagement. Eggleton then wrote to his parents. He was not yet 21 and had been away from home less than 2 years. They would probably think he was infatuated with the first nice girl he had met. Mary was actually four years older than him. In reply, they urged him to think long and hard about any decision but would not stand in the way.

While pondering an uncertain future, the ABC unexpectedly promoted him to 'C' grade journalist with the offer of a position in the Adelaide newsroom, starting in February 1952. He went to Adelaide for a few days and met his prospective new colleagues. ABC management in Adelaide were prepared to let him report for duty and then take a month's leave. Eggleton was initially assigned to reporting duties but, as in Melbourne, the news editor began to ask for his assistance with sub-editorial responsibilities. He returned to Melbourne at the end of February with his mind made up. He bought a ring at Gaunt's Jewellers for £50 – almost all his worldly wealth. At a scenic and tranquil spot alongside the ornamental pond in Fitzroy Gardens, he slipped the ring onto Mary's finger and she agreed to marry him. The wedding was set for 3 January 1953. He went back to Adelaide on his own at the end of March 1952. This was his third job within two years of leaving England. Over the next few months he made several short trips to Melbourne in another slow Dakota aircraft from Parafield Airport in Adelaide. After their marriage at St John's Catholic Church in East Melbourne, the newlyweds returned to Adelaide together on Trans Australia Airways (TAA) flight 508 at a cost of £7–12 each. They had few possessions and embarked on married life with the assumption that, at an early stage, they would probably live in England. They rented a self-contained flat in Adelaide and Mary soon found work as a kindergarten teacher.

At the ABC, Eggleton continued to enjoy faster than expected promotion. The news editor, Bob Morrison, was dissatisfied with the chief sub-editor and decided to trial Eggleton in the role. He was soon regularly rostered to edit the primetime evening news bulletins. His rapid rise to chief sub-editor had its disadvantages. Several senior reporters and the typists who had worked with them for many years were dismayed by his sudden elevation. He was not yet 23 years old. There were times when the work atmosphere was sullen as the aggrieved staff attempted to make his life as difficult as possible. Eggleton was undeterred. He enjoyed the confidence of the news editor, was coping well with his new responsibilities, and had a loving and supportive wife at home. He learnt about human disappointments and personal sensitivities, and became better at dealing with difficult colleagues and awkward situations. These lessons were to prove invaluable in future appointments.

Eggleton further consolidated his professional experiences while in Adelaide. He managed arrangements for reporting Queen Elizabeth's visit to South Australia in early 1954 and the coverage of a 5.6 earthquake which shook the city at 3.40am on 1 March. It was the strongest event of its kind to strike a major Australian city until the 1989 Newcastle earthquake. Centred a little to the south of the Adelaide city centre, property damage was recorded over a 700 square kilometre area. Mary rushed outside to see many of her neighbours. Her husband stayed in bed until he departed for work and the morning shift at the ABC. Acknowledging his superior performance in South Australia, he was promoted to 'B' grade journalist in August 1953.

The editor-in-chief from Sydney, Wally Hamilton, visited Adelaide in early 1954. He was impressed with Eggleton and floated the idea of promoting him and sending him back to Melbourne. After applying for an 'A' grade position in Melbourne only five months after being promoted to 'B' grade in Adelaide, the interviewing committee recommended:

> Mr Eggleton has progressed quickly in the ABC News Service but has justified all his promotions to date. He is a young man, only 23, but is a journalist of exceptional ability, and is equally capable as a reporter – particularly where descriptive writing is called for – and as a sub-editor. A year or so ago, Mr Eggleton was singled out by our News Editor for the responsible job of night sub-editor, and in his hands the evening state bulletins have been raised to a standard which we had never consistently maintained. Mr Eggleton subbed most of the Royal Tour copy handled in the Adelaide office, and did this with great credit, as he has performed all other tasks given to him in this office.
>
> He is a young man of very good judgement, good personality, tactful approach, and there seems little doubt that he will go a long way in our service. We feel that Mr Eggleton could at this stage capably undertake whatever duties he was assigned as an 'A' Grade Journalist, even though his promotion already has been rapid, and even though he would be an unusually young man to hold such a senior grading.

At the end of 1954, the Eggletons made their way back to Melbourne. The newly promoted 'A' grade journalist was made responsible for the morning bulletins and occasional editing shifts with Radio Australia.

After eventually finding suitable housing and settling into a stable domestic routine, the Eggletons welcomed their first child, Stephen, on 30 September 1955. Realising they needed something bigger and better than a flat, they sold their car and raised enough money for the deposit on a house in the outer Melbourne suburb of Montmorency. They moved into McCarthy Grove in autumn 1956. At the cost of £3,000, it was a simple timber bungalow in an attractive bushland setting. The road was unsealed and there was no sewerage. The toilet was a little walk from the house in the back garden.

No sooner had he established a work routine in Melbourne radio when Eggleton was approached by Jack Taylor about the advent of television. He had been selected to develop television news in Victoria. His task was to initiate start-up arrangements and locate visual resources for use during televised bulletins, such as still pictures of people and places. Eggleton was included in one of the ABC's first television training courses held in Sydney in January 1956. He learnt alongside staff destined to become the ABC's pioneer producers, technicians and presenters. They became familiar with the different aspects of getting television programs to air and, in his case, news production and script writing. Shaping the scripts to match the visual images proved a complicated task. The standard approach was to count the number of words to synchronise with each foot (30 centimetres) of film. This was a career enhancing opportunity and one Eggleton relished as the ABC strived to be ready for television coverage of the 1956 Melbourne Olympics.

The ABC's Melbourne office began its television news service shortly before the Olympic opening ceremony. As the new purpose-built television studios at Ripponlea were still under construction, makeshift facilities were erected on a building site with excavations, foundations and plenty of mud. The staff were issued with gum boots and lanterns to ensure their safety. As preparations continued, Eggleton was formally appointed Chief of Staff of the ABC Television News Service in Melbourne. His job was anticipating and identifying the main news stories of the day. Even before the first broadcast went to air, the ABC was commissioned by a television news agency in London to provide footage from the main Olympic event sites. Eggleton chartered a light aircraft and set off with a cine cameraman to film a series of aerial shots. A skilled and experienced cameraman, the twists, turns and dives that were necessary to obtain the best angles were too much for the cameraman's stomach. Eggleton spent most of the flight passing him air sickness bags.

At that time all exterior news coverage was recorded on cine cameras. Getting stories to air was a slow and laborious process. The film was delivered to the processing studios at a commercial plant in Melbourne before the time-consuming process of cutting and editing the footage. The first day on air coincided with the crash of a small aircraft a few kilometres north of Melbourne. Although the accident happened early in the morning, by the time the cameraman reached the site, returned to Melbourne and processed the film, the story could not be presented with film of the crash site until the following day. To overcome delays with urgent stories, reporters and producers relied on still photography, stock footage and rudimentary graphics. As he settled into his new job and acquired more experience, Eggleton prepared comprehensive guidance notes for his colleagues headed 'Getting the Film Story'. His ideas and suggestions were welcomed by Wally Hamilton and circulated to news staff around the country. Eggleton explained:

> The coverage man has a complex role ... chief-of-staff, contact man, reporter, researcher, public relations man, transport coordinator and film director. He must have a basic knowledge of cine cameras, film equipment, film stock, processing and filming techniques.

Pioneering television news in Australia proved to be a stimulating experience. As chief of staff, Eggleton's life revolved around identifying good stories, assigning reporters and cameramen, supervising newsroom management and logistics, and assessing the film 'rushes' in the viewing room. With his office in a prominent corner of the newsroom, he was close to all the drafting, editing and production. The Eggletons also bought a new home nearer to the studios. They relocated just as their second son, Andrew, was born in September 1957. Mary's mother Virginia played a vital role during the move, caring for an infant as the boy's father continued his busy job. The couple's fifth wedding anniversary in 1958 was celebrated with the purchase of their first television set.

Eggleton was enjoying his work but remained ambitious and eager for promotion. Having had more than his fair share of advancement at the ABC, he realised there would be few new opportunities and wondered where his next big break would come from. It did not take long to appear.

Endnotes

1   *Journalist*, vol. 32, no. 4, May 1949, p. 69.
2   Cecil Hunt, *You Want to be a Journalist?*, pp. 82–3.

CHAPTER 3

Making news   1959–65

The Melbourne *Sun* newspaper carried an advertisement from the 31 October 1959 edition of the *Commonwealth Government Gazette* seeking a 'Coordinator of Naval Public Relations'. Applicants needed experience in newspapers, radio and television, and be willing to work in Canberra. Eggleton decided to apply and thought that, so soon after the advent of television, there might not be many journalists with first-hand experience in all three media. He was interviewed in Victoria Barracks at St Kilda Road, Melbourne. The initial panel included the Secretary of the Department of the Navy, Tom Hawkins. A subsequent interview was chaired by the Minister for the Navy, Senator John Gorton, who remembered his meeting with Eggleton several years earlier for the story that appeared in the *Bendigo Advertiser* on his election to Federal parliament.

The 27 year old Eggleton told the Minister that he would not be interested in the position unless given scope to lead his 'own part of ship'. He did not want to be a 'glorified clerk'. Gorton produced an amused, knowing smile that gave little away. Gorton felt the same way about his role as Minister; he would not be a mere rubber stamp for decisions made by admirals and bureaucrats. Gorton advocated a proactive public relations strategy and responded warmly to Eggleton's answers to the interview questions. Hawkins was not keen on the young man whom he privately felt was too young and brash. Gorton was determined to have his way mainly because, of all the applicants, Eggleton was easily the most experienced in television. The Minister also sensed that Eggleton would be more responsive to him personally than the uniformed and civilian hierarchy. A formal letter of appointment arrived on 3 March 1960. He needed to move to Canberra within three months.

After nine years at the ABC and with a good chance of eventually becoming a senior executive, Eggleton's decision was bold and brave. The ABC was sad to lose him. For his send-off, the Melbourne newsroom was decorated with nautical paraphernalia and the ABC's graphics staff produced a card depicting him in ostentatious naval regalia. Unusually for a newsroom farewell, there were representatives from management and a cross-section of departments. Jack Taylor paid Eggleton a warm tribute, reflecting on his career with the ABC and noting that Eggleton's departure marked the end of an era. He emphasised Eggleton's pioneering work in television. He had gained a great deal personally and professionally from his time at the ABC but was eager for fresh challenges. Eggleton felt it was time to explore new horizons. Little did he know the Royal Australian Navy (RAN) was about to experience the five most controversial years in its relatively short history.

Eggleton's predecessor as Coordinator of Navy Public Relations had been based at Navy Office which was then at Victoria Barracks in Melbourne. Most of the naval staff were now moving to Canberra and new offices at Russell Hill, not far from Parliament House, although some directorates remained in Melbourne for the time being. Gorton insisted Eggleton work in Canberra. After agreeing to move on 6 June 1960, the Eggleton family was allocated a government house, as well as 60 complimentary trees and shrubs, in the suburb of Dickson. The Navy's new media man was warmly welcomed by the civilian and uniformed staff although most were unfamiliar with his role. Eggleton was given an office with amenities that were consistent with his institutional standing. As carpet covered two-thirds of the room, he was considered a senior official. The Department's deputy secretaries and assistant secretaries made sure he understood public service protocols and then left him alone.

The departmental secretary, Tom Hawkins, had spent much of his professional life in naval administration. Aged 61, he was in the twilight of his career. He told Eggleton he needed to be kept informed of every communication he had with the Minister. If Senator Gorton wanted to see Eggleton at the Department's offices, he was directed to enter and leave the Minister's suite through the Secretary's office. This puzzled Gorton who told Eggleton to ignore the Secretary's instruction and deal directly with him as Minister. Hawkins was unhappy but deferred to Gorton's wishes. Although the Navy was the most junior Federal portfolio at that time and its Minister was not entitled to a press secretary, Gorton wanted to use Eggleton in that role, in addition to his departmental public relations responsibilities.

Eggleton found the senior civilian staff to be genuinely helpful. Their goodwill made it possible for him to establish a positive relationship with uniformed personnel. His predecessor was a much older man who displayed little interest in naval activities and had never been to sea. The new man was energetic and enthusiastic. Eggleton arrived as the Navy was preparing for its 50th anniversary celebrations in 1961. He produced an attractive commemorative Golden Jubilee booklet and demonstrated a close and continuing interest in ships and naval aircraft. Eggleton went to sea and visited shore establishments to promote the Navy and to lift recruiting at a time when the Army and the Air Force were more attractive to teenagers interested in the armed forces.

With easy access to officers and sailors, Eggleton was quick to identify potential news stories and adept at having the media promote them. Gorton was delighted with his initiative and industry. The Minister could now distribute his own media releases. Eggleton devised a strategy of issuing ministerial announcements on naval affairs late on Sunday afternoons when news stories were often in short supply. The Minister's name was frequently on the Sunday evening radio and television news bulletins, and in the Monday morning newspapers. The Liberal Party began to take note of the Victorian senator's emerging profile. Gorton was soon made Minister Assisting the Minister for External Affairs (Sir Garfield Barwick) and later Minister-in-Charge of the Commonwealth Scientific and Industrial Research Organisation (CSIRO). The political correspondent for the *Age* remarked on 28 January 1963 that 'Gorton has emerged as one of the most capable and personable junior ministers, with a healthy mixture of imagination and tough-mindedness'. He had Eggleton to thank for his public prominence.

Gorton was always willing to give Eggleton a free hand which he used to establish a separate Navy Film and Photo Unit to reduce departmental reliance on external sources for the raw material needed to support positive news stories. The first civilian cine camera operator to be employed by the Navy, Phil Hobson, had worked with Eggleton at the ABC in Melbourne. Hobson had been an army photographer in Asia and the Pacific, and brought considerable experience, expertise and professionalism to the new unit. In cooperation with a commercial film production company, Eggleton's team compiled Navy Newsreels for distribution to Australian television stations. Proving to be popular, they were circulated within the Navy as well.

Before long, Eggleton was known throughout the Navy and his assistance was widely sought by officers eager to become better known. He often embarked in the Navy's flagship, the aircraft carrier HMAS *Melbourne*, during international exercises and foreign visits, raising the Navy's public profile at home and abroad. In addition to regular media releases and press hand-outs, Eggleton began submitting feature articles on the RAN for the major Australian daily newspapers. These pieces also found a ready readership in the major provincial papers. He usually travelled with a broadcast standard tape recorder and sent radio reports to the ABC and commercial radio stations. In an era when there were few Australian correspondents posted abroad, he had considerable success in placing these 'voice pieces' with media outlets.

Eggleton was committed to his profession and eager to do well. After being away from Swindon for more than a decade, he seized an opportunity to travel to Britain and the United States for a study tour. He would compare and contrast the approach being taken by the Royal Navy and the United States Navy to media relations. Accompanied by his wife and sons, the Eggletons flew to England for his parents' first meeting with their Australian daughter-in-law and two grandsons in September 1961. Much had changed in the country of his birth. Eggleton noticed the spread of houses, the density of traffic and the increasing multiculturalism of British society. Food and petrol rationing were now distant memories and many ordinary families were earning sufficient to own motor cars. After a family holiday, Mary and the boys flew home to Australia. They would not return to England for another decade. By then, they would be joined by the youngest of the three children, Judith, who was born in 1962.

Eggleton commenced his study tour with visits to ships and shore establishments, and meetings at the Admiralty in London. In the United States he made similar visits and met staff at the US Navy's School of Journalism. He did not realise then the importance of the insights and innovations to which he was exposed. After 1945, there were a series of naval accidents in Australia that became progressively more serious. They began with an explosion on board the landing ship *Tarakan* that killed nine men in 1950 and continued in 1954 with the drowning of two sailors from the aircraft carrier *Vengeance* in Port Phillip Bay. The newly completed destroyer *Vendetta* struck the caisson at Williamstown Naval Dockyard in 1958, the destroyer *Anzac* mistakenly fired a sand-filled practice round into her sister-ship *Tobruk* in September 1960, and an explosion in the stores carrier *Woomera* killed two men the following month. From a wartime peak of 337 ships in commission and 39,600 personnel, the RAN now consisted of 41 ships and just over 10,000 officers and sailors. Many of its ships were old and its people increasingly aware they were operating obsolete equipment. The RAN's future appeared bleak. The admirals possessed few political skills and the public were unconvinced of the continuing need for a 'blue water' navy. The number of embarrassing mishaps suggested the Navy's professional standards were in decline as well. Below the surface, there were serious problems that were partially obscured by Eggleton's effective promotion of the Navy's activities.

The Navy had two options in dealing with public criticism of its performance. The first was simply to ignore the press and deflect political concerns. The second was seeking an empathetic response from the media in the hope of securing better funding for the fleet and boosting the morale of uniformed personnel. The latter was Eggleton's preferred strategy. After the accident that had left *Tobruk* beyond economical repair, rather than expressing embarrassment and dismissing the consequences, Eggleton secured the Minister's approval to fly a group of Canberra-based reporters in an aircraft from the Naval Air Station HMAS *Albatross* to the airstrip at Jervis Bay where the damaged *Tobruk* was anchored. As the press party was transported by boat from the shore to the destroyer, the ship's captain had already used his initiative and covered the damaged hull with grey painted tarpaulins. Eggleton briefed the media and showed them around. A malfunction in *Anzac*'s gun direction equipment had nullified the shell's 6 degree 'throw-off'. The shell struck *Tobruk* when it was intended to miss. The problem had not been encountered before and was anything but foreseeable. The reporters saw the event in its proper perspective and the ensuing coverage was essentially positive. The Minister and the Naval Board acknowledged the advantages of transparency and openness. But this would not always be the case.

The run of naval accidents continued into 1963 when the frigate HMAS *Queenborough* collided with the submerged British submarine HMS *Tabard* in May. Five months later, a party of five junior officers under training from HMAS *Sydney* were drowned during a training exercise off Hooke Island in the Whitsundays. The men sailed a naval whaler around Hooke Island before the boat, by then out of sight, capsized in the forenoon. A search party was not sent until 7pm by which time they were all dead. Gorton decided to convene a Naval Board of Inquiry which he opened to the press and the public. Eggleton was sent to Hayman Island to handle the media and to provide the Minister with daily progress reports. These proceedings further consolidated his close working relationship with Gorton. The Board of Inquiry's report was not released to the public. Three officers were court-martialled and acquitted. It looked like a cover up. Newspaper editorials and letters to the editor expressed intense public dissatisfaction with the Navy's handling of the affair. The RAN's reputation was badly damaged. Trust in the Navy's leadership had been greatly diminished.

Gorton relinquished the Navy portfolio after the November 1963 Federal election. Although the Navy's standing had deteriorated, the Victorian Senator was promoted. Prime Minister Menzies believed Gorton had done well in the portfolio despite the Navy's problems. The new year did not start well for the embattled RAN. In January 1964, the Fleet Tanker, HMAS *Supply*, suffered severe engine-room flooding as the ship sank to the sea floor alongside a wharf at Garden Island naval dockyard. Fortunately, such was the draught of the ship and the shallowness of the water that the upper decks were not awash. This incident was not how the Navy wanted to welcome its minister-designate, Fred Chaney, a decorated former RAAF pilot from Western Australia. [Chaney remained the 'minister-designate' for several weeks until legislation was passed authorising an expansion to the Ministry.] Much worse was to come.

Just before 9pm in the evening of Monday 10 February 1964, the aircraft carrier, HMAS *Melbourne*, collided with the destroyer, HMAS *Voyager*, 30 kilometres south-east of Jervis Bay. *Voyager* was cut in two. The forward section sank within minutes while the after section disappeared below the waterline three hours later. The death toll of 82 men made the collision the Navy's worst peacetime disaster. Half an hour after the collision, Eggleton received a call at his home from the duty officer at Navy Office. He was advised there had been an incident off Jervis Bay and that '*Voyager*'s stern had parted from its bow'. Eggleton replied: 'That sounds serious'. The duty officer responded: 'Yes, sir, I think so'. The first signal from *Melbourne*'s commanding officer to Fleet headquarters concluded: '*Voyager* is down by the bows'. In fact, *Voyager*'s bow had sunk taking dozens of men with her. The duty officer informed Eggleton that he was not to come into Navy Office because there would be no contact with the media. This was an absurd direction. There had plainly been a serious accident and the press would want details. The unreality of the Navy's initial response to this terrible disaster was already apparent.

Despite being told to stay away, Eggleton went directly to his office at Russell Hill and began preparing for media calls. The newly appointed departmental secretary, Sam Landau, was then in Sydney with the Minister-designate, Fred Chaney. Neither could be located after they changed hotels at short notice and failed to inform their respective secretaries. They were finally contacted at 10:15pm which was about the same time Prime Minister Menzies was advised. The Navy naturally made a priority of establishing the extent of the disaster and dealing with next-of-kin. The Chief of Naval Staff, Vice Admiral Sir Hastings Harrington, was finally persuaded to provide Eggleton with a few lines that he could use in response to media calls. The floodgates opened soon after 11pm when Eggleton received a call from Australian Associated Press. Just after midnight, Fleet headquarters received a signal from *Melbourne* which had been recovering survivors from the sea: '*Voyager* has sunk'.

With the Naval Board preoccupied with operational matters and arranging an inquiry, Eggleton refused to be sidelined. He saw no point in continuing resistance to a media briefing and took matters into his own hands. He made direct contact with the Naval Air Station HMAS *Albatross* at Nowra and the Naval College HMAS *Creswell* at Jervis Bay. He asked their staffs to cooperate with the media who would soon be descending upon them. By this time calls from reporters were coming from all parts of the world. He had already summoned his assistant to help with telephone inquiries. Eggleton managed to slip home for an hour's sleep at 6am and then spent the morning dealing with the journalists. In the afternoon, Eggleton accompanied the Acting Minister for the Navy, Dr Jim Forbes, and members of the Naval Board on a flying visit to the damaged *Melbourne* which was slowly making its way up the coast to Sydney Harbour. The helicopter conveying the contingent from Canberra landed on the flight deck and met the carrier's commanding officer, Captain John Robertson, and many of the survivors. Eggleton recalled Robertson looking gaunt and grey with disbelief and sadness lining the faces of *Melbourne*'s ships company and *Voyager*'s survivors. This was an unimaginable human tragedy.

After returning to Canberra, Eggleton assisted with ministerial press conferences and briefings for the Prime Minister. The parliament, the press and the people wanted answers. The Navy could no longer hide; there appeared to be something seriously wrong with the way it conducted operations and the admirals seemed unwilling or, worse, unable to address the most pressing issues. Eggleton was praised for his independent action in ensuring a continuing flow of accurate information to those with a need and a right to receive it. For the greatest part he had acted with formal approval but without it when the wheels of government turned too slowly. The media realised he understood and appreciated their needs, and the entitlement of the public to be told about what had happened and why.

The Prime Minister announced a royal commission would be held. It would be open to the press and the people. After 55 days of public hearings and a report that was critical of the officers on *Melbourne*'s bridge (a finding that was overturned by a second royal commission convened in 1967) and the general state of the Navy's preparedness for operations, Captain Robertson resigned when he was not re-appointed in command of *Melbourne* after being temporarily relieved to attend the royal commission. An air of despondency settled over the Navy that did not lift until the following year (1965) when Australian forces were deployed to the steadily escalating civil war in South Vietnam.

Away from the media spotlight and with the RAN's reputation tarnished, Eggleton recommended the strengthening and restructuring of naval public relations. After the battering the Navy had endured at the hands of parliamentarians and the press, the Naval Board was finally prepared to listen. New approaches to dealing with the media were approved and all ships and shore establishments had designated officers for handling the media and public relations. Eggleton arranged for their selection and training, something that would have been unthinkable 12 months earlier. He was one of few people at Navy Office whose reputation was enhanced by the *Voyager* tragedy.

At the end of 1964, Eggleton was unexpectedly seconded to the office of the Minister for Defence, Senator Shane Paltridge, to serve as press secretary. Paltridge's press secretary, Len Owens, was seconded to the Prime Minister's office following the sudden death of the 52 year old incumbent, Ray Maley, who had been a journalist at the *Sydney Morning Herald*. After surviving two heart attacks earlier in the year, Maley suddenly collapsed and died in King's Hall of Parliament House on the night of 29 September 1964 during a state function for Princess Marina. Maley, a lifelong smoker until the previous year, had been Menzies' fourth press secretary since 1949. Menzies was present when Maley died and issued a public statement the next day:

Ray Maley was a fine servant of the Crown. His Public Service career extended over a period of 12 years, which was made up chiefly of six years as Press Officer at the Australian Embassy in Washington where he served the Ambassador with high capacity and distinction, followed by three and a half years as Press Secretary to the Prime Minister. I, as Prime Minister, and other members of the Government, have been greatly assisted by his rich talents in journalism and its related fields. He displayed a meritorious insight and application in his work, linked with the attractive personal qualities of great cheerfulness and dignity.[1]

When seconded to Paltridge's office, Eggleton could draw on his experience of working with Gorton but was without any exposure to electioneering although his principal task was preparing for the 1964 Senate campaign. As Paltridge represented Western Australia, Eggleton spent much of this period working in Perth. It was a surprising appointment in every sense. He was not known for any party affiliation nor, indeed, for showing any interest in partisan politics. As the Navy Minister, Fred Chaney, represented a Perth electorate and knew Paltridge well, Eggleton presumed the idea for his secondment had come from him.

Unknown to Eggleton, the secondment was actually a trial that had been suggested by the Prime Minister who wanted to see how Eggleton handled the role of press secretary to a senior minister. Paltridge was re-elected and Eggleton returned to the Navy in early 1965. Having proposed a new public relations strategy in the wake of the *Voyager* disaster, Eggleton was obliged to ensure its implementation was smooth and sustainable. In mid-1965 he embarked on an extensive overseas trip to highlight various RAN initiatives and the construction of new vessels for Australia in the United States and Britain. He also looked at how Western navies were selling their message to domestic audiences who believed the advent of fast jets and nuclear weapons heralded the end of warships and conventional forces.

On his return to Australia in early August 1965, Eggleton was asked to confer with the Secretary of the Prime Minister's Department. Sir John Bunting revealed that Eggleton was on an interview short-list for the Prime Minister's new press secretary. Bunting explained that the Prime Minister 'has asked me to ask whether you would do the job; he does not mind whether you vote Liberal or what, so long as you feel comfortable working with the Liberal Party'. Eggleton was willing to be considered for the influential post but mentioned he was 'more interested in government than politics'. Furthermore, although he was not a member of the

Liberal Party, he would want to be kept informed of party matters and not left in ignorance. Bunting assured Eggleton that the Prime Minister would not be troubled by anything he had said.

On 1 September 1965, some 11 months after Maley's death, Eggleton met Sir Robert Menzies in his Parliament House office. He received a warm welcome from the formidable Prime Minister who, much to Eggleton's surprise, referred to him as 'laddie'. Menzies assured Eggleton there was no need for him to worry about writing speeches because, he declared, 'I have a reasonable command of the English language'. Menzies had no interest in Eggleton's 'personal politics' which remained an entirely private matter. The most important thing, the Prime Minister remarked, was that Eggleton should feel comfortable serving him and the Coalition Government. Having dealt with his reservations, Eggleton eagerly accepted the position. He would advise the Secretary of the Navy Department and negotiate a release date. Menzies told Eggleton that others were attending to these matters and that he would start work in the Prime Minister's office that day. The rush was difficult to understand given the position had been vacant for nearly a year.

Eggleton's appointment was announced immediately, generating scores of messages from family, friends and journalistic colleagues. The *Sunday Mirror* reported under the heading 'Survivor' that Eggleton 'clinched the job' because he had done a good job in the aftermath of the *Voyager* tragedy. The newspaper suggested 'he's possibly too quick on his feet to be popular with the press but he should make a good man for Sir Robert'.[2] The Acting Controller of ABC News, JG 'Gil' Oakley, remarked that Eggleton was 'the first Press Secretary to the Prime Minister who has had such extensive background of radio and television news experience, and perhaps in some way this may reflect the growth of these two mediums in the Australian scene'.[3]

The duties of the Prime Minister's Public Relations Officer and Press Secretary were traditionally combined in one position until separated in May 1951. The previous incumbents – Stewart Cockburn (May 1951–August 1953), Hugh Dash (August 1953–June 1960), BJ Anderson (September 1960–January 1961) and Ray Maley (February 1961–September 1964) – had not come to the job via a public relations path. They were journalists experienced in political reporting. By 1965 the position description was still minimal but constantly evolving as media interest in political rivalry was intensifying with the growing popularity of television. Voters wanted to hear and see those who were spending their taxes and furthering their interests. Eggleton saw himself as 'the link between the prime minister and all the media of public communication. [The press secretary] is a readily available point of contact – I regret to say 24 hours a day and seven days a week – and the main day-to-day source of prime ministerial and government information'. His 'first loyalty' was to the prime minister but did not think he would be of much value 'if he became nothing more than a one-eyed propagandist'. The challenge was simultaneously serving the prime minister and the press, and 'it is fatal if this balance is not maintained. A press secretary is useless if either side loses confidence and trust in him'.

Eggleton's personal philosophy of government was nuanced but not complex. He was committed to the public's 'right to be kept fully and accurately informed'. Although there were 'good journalists and bad journalists', in his experience 'few have deliberately set out to misrepresent and distort'. In terms of a press secretary's necessary attributes, Eggleton thought they included 'a considerable amount of patience and tact ... it is also handy to have a fairly even temperament to cope with frequent, rapid changes in plans, and unexpected developments at any time of the day or night'. He saw it as 'something of a challenge to remain courteous at whatever time the phone may ring'. Being available meant he needed the 'ability to anticipate ... likely press and public reactions' to ensure the prime minister was 'forewarned and forearmed'. It was crucial that the press secretary did not 'presume to advise him in fields where there are other experts and specialists who should be far better informed'. He saw his position less as a job and more 'a way of life' that involved a 'never-ending game of chess, calling for constant concentration'. He declared that 'I do not have any special ambition to enter politics personally ... the important thing is to have a job which one can do and do reasonably well'.

Eggleton was quietly surprised at his appointment. Apart from the loss of *Voyager*, his only other previous contact with the Prime Minister concerned the National Press Club. In 1962 at a meeting in the Kingston Hotel, about one kilometre from Parliament House, Eggleton promoted the idea of establishing a National Press Luncheon Club in Canberra after becoming familiar with the Press Club in Washington. [4]An institution of this kind could raise the profile of journalists while giving them an opportunity to play host to significant and newsworthy people. A local group from the Australian Journalists' Association

(AJA) had already explored such an initiative but needed Eggleton's organisational skills to ensure focus and direction. His energy was rewarded with election to the chairmanship of a planning committee consisting initially of 11 members – Harry Keen and Norman Hoffman (Immigration Department public relations), Christopher Forsyth (Melbourne *Age*), Neil O'Reilly (Sydney *Sun*), John Rich (*Sydney Morning Herald*), Nyle Browning (*Canberra Times*), Eric Sparke (News & Information Bureau) and Noel Tanswell (Air Force Public relations) – and two ex-officio members, the AJA president, Harold Eather, and secretary, George Randall. The committee met for the first time on 7 September 1962. They were soon joined by Lee Catmull (Melbourne *Sun*) and Don Lawler (Immigration Department public relations). The committee settled on the preferred inaugural speaker: Prime Minister Menzies.

Eggleton approached Menzies's office and was told that February 1963 would be a convenient time. On 12 February 1963, Eggleton received a personal letter from Menzies informing him that 'it is clear that I cannot be with you this month and I doubt that March will prove any easier. In the circumstances, perhaps you would like someone else to do the first address, and I assure [you] I will completely understand should you decide to do this'.[5] The first official luncheon would be held at the Hotel Canberra on 17 June 1963 and the inaugural speaker would be the Minister for External Affairs, Sir Garfield Barwick. At 30 shillings a seat, the event was well attended and judged a great success. Others soon followed. With the Press Club's standing on the rise and its capacity to attract significant speakers gradually increasing, Parliamentary Press Gallery journalists began to show more interest in the initiative. Eggleton served as foundation chairman for two years before handing over leadership to a senior political correspondent, John Bennetts, of the *Age*. It was during a later luncheon addressed by the Prime Minister on 14 September 1964 that Eggleton again had contact with his future boss.

In contrast to the contemporary Prime Minister's Office (PMO), Menzies was served by a small staff numbering a dozen members, mainly female clerical officers, headed by his long-serving and highly respected private secretary, Hazel Craig. Eggleton moved into Maley's office which was a few steps from the Prime Minister's suite and the Cabinet room. It was small and, during an earlier era in the building's life, had been a men's toilet. Longer serving parliamentarians occasionally dashed into Eggleton's office, assuming it was still serving its original purpose. As Press Secretary, Eggleton was assisted by Mary Newport who worked in an adjoining room. She was experienced in the workings of Parliament House and helped Eggleton come to terms with his new role. One of her tasks was transporting a large and antiquated tape recorder to preserve the Prime Minister's remarks for posterity. All of Menzies' public utterances were later transcribed. In some 'Posterity Notes' he drafted in 1966, Eggleton admitted to being 'somewhat in awe of the great man, particularly in the early days. But he was always very reasonable and very friendly. I felt my way gently, and he was always prepared to listen to ideas'.

Menzies tended to do most of his work at Parliament House, coming and going through a nondescript side door, rather than arriving and departing from the main front entrance that faced Lake Burley Griffin and the Australian War Memorial. Although President John F Kennedy had recently been assassinated in the United States, the Australian Prime Minister was not afforded round-the-clock police protection and there were no restrictions on access to Parliament House. The public could move freely through the building. Visitors often strayed down the Government corridor and peered into the entrance of the prime minister's suite. The solitary guard politely advised that this particular area was 'off limits' and sent visitors on their way. Menzies regarded the prime minister's official residence in Canberra, known as The Lodge, as his family home. When in Melbourne, Menzies stayed at The Windsor (Hotel) which made special provision of a large suite.

In addition to handling the media and keeping journalists at a distance, the press secretary accompanied Menzies on official duties, ensuring the Prime Minister was on time, in the right place and adequately briefed in the event of questions from reporters. Eggleton exerted 'no great effort' becoming accustomed to travelling in the prime ministerial Bentley. When not with his wife, Dame Pattie, Menzies would sit in the front of the vehicle alongside the driver. Eggleton sat in the rear seat. A similar pattern was followed across the country. He was also asked to provide occasional valet services. Shortly after Eggleton joined the Prime Minister's staff he went with Menzies to the opening of the Molonglo Observatory at Hoskinstown near Canberra. As they neared the venue, Menzies instructed the driver to pull the Bentley to the side of the road and then invited Eggleton to get out with him. Menzies then produced a can of fly spray which he directed Eggleton to apply liberally to the back of his jacket and his collar, hoping to discourage the presence of bush flies during his speech at the opening. Domestic concerns were never far from the mind of the nation's leader. This kind of interaction established a close personal rapport between the 70 year-old prime minister and his 33 year-old press secretary.

While in Canberra, Eggleton briefed the Prime Minister every day on emerging media issues. Menzies' large desk was uncluttered, apart from an inward and outward correspondence tray which were cleared regularly.[6] There was also a lined notepad on which, with fountain pen or pencil, Menzies drafted his notes and correspondence. The Prime Minister disliked the telephone and, when Eggleton was in his office, expected him to take any calls.

Having been Prime Minister for more than 15 years, Menzies had well-established and finely-tuned rules governing his media relations. He expected Eggleton to generate ideas for positive stories but said his new press secretary should not be discouraged if, in the first instance, his ideas were rejected. Menzies hinted that he might even change his mind if the suggestion were offered a second time. When Menzies was appointed to succeed Sir Winston Churchill as Lord Warden of the Cinque Ports, a ceremonial office in the United Kingdom, on 7 October 1965, Eggleton proposed holding a press conference for the political correspondents. Surprisingly given his previous reticence, Menzies agreed. This was new ground even for a national leader with long experience of public life. Eggleton persuaded Menzies to be more accessible and less guarded, believing reporters were more likely to speculate when they had nothing factual to write about. It was a successful event and made Menzies generally less resistant to meeting groups of journalists although he disliked being 'door stopped' – impromptu encounters for which he was unprepared.

Although Menzies had personal reservations about many of the journalists employed in the Parliamentary Press Gallery, he was usually tolerant and courteous. A notable exception involved a UAP journalist named Jack Allsopp. In a private note Eggleton recorded that Menzies was in 'great distress over being rude' to Allsopp during

> some encounter as the PM was going to his car one evening. Menzies felt that he had been ruder than he should have been. He wanted to see me after dinner for some ideas on how he could make amends. It paid dividends for Allsopp

because the PM gave him a private interview in his office ... one of the very
few pressmen to see Menzies privately in the time that I was with him.

As Eggleton's confidence grew, Menzies was content for him to brief the media
on day-to-day issues, resulting in a steady stream of correspondents visiting the
press secretary's office.

As well as wanting protection from the prying media, Menzies sought a
degree of privacy when travelling. As the Royal Australian Air Force (RAAF)
VIP Squadron was limited in both size and scope, Menzies often travelled by
commercial aircraft. Eggleton sat in the aisle seat to discourage passengers from
disturbing the Prime Minister. On a flight to Perth in November 1965, Eggleton
was summoned to the flight deck and told that Dr Herbert Vere Evatt, the former
High Court judge and Labor Opposition Leader, had died. Eggleton advised the
Prime Minister who produced a pencil and immediately drafted a tribute which
was relayed to Canberra by the flight crew. Evatt, first elected to Federal parliament
in 1940, was Menzies' principal political foe for nearly a decade. Eggleton kept
the handwritten draft in his personal papers. Those who had served in parliament
during the war years were now few in number. Menzies was about to mark his
71st birthday and had become Australia's oldest prime minister.

On Christmas eve 1965, Menzies asked Eggleton to spend the holiday break
with him. The Prime Minister planned to have Christmas lunch with Dame Pattie
and his family in Canberra and then go to Kirribilli House in Sydney where he
could relax, watch the ferries at the bottom of the garden, and listen to tennis
and cricket on the radio. The invitation disappointed the Eggleton family, especially the three children, but Mary thought her husband should accept. Eggleton
joined Menzies at Kirribilli. They were the sole occupants of the house and were
feted by the housekeeper. Menzies was totally relaxed and completely at ease.
Over meals, the Prime Minister reflected on his life and times, and recounted
the contributions of his current parliamentary colleagues. His only reservations
were about Billy McMahon, the Member for Lowe and Minister for Labour and
National Service, whom he professionally distrusted and personally disliked.
Menzies believed McMahon was disloyal and was too willing to leak information
to the press for his own purposes.

Over dinner one evening, Menzies told Eggleton that he had decided to retire
at the end of January and would be advising his colleagues at the right time.

Eggleton was touched that Menzies had entrusted him with this information. Menzies seemed glad that Harold Holt, his long-serving Liberal Party deputy and the Treasurer since 1960, would finally get his opportunity. 'Young Harold', as Menzies routinely referred to him, was aged 58. He would, Menzies believed, make a good prime minister. Enjoying strong support within the parliamentary party, Menzies thought Holt would be elected to the leadership unopposed. In this event, Menzies would be recommending to Holt that Eggleton be retained as press secretary. He had been pleased with the way Eggleton handled the role and regretted their partnership had not begun sooner. Menzies said he had happy memories of former press secretaries but had especially appreciated Eggleton's management of the evolving demands of television. The relaxed setting presented an ideal opportunity for a candid discussion about handling the announcement, particularly the media arrangements.

Menzies wanted to bow out quietly but was eventually persuaded to hold a final news conference. Invitations would not be restricted to bureau chiefs. He would announce his retirement during a full-scale news conference to be held in the main members dining room at Parliament House. It would be broadcast on radio and be the first live telecast from Parliament House. It represented a significant logistical exercise that required Eggleton to work closely and confidentially with the ABC in making the necessary preparations. He felt it was important that the Prime Minister should walk into the news conference at the appointed time with the telecast to start as he entered. Given the tight schedule, Eggleton rehearsed the walk from the prime minister's office to the parliamentary dining room. To be safe, Eggleton decided they should allow five minutes. If they were a little early, he and Menzies could always loiter for a minute or two.

Eggleton went to see Menzies 20 minutes before the press conference. The retiring Prime Minister reviewed all the arrangements and then asked how long had been allocated for his walk to the dining room. When told five minutes, Menzies held up his hand and said 'Wait. You haven't allocated time for my nervous pee'. Eggleton could not hide his astonishment. Menzies revealed that, despite public perceptions of confidence and calm, he needed to visit the toilet prior to every major speech. The preparation time was adjusted accordingly and Eggleton was able to guide the Prime Minister into the dining room on cue. It was 20 January 1966. More than 100 journalists and commentators were present. Most recognised it was the end of a political era.

Eggleton's handling of the retirement press conference attracted extensive praise from his journalist colleagues. Herschel Hurst of the Melbourne *Sun* newspaper told Eggleton he 'went far beyond the call of duty in the way you worked to keep us informed of happenings. I also want to thank you on behalf of our own photographer and TV camera team, whose job was made much easier by your thoughtfulness and assistance'. Writing on behalf of the Parliamentary Press Gallery, Alan Reid thanked Eggleton for his 'really magnificent handling of the involved and difficult arrangements ... you gave us effective, efficient and courteous cooperation which made it a professional and personal pleasure to work with you'.

As expected, Harold Holt succeeded Sir Robert Menzies as leader of the Liberal Party and Prime Minister. Although the Labor Opposition led by Gough Whitlam portrayed Holt as a veiled version of Menzies, Holt was temperamentally very different to his predecessor. Eggleton immediately noted differences in their manner and style. A few days before Holt was sworn-in as prime minister, a funeral was held for the former Minister for Defence, Senator Sir Shane Paltridge. Eggleton travelled to Western Australia with Menzies on 24 January 1966. He stayed at the old Esplanade Hotel with Menzies in a room on one side and Holt on the other. The next morning there was a loud knock on the wall. Eggleton went quickly to Holt's door and was greeted by the prime minister-designate clad only in his underpants. Holt asked whether an Australia Day message had been prepared for him to consider. A text had indeed been produced and Holt was handed a draft. Holt said he would read it while sitting on the toilet. The suggested form of words survived the bathroom scrutiny. So began the Holt era.

Despite being Australia's longest serving prime minister, Menzies told Eggleton 'there is no greater has-been than a has-been prime minister'. The retiring Menzies would not pose any problem for his successor. He walked away from public office and was true to his word. He did not interfere in Liberal Party affairs or criticise decisions he personally felt were poorly considered. For Eggleton, however, there was a nervous wait. Would Holt accept Menzies' final piece of advice and retain Eggleton or bring his trusted Treasury press secretary with him and send Eggleton back to the Navy? There was no guarantee that Eggleton would continue working at Parliament House when Harold Edward Holt became the 17th Prime Minister of Australia on Australia Day 1966.

Endnotes

1   https://pmtranscripts.pmc.gov.au/release/transcript-995

2   *Sunday Mirror*, 5 September 1965.

3   Private letter to Eggleton from JG Oakley, ref 55/511/654, dated 31 August 1965.

4   *National Press Club Journal*, vol. 8, no. 2, May 1983, p. 2.

5   Steve Lewis, *Stand & Deliver: Celebrating 50 Years of the National Press Club*, Black, Melbourne, 2014, p. 1.

6   The desk is now on display in the John Howard Prime Ministerial Library at Old Parliament House in Canberra.

CHAPTER 4

Political prominence   1966–67

The retirement of Robert Menzies as the Prime Minister of Australia marked a change in the tenor of national affairs. Menzies had exercised national leadership for more than 18 years (April 1939–August 1941 and December 1949–January 1966) and his imposing presence had shaped every facet of Australian public life. His successor, Harold Holt, was portrayed as young and energetic although he was 58 years old and suffering from a few well-hidden physical ailments. After more than 30 years in Federal parliament, Holt was highly regarded by his fellow parliamentarians and most members of the press gallery. He had maintained a substantial public profile throughout 1965 as the public face of Australia's transition to decimal currency which would occur on 14 February 1966.

Few Australian prime ministers have ever enjoyed the orderly succession of power that saw Holt ascend to the nation's highest political office in January 1966. Menzies had departed at a time of his own choosing and without any pressure being applied by his colleagues. Although Holt was Menzies' deputy as leader of the Liberal Party for nearly a decade and had high hopes of being the next leader, painful memories of Menzies' resignation as prime minister in 1941 and the subsequent demise of the United Australia Party prevented him from ever contemplating a challenge. Holt believed that Sir Robert was entitled to his loyalty and never wavered. He had avoided stepping 'over anyone's dead body'.

Eggleton had been Menzies' press secretary for five months. He had merely been seconded from the Department of Navy and was not a member of the Prime Minister's Department. Holt had known and worked with many press secretaries as a Cabinet minister over the previous 16 years and might have had another journalist in mind. Eggleton's uncertainty continued until the day after the funeral for Senator Paltridge which he had attended with Holt. During the return journey to Canberra in a RAAF VIP aircraft, Holt quietly invited Eggleton to continue as press secretary but, he added, it would be a trial arrangement to ensure they could work together. Senator John Gorton, the Minister for Education and Science, was on the same plane and approached Eggleton about working for him. Holt responded: 'You're too late, John. I've already signed him up'.

During the long flight Holt talked about changes to the existing ministry and made a point of highlighting the appointment of Malcolm Fraser as Minister for the Army. He felt it was time Fraser was given an opportunity to demonstrate his abilities, albeit in a relatively junior portfolio. Eggleton would need to present the slightly modified Cabinet to the press gallery as evidence that Holt had confidence in the ministerial team he had inherited from Menzies and would continue his predecessor's style of government. Holt was, he told Eggleton, 'eager to have a much more friendly relationship with the press'. The new Prime Minister was able to pursue such a relationship because he was well liked by the media and on first-name terms with many of the Canberra-based newsmen.

Like Menzies, Holt enjoyed the goodwill of his colleagues. First elected in 1935 and elevated to the Menzies' Ministry in 1940, he was a seasoned politician and hardened parliamentarian. Whereas Menzies tended to be aloof, Holt was accessible. Although well into middle age, the media were fascinated by the contrasts between the two men. Photographs of 'Sir Robert' in his double-breasted suit seated at his parliamentary desk were contrasted with pictures of 'Harry' in a wet suit surrounded by his attractive bikini clad daughters-in-law. The media readily warmed to the informal, beach-loving prime minister, his trendy fashion-designer wife, Zara, and photogenic sons, Nick, Andrew and Sam. The television channels wanted film of Holt snorkelling at Cheviot Beach and relaxing at his Portsea retreat. These images helped Eggleton to present the new prime minister as someone connected to popular culture and appreciative of everyday pleasures.

Consistent with his minimalist approach to Cabinet appointments, there were similarly few changes to Holt's personal staff. In addition to the retention of Eggleton, Holt kept the official driver, Ray Coppin. Menzies' private secretary, Hazel Craig, entered a well-deserved retirement and was replaced by Holt's loyal private secretary at the Treasury, Pat de Lacy. Holt chose a senior official from the Prime Minister's Department, the measured and thoughtful Peter Bailey, as his principal private secretary. The daily office routine also changed. Holt started work earlier and often left the office later than Menzies. Holt preferred to walk through the main front entrance to Parliament House where he could be seen rather than the nondescript side door used by his predecessor. The gregarious Holt looked forward to interacting with tourists and frequently spoke with visitors in King's Hall. He was unconcerned about the need for personal protection and was untroubled by impromptu approaches from journalists.

Holt and Eggleton established a mutually satisfactory working relationship and the trial soon became permanent. The Prime Minister would be met each morning by his Press Secretary in King's Hall and the two men would walk together down the 'Government' corridor. [The corresponding corridor on the other side of the building housed the Leader of the Opposition and was known as the 'Opposition' corridor]. Eggleton would canvas current issues and, if any matter required more than quick consideration, he would follow Holt into his office. Regular face-to-face contact meant that Eggleton was kept informed about new thinking and looming problems. Eggleton found that seeing Holt during the day was never difficult to arrange. For Eggleton, the day ended as it began. He would accompany Holt to his official car which would be waiting at the front of Parliament House. This afforded a last-minute chance to 'compare notes' and anticipate the next day's priorities.

Unlike Menzies, Holt agreed to speak with the media on a regular basis. Senior press gallery members were invited to the Prime Minister's office for conferences and briefings. As the Parliamentary Press Gallery was still relatively small, the correspondents were seated in chairs around the prime ministerial desk. At the conclusion of a press conference, Holt was available for separate interviews with the small number of television news crews then working in Canberra. To ensure Holt was quoted accurately, a small microphone was installed on Holt's desk. It was designed to look like a pen holder although its existence was never a secret. At the press of a button there would be a permanent record of everything that was said in the Prime Minister's office. It was considered a revolutionary innovation in that it obviated the need for a portable recorder to be set up every time Holt gave an interview. Eggleton also arranged for the installation of a 'peep hole' in the main office door to allow personal staff to see whether the Prime Minister was on the phone or speaking with someone before they entered the room.

Eggleton realised his personal influence was increasing with his professional standing.

> My office soon became much more significant. Increasingly, I was able to make information available. Holt trusted me to pass on what I thought was reasonable and proper. I rarely remember him expressing concern at anything I decided to give to the press. Of course, if in doubt I always made sure I checked with him or Sir John Bunting first.

An article in *Nation* by Maxwell Newton noted that Eggleton 'finds himself from time to time in the position of being virtually the spokesman for the Government'.[1]

As one of the first ABC journalists to receive television training, Eggleton was keen to help Holt exploit the medium. Although there was little pressure on politicians to appear on live television, Eggleton had a sense of when Holt should make himself available for interview. As junior ministers were increasingly participating in television current affairs or talk shows, Eggleton rationed access to Holt with a standard response to invitations:

> The Prime Minister feels, and so do I, that he should not appear too often on TV. Cabinet ministers may appear on television as often as they choose, but we feel that the prime minister's television appearances should be reserved for the really big occasions when he has something of particular importance to say to the people.[2]

On several occasions, Holt felt he was unprepared and exposed to significant risk of personal embarrassment. He directed that his speaking invitations be 'more thoroughly investigated before his acceptance was recommended' and wanted his speech notes to have a standard format – more like 'President Johnson's system of small cards (about the size of filing cabinet cards) linked together with a piece of cord through the top left-hand corner' – and every lectern to have common characteristics. Making these arrangements became Eggleton's responsibility.

Although Eggleton, described by journalist Peter Bowers as 'ever obliging',[3] believed that Holt needed to be 'get-able', the Prime Minister resented being contacted by his staff and journalists when he was at his beach house in Portsea (where he would spend most weekends) or his beach 'shack' at Bingil Bay in

North Queensland. Nevertheless, Eggleton received calls from both locations whenever Holt wanted something done. The Prime Minister also disliked 'on-the-run interviews at airports [and] often annoyed local newsmen when he told them: 'If I've got anything to say I will say it to the press in Canberra". Eggleton believed that Holt's 'press 'honeymoon' lasted a remarkably long time'.

Eggleton was travelling everywhere with the Prime Minister. During their first few trips together he politely offered to carry Holt's briefcase off the plane. He inadvertently gained a new role and from that moment was the official keeper of the briefcase. It became Eggleton's constant companion and Holt always assumed that he would be nearby with the briefcase in hand. Describing it as a 'briefcase' is misleading. It was much more than a document carrier. It included pills, hairbrushes, a transistor radio, a sleeping mask and various snacks. Holt would leave packets of biscuits and cheese in the briefcase 'just in case'. His foresight was welcome on more than one occasion when the VIP aircraft was delayed and hungry travellers were left without catering. Holt was able to produce some 'emergency rations'. The sleeping mask was similar to the disguise worn by the fictional hero Zorro, without the eye holes. Holt had a great capacity for catnaps. When travelling for more than an hour Holt would slip on the mask and was soon fast asleep.

From the outset, Eggleton enjoyed a close personal rapport with Holt who trusted his judgement and relied on his discretion. In background notes on Holt that were drafted by Eggleton for *Vogue* magazine, readers were told that the Prime Minister

> makes considerable use of his Press Secretary and likes to have him in fairly close attendance. Normal policy is for the Press Secretary to attend all public events and all engagements at which press may be present ... the [Prime Minister] wants the Press Secretary available to cope with press who may try to intercept him on arrival at his hotel or other venues. For this reason it is desirable that the Press Secretary travel in a car reasonably close behind the prime minister so that he can alight quickly, ready to deal with waiting newsmen and photographers.

As Holt was comfortable with delegating duties, Eggleton knew how far he could go in dealing with the press and proposing media initiatives.

Not surprisingly, some journalists took advantage of Holt's friendly disposition to telephone him directly in the hope of getting tip-offs about impending announcements. The Prime Minister was invariably polite but encouraged them to go through the proper channels. That meant speaking with Eggleton. If Holt shared any information with the media, he advised Eggleton of what he had said and to whom. Holt's informal style, coupled with his charm and courtesy, made him a popular figure. Being accessible, however, increased the daily demands of the prime ministership which gradually sapped his vigour. He once confided to Eggleton, 'I always thought the treasurership was an important role but, as prime minister, everyone wants to put you on a pedestal. This job's not all it's cracked up to be.' Having said that, Holt also remarked, 'If you can't stand the heat, don't go into the kitchen.' Holt was fond of quoting Rudyard Kipling's poem *If*: 'If you can keep your head when all about you are losing theirs and blaming it on you ... If you can meet with Triumph and Disaster and treat those two impostors just the same ... Yours is the Earth and everything that's in it, and — which is more — you'll be a Man, my son!'

The Prime Minister had a number of interests that helped him cope with the stresses of the job. He was particularly keen on horse racing. If the Bentley was seen driving laps around Parliament House, Eggleton told the bemused staff that they had probably arrived at the office before a race was finished and Holt was listening to the radio to hear the finish. Holt also enjoyed a wide range of popular music, especially 'The Seekers'. He would hum or sing their songs while driving and was delighted to meet the group when they visited Canberra. He invited Eggleton to join them for lunch at The Lodge. Conscious that he was nearer to 60 and knowing the average life expectancy of Australian males was less than 70, Holt never contemplated spending a long time as prime minister – assuming he continued winning elections. He certainly had no intention of settling into a lengthy incumbency as Menzies had done after returning to the prime ministership just before his 55th birthday in 1949. Holt spoke of serving a couple of terms – meaning not more than six years – before retiring with Zara to Bingal Bay. He looked forward to growing tropical fruit and enjoying the warm water.

Having been a parliamentarian for three decades and a minister for 17 years, Holt was familiar with his surroundings and the ebb and flow of political life. As prime minister, however, he needed to be acquainted with the full range of government activities while selling the Coalition's political agenda. As Treasurer for the previous six years, he understood the main economic issues and knew from hard experience that managing the economy was the principal test applied by voters when deciding whether the ruling party deserved another term in office. Fortunately for Holt, his first substantial media success was the introduction of decimal currency within a month of becoming prime minister. Decimalisation attracted extensive and entirely favourable media coverage. Despite Labor's insistence that decimalisation would disrupt the economy and cause inflation, the 'new money' circulated freely and without any inflationary effect. Holt was personally credited with the success. He was also proving adept at diplomacy.

With continuing advances in air travel and mass communication, there was an expectation that Australia would play a greater role in regional and global affairs. Drawing on his seven years as Minister for Immigration (1949–56), Holt understood international affairs and personally committed Australia to a closer relationship with Asia and the Pacific. Heralding the shifting focus, Holt's first overseas trips were not to the United States or Britain but to Singapore, Malaysia, Laos, Cambodia, South Korea, Taiwan, the Philippines and Vietnam. He was the first Australian prime minister to visit some of these countries. Eggleton changed the nature of these tours by persuading Holt that Australian media correspondents should travel with them. It began a valuable practice that has persisted for more than half a century and has helped to make the Australian public more aware of regional partnerships. As RAAF VIP aircraft were relatively small, the press contingent usually travelled in a separate plane. When there was adverse comment on the cost of the small VIP fleet, Eggleton suggested the aircraft be described as 'flying offices' that enabled the business of government to be continued as the Prime Minister and his ministers travelled. Travelling in separate planes was also helpful in keeping journalists at arms' length from executive discussions. Eggleton would travel with the Prime Minister, while a press officer was assigned to the media aircraft as the so-called 'press mother'.

The arrangement worked well for all parties. No matter how remote the location, the media were able to provide detailed firsthand reporting of Holt's interactions with local dignitaries. The Prime Minister's international meetings and initiatives received far wider coverage as a result. It was a positive move that contributed significantly to raising Holt's profile beyond Australia. Greater transparency was always accompanied with elevated risk. Bringing the Prime Minister into close proximity to the media could be a disadvantage when there were verbal slips or organisational mishaps. There was also the added challenge of handling a planeload of journalists, whose collective egos were only slightly less sensitive than those of the politicians they stalked. In Cambodia a sumptuous white-tie dinner was hosted by the young Prince Sihanouk. His staff regarded the travelling media as second-rate guests and seated them in the kitchen. The journalists certainly did not see themselves as lesser beings and were enraged. Eggleton suddenly found himself negotiating a rapidly escalating diplomatic incident as the entrees arrived. Fortunately, by the time the second course was being served, Eggleton had managed to persuade the hosts to make more suitable arrangements for the press contingent.

This visit preceded the American bombing of eastern Cambodia to prevent the movement of Communist troops and supplies from neighbouring North Vietnam to South Vietnam. It was also well before the tyranny inflicted on the population by the Pol Pot regime when Cambodia was still a showpiece of South-East Asian progress. Eggleton noted the well-preserved French architecture, attractively maintained towns and villages, nuanced culture, and tangible evidence of economic development. The Australian delegation was feted across the nation. At the ancient capital of Angkor Wat there was a particularly memorable welcome. The town band had assembled to greet Holt with what they believed was the national anthem. As he stepped down from the aircraft they burst into 'Tie Me Kangaroo Down Sport'. Holt didn't blink. He held his hat across his chest and, with a straight face, took the salute.

The travelling delegation included the prime minister's personal physician, Dr Marcus Faunce, whose most valued contribution was a series of signals that were devised to let the Australians know what was safe to eat. At various banquets and receptions the visitors puzzled over the menus and looked to Dr Faunce for a discreet thumbs up or down. The Prime Minister was also accompanied by a security officer, who provided personal protection and liaised with local police. He carried a bulky revolver that was difficult to conceal under light tropical clothing. In Laos, Eggleton returned to the government guest house to find it had been locked down for the night. He was searching for an alternate way into the building when a window was suddenly thrown open and the security officer appeared, clad only in his underwear, aiming the revolver at Eggleton's head. Fortunately, the officer exercised restraint.

One of the Prime Minister's regional tours included Taiwan (the non-communist Republic of China) to which Holt had controversially appointed an Australian diplomatic representative. The Taiwanese President, Chiang Kai-shek, was in his second decade of exile from China (the communist People's Republic of China) and still harboured hopes of reclaiming the mainland and reunifying the country. The Australian delegation was accommodated in an elaborate guest house and honoured at various gala events. In a private meeting the Taiwanese President looked directly at the Australian Prime Minister and asked how many troops Australia would provide for an invasion of the Chinese mainland. Not wanting to seem ungrateful for the warm welcome he had received in Taipei, Holt went pale before managing an ambivalent response. He explained that Australia had neither plans nor provisions for military action of that magnitude. The President got the message and did not attempt to embarrass the Prime Minister again.

Behind Holt's emphasis on Asia was Australia's alliance with the United States. While Australia remained closely tied to the United Kingdom politically, socially, legally and even economically, the relationship with the United States had steadily increased in importance since Prime Minister John Curtin declared at the start of the Pacific War in 1941 that 'Australia turns to America.' The conflict in Vietnam brought Holt into contact with the American President, Lyndon Johnson. Australia had contributed a military training team to South Vietnam in 1962 and deployed its first combat battalion in May 1965. The war proved to be even more politically controversial when Holt increased Australia's commitment of ground forces and announced that national servicemen – conscripts – would be sent to resist the escalating Communist insurgency.

The relationship between Holt and Johnson was bound to be friendly. The two men were born in August 1908 and were first elected to public office in the same year. Their wives formed a warm friendship and enjoyed the same pastimes. Both Holt and Johnson had war service (Johnson had seen combat but Holt had not) and their view of the task in Vietnam was very similar although leading parties on opposing sides of the political divide. The two men formed a genuinely close bond. They were comfortable and relaxed together, and enjoyed each other's company. Their discussions began with Vietnam but soon expanded to other shared concerns.

The American President demonstrated his high regard for the Australian Prime Minister by ensuring that Blair House, on Pennsylvania Avenue opposite the White House, was always available when Holt visited the United States. An aircraft from the Presidential Flight was also provided to convey Holt from San Francisco to Washington. This was a significant gesture of friendship although Eggleton noted there were also some challenges. Passengers were encouraged to change into night attire and slip into their bunks before take-off. Eggleton found it was a strange sensation to be lying down while the plane rose steeply into the air. The tiered bunks were not separated by rank or gender. Zara Holt slept a few feet away from Eggleton. When advised they were nearing Washington's National Airport, dozens of people vied for the limited toilets and changing facilities. The Prime Minister and his wife were still trying to dress as the aircraft began its descent. Despite a less than comfortable night, and the morning's helter-skelter preparations, the Holts looked their best as helicopters whisked them to a formal welcome on the White House lawn.

It was on the South Lawn that Holt was inspired by the lavish formal welcome, including a traditional guard of honour, to conclude an otherwise unremarkable speech with the immortal phrase, 'All the way with LBJ.' It had not been in the notes and Eggleton was concerned to hear him say it. At the first opportunity, while walking to official cars after the ceremony, Eggleton asked Holt about the unexpected addition. Holt said the phrase had struck him as an appropriate off-the-cuff remark. 'It seemed like a good idea at the time.' He was surprised when Eggleton suggested it might excite the Australian media. It did. The Opposition also made much of the phrase, helping to ensure it became one of the indelible features of the Holt prime ministership.

On the way home, the Australian delegation stayed at one of San Francisco's leading hotels. Holt was greeted with another extravagantly stage-managed welcome. Some of the gloss wore off when he was escorted to his suite and found a complimentary bottle of whiskey with the message, 'Welcome to Harold Holt, Prime Minister of Canada.' He did not take offence at the mistake. He found it humorous and humbling. Holt was an unpretentious man. He was also a relaxed traveller. On international flights he was quick to get out of his suit and into more comfortable clothes. During an American commercial flight the captain entered the passenger cabin to greet the prime minister and seek out the relevant Australian staffer to discuss the whereabouts of missing baggage. He assumed the casually attired Holt was the baggage man. The prime minister simply smiled and pointed further back in the plane, where the more smartly attired officer responsible for baggage was squirming with embarrassment. Eggleton learned one more practical lesson during this trip. It involved valuable advice from staff at The Lodge in Canberra. Whenever Holt vacated a room, Eggleton needed to conduct a quick search to gather any stray official papers or one of Holt's many transistor radios. The Prime Minister had a habit of tucking them under his bed or leaving them beside the toilet.

Despite the 'All the way with LBJ' controversy that gathered momentum in Australia, the friendship between Holt and Johnson continued to deepen. Security in Asia and the Pacific were key issues at their well-publicised meetings. Once together they would openly compare each other's briefing notes on diverse social and political issues. After Holt had visited Washington, Johnson decided to demonstrate his support for Holt in spectacular fashion. Johnson became the first American president to visit Australia in October 1966. The timing was contentious. Johnson arrived as campaigning began for the Federal election scheduled for the following month. It was interpreted by some commentators as a partisan move. It was. Johnson was essentially campaigning for Holt against the Opposition leader, Arthur Calwell, who had pledged to withdraw Australian forces from South Vietnam if Labor won office on 26 November 1966. At a parliamentary event in Canberra, Johnson repaid Holt's compliment by declaring, 'Every American and LBJ is with Australia all the way'.

Eggleton travelled from Canberra to Sydney in the presidential aircraft with other key members of Holt's staff. Australian and White House staff were too busy tapping away on typewriters to bother with seat belts as Air Force One landed at Kingsford Smith Airport. Eggleton assumed the Americans were always indifferent to flight safety. The four-day presidential tour was highly successful. It boosted Holt's standing on the eve of an election and further cemented the relationship between the two leaders. It also added momentum to deepening anti-war sentiment. Many protesters seized the opportunity to register their opposition to the conflict in Vietnam and reliance of conscription as demonstrations dramatised the 1966 election campaign.

Holt was escorted through hordes of placard-waving demonstrators. There were angry scenes as official cars were surrounded by determined protestors. Shirts were torn and heads were struck by placards. Eggleton thought any physical injuries were largely accidental. Eggleton was sometimes unable to force his way to the prime minister's car and had to be hoisted into back-up vehicles – sometimes through an open window. It had become virtually impossible for Holt to travel in the front seat of an official vehicle – which was always his preference. The police decided it was safer to have Eggleton in the front seat while the prime minister sat in the rear alongside a security officer. On other occasions, particularly when arriving at evening public meetings, Eggleton sat in the back seat as a decoy for the Prime Minister. After an unsuccessful attempt to assassinate Calwell in June 1966, the Commonwealth Police took any apparent threat to Holt's life seriously.

There was one security situation in Perth that Eggleton described as 'tricky'. Holt had addressed a lunchtime campaign rally in Forrest Place. The huge crowd prevented the prime minister's car from moving. Holt and Eggleton had to push their way through the mob and the possibility that an angry protestor might have been armed. There was some hostility at first but once they were in the middle of the crowd they were just another couple of people pushing and shoving. They finally made it to the road, where they were somewhat vulnerable on the edge of the throng. In the absence of the official car Eggleton caught sight of an approaching taxi. He flagged the vehicle down and he and Holt both jumped in the back. The driver glanced in the rear vision mirror and was stunned. He exclaimed, 'My God, it's the prime minister!' As they drove towards the hotel, another dilemma emerged: neither of them had any money. The driver wanted to give them a free ride. They refused. The driver waited until Eggleton eventually managed to locate some cash.

Loud as they were, the anti-Vietnam War protesters were a vocal minority. The wider community did not share their sentiments or endorse their actions. Holt won the November 1966 election with a strong personal mandate. This gave him confidence to move on key domestic and international issues. As well as Vietnam, a central concern was Britain's withdrawal from its territories 'east of Suez', which came to be regarded as the official end of the British Empire and further justified Australia's continuing pivot towards the United States. Consequently, there were more frequent prime ministerial visits to the United States, South East Asia, the South Pacific and the United Kingdom. Significantly, Foreign Minister Paul Hasluck was rarely part of these delegations. Holt preferred to handle international relations on his own. Hasluck deeply resented his exclusion and was continually irritated by Eggleton's inclusion. Holt saw media relations during his overseas visits as a high priority. Hasluck had little interest in press coverage and thought briefing journalists was largely pointless. With complete confidence in his press secretary, Holt often left Eggleton to front the initial press conference.

Eggleton did not, and was without any desire, to act as the Holt Government's international affairs spokesman. There were always departmental officials in the travelling delegation and Eggleton placed his trust in them, never second-guessing their advice and guidance. Unintentionally, Eggleton became the messenger on one occasion. Holt and his staff were in Washington for discussions with the Johnson Administration when Eggleton was asked to give a joint media briefing to the White House Press Corps alongside the President's press secretary, George Christian. Eggleton was overwhelmed by the experience. He stood in front of a vast auditorium filled with some of the world's toughest journalists. He was surprised, and then dismayed, when they largely ignored Christian and directed most of their questions to him. At first the questions were predictable and easily handled, focussing on the purpose of the visit and the relationship between the two countries.

When the questions turned to international conflicts, Eggleton was asked if he felt war was imminent between the Soviet Union and the United States. 'No', he replied. 'The great powers are only huffing and puffing'. It was a phrase he had taken from a draft prime ministerial speech that had been written by departmental officials. Eggleton had seen a draft during the outward flight from Australia and made a mental note of what he had read. Johnson was certainly pleased by the statement. At a black-tie dinner to honour the Australian Prime Minister at the White House that evening, Johnson told Holt that Eggleton had done an excellent job with the press conference. Both Australians were gratified by the presidential praise. The next morning Eggleton picked up the morning newspapers to find he was featured on their front pages. There was little reference to the Prime Minister but considerable attention to Eggleton's remarks. When Holt joined him for breakfast, Eggleton diffidently drew his attention to the papers. Holt smiled slightly and congratulated him on getting such a good run. Holt was glad that Eggleton had tested the waters with material from the draft speech.

There were, however, two unfortunate consequences. In Australia, Eggleton was misquoted. His 'huffing and puffing' comment was associated with tensions between Israel and Egypt which were about to engage in the Six Day War (5–10 June 1967). When the delegation returned to Australia, hostilities had ended but the media were still making a fuss about Eggleton's comment. Holt was asked whether he would take disciplinary action against his press secretary for what were, they claimed, plainly mistaken views. The Prime Minister replied that the statement was made 'in good faith' and with Eggleton's 'usual capable care of what is said at these background briefings'. Eggleton's comment was consistent with Holt's own view on the likelihood of superpower confrontation. 'Huffing and puffing' was a short-hand way of defusing a complicated situation and, Holt said, 'I am not critical of Tony for that'.

Holt consistently supported Eggleton publicly and privately. He was not displeased with the initial comment (in its correct context) or Eggleton's decision to offer a view – which was simply that of the Department of External Affairs. The Prime Minister was prepared to accept whatever blame could be attributed to him and his office for any misunderstanding or misapprehension. This show of solidarity was typical of Holt although it proved to be quite unnecessary. The transcript of the original briefing was circulated to confirm the Prime Minister's account. When asked by a journalist about the incident a year later, Eggleton replied: 'It just goes to show that in this job you put your head on the chopper every day of your life'.[4] Whenever Holt wanted to tease Eggleton he referred to him as 'old huffer and puffer'. This was an apt tag on another occasion when Eggleton was literally out of breath.

An Australian delegation was in Los Angeles. Holt was to give an important prepared address to a major business lunch. The officials were running late in preparing the text as Holt wanted last-minute adjustments. The Prime Minister decided to set off with Eggleton to follow with the revised speech. With the amended version in hand, Eggleton ran to a waiting car that would convey him to the venue which happened to be on the other side of the city. The heavy midday traffic made for slow progress. To make matters worse, the driver was vague about the location and the quickest route. By the time Eggleton arrived at the venue, Holt was already on his feet. He was making some innocuous opening remarks and speaking very slowly while looking desperately towards the door. The Prime Minister and his press secretary were relieved when the speech notes changed hands.

The benefits to Australia of the close relationship between Johnson and Holt were very apparent when the Prime Minister was about to return home from a trip to London. Johnson requested an unscheduled meeting. The majority of the Australian delegation continued to Honolulu as Holt and his wife diverted to Washington accompanied by Eggleton and the head of the Prime Minister's Department, Sir John Bunting. The four Australians were treated like members of the President's family. Talks were held in the Oval Office and lunch was served in the President's private quarters. Eggleton was fascinated to see the bank of secure phones on a shelf under the dining room table. They were then flown by helicopter to Camp David where each of the Australians had their own cabin among the gardens and trees.

Talks continued over lunch and dinner in the President's chalet with Eggleton taking notes. Johnson and Holt exchanged ideas about upcoming speeches and statements on Vietnam. There were lighter moments to alleviate the stress of the serious business they were conducting. As Johnson loved cowboy movies, his sitting room was quickly converted into a cinema. After the movie, Johnson and Holt sat on the terrace, smoking and talking well into the night. The following Sunday, the president and his wife, Ladybird, took the Australians to church in their station wagon. Johnson drove, with Ladybird in the front and the Holts in the back. Eggleton and the President's secretary climbed into what Johnson called the 'dicky seat'. It had the tone of a family outing and was full of good humour. The President joked about Eggleton and the pretty young secretary in the back.

Although an informal outing, this was still a presidential motorcade with a line of black cars in front and more security vehicles at the rear. The fate of Johnson's predecessor, John Kennedy, was still a fresh memory in the United States. During the church service, Eggleton briefed the Australian press as they had not been given access to Camp David. After the service, Johnson took them for a drive into the country with the black cars and security men never far away. On an even more informal note, Holt decided to make use of the Camp David swimming pool. He demonstrated his diving skills in front of Ladybird and her daughters, Lynda and Luci. Unfortunately, his borrowed swim shorts were several sizes too large and, when Holt hit the water, the shorts disclosed more than he intended.

The convivial atmosphere did not lessen the seriousness of the issues that were discussed. While supportive of the war against Hanoi, Holt was uneasy about South Vietnamese domestic politics. On becoming Prime Minister, he wanted to speak with deployed Australian forces and to assess the security situation for himself. Vietnam was included in his first overseas trip. Holt met the troops at Bien Hoa, across the Dong Nai River from Saigon (now Ho Chi Minh

City). The journey went smoothly and was uneventful, helped by the local police manning all the intersections to ensure the Prime Minister had a fast and safe run through the city. Eggleton's driver had trouble getting his vehicle started. By the time they transited through Saigon the police had released the cars they had previously stopped. The driver had to fight his way through endless traffic snarls. By the time Eggleton arrived at the airport, Holt's plane was disappearing into the sky. It was not until halfway through the flight that Holt complained to other members of the delegation that he could not see Eggleton. Only then did the official party realise the press secretary had been left behind.

The only option was for Eggleton to travel by road which was a much more hazardous journey. There was less than 25 kilometres between Saigon and Bien Hoa in a straight line but the insurgency was unpredictable and the surrounding countryside was dangerous territory. Eggleton's only protection was a lone Commonwealth policeman with a single revolver. Fortunately, the trip passed without incident and Eggleton joined the Prime Minister for most of his official engagements. They met Australian soldiers against a background soundtrack of rifle fire, punctuated by artillery and mortars. Holt was warmly welcomed by the troops. Eggleton shared a room with Dr Faunce. A note on the door told them not to be alarmed by the sound of gunfire during the night although it did advise them to crawl under their beds in the event of a perimeter attack.

During his Asian and Pacific visits, Holt did not want his conversations with regional leaders to be unduly dominated by the Vietnam War. He was eager to warn Australia's neighbours of the implications of Britain's withdrawal. Holt was convinced that Europeans did not appreciate either the potential of Asian economies or the challenges facing their governments. Regional leaders soon regarded Holt as a well-disposed, influential spokesman for their concerns and aspirations. He won their trust as a determined advocate for the developing world. He was supported by the New Zealand Prime Minister, Keith Holyoake, who shared most of Holt's views. Similar in build and demeanour, they were described by some as the 'Anzac Twins'.

The goodwill that Holt enjoyed abroad stood in contrast to the ill-will he experienced at home. Despite having secured a stunning election victory in November 1966, Holt's position was immediately under threat. There were a series of political set-backs and looming tensions within the Coalition. Holt was privately worried about William McMahon's political ambitions and his poisonous relationship with Deputy Prime Minister Jack McEwen. Meanwhile, new Labor leader Gough Whitlam was making a significant impact in parliament and the opinion polls. Behind the façade of Coalition solidarity, concerns were expressed about Holt's performance. These were relatively muted and isolated but the Prime Minister himself knew he could do better on some fronts. He spoke with Eggleton about strengthening his personal office and enhancing his public presentations. Eggleton prepared a paper suggesting various ways of increasing electoral support and sharpening his message. Most of Holt's speeches were prepared by departmental officers. Eggleton helped coordinate the content of Holt's speeches but did not have the time to research and write the text. Nor was it seen as his job. Eggleton turned to Keith Sinclair, a former editor of the *Age*, for assistance. As part of a blueprint for the future, Eggleton proposed that Holt be more selective about speaking engagements. Eggleton thought that delivering fewer speeches of higher quality would help Holt to counter Whitlam's impressive oratory.

Holt contributed to his own difficulties as well. In the second half of 1967, he unintentionally misled Parliament over the alleged misuse of VIP aircraft and generated an entirely avoidable controversy. Eggleton worked closely with the Minister for Air, Peter Howson, and an assistant secretary in the Prime Minister's Department, Geoffrey Yeend, to draft press releases and ministerial statements that tried to absolve Holt from any suggestion that he had knowingly misled Parliament. By this time Eggleton had become a resource for many ministers wanting to know how they might manage the disclosure, and sometimes non-disclosure, of sensitive material or controversial information.

By August 1967, some of Holt's parliamentary colleagues, including the Chief Whip, were pessimistic about the political landscape and the government's electoral fortunes. They worried about how the Prime Minister used his time, particularly his accessibility to the parliamentary party, and the relevance of his public engagements. All of this was far short of questioning the future of his leadership but it was destabilising. Holt reminded himself that it was less than a year since he had achieved a resounding electoral mandate. Holt was not inclined to panic or punish his critics. The Prime Minister felt he could restore his parliamentary support and revive public confidence. His health remained robust, aided by his commitment to regular swimming and snorkelling, but his body was ageing. Holt quietly confided to Eggleton that he needed to be helped from the water during a recent holiday and was having increasing trouble with shoulder muscles. He occasionally mused that the Holt family did not 'make old bones' as none of his male forebears had lived beyond 60. Concerned that he was too cavalier about his personal wellbeing, Eggleton confronted Holt about the dangers associated with water sports and the Prime Minister's tendency to be reckless. Holt rebuffed him: 'Look Tony, what are the odds of a prime minister being drowned or taken by a shark?'

Holt's troublesome shoulder – a legacy of football injuries sustained during his university days – flared up significantly during the November 1967 Senate election. Muscle spasms made Holt appear stiff and awkward during a televised speech to launch the Coalition's campaign. He was receiving treatment from a specialist and taking pain medication. The prime ministerial briefcase contained more pills than usual. Holt tried to keep the problem from the media but his discomfort soon became apparent. During the long outward flight from Canberra to Perth he took too many pain relief tablets. As Holt stepped off the VIP aircraft he seemed unsteady on his feet. At the traditional lunchtime election rally at Forrest Place he shuffled awkwardly onto the platform. He delivered the speech but slurred some of his words. The media were chattering among themselves and jumped to the conclusion that Holt had drunk too much alcohol on the plane. In damage control mode, Holt asked Eggleton to gather the press for an informal meeting over afternoon tea before he returned to Canberra. Holt then explained why he was not his usual self. This killed off drinking stories but there were a few press reports about his shoulder problem and the first doubts about his continuing fitness for office.

Eggleton did what he could to present the prime minister as a man at the peak of his profession but he could do little about the gathering political storm clouds or Holt's tendency to push his body beyond its physical limits.

Endnotes

1   Maxwell Newton, 'In-between Men', *Nation*, 11 March 1967.
2   Ray Aitchison, *From Bob to Bungles: People in Politics 1966–70*, Sun Books, Melbourne, 1970, p. 63.
3   Peter Bowers, 'So keep away from Bingil Bay', *SMH*, 28 July 1966, p. 6.
4   *Australian Women's Weekly*, 21 February 1968, page 5, 'Tony Eggleton, the reluctant celebrity'.

CHAPTER 5

Death's shadow   1967

A 'half Senate' election was held on 25 November 1967. The contest for 30 of the 60 Senate seats produced a disappointing result for the Coalition. After their substantial victory in the general election a year earlier, the Liberal party lost two Senate seats to the Democratic Labor Party (DLP) which would hold the balance of power in the Senate until 1974. It was small consolation that Labor had not gained any seats either in the first electoral contest under new leader, Gough Whitlam. The Coalition was expected, however, to have done better adding to earlier political disquiet over Harold Holt's leadership.

In a private note Eggleton recorded that 'things had not gone well since the middle of the year, and the inept handling of the VIP issue had disturbed many members' of the government. He did not think Holt 'was conscious of any general unrest. He was too preoccupied with such things as devaluation, and the Country Party's stand'. There was no 'chance of Holt being replaced. Only a year before he had led his party to a record victory. He still remained personally extremely popular'. Eggleton thought 'a coup at this stage would have been abortive. Anyway, there was no-one in a position to vie for leadership and there was no clear-cut successor ... this was the cause of much of the worry'. Still, Holt remained resilient as ever. More than 30 years in parliament had taught him that political fortunes wane without warning and then rise unexpectedly. He was particularly encouraged by the positive response of both the Liberal Party and the public when he succeeded in a confrontation with the Country Party leader, 'Black Jack' McEwen, over the value of Australia's currency.

Holt was characteristically cheerful as the parliamentary year ended and summer holidays approached. He saw the New Year as an opportunity to make changes and reassure his political colleagues. Although the Holt family was planning to spend Christmas and New Year at Portsea, the Prime Minister decided he would spend the previous weekend there too. Zara had a house guest at The Lodge and was looking forward to several Christmas parties, so she chose to remain in Canberra. On the morning of Friday 15 December, Eggleton walked with Holt to his car at the front of Parliament House. The Prime Minister was in good spirits and said he would telephone the next morning for a rundown on the weekend media. They exchanged a wave as Holt's car set off for the airport.

Holt rang Eggleton about 8.30am the next day (Saturday 16 December). They compared notes about some favourable media coverage and Holt reflected on the events of the past year. Despite the problems, he felt there had been some worthy achievements. He said the trouble was that many people 'could not see the wood for the trees'. He planned to use a news conference proposed for the following week to put a few issues in perspective. Eggleton was asked to seek relevant briefing notes and other documentation from the Prime Minister's Department, then arrange his own travel to Melbourne on Monday. He and Holt would review the material and prepare a positive statement that would set the scene for the scheduled news conference. They spoke on the telephone for almost an hour. Holt was looking forward to the coming year and planning international priorities. He felt it was time to put a stronger focus on communications with Europe where there was a lack of appreciation for the growing significance of Asia and the Pacific. He would visit a range of European capitals with the goal of highlighting the challenges and opportunities that existed in the region. Holt was determined to make the European nations, including Britain, see that Asia and the Pacific would be the powerhouse of the future and collaborative partnerships made long-term strategic sense. Later in the day and despite orders from his doctor to rest his troublesome shoulder, Holt played tennis and socialised with friends.

Sunday 17 December 1967 was to prove a fateful day. It was a warm summer morning in Canberra. Eggleton was working in the garden. That afternoon he and Mary were to attend a party hosted by Herschel Hurst, the head of the Melbourne *Sun*'s parliamentary bureau in Canberra. Shortly after lunch, Eggleton received a phone call from Hurst. He assumed it would be to confirm arrangements for the party. Instead, Hurst asked about Holt. He apologised for raising a work matter but said his Melbourne office was insistent that he clarify vague reports of a dignitary, possibly Holt, missing in the sea off Portsea. Eggleton remarked that there were a lot of very important people at Portsea but promised to check with The Lodge. He was still making preliminary enquiries when Hurst rang back to say the reports were now referring specifically to the Prime Minister.

Eggleton phoned the housekeeper at Portsea, Patricia 'Tiny' Lawless. She said the Prime Minister was out with friends although there was a degree of anxiety in her voice. He next phoned the police headquarters in Melbourne and was soon speaking to a senior officer who was able to confirm reports that Harold Holt was missing at Cheviot Beach. The officer said he was about to inform Mrs Holt but suggested Eggleton might handle that. Eggleton phoned The Lodge but Zara was at a Christmas Party. He asked the Prime Minister's driver, Ray Coppin, to find her and arrange for her to speak with him over the telephone. In the meantime, Eggleton alerted the Prime Minister's principal private secretary, Peter Bailey, to the developing situation. They agreed it would be prudent to have an aircraft on standby at Canberra Airport. Bailey said he would make contact with Sir John Bunting who was holidaying at the coast.

When Eggleton managed to speak with Zara she was not unduly concerned about her husband's welfare. She said it was not unusual for her husband to swim out to an exposed rock and sit in the sun. She did not see any immediate need to consider flying to Melbourne. The situation was escalating quickly. It was not long before domestic staff at The Lodge telephoned Eggleton to say Zara had changed her mind and would travel to Portsea. The official car would collect Eggleton en route to the airport. As he prepared to depart, Eggleton was being contacted by media from across Australia and around the world. Mary began taking messages while he packed a few personal items in a bag. He alerted his assistant, Mary Newport, and asked her to deal with the media while he was travelling to Melbourne and Portsea. At about 3.15pm the sound of a car horn announced the arrival of the prime ministerial Bentley. Zara was accompanied by her house guest from Queensland, Alison Buest, as well as the prime minister's personal physician, Marcus Faunce. At RAAF Base Fairbairn, a group of photographers were waiting to record their hurried departure for Melbourne.

During the flight Zara was initially cheerful and confident. She was hopeful an 'all clear' message would soon be conveyed through the aircraft's communication system. With the absence of any news, however, she became increasingly uneasy. The pilot passed a message to Eggleton, asking whether Zara would like a helicopter to be on standby in Melbourne to fly her directly to Portsea. Grateful for the pilot's thoughtfulness, she insisted that all available helicopters should be diverted to the search at Portsea. Her preference was a swift car with a police escort. For the 130-kilometre dash from Melbourne Airport to Portsea, Eggleton chose to travel in the back-up Commonwealth car. His plan was to monitor developments and radio broadcasts without upsetting Zara. The Commonwealth Humber Hawk did not have an in-built radio. Fortunately, the driver had a transistor clipped to the windscreen shade. That afternoon, radio programming was devoted entirely to the search for the missing prime minister.

People were gathered along the roadside on the route to Portsea in silent groups, curious and concerned, as Zara made her way to Cheviot Beach. They were dressed for Sunday-by-the-sea but had abandoned the beach. Media reports were leaving listeners in no doubt that Australia, on that pleasant Sunday afternoon, was being plunged into a political crisis. The nearly two-hour drive to Portsea allowed Eggleton to consider the immense challenges he was suddenly facing. The eyes of the world were on Portsea with all the inevitable media implications that came with an unfolding tragedy. There was no pre-arranged plan for this kind of drama. His only option was to take it one step at a time and try to respond appropriately, and with calm dignity.

Zara arrived at Portsea around 6pm. The beach house was full of distressed family members. The senior Army officer at Portsea advised that he was holding a large team of media outside the military base and wanted to know Eggleton's wishes on their management and movement. The media were to be given access to the Army base as a suitable venue for press briefings was organised. He stressed that media arrangements should not hamper the search in any way. Eggleton then received a host of messages from Liberal parliamentarians, key government figures and departmental officers asking to be kept informed and pledging their assistance. Zara asked Eggleton to check the Prime Minister's briefcase to see whether any of his papers needed urgent attention. As the man on the scene, Eggleton was given complete freedom by the Prime Minister's Department to handle the situation as he saw fit, liaising with the Army and Victoria Police. Bunting suggested that he not abandon hope for the Prime Minister during the Sunday media briefings, a position that would need to be reviewed the following day.

The first in a series of press conferences began at 8pm in Badcoe Hall at the Portsea Army base. Eggleton was joined by military and police representatives, who asked him to take the lead and coordinate the conference. This was no ordinary press briefing as the event was being telecast live around the nation. It would be the first of six televised press conferences over the next three days. On returning from the press conference, the Holt family arranged a late meal for those staying in Portsea overnight. They then tried to catch up with sleep in various parts of the relatively small beach house. Eggleton camped in the sitting room with Holt's sons and Dr Faunce. There was a loud thunderstorm during the night and Zara came around making sure they were all as comfortable as possible.

Eggleton woke at dawn the next morning. The beach was damp and the sky heavy with menacing grey clouds. It was a daunting sight. The Prime Minister's personal secretary, Pat de Lacy, cancelled a Pacific cruise and drove to Portsea to help establish a temporary office. They watched her cruise ship sail out of Port Phillip Bay in the early afternoon. It was near impossible to run an office within the crowded beach house. Fortunately, neighbours made their vacant house available to Holt's staff.

De Lacy then organised a meeting with Marjorie Gillespie who had been with Holt on the beach when he disappeared. She gave an emotional and detailed account. Mrs Gillespie lived nearby and was visibly overwrought by the tragedy. She explained that Holt had picked up a group of four friends on Sunday morning, taking them to watch the solo English yachtsman, Alec Rose, sail his boat *Lively Lady* into Port Phillip Bay. The Prime Minister had been keen to cool down at Cheviot Beach although the water was choppy and uninviting. With traditional bravado, Holt proposed they should all go into the water but only one of the group shared his confidence. Holt emphasised that he 'knew this beach like the back of his hand' but the elements were against him. Within minutes he was being swept out to sea in a strong current. His silver hair was seen bobbing among the waves and then he was gone. It was a typical incident of someone misjudging the seas; it was atypical as a national leader was involved. No other factors seemed relevant.

Eggleton spent most of Monday giving interviews, convening press conferences and communicating with the Victoria Police, the Liberal Party and the Governor General. Zara was trying to remain composed and spent much of her time playing with grandchildren. According to Eggleton, the media were considerate and cooperative, even when Zara made her way along the beach to thank the rescue teams. They kept a respectful distance. At the end of the walk she stopped to say a few words to the journalists. Eggleton was also on the beach with the media and search parties when he was summoned to an urgent phone call. When he arrived at the Holt's beach house an American voice told him that the President of the United States wished to speak with him. Johnson said, 'Tony, this is LBJ. I'm shattered by Harold's death, absolutely shattered. I'm coming to the funeral. I know there are protocols for invitations, but make it clear to everyone that LBJ will be there. I want to see Zara.'

After two days back in Canberra (Tuesday and Wednesday), Eggleton returned to Melbourne with Zara on Thursday afternoon, ahead of the memorial service the next day (Friday). The house in Toorak was swarming with American secret service officers who were making preparations for the presidential visit. Eggleton met LBJ when he arrived and took him to Zara. He left them alone as they were both very emotional. The service was held at St Paul's Cathedral in Melbourne. The presence of 19 presidents and prime ministers made it the largest gathering of world leaders on Australian soil. It was a remarkable tribute to a man who had been prime minister for less than two years. The cathedral was overflowing with crowds spilling onto the surrounding streets. Eggleton was invited to attend the service with the Holt family as well as the state reception afterwards at Victoria's Government House. He struggled to believe that Holt – his boss and his friend – was gone.

Some Australians found it hard to accept that a prime minister could drown, assuming his personal security detail would have rescued him. But Holt was accompanied only by friends and the seas had shown no respect for public office. Without a post-mortem or a coroner's report, the events preceding Holt's disappearance were shrouded in supposition and speculation. There was even talk of political intrigue. Eggleton never doubted that Holt's death was misadventure:

> He misjudged the currents and the tides, a simple mistake that changed the course of Australian politics ... The prime minister had been in good spirits, looking to the future. He was his usual cheery and positive self. Harold's drowning was the kind of sad and distressing event that takes place all too often during an Australian summer.

Privately, Eggleton wrote on 2 January 1968 that 'the PM's pride, and his weakness for a little exhibitionism, were the factors that contributed to tragedy on the wild surf beach that fateful Sunday morning ... he had a 'show off' streak in him, which seemed to have become more pronounced in the last year or so. This showed through particularly when he was in the presence of women – especially attractive women'. Notably, Eggleton referred to Mrs Gillespie as a mature woman who was 'still very attractive' and that Holt 'gave the impression sometimes that he was trying to turn the clock back'. He ended these contemporaneous reflections with the observation: 'Rather foolish and careless perhaps, and motivated by an almost childish pride. But so human ... and so Harold Holt'.

There were personal consequences for Eggleton beyond losing his boss and friend. The five dramatic days in the international spotlight had left an indelible mark on his professional identity, transforming him into a recognised public figure. He would forever be the man that fronted the press conferences following Holt's disappearance. Eggleton was now a household name. News organisations and magazines carried feature stories about him and his family. There were rumours that a few Liberals wanted Eggleton to replace Holt as the Federal member for Higgins. Bruce Juddery writing in *Nation* revealed that a group of journalists 'asked him, not quite facetiously, if he would consider standing for Higgins. It had been agreed in a lounge of the Hotel Nepean at about two that morning that Mr Eggleton would make the ideal candidate'.[1] He had managed the media and the military at Portsea with confidence and conviction. But a move into party politics was not on Eggleton's agenda. He also received a phone call from Sir Frank Packer, saying there were opportunities within his organisation if he did not have a role with the new prime minister.

Eggleton received hundreds of complimentary notes and letters on the manner in which he handled the aftermath of Holt's disappearance. Sir Robert Menzies wrote: 'I want to tell you how much we all admired your own skill, balance and dignity, in the handling of your most difficult task. You have my unqualified admiration'. Sir John Bunting told Eggleton he had conducted himself 'with great dignity and high responsibility. This was reflected in your television appearances which have attracted the most complimentary references, inside and outside of Government. I know it was a period of intense personal strain for you as well as an arduous one ... you carried the load wonderfully well'. One of his former colleagues at the ABC Melbourne newsroom, Perc Mooney, wanted to 'express my admiration for the efficient and dignified manner in which you conducted the news conferences ... Knowing your deep respect for the bereaved family, and your obvious close relationship with the PM, a lesser person would have lost tolerance with some of the inane and tactless questions asked by a few of my colleagues in the news business'.

The Public Relations Institute of Australia resolved to present him with an 'Award of Honour'. The Institute's president, Jack Allan, explained that 'this award is unique in that we have created it in your honour; it has been awarded to no other and we do not expect to make a similar award in the foreseeable future'. In reply, Eggleton told the Institute that when he came to Australia in 1950 he 'could hardly claim to be a 'journalist of considerable standing' although he had 'received a pretty thorough journalistic grounding in two years with British provincial newspapers'. At the award presentation, Eggleton explained that he tried to see himself 'not as an obstacle but a channel, with a two-way flow, between authority and the man in the street'. He declared himself 'a great believer in the public's right to be kept fully and adequately informed' and concluded that no reporter was forced to speculate on the prime minister's death because of 'a lack of information'. Hence, his role was less with managing public relations and more with facilitating public information.

The *North-West Star* observed that Holt's death 'brought to the public eye a remarkable young man who in the normal course of events would only be known to newspaper and other news media representatives'. He had taken a 'fresh approach to the image of press secretaries' and had impressed in being 'always immaculately dressed ... even when called from his mattress on the floor after a 20-hour day'. The Sydney *Mirror* thought Eggleton was the 'most memorable personality' to emerge from Holt's disappearance. The *Daily Mirror* reported that, with Holt's death, 'technically, he is out of a job. But the Government is sure to find a job for him'. The *Australian* reported that the press gallery's 'betting is that he will stay [in the prime minister's office]. But if it is wrong, more than one Canberra journalist will believe that Mr Holt's successor has done the wrong thing'.

On 4 January 1968, Eggleton produced his own private 40-page summary of the previous fortnight 'while the various episodes are still in my mind. In this rough form they are merely a record for future reference. The material might also be useful for incorporating in articles at a later stage'. After setting down a detailed chronology, Eggleton made a series of 'background observations'. Throughout 1967 he saw the weight of office beginning to tell on Harold Holt. The cares and responsibilities took some of the lightness out of his step, and he began to look his age ... at the end of a hard week in Canberra he could look quite grey and old. At The Lodge it was noticed that he was inclined to spill his food, and show even greater irritability early in the mornings. He could be particularly shaky at lunchtimes, especially on those days when Parliament was sitting.

Eggelton was surprised by the extent of the therapeutic benefit Holt derived from weekends at Portsea. It was a change more than a rest. He always took 'a briefcase full of papers ... but there was no guarantee that he would do much work on them'. Eggleton noted that Holt was 'increasingly obsessed with Portsea over the last 12 months. He would go to ridiculous lengths, if only to spend one night there. His itineraries and programs had to be planned with this in mind'. Although time away from Canberra was plainly restorative, Eggleton doubted 'whether he could really afford the time. He was inclined to neglect his 'homework' and take shortcuts in order to hang on to his Portsea pleasures'. The consequences were 'loose and short-sighted political decisions during the year, as highlighted by the VIP [aircraft] fiasco'.

Ironically, given Eggleton's later rejection of the criticism that Holt's successor thought he could be a five-day-a-week prime minister, he cited the same phrase to summarise many of the criticisms of Holt in 1967. So determined was Holt to spend time at Portsea that 'he often had only three full days of each week in Canberra'. In effect, 'he tried to take everything on the run, and rarely gave enough advance thought and planning to the tasks he had to undertake'. His generally poor performance could be 'traced back to the five-day week and the Portsea obsession'. Eggleton detected an element of fatalism: 'towards the end I had a feeling that he had been carried away by the idea of living life to the full ... almost as though he expected each week might be his last'.

Some effort was expended by Eggleton and others to avoid any mention of Marjorie Gillespie, the neighbour who was on the beach with the Prime Minister before he drowned. She was distraught and Eggleton thought her 'story struck me as rather confused'. At the first press conference he was 'not put in a position of having to reveal that the Gillespies were involved'. The *Australian* telephoned Eggleton near midnight to ask about Mrs Gillespie. He told the reporter that 'this was not all that relevant'. On Wednesday morning, a reporter from the Melbourne *Sun* told Eggleton his editor 'was trying to read sinister implications into some aspects of the tragedy, including my failure to mention the Gillespies on Sunday night'. Eggleton thought he 'was able to clear up all the matters without any problem'. There was, however, a problem and its essence would not be revealed for nearly two decades.

In 1985, the then Dame Zara Bate gave a forthright interview to a women's magazine in which she confirmed that her late husband and Mrs Gillespie were engaged in an intimate relationship and that she was 'very aware' it had been taking place. She told a television documentary crew that Holt 'was a womaniser. He loved them … [and] I felt like telling Marj [Gillespie] about the other half dozen in the same position … He didn't have any men friends, or many. He had friends, but he didn't have one great friend … a man, but he had a lot of women. He was a menace'. She was also aware he was trying to hide these relationships from her:

> he was charming to me. He really hid them beautifully. I might know, and I saw … and I didn't see, for I knew if I saw I'd have to make a fuss and that'd be it, and I'd have to leave him and have to bring up three children. Anyway, I loved him. I had to make my mind up about that very early in my marriage and I decided alright, if that's it, I'll look the other way. Which I did.

One of those on the beach with the Prime Minister was Martin Simpson, the boyfriend of Mrs Gillespie's daughter, Vyner. He later remarked: 'my lasting recollection is that they were in love. To see them together even briefly, the way they leaned into one another, they were obviously connected … Marjorie was a beautiful, extremely elegant woman, with a bohemian touch'.[2] The existence of this relationship explained why Mrs Gillespie was so distraught after the Prime Minister was swept out to sea and why Holt was so keen to be in Portsea during 1967.

Eggleton was surprised and bemused by the enormous personal attention he had received. He reflected: 'it seemed an ironic way to obtain fame … as a result of the death of my boss, who had always taken great pride in avoiding 'bodies' in his climb to the top'. He had worked with Holt for 692 days – the entirety of Australia's 17th prime ministership. Eggleton had refashioned the role of press secretary, partly as a function of his own capacities and capabilities, and partly because Holt needed a constant companion to deal with distractions, disruptions and the difficulties of dealing with an ever more intrusive press gallery.

Eggleton was highly regarded by Holt's ministerial colleagues and the public service staff at Parliament House. He had gained a reputation for diligence and discretion, punctuality and attentiveness. His invariably perfect manners and constant good humour lessened the number of actual and potential adversaries with which he had to contend in trying to promote the Prime Minister and his government's plans. The press considered him one of their own. He was a highly effective and efficient operator who understood their needs and empathised with their challenges.

Eggleton's most vehement critic was not a hostile newspaper proprietor who was concerned with restrictions imposed by the press secretary on access to the prime minister but a senior member of the government. The Minister for External Affairs in the Holt Cabinet, Paul (later Sir Paul) Hasluck, revealed his personal and private feelings about Eggleton in some notes penned in March 1968. These character 'portraits' were not discovered until the 1990s and were then published by Hasluck's son, Nicholas, in a volume he titled, *The Chance of Politics*. After claiming that Holt was out of his depth as prime minister, and complaining that the Holts were 'vulgar' people, Hasluck turned to Eggleton.

> I think his public relations officer, a young chap named Eggleton, immensely devoted to his task of promoting publicity for the prime minister, had an unfortunate influence. Naturally his interests were focused on getting favourable stories and if he found the journalists responding to a particular line he influenced the PM to continuing that line regardless of whether it was a sound expression of policy. I suspected Eggleton, too, of adding to the dissatisfaction of ministers by pushing the prime minister into a somewhat ungenerous monopoly on all the good news and leaving all the bad news to other members of Cabinet.
>
> It was an unfortunate association and did Harold a lot of harm. Indeed, Holt might have done much better in his job if he had been fortunate enough to inherit someone other than Eggleton in the public relations job and if he had paid much more attention to the counsel of John Bunting, the permanent head of his department, and faced up to such realities as might have been presented to him by his senior ministers, rather than being lured into Eggleton's strange and glamorous but quite fanciful world of 'public relations'. This loyal and devoted minor member of his personal staff undoubtedly thought he was building up the prime minister but I think he really damaged the possibility of Holt's growing up himself.[3]

Hasluck conveyed similar sentiments to Gerard Henderson for his 1994 work on the Liberal Party, *Menzies' Child*. By then, Hasluck was even more voluble.

> The chief disability under which Holt suffered was having this wretched fellow Eggleton as his public relations officer. I thought that was one of Holt's tragedies … this little twerp, who was just a minor public relations chap, was always trotting in and saying: 'The press gallery is saying, the press gallery is saying …'. Eggleton thought he was serving his master very loyally but he did more to destroy Holt as prime minister than any other cause … Holt needed somebody to conquer his own weakness but this chap was feeding his weakness, not intentionally but just in the nature of his own trade.

Henderson then remarked, with an element of admiration, that 'Eggleton would always know what every editorial had said by half past six in the morning and what every journalist was writing. Beyond that he didn't have any direction'. Whether this was Henderson's defence of Eggleton – that he was merely doing his job as the press secretary (rather than as a public relations officer, which he wasn't) – or that he did not try to direct Holt's discernment or decisions, is not clear. That it was interpreted as a criticism was reflected in Hasluck's reply:

> [Eggleton] knew nothing of politics. He just attached himself to Holt and played on what was Holt's weakness – paying too much attention to what they were saying in the press gallery, what somebody was going to write tomorrow about this or that. I think Eggleton spoiled whatever chance Holt had of becoming a good prime minister.

In personal notes produced in February 1997 upon which he could rely if approached for public comment, Eggleton remarked: 'I find it awkward commenting on the opinions of an author who is no longer with us'. Hasluck died in 1993. Eggleton thought 'Hasluck does Harold a considerable disservice'. Holt did not see himself as an intellectual but as 'a realist and a politician'. Eggelton suggested that Hasluck's 'personal notes should be seen in perspective. He was not an independent observer of the political scene'. Eggleton was interested in Hasluck's views but felt 'it would be wrong to see them as a definitive and totally objective assessment of the events and personalities of the period' and found it 'disappointing that Sir Paul had such a low opinion of many of his Liberal colleagues'. Eggleton's response was diplomatic and dignified – and better than Hasluck deserved for prose he termed 'gossip to myself'.

Hasluck's scathing judgements about Holt and Eggleton – indeed, much of the content of *The Chance of Politics* – were inaccurate and self-serving. Eggleton's job was informing the prime minister of press reactions to his public statements and parliamentary performance. What Holt did with this information was entirely a matter for the prime minister. Holt had the authority to make decisions and the power to implement them. Although Holt is not ranked among the best or the worst prime ministers, I argued in *The Life and Death of Harold Holt* that he was an effective public administrator who barely had time to demonstrate his capacity for national leadership. After his unparalleled election victory in October 1966, Holt began to transform the economy and Australian diplomacy. He was often too cautious and sometimes lacked imagination. In the view of his colleagues, Holt was a far more attractive and engaging figure than the dour, and plainly judgemental, Minister for External Affairs, Paul Hasluck.

Hasluck also overlooked the dynamics of the prime minister's office. He did not seem to realise it was more Holt wanting Eggleton by his side than Eggleton trying to ingratiate himself with the prime minister. As press secretary, Eggleton was conscious of the limits of his expertise and his experience. He remained either in the shadows or at the margins and showed neither the interest nor the inclination to increase his influence. There is no evidence that Sir John Bunting or Holt's principal private secretary, Peter Bailey, was ever concerned that Eggleton was exceeding his brief or exerting a detrimental influence on the prime minister. Eggleton maintained positive relations with every member of the Cabinet and there were no complaints from them (or none that were ever recorded) of Eggleton manipulating the media to have Holt receive credit for achievements that were primarily the work of others. If Hasluck was displeased with Eggleton's performance, he might have approached Holt or Eggleton with his concerns but there is no record that Hasluck ever did.

Although he was a very able minister, Hasluck was considered one of the poorest politicians in the Menzies and Holt Cabinets. He had a 'tin ear' when it came to public opinion and popular culture. The high-brow Hasluck failed to connect with the aspirations of 'middle Australia'. The electorate did not warm to him. Hasluck personally resented Holt for not including him in official delegations during several of his overseas trips. In Holt's judgement, Hasluck struggled to develop personal rapport with foreign leaders and he was unable or unwilling to 'sell' the government's message to reporters. The newsletter *Incentive* reported that 'the prime minister himself has had to take over more and more of the routine work of diplomacy, even to the point of conducting interviews with visiting journalists and television men, whom Mr Hasluck simply refuses to see'.[4] It was even suggested that Hasluck might be sent to Washington as Australia's ambassador and be replaced in the External Affairs portfolio by Senator Gorton.

As a senior minister, Hasluck naturally considered himself a candidate for the leadership of the Liberal Party after Holt's disappearance. There was no doubt that Eggleton would lose his job and return to the Department of the Navy were Hasluck to succeed in the party room ballot. As with the transition from Menzies to Holt, there were still no guarantees that the election of someone other than Paul Hasluck as the new prime minister would mean that Eggleton remained the prime minister's press secretary. Once again, his future was uncertain.

Endnotes

1   Bruce Juddery, 'Mr Eggleton at the helm', *Nation*, 20 January 1968, p. 5.
2   https://www.oversixty.com.au/news/news/
    the-last-person-to-see-harold-holt-alive-speaks-out
3   Paul Hasluck, *The Chance of Politics*, Text, Melbourne, 1997, pp. 145–46.
4   'Topic of the Week', *Incentive*, no. 88, 8 March 1967.

CHAPTER 6

Managing the messenger   1968–69

With Harold Holt missing presumed dead, Country Party leader John McEwen became Australia's eighteenth prime minister. There was an understanding he would remain in office until the senior Coalition partner, the Liberals, found a new leader. In the wake of the dramatic events of the previous few weeks, the head of the Prime Minister's Department, Sir John Bunting, suggested to Eggleton that he take some leave and return to Parliament House to liaise with the press gallery ahead of the leadership ballot which was scheduled for 9 January 1968.

Eggleton arranged for the assembled photographers and cameramen to enter the government party room to record some visual images before the ballot was held. His instructions were brief: 'Only two minutes, chaps. That'll be all you're allowed'. There were four candidates for the leadership: Billy Snedden, Leslie Bury, Paul Hasluck and John Gorton. They sat alongside one another on a bench facing those who would determine their future. There was no obvious frontrunner as each tried to avoid looking at the cameras as they chatted about everything but the solitary matter that had brought them together. True to his word, after two minutes Eggleton announced: 'Right, thank you gentlemen'. Deputy Liberal leader, Bill McMahon, chaired the meeting and announced, to some surprise, that his position was not vacant and would not be contested. Snedden and Bury were excluded after the first round of voting. At 3.16pm, Eggleton walked into King's Hall at Parliament House to declare that Senator John Gorton was the new leader of the Parliamentary Liberal Party.

Given their friendship and previously productive relationship, it was unsurprising that Gorton asked Eggleton to serve as his press secretary. He was pleased to accept. Eggleton was the only key member of Holt's staff to make the transition to Gorton's office. By this stage, Eggleton had a fixed daily working routine that would continue under the new leader. He was out of bed by 6.40am and listened to the 6.45am ABC news bulletin as he showered and shaved. He listened to the BBC's 'World Report' as he was dressing, just after 7am. Over breakfast he would read the *Canberra Times*, *Sydney Morning Herald*, *Australian*, Sydney *Telegraph*, Melbourne *Age* and the *Australian Financial Review*, clipping relevant stories for the scrapbooks he assiduously maintained. He would field a few calls from newsrooms before arriving at Parliament House around 8.40am. Eggleton dealt with paperwork during the forenoon and with a steady stream of journalists in the afternoon: 'they would hang around in my outer office like patients waiting to see the doctor. They preferred to consult with me one at a time. I would chat to each of them for 10–15 minutes, giving them what guidance I could and picking-up their pieces of gossip.' He would usually leave for home by 6pm unless parliament was sitting, when he was rarely home before midnight. His 'average' day during a non-sitting week was over 11 hours and customarily around 17 hours during a sitting week. The pace was unrelenting: 'for the whole of the time I did the job, I did not have a lunch hour. I always worked straight through, without eating. All I had during the day were a couple of cups of tea or coffee, and the odd biscuit'.

Eggleton now faced a dual challenge. Not only did he have to launch a new prime minister, Eggleton had to help Gorton win a seat in the House of Representatives. He was the first senator to be elected party leader and needed to move from the 'Upper' to the 'Lower' house of parliament. Section 64 of the Australian Constitution stipulated that no minister 'shall hold office for a longer period than three months unless he is or becomes a senator or a member of the House of Representatives'. Gorton had three months to complete the transition. He resigned from the Senate on 1 February 1968 to contest the seat of Higgins that was made vacant by Holt's death. He was elected to the House of Representatives at a by-election held on 24 February 1968.

The veteran journalist Alan Reid described Eggleton as 'highly professional and discreet' who had the task of 'loyally struggling to present attractively to the Australian electorate the figure of a much less conventional occupant of Australia's highest political office'.[1] Gorton wanted to be prime minister but also insisted on being himself. He was not prepared to change his style to conform to the views of others. At press conferences, Eggleton thought Gorton was 'inclined to say precisely what he thinks, without any qualification. It would seem in retrospect that he has sometimes been 'thinking aloud', rather than expressing any firm policy line or decision'. Eggleton also noted that Gorton had a 'tendency to become a little irritable and impatient ... he has sometimes become so defensive (in complete contrast to his previous frankness), that his comments at press conferences have been cautious to the point of nonsense'. The solution, Eggleton believed, was to prevent Gorton 'thinking on his feet'. He needed to 'do everything possible to dispel the atmosphere of inconsistency and indecision. The future must produce clear, concise statements without ambiguity ... showing the PM as a man of action who knows precisely where he's heading'.

According to Eggleton, Gorton resembled Holt in believing he could be prime minister for five days a week and then revert to being 'John Gorton, orchardist' on the weekends. Eggleton thought Gorton never adjusted to the pace of the prime ministership and was perennially tardy with paperwork. A suitcase of official correspondence was always taken when Gorton was travelling in the hope the prime minister might be persuaded to read briefings and sign documents. Gorton's biographer, Ian Hancock, challenged Eggleton's assessment of the 'Monday to Friday' prime minister based on office hours, suggesting Eggleton 'may not have taken sufficient account of Gorton's preference for reading his papers at The Lodge either in bed or at breakfast in the morning'.[2] Hancock agreed, however, that Eggleton had correctly discerned Gorton's belief that the prime minister should be able to lead 'a normal life'. Hancock disputed another of Eggleton's personal observations. Eggleton thought there was 'no question' that Gorton's drinking affected his judgement because the standard applied by his 'abstemious' press secretary was inconsistent with those of his Cabinet colleagues who thought alcohol had no influence on his performance. Unlike those who saw Gorton during working hours, Eggleton's perspective was drawn from accompanying Gorton on domestic and international trips, seeing him at night after others had gone home, and first thing in the morning at Parliament House. Eggleton was better placed than most members of Cabinet to offer a reliable assessment.

Despite his lack of diligence and attraction to alcohol, the new prime minister had a lot going for him in terms of public presentation. Gorton's self-portrayal as a 'very Aussie bloke' was not concocted for the cameras. He loved sport, a smoke and a beer. Gorton was not attracted to the luxury hotels that had been favoured by his predecessors. When in Melbourne he did not stay at the Windsor but a slightly down-market alternative. Gorton's break from the conservative mould was generally welcomed by the Australian community. He was seen as more typically Australian than his two Liberal predecessors, Robert Menzies and Harold Holt, with a battle-scarred face that bore testimony to his wartime service as a RAAF fighter pilot. Veteran press gallery journalist Wallace Brown thought that the 'ubiquitous' Eggleton 'had succeeded in casting Gorton as the 'educated battle hero'.[3] It was largely Gorton's own work.

Gorton delighted in demonstrating that he would indeed do things his way. His style led to tension with world leaders, federal ministers, state premiers and members of his own party. But he would not be restricted by convention or bound by tradition. Gorton detested the affected formalism and rigid decorum that he encountered among longer-serving officials. To their discomfort, they soon discovered the new prime minister was very different to his predecessors. Gorton dismissed a series of respected public servants and insisted, against formal advice, on installing the young Ainsley Gotto as his principal private secretary.[4] Her predecessor, Peter Bailey, was aged 40 and held the rank of First Assistant Secretary in the Prime Minister's Department. He was widely experienced and highly regarded. Gotto was aged 22 and had been working at Parliament House for less than two years as secretary (clerical assistant) to the Chief Whip. She was intelligent, assertive and made parliamentary staffers know that she spoke with the authority of the Prime Minister.

Gorton initially took advice from a small group of trusted officials. The core group were the new head of the Prime Minister's Department, Len Hewitt, Gotto and Eggleton. When travelling abroad Gorton tried to avoid being accompanied by departmental officials from External Affairs, Trade and Defence, and dismissed the suggestion he needed their advice or guidance. Worse, he often asked, to the embarrassment of his hosts, whether he could be accompanied by Eggleton and Gotto at social or informal occasions to which they had not been invited. When President Johnson honoured Gorton with an invitation to be his guest on the presidential yacht, Gorton asked whether Hewitt and Gotto might come too. This was poor form but Eggleton managed to keep the Australian press from noticing the *faux pas*.

A recurring theme throughout Gorton's prime ministership would be his relationship with Gotto. There were frequent insinuations, fuelled by the media who took every opportunity to shine a spotlight on the pair. Eggleton saw them constantly at close quarters, often behind closed doors. He says they were undoubtedly close but the nature of the relationship was often exaggerated and deliberately distorted. Gorton was fascinated by Gotto. He greatly enjoyed her company and had a high regard for her abilities. Much later he said publicly that he 'loved Ainsley but was not in love with her'. Gotto, in turn, relished the intimacy of their friendship and the opportunity to be an influential adviser. She evidently enjoyed the status this gave her. In a private note, Eggleton observed that 'no-one has more influence on him' than her because she

> has woven herself into his life in such a way I believe he would find it almost impossible to face the future without her. His dependence on her is frightening ... I wondered whether he was just a fool or whether he just could not bear the thought of being without her ... if he is not man enough to do without her, then he must fall with her.

Although the relationship was clearly an indulgence for both of them, Eggleton never saw any evidence of impropriety. Gorton also knew that Gotto was in a romantic relationship with Race Matthews, the chief of staff to the Leader of the Opposition, Gough Whitlam.

From the time she arrived, Gotto was a highly divisive figure in the Prime Minister's office. Eggleton felt 'there was no concealing her ambition, and she made sure that no one got in her way. If they did, they did not last long'. It was not long before Hewitt wanted her moved out of the job but knew Gorton would not agree. Hewitt's response was to compete with Gotto for the Prime Minister's time and attention. Within six months, the trust between Gorton and Hewitt had turned to hostility. Eggleton observed a 'very noticeable change in the PM's manner to Len. He was pointedly brusque and rude'. Gorton was giving Hewitt less of his time and was openly critical of his performance in Eggleton's presence. This troubled Eggleton who noted that although Hewitt 'put on a good front, he was obviously very hurt. He found it increasingly hard to be nice to Ainsley. Whereas he once kept in close touch with her while we were away from Canberra, he began using me as his main point of contact'. Hewitt began to speak with Eggleton 'much more openly, and to confide in me. He saw me as a friend, and also as someone who could provide inside information on the Ainsley-PM relationship. I could judge the temperature for him'. By way of contrast, Eggleton was not involved in scheming against those he disliked or attempting to increase his influence. His practice was never to take sides. He would focus on political objectives and administrative imperatives.

Hewitt's increasingly fraught relationship with Gotto was, Eggleton conceded, partly Hewitt's own doing. As the nation's most senior public servant, Eggleton thought Hewitt could be

> somewhat overbearing, and is inclined to wear out his welcome by persisting when he would do well to wait for a more opportune moment. Also, he cannot delegate. He tries to do everything himself. The result is that things get delayed. He has terrible staff relations in his department. His officers are all scared to death of him, and are frightened to take action or do anything without consulting Hewitt.

Hewitt knew that if a choice had to be made, Gorton would retain his principal private secretary and dispense with his departmental head. Eggleton often felt caught in the middle of a conflict in which there would only be losers, with the Prime Minister likely to lose most. Despite the disagreements, Hewitt was knighted during Gorton's prime ministership.

When all was going smoothly and Hewitt was 'in his place', Gorton and Gotto were a close-knit team. They would drink and debate together well into the night. Eggleton was not invited to these sessions but had no desire to join them. The intensity of the bond between Gorton and Gotto inevitably led to problems. Gorton could suddenly, and without obvious reason, become unreasonably antagonistic towards Gotto, causing her considerable distress. On one occasion – at a dinner with the Administrator of Papua New Guinea and his wife in Port Moresby – Eggleton noted that a 'deep freeze' descended over the whole evening as Gorton openly humiliated Gotto. Their hosts were dismayed and embarrassed. On such occasions Eggleton tried to intervene, sometimes with success.

Gorton's accomplished wife, Bettina or 'Betty' as she was widely known, tried to avoid any outward sign of concern over the relationship between her husband and his young principal private secretary. She was, however, upset by her reduced involvement in his parliamentary career. Betty had been the driving force and guiding hand throughout his political life. Her influence waned when he became prime minister and she greatly missed the closeness of her former role. She was clearly irritated at being 'replaced' by the young and inexperienced Gotto. When the irritation became unbearable, she asked Eggleton to visit her at The Lodge. She disclosed her resentment at being overlooked and marginalised.

Why Gorton needed Gotto at all was a mystery to Eggleton. Like his predecessors, Menzies, Holt and McEwen, Gorton was a highly experienced politician. He was first elected to the Senate in February 1950 and held a number of senior parliamentary posts, including Leader of the Government in the Senate. After five very productive years as Minister for the Navy, he held the Interior, Works, and Science and Education portfolios. He had not had any direct exposure to the conduct of international affairs. Although he had travelled overseas on government business many times before becoming prime minister, Gorton's personal style was to have an adverse effect on Australian diplomacy.

Relations between Australia and the United States had become particularly productive as a function of Harold Holt's friendship with Lyndon Johnson. Early in his prime ministership, Gorton visited the United States for talks on South Vietnam, American policy in the Asia-Pacific region and the acceleration of Britain's planned 'east of Suez' withdrawal. The President went to great lengths to welcome Gorton and to consolidate further the Canberra–Washington nexus. Johnson invited Gorton to his ranch in Texas where he had arranged for key figures in his administration to brief the Prime Minister on security issues. The President sought to create an air of informality with some of the discussions held in the gardens. Johnson had also instructed General William Westmoreland, the commander of American forces in Vietnam, to be present. Unlike Holt, Gorton had growing reservations about the efficacy of the war and did not feel personally well-disposed to Johnson. Gorton did not make any great effort to hide his attitude; a charm offensive would not succeed with him. When the time came to leave the ranch, Eggleton was the last to board the presidential helicopter. Johnson shook his hand warmly, then leaned close enough to whisper, 'Tony, it's not the same, sorry, but it's not the same.' Gorton could not replace Holt in the President's affections.

Gorton's unpredictable streak was on display during the return journey to Australia when the delegation rested for a couple of days on the Hawaiian island of Maui. Gorton was angry about the highly intrusive security measures adopted by the Americans who were understandably anxious about avoiding any problems on their territory. The former Australian prime minister (Holt) and the previous American president (John F Kennedy) had both died in office. A special team of security agents was flown from Washington to protect Gorton. Every time he entered the water there were boats and divers on hand. The security for his bungalow featured constant monitoring, including one man who climbed to a nearby tree to act as a look-out. The resort staff had kept these details from Gorton because they were made aware of his disdain for personal protection. During their stay, Eggleton was briefing Gorton when the look-out's two-way radio suddenly burst into life. Gorton was incensed to discover a 'talking tree' in the garden of his bungalow. Eggleton and Gotto were instructed to restore his privacy 'by whatever means'.

During dinner one evening, Gorton and Betty decided to 'give the guards the slip'. They jumped into their motorised cart and, with Gorton applying all the power the cart could generate, disappeared into the night. The security men were not amused and pursued them. Gorton claimed afterwards he had simply lost his sense of direction in the dark. The Australian journalists were greatly amused and found Maui a rich source of entertaining copy for their readers.

A not dissimilar episode occurred during an official visit to Canada. Gorton scheduled a private recreational stopover at Jasper National Park. The Prime Minister's ire was aroused by the arrival of a couple of journalists at what was meant to be a non-media occasion. Gorton and Betty set off on a guided fishing and hunting trip. They had to cross a ravine by flying fox and, knowing the press were not far behind, refused to return the swing seat to the other side. Not to be out manoeuvred, the press finally managed to clamber across the ravine. The story later emerged that the Prime Minister had brandished a rifle to keep the intruders at a distance. The journalists also claimed there was much bad language. On his return, Gorton was less than forthcoming about the precise circumstances of the encounter. The media contingent were certainly scared off but colourful news stories echoed around the world. It was not the sort of incident that even an accomplished press secretary could easily explain or credibly contain.

Firearms also featured in Gorton's visit to Papua New Guinea and the island of New Britain which had recently experienced civil unrest. In May 1969, a group of Tolai, the local people of the Gazelle Peninsula in East New Britain, formed the Mataungan Association (MAS) in the island's largest town, Rabaul. They opposed the establishment of a multi-racial Gazelle Peninsula Local Government Council by the Australian colonial administration. The MAS boycotted the Council elections and organised demonstrations and mass meetings. In December 1969 violence broke out between MAS members and some of the Council's supporters. By then the MAS had expanded its grievances to include the proposed lease of land to the local people for cocoa and copra production. The MAS argued that the land belonged to the Tolai not the colonial Administration and they were entitled to make such decisions, not the Australians.

Against the backdrop of civil unrest there were serious security concerns about including Rabaul in the Prime Minister's itinerary. Officials in the Department of External Affairs were opposed to Gorton visiting Rabaul because they genuinely feared, given the strength of local emotion, the possibility of something being said or done that might provoke violence. Gorton was undeterred. He insisted on seeing Rabaul. It seemed he was determined to make a point. Gorton asked Eggleton to 'discourage press stories that he would not make the visit if there was the possibility of violence or injury ... He couldn't call off such a visit just because some people might get hurt'. Eggleton was incredulous.

> I find it hard to believe that a prime minister could adopt such an irrespon-
> sible attitude. He will probably get away with it provided no violence does
> occur. But that is really not the point. The thing that concerns me is that the
> man responsible for our country could take such a gamble ... a gamble with
> life, with property and the future of Papua New Guinea (not to mention the
> reputation of Australia).

Against Eggleton's strong advice, the Prime Minister decided he would visit Rabaul armed with a revolver. Gorton was probably the first Australian prime minister to carry a personal firearm on an official overseas visit. Eggleton managed to ensure that Gorton's decision to be armed was not disclosed to the media until much later.

When the official party flew into Rabaul, a large, angry mob of warriors brandishing spears and clubs had assembled as expected. Contrary to standard operating procedures, the media plane was instructed to land first. This was at the direction of Australian security officials who wanted to test their ability to control the crowd prior to Gorton's arrival. Eggleton embarked in the media plane. Once on the ground and in receipt of local approval, he would clear the official party to make their descent. The press wondered why they had received favoured treatment, not realising that they were, at best, a decoy and, at worst, bait.

Gorton's sometimes reckless approach to foreign affairs continued during the Five Power Defence Conference which was held in Canberra in June 1969. Gorton had already made plain his firm belief that with the withdrawal of British forces east of the Suez Canal, Australia could not replace the United Kingdom as the primary protector of South East Asia. At the time Malaysia was dealing with internal race riots, the prospect of renewed violence from communist insurgents, and tension with the Philippines over the sovereignty of Sabah. At the Conference, Gorton told the Malaysians they should not presume Australian military assistance in their struggle against internal forces and external threats. He said that Australia would be ready to fight in 'Malaya' but only under certain conditions. The journalists covering the conference asked Eggleton whether Gorton had meant to say 'Malaysia' which included the Federation's 13 states and three territories covering the Malay Peninsula and North Borneo. Eggleton presumed the same thing, telling journalists: 'I doubt that the prime minister would make a mistake like that.' He conferred privately with Gorton who indicated that his reference to Malaya was intentional. The implication was that Australia's role in regional defence was restricted to the Malay Peninsula and not Sabah. The Malaysians, especially its deputy prime minister Tun Razak, were angered by Gorton's comment at a time when the government in Kuala Lumpur was struggling to preserve national unity. Eggleton could do little to smooth the ruffled diplomatic feathers. Gorton did not seem to care who he offended.

Eggleton was required to intervene in yet another diplomatic incident caused by the Prime Minister's ill-considered comments. Eggleton received a visit at Parliament House from the South African High Commissioner, Johann Kunz Uys, who complained that Gorton had insulted his wife. He alleged that Gorton had become uncomfortably familiar with his wife at a reception, remarking that he 'was partial to a bit of black velvet.' The press secretary promised to take up the issue with the Prime Minister. The High Commissioner expressed his gratitude and said he would return in a few days. Gorton seemed genuinely nonplussed when informed of the complaint. He remembered the function but struggled to believe he could have caused any offence. On his return, Eggleton suggested to the High Commissioner that light-hearted banter may have led to some misunderstanding. Although unconvinced, Uys decided to let the matter rest. Unfortunately, rumours were already circulating in diplomatic circles and references appeared in political newsletters. There were reports that this essentially private matter had strained official relations between the two countries. The High Commissioner found it necessary to issue a public statement to take the heat out of the controversy and to clear the air.

Discomfort over the Prime Minister's judgement reached a crescendo during the annual dinner of the Parliamentary Press Gallery on the evening of 1 November 1968. The venue was the Park Royal Motor Inn in the Canberra suburb of Braddon. The first public mention of what had occurred after the dinner was in the 10 February 1969 edition of Max Newton's *Insight* newsletter. Newton loathed Gorton for partly personal and partly professional reasons. Newton was excluded from the Prime Minister's occasional briefings with heads of news bureaus because he was a lobbyist rather than a political reporter. On 19 March 1969, during an adjournment debate, Labor backbencher Bert James referred to an account of the evening in the Canberra scandal sheet, *Things I Hear*, published by Frank Browne, which was known colloquially as 'Things I Smear'. The Liberal Party room loyally rallied behind Gorton with one notable exception, the maverick Member for Warringah, Edward St John QC. Having previously disagreed with Gorton on both policy issues and procedural matters, St John saw this incident as a chance to chide Gorton over his personal conduct.

There were several versions of what occurred on 1 November 1968. Eggleton's account is the most detailed and candid because it was never intended for publication. He attributed the genesis of the incident to Gotto although her 'part in this never really came out … because she asked me to 'protect' her. But she was, in fact, the one who got the PM embroiled in the whole business'. The day had begun badly. The Johnson Administration had announced a halt to its bombing campaign over North Vietnam but had been tardy in advising the Australian Government of its intentions. When the American Ambassador, William 'Bill' Crook, arrived at Parliament House to brief Gorton, he was kept waiting and then treated disrespectfully by the Prime Minister who clearly felt the need to convey his displeasure.

That evening, Gorton was the guest of honour at the Press Gallery dinner but arrived late because he insisted on watching the television evening news at The Lodge. During the dinner, Eggleton received a call from Gotto who was at the American Embassy saying the American Ambassador hoped the Prime Minister might call on him later in the evening for a drink to confirm the Prime Minister's anger had subsided and cordial relations with the Embassy had resumed. Eggleton was 'less than enthusiastic but promised [Gotto] I would mention the invitation'. As the night wore on, Gotto telephoned Eggleton again, 'wondering how much longer we were likely to be'. At the conclusion of the dinner, Gorton started drinking with a few journalists. An hour or so later, he was persuaded to leave. Eggleton is unsure of when he told Gorton about the invitation to the Embassy but felt it was nearer to the conclusion of the dinner.

As Eggleton was walking towards the Prime Minister's official car he noticed that Gorton was accompanied by Geraldine Willesee, a 19-year old junior reporter with Australian United Press (AUP). Her father was Don Willesee, a Labor senator representing Western Australia; her brother was the ABC television journalist Mike Willesee. Most of the journalists attending the dinner looked on with a mixture of amazement and amusement. Gorton had apparently offered Willesee a lift home. Much to Gorton's annoyance, Eggleton thrust Willesee into the back of the Bentley and jumped in alongside her, leaving the Prime Minister with no other option but the front seat alongside the official driver, Ray Coppin. Eggleton thought it was 'extremely indiscrete to give this young woman a ride in his Bentley' especially as 'they were both considerably the worse for drink'.

Gorton then announced that he was taking Willesee to a charity ball at the Hotel Canberra. Eggleton said he thought it was unwise and, in any event, he explained that Ambassador Crook was expecting them at the American Embassy. Loudly objecting that John Gorton would not be told what to do and that he did not need any 'protection', Eggleton responded: 'It would take a better man than me to protect you'. Gorton then reached back to hold Willesee's hand. Eggleton thought Gorton 'was behaving like a schoolboy out with his first girlfriend, and was nattering away in a boastful and foolish fashion. She was encouraging him … I felt most embarrassed'. Finally, Gorton agreed to go to the Embassy but said, regardless of any objection from his press secretary, he would take Willesee with him.

On arrival at the Embassy, Eggleton went straight to the front door where he was met by Ambassador Crook. Before becoming President Johnson's nominee as Ambassador to Australia, Crook had been a Baptist minister and school headmaster in Texas. Eggleton explained the situation before the Prime Minister appeared hand-in-hand with the young journalist. The situation went from bad to worse once they were inside. Eggleton recalled: 'what then transpired in the residence was incredible. It seemed unreal at the time, and even more so in retrospect'. The Ambassador had been entertaining a few people for dinner, including Gotto and one of his attachés, Jeff Darman. Gorton was not pleased to see her with Darmon and Gotto was appalled that Gorton was accompanied by Willesee. To register his annoyance, Gorton took Willesee off to a corner of the room and gave no indication of wishing to speak with the Ambassador. He upset Gotto by studiously ignoring her. When Gotto approached Gorton, he said: 'Ainsley, we're in the middle of a private conversation' and told her to go away.

Ironically, shortly afterwards Willesee wrote a brief profile of both Gotto and Eggleton for the *Independent*.[5] She described Gotto as 'attractive' and 'one of the most competent secretaries around Parliament House'. Willesee had heard stories of Gorton abusing Gotto in the presence of journalists and suggested that 'although his personal secretary may now annoy him and although he obviously no longer likes her, Ainslie [sic] Gotto is probably the most loyal secretary he will ever find'. She also noted that 'the non-smoking, non-drinking Mr Eggleton does not have a lot in common with Mr Gorton'. Willesee described him as 'hard-working and able', and an invaluable asset to the prime minister. Given his experiences and knowledge (including of what occurred after the press gallery dinner), she thought Eggleton 'would have the material for an extremely interesting book'.

Gorton asked Willesee, the only female member of the Parliamentary Press Gallery, what her colleagues thought of him. She mentioned his reputation for drinking and womanising. Gorton then apparently revealed that he wanted to withdraw all Australian military forces from South Vietnam but was prevented by Liberal Party policy from doing so. This indiscrete comment would have created an international controversy and probably lost Gorton the prime ministership had it appeared in a reputable newspaper. In a statutory declaration dated 21 March 1969, Willesee assumed that 'anything I discussed with Mr Gorton was in club [meaning private and non-attributable] and not usable by me for a story in any newspaper'. This was not what she told the chief of the AUP's Canberra bureau, Ken Braddick, in November 1968. She felt that Gorton's comments could be reported because they were not conveyed in a social setting but at the American Embassy. Braddick disagreed.

In the hope of circumventing the embarrassing impasse, Crook suggested Eggleton accompany him to the Ambassador's study where they could discuss the war in Vietnam. Between 2am and 3am, Eggleton finally managed to persuade the Prime Minister to leave. Willesee was taken to her home in Yarralumla (where her father also resided) before the Prime Minister returned to The Lodge. The next morning, according to Alan Reid, accounts of the previous evening were 'given some nasty and malevolent twists' that were intended to impugn Willesee.

These accounts found their way to the AUP's management who decided that Willesee had embarrassed the company and would lose her job under the guise of a staffing review. An unhappy Braddick then informed Eggleton of the direction he had received to terminate Willesee's employment. Eggleton recognised the potential of this decision to harm Gorton, especially if Willesee decided to make a public statement. After informing Gorton of Willesee's fate, the Prime Minister asked Eggleton to contact Arthur Shakespeare, the former owner of the *Canberra Times* and an AUP board member, and explain that Gorton was willing to speak on Willesee's behalf. Apparently, the journalist had already made an appeal for Gorton's help. Eggleton strongly advised the Prime Minister against interfering. He might not save Willesee's job and could have drawn attention to what had occurred after the dinner. Eggleton continued to believe the incident had enormous potential to harm Gorton's reputation – fairly or otherwise.

By this time, Gotto had asked Eggleton to 'blur the fact' that the invitation to the Embassy had not originated with Ambassador. Eggleton thought she had 'big-noted herself with the Ambassador [and] ... for once in his life, Gorton appeared to see through Ainsley on this occasion'. Len Hewitt also got involved. This incident marked, according to Eggleton, 'Ainsley's all time low with John Gorton, and Len Hewitt's peak of influence'. Gorton telephoned Eggleton to tell him 'not to trust Ainsley, and not to take any notice of what she told me'.

Unsurprisingly, it was only a matter of time before gossip-fed rumours were publicly reported. By the time St John decided to make an issue of Gorton's behaviour, more than four months had passed since the dinner. Having shown no reticence about criticising his own party or reluctance in attacking his colleagues without any remorse, St John concluded his highly personal attack on Gorton with a public appeal.[6]

> I have no doubt what the American people and the American President would think of this kind of conduct. I am quite content to leave it to the Australian public to say whether they are going to set the seal of approval on this standard of conduct or whether they will in fact utterly repudiate it.

Gorton replied with an air of disdain:

> I do not propose to spend more than perhaps five minutes on this matter. But it is an interesting exercise in how something which I believe is a perfectly

reasonable and proper thing can be twisted, turned and slimed over, as it has been tonight.

The Prime Minister explained that when he was leaving the dinner 'a girl journalist there, whose father I have known for a long time, asked could she be given a lift home. It is perfectly true that she got into the back seat of my car – with Mr Tony Eggleton. I hope nobody is going to attack Mr Tony Eggleton. I got into the front seat of the car'. Gorton then claimed that 'we stayed about thirty minutes and then went home – all of us – in the same order, with Mr Eggleton and the girl in the back seat'. He then protested: 'I think it is utterly absurd that a story of that kind can be twisted in this way'.

Gorton had not said the dinner started late because he had intentionally arrived late. He then told parliament he arrived at the Embassy at 11:45pm when it was actually 1am and stayed for nearly two hours, not half an hour. St John had enough facts to refute Gorton's account of the evening. He chided the Prime Minister for not mentioning that Willesee was 'the daughter of a Labor Senator with whom, despite denials, Mr Gorton had quarrelled some years ago'. She was not, therefore, the daughter of a close friend. Further, Gorton 'actually argued the toss with two young journalists as to who should take the girl home. He persisted in doing so, despite the warnings from his Press Secretary [Eggleton] as to the gossip it would cause'. St John chided Gorton for ignoring national affairs and the importance of informing himself of the latest developments in South Vietnam while indulging himself in idle 'chatter' with a young woman.

By this time Willesee had published her statutory declaration. She recalled that 'the prime minister asked me if I would like a lift home. Before I gave him a reply we both discussed the gossip we both felt would be inevitable if I accepted his offer'. As Willesee was leaving the dinner, another journalist offered her a ride. It was then that 'Mr Gorton walked up and said 'I am giving her a lift home''. After arriving at the Embassy, Willesee saw Gotto and 'chatted with her about the Gallery Dinner … Mr Eggleton was still at the other end of the room talking to the Ambassador'. During their two hours at the Embassy, 'Mr Gorton and I were together at one end of the room talking and Mr Crook, Mr Darman, Mr Eggleton and Miss Gotto were talking and dancing to music from a record player at the other end of the room'.

Stories about the episode were widely reported. There was embarrassment for Ambassador Crook, who was subsequently obliged to make two formal public statements about the episode. The press was divided on the seriousness of Gorton's conduct or, misconduct, as some saw it. Several newspapers were critical of St John's scurrilous and puritanical campaign against the Prime Minister. Brisbane's *Courier Mail* thought Gorton had 'acted in a foolish and ill-advised manner'. The editorial went on:

> The girl was not invited to the Embassy and Mr Gorton committed a ridiculous *faux pas*. He had no right and no business to take her along when he was going to the Embassy on a matter of serious State affairs; to discuss a change in US tactics in the Vietnam war.

The *Canberra Times* adopted a similar stance.

> It is legitimate to ask whether at midnight a Prime Minister ought to take a young woman to the home of an official representative of a foreign power, however innocent the visit might be. The consequences [the need for the American Ambassador to confirm the accuracy of public statements made by the Australian prime minister], as we are seeing, can be damaging and danger-ous. In this case, the representative was not only placed in a position where he could, if he wished, make a judgement affecting our international relations. The foreign power itself has become involved.

The passage of time had naturally influenced the accuracy of most recollec-tions. Those involved remembered the night differently. Why had it taken so long for the media to report Gorton's behaviour? As press gallery journalist Wallace Brown later explained: 'this was an era when the 'off-the-record' convention that applied to a Press Gallery dinner – meaning nothing that was said or done was reported – was observed. In more recent years, of course, this custom has been disregarded'.[7]

Gorton had fallen short of every standard of acceptable behaviour. Fortunately for him, he was saved by Eggleton's professional reputation and personal integrity. Journalists knew that Eggleton did not drink alcohol and would not be party to misbehaviour – either its commission or cover-up. In fact, Gorton cited Eggleton's presence as evidence that nothing untoward could have happened. It was a tawdry affair and the treatment of Eggleton could only be described as shabby. The 'US Embassy visit' also marked a turning point in the relationship between Gorton and the press gallery.

This was not, of course, an isolated incident nor was it the first time that Eggleton needed to make excuses for Gorton's undisciplined behaviour. According to journalist Ray Aitchison, Gorton had developed a reputation for being 'inconsiderate to others, and was unconscious of time, and that he had become so much the prime minister that he had forgotten ordinary courtesy, and kept people waiting and inconvenienced them unnecessarily'. He had gained this reputation after a series of events that Eggleton could not conceal, such as his failure to attend a Cabinet meeting the day after he attended the marriage of Holt's widow, Dame Zara, to Liberal backbencher, Jeff Bate. Curiously, after being unable to attend Cabinet Gorton was able to attend an evening reception at the British High Commission for Lord Carrington. Eggleton explained to journalists that his absence from Cabinet was a consequence of the prime minister feeling 'a bit fluey'. The influenza story persuaded none of the journalists who presumed Gorton had drunk too much at the wedding reception and was hungover the next morning. Eggleton remained the soul of discretion and insisted Gorton was laid low by a virus. While Gorton preserved a measure of electoral appeal and the prospect of replacing him would serve only to increase the chances of the Labor Opposition winning the next election, his conduct was not sufficiently grave to provoke a leadership challenge. But there would be little to save him or his prime ministership once his standing in the electorate began to decline.

Endnotes

1   Alan Reid, *The Gorton Experiment*, Shakespeare Head Press, Sydney, 1971, p. 4.

2   Ian Hancock, *John Gorton: He Did it His Way*, Hodder, Sydney, 2002, p. 169.

3   Wallace Brown, *Ten Prime Ministers: Life Among the Politicians*, Longueville Books, Sydney, 2002, p. 79.

4   Gotto was initially titled 'Personal Private Secretary' until confirmed in the position.

5   Geraldine Willesee, 'Reaction' column, *Independent*, 15 June 1969.

6   Edward St John, *A Time to Speak*, Sun Books, Melbourne, 1969, chapters 8 and 9.

7   Wallace Brown, *Ten Prime Ministers*, p. 92.

CHAPTER 7

Protracted end   1969–70

John Gorton had much less experience of electoral campaigning than Harold Holt. Gorton had been a senator for much of his parliamentary career and was usually assured of re-election because of his place on the party's Senate 'ticket'. When Gorton campaigned, it was usually on behalf of his colleagues. As prime minister, he would be central to the Liberal Party's strategy and hopes of retaining office. At the election which was due at the end of 1969, Gorton would be seeking re-election to the House of Representatives *and* leading his party.

In mid-1969, Gorton hinted at the possibility of an early election. He had not spoken to his advisers nor the leader of the Democratic Labor Party (DLP), Senator Vince Gair, which usually directed its second preference votes to the Liberals. With expectation of an early poll gaining ground, Gair informed Gorton that an early election was not justified and the Liberals would not receive DLP preferences. There was little Gorton could do. He directed Eggleton to advise the press gallery that the election would not be held until the end of 1969. Eggleton was placed in a precarious position because he was unable to give journalists a cogent explanation for the Prime Minister's apparent change of heart. To make matters worse, Gorton evaded questions from the Opposition about why he had floated the prospect of an early election only to claim these were never more than rumours that did not originate with him. It looked like Gorton was playing political games with little point or purpose.

Gorton finally called an election for 25 October 1969. It would be his first as Prime Minister and Whitlam's first as Opposition leader. Gorton's laid-back and almost lethargic attitude nearly derailed the Liberal's quest for another term in office. As much of the campaign was conducted in Melbourne, Eggleton observed that Gorton 'never once attempted to work efficiently' in his nearby office. 'Instead he remained in the hotel. As usual, he rose late and never really did his homework or made adequate preparation'. It had been agreed that Gorton's advisors would finalise his main policy speech a few days ahead of the campaign launch. Instead, the Prime Minister locked himself in his hotel room and rebuffed every attempt by Eggleton and Gotto to make him focus on the task. Gotto resorted to pushing drafts under the door. When all else was failing, they urged Gorton's departmental secretary, Len Hewitt, to travel to Melbourne in the hope he would prove more persuasive.

At the eleventh hour, Gorton began to take an interest in what he would say to the nation. He asked Eggleton to take responsibility for writing elements of his speech and shaping the Liberal party's policy although, as press secretary, Eggleton knew next to nothing about what Gorton wanted to say or the objectives to which the Party was committed. Eggleton then realised that 'Gorton was depressed and despondent, and was struggling with every word. What horrified me was the way this key speech was being thrown together. It had no cohesion. It was just a series of papers on different subjects being tacked together ... What a hotch-potch ... what a way to prepare a policy speech'. Eggleton was also annoyed that Gotto had prevented Hewitt from having any influence on the content and the delivery until the final moment when there was a 'general state of confusion' and he was exhorted to intervene. Hewitt quickly noticed inconsistencies in what the Prime Minister would be promising. There was also a factual error in what had been circulating to advisers as the penultimate draft. Gorton resented Hewitt's assistance, especially his correction.

As Gorton and Eggleton drove to the television studio for the launch, they were still shuffling through the speech notes and trying to get pages in the right order. Gorton told the television producer, Ron Davis, that he 'did not want to know anything about technique. He had always managed to do pretty well on TV ... so he just wanted to do what came naturally'. Gorton's presentation was assessed by commentators as adequate but the substance in his speech left a great deal to be desired. Eggleton was exasperated. He thought the text 'had nothing forward looking or imaginative about it, it was badly written and the promises and policy were pedestrian. What had happened to the man of destiny ... the man of change ... the man with great ideas for the future?'

The Minister for Defence, Malcolm Fraser, was far from satisfied with Gorton's performance let alone shortcomings in his text. Fraser later commented:

He wasn't able to answer questions he'd been asked, and he'd been ill-prepared. He'd ring me up in the morning and say 'what's the answer to this, and what's the answer to that? And he got the answers, but his staff should have prepared him and he wasn't. He did his policy speech in a television studio in front of thirty or forty of us, and just read it out. Eggleton said on the morning of the day in the car going to the studio, 'There's nothing about transport in the speech'. Eggleton had written something into a suitable form that morning and it was assembled into the speech there in the car. 'Here, do you want to read it?' [Eggleton asked]. 'No'. He hadn't read it before he got up onto the podium to read it.[1]

There were also Gorton's attitudes which required some moderation. What he considered harmless 'larrikinism' was always a potential problem. During the campaign the virulent side of his larrikinism was provoked by anti-Vietnam war demonstrators. The Prime Minister decided he would like his own anti-demonstrator placard. Gotto had one made up for him that read, 'I hate you too'. As far as possible, Eggleton discouraged him from displaying the placard in the window of his official car. There were times when he insisted on doing things his way and Eggleton was powerless to restrain him.

The campaign was largely dominated by Gorton although he avoided public gatherings and turned on Eggleton when he tried to offer constructive feedback on a number of recorded radio talks. After enduring his anger and aggression, Eggleton remarked in a private note: 'I've never seen such hard work made of such a simple task ... the preparation and reading of short radio talks. The ABC people were staggered'. Eggleton thought the press had become hostile because Gorton had given them precious little of substance to report. The policy speech was dull and lifeless with the critics complaining that the nation deserved better. Although he was not responsible for campaign arrangements – that was a task for the Liberal's federal director – Eggleton believed the Prime Minister and his party attracted 'a very bad press'. He had firm views on what needed to change the next time the government went to the polls. In a private note, Eggleton considered the third-quarter of 1969 to be 'the worst period in my four years in this job. The PM insisted on doing things his own disastrous way'. He was excluded from some decisions because Gorton and Gotto 'were largely keeping their own counsel'. When Gorton told the press in Perth that all of the Coalition's policy promises had been costed, Eggleton was told to supply journalists with a 'supplementary statement' outlining the proposed expenditure although the work had not been done by either the public service or the Liberal Party. Eggleton mused: 'I put up a smoke screen suggesting that the figures had accidently been left in Canberra, not wanting to admit that no costings had been done. Of course, it was a surprise to me to learn that there were no figures. It seemed so basic.'

Similarly, Eggleton was astounded that Gorton and Gotto had arranged for a private public relations firm, Eric White & Associates, to help with the Prime Minister's speeches without telling either the Liberal Party's campaign director, Bede Hartcher, or the party's own public relations officer, Edgar Holt. When the Labor Party and the press learned that Gorton had sought outside assistance, the newspapers suggested the Prime Minister was engaging in a 'desperate last minute bid to rebuild his image'. Despite his personal misgivings about both the campaign strategy and the Prime Minister's approach, Eggleton's outward demeanour never wavered. Reporters appreciated that he was 'scrupulously fair in his dealings with the press; there are no favourites, no whispered 'scoops', no preferential treatment whatsoever'.[2] When travelling with journalists on the campaign trail, he 'shuttled up and down the [prime minister's] plane ostensibly to chew the fat, to brief reporters or to borrow a paper, but more calculatingly to feed back to the prime minister questions he's likely to be asked at the next hurried stopover'.

Late on election night, Gorton entered the national tally room in Canberra and was mobbed by a surging crowd of journalists. He had been drinking whisky throughout the evening with a small group of invited guests at The Lodge. His face was visibly flushed as he tried to shove some of the reporters out of his way. One of the journalists, Ray Aitchison, noted that Mrs Gorton was 'silent and impassive, and behind her was the urbane Eggleton, finding circumstances for once beyond his management'.[3]

The election result was nothing short of a disaster for the Coalition although Eggleton recalled Gorton being 'far too optimistic' when claiming at the tally room on election night that the Coalition might secure a 14-seat majority. By Eggleton's own reckoning, it was still possible the Government might lose by one seat. Labor had enjoyed a 7.1 per cent swing and secured 50.2 per cent of the two-party preferred vote. This was the largest swing in electoral history not to have resulted in a change of government. The Opposition had come within four seats of claiming victory. Holt's 40-seat majority had been reduced to just seven seats. Whitlam, and most commentators, sensed Labor would win the next election and end two decades of unbroken Coalition rule. The public had warmed to Whitlam and expressed their dissatisfaction with Gorton who refused to acknowledge any blame or accept any responsibility for the Coalition's poor showing at the polls. It was only when he was challenged by David Fairbairn for the party leadership after the election that Gorton showed, according to Eggleton, 'signs of contrition'. Highly personal attacks on Gorton's performance during the campaign by Sydney's *Daily Telegraph* also appeared to have had an influence on the outcome. Eggleton thought the tenor of this reporting was 'vicious' and intended to boost the profile of the Treasurer, Bill McMahon. According to Eggleton, the 'main hatchet man' was Alan Reid who 'appeared to relish the job. It was a case of boots and all, and I felt it damaged the standing of the paper and the reputation of a respected political journalist more than it hurt the PM'.

Eggleton now had very 'mixed feelings' about Gorton. He wrote privately:

> I am doubtful about the future. John Gorton has many limitations, and I am doubtful he will make a successful prime minister. I don't believe I will be able to change his ways. I will be surprised if he sees out another full three year term. But as things stand, he probably is the best man available. I share the view of the backbencher [Don Cameron, the member for Griffith] who said to me: 'I wonder if the leopard can change his spots?' Personally, I doubt it.

Eggleton was obliged to tell Gorton that a story was doing the rounds that he would 'retire on health grounds in about a year's time'. Gorton replied: 'They can forget it. I may be beaten on a vote of the party room – *but not eased out on health grounds*' [emphasis retained].

Despite his own rather sanguine views, Eggleton resolved to pursue a fresh approach with Gorton in the new year, beginning with rehabilitating his standing among press gallery journalists. At the start of 1968, Gorton had enjoyed a positive relationship with the media. As criticism increased, his attitude hardened until he resisted media contact and refused to hold press conferences. Eggleton shared many argumentative meals with Gorton and Betty in which they disagreed with Eggleton about the inherent worth of the media in a democratic society. The Prime Minister wanted to create a list of correspondents who would be deemed *persona non grata* and barred from the prime minister's press office. Eggleton made it clear that he would not continue in the job if there were 'black lists'. He was determined to treat all journalists fairly and equally.

A new approach had to be introduced gradually. Gorton had never been willing to stand before a group of assembled journalists and answer questions without notice. Nor was he willing to hold regular press briefings. News bureaus would be given public statements when Gorton and Eggleton decided they were needed. Gorton preferred to seek Eggleton's advice before speaking with individual reporters or he would allow Eggleton to decide which of the reporters should be granted an interview. Whitlam displayed none of Gorton's reluctance. He was always willing to speak with journalists individually. Every Wednesday, following the weekly meeting of the Labor Party caucus, Whitlam held an open press conference. The Leader of the Opposition was articulate and credible.

Early in 1970, Eggleton persuaded Gorton to hold two televised press conferences. They began with a detailed policy speech delivered directly to the camera followed by well-rehearsed answers to questions that were posed by assembled journalists. The aim was to have Gorton address the electorate whose views mattered more than those of journalists at election time. Rather than face his detractors in the media, Eggleton hoped Gorton would appeal directly to the voters. With thorough preparation and Eggleton's urging that he remain calm and not lose his temper, Gorton appeared more controlled and convincing. He continued to distrust the press and avoid close scrutiny but the people had seen a more engaging and attractive side to a prime minister who often seemed unprepared and irascible.

It was becoming plain that media coverage and commentary were prompting shifts in public administration. Gorton's colleagues were unnerved by the growing profile of the media in political life, believing it came at the expense of parliamentary processes. Rather than ministers making statements to parliament on matters of public importance, they would issue media releases and looked to the nation's newspapers as the principal venue for the contest of political ideas. Eggleton was blamed for encouraging and facilitating this trend but he was merely reflecting changes in the way that information was conveyed and voters participated in Australia's model of democracy. Television, radio and newspapers were voracious consumers of political content. The audiences they served wanted clear and concise accounts of government decisions and policy proposals, and impartial summaries of opposition to its priorities and plans. The public were unconcerned with whether parliament happened to be in session and was unwilling to endure long and protracted parliamentary debates to discern what the government was intending to do about pressing matters. Journalists were much more than reporters and chroniclers; they were expected to be interpreters and commentators as well. Parliamentary proceedings were only one element of participatory democracy. With declining memberships and fewer 'rusted on' supporters, all political parties needed to find new ways to communicate with voters who were increasingly unlikely to commit their vote to only one party, irrespective of its policies and performance. Politics was changing and Eggleton was at the forefront of ensuring that the Gorton Government was not left behind.

After five years as the Prime Minister's press secretary, an interview with the *Canberra Times* began with a question about whether he still had a sense of humour.[4] Eggleton replied: 'I hope so – I need it'. The unnamed interviewer then added: 'And to prove that he had a sense of humour, Tony Eggleton's features – the smooth, grave face he shows in public – cracked into a grin. 'If I'm not smiling people say, 'what are you worried about?' but I'm not worried; I just happen to be not smiling''. Despite his elevated public profile, Eggleton was described as 'modest' and the 'pressman's pressman'. A Les Tanner cartoon in the *Age* had one character asking another as Gorton walked barefoot away from Parliament House: 'when his press secretary leaves what do we do for a prime minister?'[5]

Eggleton had also been linked with Liberal candidacy for the Australian Capital Territory's sole seat in federal parliament. The first occasion was September 1968. The *Sun Herald* reported that 'party organisers have had three meetings with Mr Eggleton over the past two months, despite assurances from the outset that he was not really interested … party organisers who for more than a decade have been trying to find a good candidate, regard [Eggleton] as capable of unseating the present Labor member [Jim Fraser]'.[6] Eggleton was considered to be 'one of the most astute public relations men to have graced Canberra's political scene and he is probably being politically wise in avoiding a contest at this stage with Mr Fraser'. The second occasion was in March 1970 when Fraser was recovering from an abdominal operation and there was speculation he would not resume his parliamentary duties. Fraser died from cancer on 1 April 1970. Eggleton was approached for comment by the *Daily Mirror* and said 'he knew of no plans for him to contest the seat if it became vacant'.[7] The *Australian* reported that Eggleton would be nominated by the ACT Branch of the Liberal Party although he was not even a party member.

> Mr Eggleton was approached before the last Federal election to stand as a Liberal candidate but indicated then that he was not interested. However, he said yesterday he would not make a decision this time before the approach was made.[8]

A non-Labor candidate was still considered unlikely to achieve success in a solidly Labor held seat. Eggleton was content to remain in his present position for the time being. There was still a few things he wanted to achieve with Gorton who seemed increasingly content to make decisions without consulting his Cabinet.

The parliamentary Liberal party was slow to recognise the rise of prime ministerial government. Although Gorton (and Holt before him) was often chided for practising a 'presidential' style of administration modelled on the United States, the increasing size and remit of the Australian prime minister's office mirrored changes elsewhere in the Western world. Demands on national leaders were growing exponentially. By modern standards, Gorton's office was very modest. The point of friction was the resentment of ministers and backbenchers at the requirement to liaise with a senior public servant, Len Hewitt, and a young personal staffer, Ainsley Gotto, over their concerns rather than dealing with Gorton as they had done with Holt. As Aitchison remarked: 'they did not think it was a healthy trend. They were baulked and bothered by the difficulty of having to break through the invisible wall of officialdom which the prime minister had built up around his office.'[9] Occasionally it was Eggleton, but usually it was Gotto, who experienced the backlash against Gorton's desire to keep other people at a distance. This backlash included slurs against Eggleton's integrity.

One such incident involved anti-Vietnam war protests outside Parliament House. On 2 October 1970, Whitlam was photographed by the Australian News and Information Bureau (ANIB), a federal government agency, addressing a group of protestors. The photographers were acting on Gotto's advice. Of the 70 photographs that were taken, 11 depicted Whitlam speaking in front of the flag associated with the Vietcong insurgency. The government was able to exploit these images to further its claim that Whitlam stood with Australia's enemies while the Opposition complained that the apolitical ANIB had been exploited for partisan purposes. As a fellow public servant, Eggleton recognised the damage that had been done to the impartiality of the entire public service by the clearly polemical use of its work. Eggleton took personal responsibility for ordering the offending ANIB photographs of Whitlam and the Vietcong flag while making the point that the ANIB had simply produced a public record of what had occurred outside the national parliament. None of the photographs were altered. Gorton was not implicated in the controversy although Gotto's role almost certainly originated with him.

There were also incidents in which Eggleton was accused of leaking information against ministers at Gorton's request. In October 1970, the same month as the ANIB controversy, the Coalition was divided over setting a reserve price for the sale of wool and establishing a new statutory marketing authority (the Australian Wool Commission). Peter Howson, the Member for La Trobe in Melbourne, was rumoured to be against the scheme. Howson attributed the origin of these rumours to Gorton and two other Liberal backbenchers, Les Irwin and Harry Turner. In his private diary, Howson wrote that

> Tony Eggleton had repeated the rumour to some of the Press Gallery, who came to see me about it. I took the opportunity to remind Tony that I was not too pleased with his performance and he'd repeated rumours without any foundation; it might be useful to remember this in the future.[10]

Eggleton had not started the rumour nor had he helped it to spread. He merely told journalists that Howson had been associated with Liberal party room opposition to the government's proposals. Gorton was willing to wound his ministers but was unwilling to strike them. Other people, often Eggleton, were Gorton's preferred weapons especially if they were unaware of his malevolent intentions. Eggleton was against the leaking of government information and refused to be complicit in the unauthorised release of official documents.

Eggleton was accused by journalist-turned-Labor Senator, James Ormonde, of exceeding his authority when he appeared to moderate a remark that the Prime Minister had made at the National Press Club in Washington. Gorton revealed his interest in a citizens army that would be 'properly armed, properly equipped and ready to go into action at a moment's notice, just as the Israelis were'. In answer to a later question from a journalist, Eggleton hosed down any speculation that detailed proposals were being seriously considered. Ormonde complained that Eggleton was making 'comments on matters of policy ... a good deal of late'. He feared Australia might 'follow the experience of the United States where public servants speak for parliamentarians and ministers'. Eggleton was defended by Senator Ken Anderson who 'would not accept for one minute that [Eggleton] had been making statements on policy in the sense suggested by [Ormonde]'. This was the only occasion in Gorton's time as prime minister when Eggleton was accused of independently making policy. The story never gathered momentum because, as ever, Eggleton was only reflecting the views of Gorton and his Cabinet – which sometimes needed the clarification he was permitted to offer.

To avoid the need for leaks and the need for constant policy clarifications, Eggleton confidentially proposed the establishment of an 'Office of Public Affairs and Information' within the Prime Minister's Department. He had in mind a 'small, relatively inexpensive unit, with the task of keeping a watchful eye on government public relations in general, but working through – and coordinating when necessary – the existing ministerial and departmental press and public relations machinery'. This office would also scrutinise 'the agencies responsible for Australian publicity overseas' and ensure they are 'presenting a properly coordinated image of Australia'. Eggleton pointed to the public information 'mess' in Canada and the appointment of a Canadian national taskforce to finding 'ways of bringing some order out of chaos'. In Australia, the enhanced flow of information would help 'a government whose public image and credibility are suffering the inevitable strains of long tenure'. His proposal was ignored and the problems remained.

Although he had persuaded Gorton of the need for televised press conferences, there was little evidence the Prime Minister was more aware of the need for clearer communication with the electorate or that he had been chastened by the disastrous 1969 election result. Gorton was still managing his time poorly. He was not discerning the mood among backbenchers or seeking advice from a broader range of sources. Most egregious to his senior colleagues was Gorton's increasing propensity to make decisions without consulting Cabinet and his readiness to ignore the guidance of ministers.

On 22 April 1970, Gorton proposed announcing the withdrawal of a combat battalion from Vietnam and further withdrawals over the next 'twelve-month period' if the South Vietnamese assumed a greater burden for the fighting. As Minister for Defence, Fraser advised against any mention of a timetable for withdrawal. Gorton ignored Fraser and his advice. The press interpreted Gorton's announcement as a firm commitment to the return of Australia's remaining combat forces at the start of 1971. The leading newspapers informed their readers that the nation's most controversial deployment of military force would soon be ending and there would be no continuing need for conscription. The Australian government was being tethered to a timetable that Cabinet had not even considered and a course of action that had not been communicated to either the Americans or the South Vietnamese.

Eggleton immediately recognised the problem and wrote to Gorton:

> The press are beating up stories implying Australia may soon be taking a decision to further reduce its forces in Vietnam. The *Sunday Observer* went as far as stating that Australian troops would be relieved of combat duties by late April [1970]. Before press speculation becomes folklore, is there anything I could or should say for background to keep this matter on the rails?

Gorton replied: 'There is no basis whatever for the press inventions – the position now is exactly as it was stated previously. Further decisions will be made in the light of further events.' This badly written reply was an inadequate response. The press had heard nothing to suggest that 'Vietnamisation' was not proceeding to plan. It was reasonable to assume that combat troops could (and would) be withdrawn. There was nothing more Eggleton could do to prevent political uncertainty and public confusion. The last major battle involving Australian forces was fought at Nui Le in September 1971, resulting in five Australian deaths and 30 wounded. The Australian base at Nui Dat was handed over to the South Vietnamese in October 1971. A headquarters protection detachment from the Fourth Battalion, Royal Australian Regiment, was not withdrawn until March 1972 – nearly two years after Gorton's poorly worded statement.

Eggleton did, however, have more success with Gorton's performance on television ahead of the Senate election scheduled for 21 November 1970. The Liberal Party had already perceived the Prime Minister's need for training in the art of television communication. Eggleton 'was equally concerned but did not accept that self-assurance and a liking for the television medium were good substitutes for proper training' – which Gorton had never had. Gorton preferred interviews rather than looking at the camera. He also disliked the auto-cue and did not seem to grasp the mechanics of its operation. Having observed that Gorton was not on the best of terms with the owner of Channel Nine television, Sir Frank Packer, Eggleton thought the ABC might be able to assist. He wrote to its general manager, Talbot Duckmanton. He began by noting 'there has been the feeling that the ABC has been casual in its handling of Liberal Party recordings, and there have been those who would go so far as suggesting some ABC production staff would deliberately produce second-rate material'. The letter continued in typical Eggleton style: 'I don't share this view, and I am sure that you will do all in your power to prove that such fears were without foundation'.

Eggleton first had to persuade Gorton that he would benefit from formal training. The second task was finding the right producer to deliver it. Eggleton then needed to devise a cover story in the event that reporters learned the Liberal Party thought their leader had a television image problem. Despite Eggleton's careful efforts, hopes of avoiding publicity were

> dashed when the *Sunday Observer* of 20 October reported that the producer of the ABC's Four Corners program had gone to Canberra to instruct the prime minister on the use of the auto-cue. Eggleton was forced to claim that Gorton had merely visited the Canberra studios in case it was decided to use them for the Senate [campaign] broadcast. The prime minister was not being coached (which he was) but was interested in seeing how the auto-cue worked (which he was not).

In subsequent television appearances, both Eggleton and senior Liberal Party figures believed that Gorton had put in 'a vastly improved performance'. He showed restraint when it was needed and aggression when it was required.

Eggleton was given little to no credit by anyone for his patience and persistence with the irascible prime minister. Gorton thought a press conference held in Brisbane on 6 November 1970 in which he had been asked about increasing age pension payments had been 'a disaster'. Gorton believed Eggleton 'was to blame for talking him into it. The strange thing was that the press ... had a very different picture. They were busy writing stories about the successful opening' of the campaign and 'giving him high marks for the handling of the press conference. Little did they know just how the PM was feeling'. As Whitlam campaigned on the need for pensions to be increased, Gorton's anger with Eggleton persisted. To his credit, Eggleton did not take the Prime Minister's bluster to heart. He privately mused: 'I was not particularly disturbed by his illogical turn of mind. I had experienced similar blockages of reason before ... he wanted a scapegoat and I fitted the bill'.

More telling, however, was that Gorton had convinced himself that 'all his press conferences would be disasters. They would all detract from his nightly [public] meetings, and would be of no value whatsoever. Press conferences were only of help to the Opposition, there was nothing in them for the Government, and so it went on'. Eggleton had already decided that arguing with Gorton 'put him in an even worse frame of mind'. It was, he thought, 'just as well that I have a placid temperament'. As the Prime Minister's emissary to the Parliamentary Press Gallery, Eggleton was disturbed that Gorton 'really does hate the press. He would only be content in a dictatorship where he had complete control over the media to ensure that they wrote only what suited him!'. When the next day's press conferences went surprisingly well, Gorton's mood was vastly improved although he 'didn't make any admissions' of regret over his previous jibes at Eggleton. Gorton wanted to 'be friendly and pretend that yesterday didn't happen'. Journalists were now talking about the 'new John Gorton'.

Commentators noted that the Prime Minister had fought a strong campaign on the back of better relations with the press and more polished public performances. But the training and Gorton's genuine effort were ultimately to no avail. The Senate result was the second-worst for a non-Labor party since Federation although the spread of votes would not have led to a Coalition defeat if translated to a House of Representatives election. Nonetheless, Gorton had no choice but to state publicly his disappointment at the government's declining primary vote. The Liberal Party as a whole had a problem but Gorton was made to accept blame for another 'disastrous' result by those who wanted him replaced as leader. The chances of the Coalition being returned to office at the next election continued to look slim.

After six tumultuous years serving three prime ministers,[11] Eggleton was ready for a change. His appointment as Menzies' press secretary had come as a surprise. Having served Menzies for five months, it made sense for him to continue with Holt, assuming the new prime minister wanted him. He was engaged by his third prime minister in three years when Gorton asked him to stay. There was no formal agreement nor even an informal understanding about how long Eggleton would remain in the high-pressure post. Indeed, under Gorton the press secretary's unofficial job statement widened even further as Gorton recognised he needed Eggleton's wise counsel and sound judgement. Eggleton refused to 'produce sterile handouts, cover-up and make excuses for the government and keep at bay reporters who are trying to get at the facts'. Gorton was relying solely on Eggleton for the kind of assistance that the Leader of the Opposition, Gough Whitlam, was receiving from three staffers: Race Matthews, Richard Hall and Graham Freudenberg.

Eggleton was anything but a faceless public servant. The *Sun-Herald's* political correspondent Max Walsh explained that the prime minister's press secretary had become a 'one-man intelligence network'. He was thrust into this role, previously undertaken by the Liberal Party's deputy leader, because neither Holt nor Gorton were prepared to trust McMahon as their intermediary with the parliamentary party or the Liberal secretariat. According to Walsh, Gorton was more isolated because he had relied on too many self-interested 'cronies' to secure the prime ministership and was now beholden to them. Walsh asserted that 'Eggleton arrived at this role not by a conscious process of empire building but through the coincidence of circumstances'. To Eggleton's credit, Walsh did not think he was 'some sort of Svengali. He is a very efficient machine politician – which is something entirely different from the parliamentary politician which John Gorton tried to persuade him to become by seeking Liberal pre-selection for the ACT'. Eggleton was better at 'keeping an eye on party responses to the issues ... [and] getting the feedback up the line of rank-and-file reaction to the leadership in Canberra and the direction of policy'. Walsh's only lament was that Eggleton did not have the extensive experience of the public service that he needed to repair the damage that he thought had been done by Hewitt and Gotto.

Eggleton was still one of the most recognisable men in Australian public life. The business magazine, *Rydges*, remarked in an August 1969 article headed 'Well done, Jeeves', that Eggleton had enjoyed a 'meteoric rise to a position of political power in the last few years ... and was going to be a difficult man to replace'. It claimed he had moved from being 'little more than a message runner and carrier of bags ... to a national figure'. It described him as 'quiet and restrained' but the only effective link between the prime minister's office and the Prime Minister's Department. He was 'always accessible, always helpful, never short tempered and never bumptious'. Eggleton 'inevitably reminds one of PG Wodehouse's memorable character Jeeves'. The magazine claimed that Eggleton 'has let it be known that he is looking for something less strenuous'. He had apparently been 'approached by quite a few organisations ... so far he has not been tempted but ... he may be persuaded to move out into the private sector'.

The following year he was approached to work for British Tobacco as their public relations manager in Sydney. He would follow Bill Bengston who had previously worked as a research officer in the Liberal Party's federal secretariat. An issue for Eggleton was that Bengston had been appointed to the company's board and would have general oversight of his work. Eggleton thought 'this could be an uncomfortable arrangement'. He was never enthusiastic about the position because he 'had some reservations about such an appointment in the commercial sphere'. He drafted a 'personal check list' to help him decide. It featured a number of considerations that involved judgements about his present position.

> Want more personal satisfaction – tired of 'reflected glory'; no future (good experience but much now is repetitious); tiring of incessant demands; not as satisfactory a relationship as with Holt; do not feel I enjoy as much confidence as with Holt; PM's difficult personality (inconsistent, bad tempered, prejudiced); little respect for him personally or for his approach; no guarantees of future employment on completion of term; tired of being 'staff'; want a position in my own right.

After thinking deeply for some months about his future, he did not 'think it was a position or type of industry that would really satisfy me'. The negotiations between Eggleton and British Tobacco were later reported in the *Australian* as part of a story on government efforts to highlight the health consequences of smoking.[12] He was also reported to have been offered the chief executive's position with the Margarine Manufacturers Association.[13]

There were rumours in March 1970 that Eggleton was being 'edged out' of the press secretary's job rather than wanting to leave. The former Chief Whip, Dudley Erwin, told Eggleton that Gorton might have seconded him to the Royal Visit organising team to better position Bill Arthur, the Prime Minister's newly appointed Research Officer, to succeed him. Eggleton took little notice. He did not think Erwin was a reliable source and doubted his judgement. Arthur had been the unsuccessful Liberal candidate for Barton in the 1969 election and apparently 'had his eyes' on Eggleton's job. There were days when Eggleton would have said he was welcome to it. The satirical magazine *Oz* featured a story on the rumours, claiming the replacement of Eggleton with Arthur would be the source of impending disaster for Gorton who had been 'salvaged' many times through Eggleton's timely interventions. Gotto told Gorton of the rumours. He gave Eggleton an assurance 'that they were quite untrue. He certainly did not want me to go. He could understand if I wanted to leave but he did not want me to go'. Eggleton said he 'did not believe the rumours (which I did not) and that I was not in the least concerned (which I was not)'.

The personal and professional turning point for Eggleton was the Commonwealth Heads of Government meeting which was held at Singapore in January 1971. Gorton had been reluctant about attending as his enthusiasm for the Commonwealth as a vehicle for policy development and economic progress was rapidly dissipating. Eggleton was among those urging him to participate before he finally agreed. But Gorton was not prepared to have the Minister for Foreign Affairs, Bill McMahon, accompany him on the VIP aircraft. McMahon and his staff would have to travel separately. Eggleton thought it was petty and petulant behaviour on Gorton's part.

On the first night in Singapore there was considerable socialising among the delegates. Late in the evening Gorton sent for Eggleton. He had decided that McMahon should be put in his place and asked that, when briefing the Australian journalists the next morning, Eggleton should make it clear that they should not approach McMahon for information on the conference. All queries were to go through Eggleton to the Prime Minister himself. Eggleton bluntly refused, saying he was not prepared to undermine McMahon in that way: 'it was another of those occasions to stick my toes in, because I was convinced that he'd worked himself up into such a state he didn't really understand the significance of what he was saying'. Marginalising McMahon was something Gorton would have to do himself although Eggleton advised strongly against it. The next morning Gorton asked, rather irritably, whether Eggleton had briefed the media as he had been directed the previous evening. Eggleton said he had not. He reiterated his position: it was inconceivable for him to act as Gorton wanted. There was a long silence. Gorton then said: 'In that case, maybe it was just as well that you didn't brief the press'. Eggleton described the episode as a 'piece of nonsense'. Ironically, the relationship between Gorton and McMahon greatly improved during the conference.

Having decided against adding any discussion items to the meeting agenda, Gorton was determined to thwart several draft resolutions he thought involved matters that members were entitled to consider individually and independently as sovereign nations. When three African leaders urged the meeting to oppose British arms sales to the apartheid regime in South Africa, there were two minds in the Australian delegation. The British Government naturally looked for Australian support but the Department of Foreign Affairs counselled against supporting arms sales anywhere in Africa because they would create problems in the Indian Ocean region. Eggleton drafted a 'for and against' inventory and concluded the case for opposing arms sales was significantly stronger. Gorton took no notice and insisted the meeting had no authority to direct member nations in such a manner. He also opposed resolutions binding member nations to punitive action against the all-white government in Pretoria.

For Eggleton, the most significant outcome of the conference was the decision to establish a Commonwealth Information Department in London. He had received soundings about the possibility of directing the new department from the Queen's assistant press secretary, the former Australian public servant, Bill Heseltine. After the Singapore meeting, the Commonwealth Secretary-General, Arnold Smith, visited Canberra for an Education Ministers conference.

> I asked Gorton if I could steal Eggleton ... Gorton reluctantly agreed, but asked me to announce the appointment, which I did at a press conference in Canberra [on 10 February 1971]. After I did so, one hard-headed journalist paid an unusual compliment to Tony: 'Now you have made it inevitable that Gorton loses the next election'.[14]

Eggleton thought otherwise. In his opinion, Gorton's position within the Liberal party was secure although he was not persuaded the Coalition would win the next election. Taking a new role at that time would give the incoming press secretary a chance to consolidate his position before the election that was scheduled for the end of 1972. His only remaining motivation in working for Gorton was a sense of professionalism: 'I could hardly be motivated by admiration and respect'. As he prepared to depart for London, yet another unnecessary drama enveloped the Prime Minister. On this occasion Eggleton was unable to save Gorton from himself.

Endnotes

1   Philip Ayers, *Malcolm Fraser*, Mandarin, Melbourne, 1989, pp. 143–44.

2   Denis O'Brien, 'Not getting into the vaudeville act', *Bulletin*, 25 October 1969, p. 24.

3   Aitchison, *From Bob to Bungles*, p. 226.

4   Capital Letter column, 'Pressman's pressman', *Canberra Times*, 13 August 1970.

5   *Age*, 10 March 1971.

6   'Pressman shy of Liberal pre-selection offers', *Sun Herald*, 22 September 1968.

7   'Eggleton is silent', *Daily Mirror*, 24 March 1970.

8   Mungo MacCallum, 'PM's press secretary may contest ACT seat', *Australian*, 24 March 1970.

9   Aitchison, *From Bob to Bungles*, p. 262.

10 Peter Howson, *The Howson Diaries*, Viking, Melbourne, 1984, p. 663.

11 Eggleton remained the prime minister's press secretary after Holt was presumed dead on 21 December 1968 but did not work directly for John McEwen during his brief prime ministership of 23 days.

12 Owen Thomson, 'Fire and smoking', *Australian*, 15 March 1971, p. 9.

13 'Media Tedia', *Oz*, no. 42, 14 April 1970, p. 4

14 Arnold Smith, *Stitches in Time*, p. 289.

CHAPTER 8

Time of change   1971–74

Almost from the day he was chosen by his colleagues to lead the Liberal Party, John Gorton slowly alienated his supporters and eventually even his friends. He was the source of a series of grievances and the subject of more than a few complaints. If he continued to antagonise his allies and inflame his adversaries, a challenge to his leadership would be inevitable. Typical of the rising tide of ill-will was the Speaker of the House of Representatives, Bill Aston. He invited Eggleton for a drink to 'make it very clear that he was disenchanted. He seemed to be particularly hurt over the PM's treatment of him. He felt the PM had been rude to him, and did not consult him sufficiently'. More broadly, Aston objected to Gorton's cronyism, refusal to contemplate an elected ministry, and handling of foreign affairs. He also told Eggleton that 'he had a list of members who would be prepared to support McMahon' in the event of a leadership spill. The Defence Minister, Malcolm Fraser, was not among them although tension between Gorton and Fraser had been slowly escalating.

Fraser felt that Gorton was unnecessarily involving himself in defence and security matters and undermining Fraser's credibility with the uniformed Service Chiefs. Unlike the 59 year-old Gorton, Fraser was born in 1930 and was too young for active service in the Second World War. Unlike his immediate predecessors in the portfolio, the 40 year-old Fraser had no personal military experience – not even national service – although he did think of joining the British Army after completing his tertiary education at Oxford University. Both men had experienced an armed services ministry. Gorton had been Minister for the Navy from 1958–63 and Fraser was Minister for the Army from 1966–67.

Eggleton believed that Gorton and Gotto thought Fraser needed to be 'taken down a peg'. There was an echo here of Gorton's attitude to his Minister for Foreign Affairs, Bill McMahon, leading into the January 1970 CHOGM meeting.

Eggleton had 'picked up some snippets of conversations to that effect that surprised me, because I thought Malcolm was doing well – almost the Defence Minister from central casting'. The basis of their attitude was not clear, at least to the press secretary. Eggleton 'thought at the time and I have always thought since that when the civic action affair blew up, they saw it as an issue on which they could cut Malcolm down to size'. He later remarked: 'what they had in mind was some sort of controlled burning-off exercise which unfortunately became a bushfire'. Eggleton thought that Gotto was angry that Fraser had not 'paid her enough attention and respect. She often made disparaging remarks about him'.

'Civic action' was the name given to a number of 'hearts and minds' initiatives designed to improve local living conditions and persuade the South Vietnamese civilian population that their future lay with the government in Saigon and not with the Communist insurgency. Fraser was a strong supporter of civic action and believed it needed to be extended once combat forces were withdrawn. The Chief of the General Staff, Lieutenant General Sir Thomas Daly, was concerned that without adequate protection, the civic action teams consisting of engineers and medical personnel would be more vulnerable to insurgent attack. The media discerned growing tension and distrust within the political-military interface. General Daly thought the Army Minister, Andrew Peacock, was waging a media campaign against Fraser. Peacock disliked Fraser and considered him a future rival for the Liberal Party leadership. Fraser was certainly critical of the Army. He thought the Task Force commander was 'hidebound and insensitive'. Fraser told Eggleton that the Army was 'not keeping him properly informed. He clearly felt that his discomfort was a result of the Army's bungling'.

In reality, Gorton was doing his best to discredit Fraser by giving journalists the impression that the Army had lost confidence in its minister and was 'in revolt'. The Prime Minister met Daly and, rather opportunistically, expressed his empathy. Gorton is reported to have stated: 'if these attacks continue, the Army and its leaders will have my fullest support'. Fraser's name was apparently not mentioned during the discussion although the press gallery heard rumours that Daly had accused the minister of disloyalty. Eggleton was intrigued by the source of the rumours: 'whomever it was played a key part in this political upheaval. There is no doubt that it could have been Ainsley, either directly or indirectly. She was inclined to chat away to people who were close to her, perhaps even her current boyfriend, Race Matthews'. Many years later Ramsey revealed his source to Eggleton. It was Susan Peacock – the wife of Minister for the Army, Andrew Peacock. Daly telephoned Mrs Peacock to ask about her husband's health after a recent hospitalisation. During the conversation, and conscious of her distress over media stories that were damaging her husband, Daly relayed the details of his conversation with Gorton. Shortly afterwards, the *Australian's* Alan Ramsey also telephoned the Peacock home to inquire about the Minister's recovery from surgery. Mrs Peacock repeated what Daly had told her. Ramsey had a story.

Ramsey asked Eggleton for a meeting with Gorton to clarify and confirm what had been said in his meeting with Daly. Eggleton had earlier told Gorton that 'Ramsey still has a warm feeling for you but there is some disenchantment' and that Rupert Murdoch, owner of the Australian newspaper, had told Ramsey that he 'certainly did not want to see McMahon become prime minister'. Murdoch instructed the *Australian's* office in Sydney to 'fix' McMahon. Eggleton urged Gorton not to speak with Ramsey. The Prime Minister insisted but not before he accepted Eggleton's advice that Ramsey's questions were to be submitted in advance. In his meeting with Ramsey, Gorton would not outline what he had said, only what Daly had said. This led Ramsey to believe that Daly had indeed accused Fraser of 'extreme disloyalty' and Gorton did nothing to dissuade him from that belief. In a detailed article published in the Australian, Ramsey reported that Fraser had been critical of Daly and the Army.

Fraser was incensed. He accused Gorton of disloyalty and a stand-off ensued. There appeared to be only two outcomes: Fraser would resign or Gorton would sack him. Fraser drafted and then delivered his letter of resignation to the Governor-General – his former ministerial colleague, Sir Paul Hasluck, rather than to the Prime Minister which was the usual convention. Gorton tried to retrieve the situation but Fraser was adamant, telling the Parliament that Gorton was an autocrat. He had displayed 'a dangerous reluctance to consult Cabinet, and an obstinate determination to get his own way'. In sum, Gorton was 'unfit to the hold the great office of prime minister'. Others had come to the same view but for different reasons. Gorton had performed poorly at the polls in 1969 and 1970. He had fallen out with the Liberal premiers of the two most populous states, Robert Askin in New South Wales and Henry Bolte in Victoria. Powerful media proprietors, such as Sir Frank Packer and Rupert Murdoch, were finding common ground with disillusioned senior Liberals who started to consider McMahon as an alternative prime minister.

When Gorton responded to Fraser's speech in Parliament, the Prime Minister mentioned his meeting with Ramsey. Explaining that he was unable to discuss publicly what Daly had said privately, Gorton claimed that Ramsey had replied: 'Fair enough'. Ramsey, who was sitting in the press gallery above the speaker's chair, yelled: 'You liar'. Recognising the seriousness of his offence, Ramsey quickly left the chamber for Eggleton's office. He wanted to offer an apology and asked for advice on what he should say. Labor wanted Ramsey called to the Bar of the House where the journalist could be quizzed on his meeting with Gorton but after receiving a handwritten note from Eggleton explaining that Ramsey had offered a fulsome apology (of which Eggleton had contributed perhaps a third of the words), Gorton moved to adjourn the debate.

Persuaded that he probably had the numbers to retain the leadership, Gorton called a meeting of the Parliamentary Liberal Party the following day (10 March 1971). The gravity of the situation was now apparent to Gorton and Gotto. Their plan to humble Fraser had backfired. On his way out of Parliament House, Eggleton found Gorton and Gotto in a 'sombre but pessimistic mood'. Gorton had already overcome one challenge to his leadership after the disappointing 1969 election result but this challenge seemed different. Gorton had brought this contest on himself.

After the party meeting, Eggleton faced a media scrum to announce that a vote of confidence in Gorton's leadership was tied 33–33. Gorton could have continued but stated: 'Well, that is not a vote of confidence, so the party will have to elect a new leader'. He used his casting vote to remove himself from office. Eggleton then went back to the Government party room before returning to announce that McMahon had won the leadership ballot over Billy Snedden. Shortly afterwards Eggleton reappeared again to announce that Gorton had been elected Deputy Leader of the Liberal Party ahead of Fraser and David Fairbairn (who stood against Gorton after the 1969 election). One of the journalists responded in disbelief: 'You must be joking'. The reasonable assumption was that Gorton would do the dignified thing and return to the backbench and then leave parliament. Alan Reid observed: 'For once Eggleton's urbanity slipped. 'I don't joke on such matters', he said tersely'. McMahon offered Gorton four different jobs including Foreign Affairs and the Treasury. Gorton also expressed an interest in being High Commissioner in London. Eventually, and in what appeared to be an act of pure spite, Gorton accepted the Defence portfolio – Fraser's former job.

Eggleton accompanied McMahon to Government House for the official swearing-in of the new Ministry. After what had happened, Eggleton was not surprised that 'Gorton looked grey and ill. McMahon was full of bounce. In front of the Government House staff, he asked me to work for him. John Gorton agreed that it would be the best idea in all the circumstances'. McMahon knew that Eggleton was preparing to leave for his new job in London but hoped to change his mind, offering him various inducements including a senior diplomatic appointment if he agreed, for the foreseeable future, to remain as press secretary. Eggleton was not even vaguely tempted. He was looking forward to working at Marlborough House in London and definitely felt that time was running out for the Coalition government. He would probably be out of a job in 20 months if he stayed in the prime minister's office.

There was one more twist to what had proved an eventful day. On the evening of the leadership change, Eggleton noticed Gorton and his wife walking to the parliamentary dining room. The now Deputy Leader of the Liberal Party asked Eggleton when he would likely be returning from London. When Eggleton replied, 'in about three years', Gorton responded: 'well, you can come and work for me again ... as prime minister'. It did not take long for Eggleton to detect that "the Gorton group' were working actively against McMahon'. Eggleton would never contemplate working for Gorton again. Unlike Gotto, who constantly threatened to resign from the prime minister's office, Eggleton had persevered with what he considered were the standards expected of a public servant. In a private note written the following day, Eggleton said he was 'not disappointed at Gorton's defeat. He was not a good prime minister'. Gorton was, in his view, a 'dangerous man to have leading a government. I don't believe the party would ever have him again'.

Gorton had dispensed with all of the people who had worked for Holt with one exception. He retained Eggleton because he knew of his abilities, trusted his direction and relied on his judgement. Eggleton was creative and courageous, the very characteristics Gorton admired at a time when public servants and parliamentary staffers tended to be cautious and conservative. Eggleton monitored the newspapers for Gorton and found ways of adapting to his irregular office hours. Whereas Eggleton was a very early riser, usually around 5 am, it was usual for Gorton to retire at 3 am and arrive in his Parliament House office at 10 am or later. Eggleton also accepted the close relationship that existed between Gorton and

Gotto and never sought to disrupt the bond between them although he thought it was damaging to both. Alan Reid observed that Eggleton was 'among the very few' who were ever welcome to join the end-of-day conversations between Gorton, Gotto and a few others.

> But Eggleton seems to have eschewed these intimate seances as much as possible. A very proper man, Eggleton probably disliked the ferocity with which personalities were dissected and their futures preordained by such a narrow and, with the exception of Gorton, unimportant gathering, and the manner in which complex and highly technical subjects were examined on a personalised basis of near primitive simplicity.[1]

After three years of constant companionship, Eggleton had seen every side of John Grey Gorton but the man remained something of an enigma. He was capable of so many contrary moods and emotions. Eggleton recalled that late on a sitting day he was approached by a woman whose six year-old daughter had some flowers she wanted to give the Prime Minister. She also hoped for a photograph and wanted to know when Gorton would be leaving Parliament House. Eggleton mentioned his encounter with the little girl to Gorton who quickly replied: 'why isn't she in here?' Eggleton tracked down the mother and her child, and ushered them into Gorton's office where the flowers were presented. Their photograph was taken on an old box camera.

John Gorton wanted to be an effective prime minister but, in Eggleton's eyes, never seemed to have the energy or enthusiasm that it required. Eggleton had witnessed the highs and lows of his leadership. His temperament and personal habits soon caused fault lines to appear. It was a roller-coaster ride and Eggleton's toughest time as press secretary. Despite his many flaws and failings, and being men of very different dispositions, Eggleton never ceased liking Gorton on a personal level. Eggleton offered a warm public tribute when Gorton died in 2002. He would not speak ill of the dead. He said: 'Many people saw John Gorton as being ahead of his time. He was something of a political gladiator of his era: bold, uncompromising, sometimes impetuous but never daunted.' But four decades earlier in one of his private notes, Eggleton conceded:

> Deep in my heart I knew Australia would be better off without this man as prime minister. He was indiscreet, arrogant, impetuous, bad tempered … and ruled by his emotions and a 22 year-old typist. But it was up to his own party

to recognise his faults ... it was not for me (a public servant) to interfere. I did my job as a professional, and to ease my conscience I kept telling myself I was serving the office of prime minister and not John Gorton ... it was up to me to keep up the best possible façade. If it was to be torn down, that was for others to do.[2]

When he re-read and reflected on these words 30 years later, Eggleton was worried that 'these notes, taken as a whole, give a negative image of John Gorton and of some other people, such as Ainsley Gotto'. He had not intended to be destructive, especially of Gotto, who had been 'a colleague and a friend, and a bright, intelligent and able young woman. But the chemistry of the relationship was damaging to the prime ministership'. Eggleton was 'sad that the promise [Gorton had] shown in his Navy minister days did not continue in his prime ministership'. Had Gorton continue to rely on the advice of Len Hewitt, 'the events that led to John's loss of the prime ministership' would not have occurred.

Eggleton had decided in 1970 that he would leave the prime minister's office in 1971 and seek new challenges. The only consequence of Gorton's demise was a slight adjustment in his departure date. Eggleton was willing to help the new prime minister settle into office and hand over to a new press secretary. The appointment of Reg McDonald, a member of the Parliamentary Press Gallery since July 1970 and a former correspondent for the Melbourne *Sun* and the *Adelaide Advertiser*, was announced on 19 February 1971.[3] Eggleton found his remaining few weeks uncomfortable. It was evident to him that McMahon had achieved the top political prize too late in life. The new prime minister was already aged 63 years and had been in Parliament for more than two decades.

Some things did not change. Eggleton was still being asked to do prime ministerial 'dirty work'. On his first day as Prime Minister, McMahon asked Eggleton to deal with the 'sacking' of Sir Lenox Hewitt as Secretary of the Prime Minister's Department. Eggleton did not know, and was not told, why this unpleasant task fell to him. Plainly, McMahon did not want to convey the news although Hewitt was the head of his department and deserved the courtesy of being told personally that he was no longer wanted. By then, Hewitt had made more than a few enemies of his own. Eggleton was not among them. He had established a positive relationship with Hewitt during their many hours travelling together. Naturally, Eggleton did not relish being the bearer of bad news. But Hewitt recognised his fate on hearing that Eggleton was telephoning on behalf of the Prime Minister.

Hewitt knew the man he had replaced, Sir John Bunting, would be returning to his old position in the renamed 'Department of the Prime Minister and Cabinet.'

Eggleton noted that McMahon was especially nervous and uneasy about aspects of his new responsibilities. McMahon agonised over his parliamentary speeches and looked for scapegoats when he felt he had not done well. Sometimes his wife, Sonia, even got the blame for making him rehearse too much. He was scrupulous in maintaining a written record of all his meetings and discussions. At the earliest moment McMahon dictated what he also liked to call 'notes for file'. These were kept handy for ease of reference, especially if anyone questioned the outcome of meetings or misrepresented any promises he had made. Eggleton was aware of McMahon's reputation as 'Tiberius with a telephone' – a mocking moniker that Whitlam had bestowed upon him. Eggleton's wife Mary realised how apt Whitlam's quip had been through firsthand experience. On his last day in the prime minister's office and over the Easter long weekend prior to their departure for London, Eggleton received eight phone calls from the ever active McMahon.

Eggleton thought 'McMahon had the most intimate relations with the press' of the four prime ministers with whom he worked. McMahon had 'built up a close relationship with them over the years' partly because he was prone to leaking official information. Journalists had assumed the habit of telephoning McMahon 'at home and at any time, and he made it clear that he did not mind this. Also, he was prepared to see correspondents at the drop of a hat'. Egggleton felt he had 'McMahon's confidence, and if I had been around for long, I have no doubt that he would have been less concerned about using the press themselves as a sounding board'. Eggleton also thought it 'was a bit dangerous' to ring journalists 'at all hours to chat about politics and events in general'.

At Eggleton's formal farewell at the National Press Club, McMahon was generous in his remarks, expressing the hope that Eggleton might return to work within the Department of Foreign Affairs. The new prime minister had privately spoken with the Departmental Secretary, Sir James Plimsoll, who was personally keen to employ Eggleton. At the same event, the Press Club's president, Alan Fitzgerald, acknowledged Eggleton's role as its foundation president. Eggleton said he had not 'established a very good record from a prime minister's point of view'. Menzies had retired; Holt had drowned; and, Gorton had been deposed. He wished his successor well. Future Press Club president, Ken Randall thought 'the

Eggleton style is almost flawless for the job' of press secretary. He also suggested that Eggleton had been wise not to have considered elected office: 'Eggleton is not a politician. His political instinct is highly developed and rarely to be faulted but more in the mould of the diplomat than the political animal'. To his credit, Eggleton had 'contributed more to the style of the last two prime ministers than they realised or could accept'.[4]

There was an invitation to the Prime Minister's home in Sydney for farewell drinks which were attended by Sonia McMahon and a few other staff members. The Press Gallery also organised a generous send-off lunch attended by 50 correspondents. In his speech, the Press Gallery President, Allan Barnes, described Eggleton as the best press officer he had known. Farewell presentations included a Larry Pickering cartoon of Eggleton dancing to the tune of Menzies, Holt, McEwen, Gorton and McMahon. The Parliament House press secretaries arranged yet another pre-departure dinner. One of the main organisers was Gough Whitlam's press secretary, Graham Freudenberg. He told the gathering that Eggleton had contributed to the status of press secretaries. In reply, Eggleton spoke about the versatility required of press secretaries, recounting that he had been 'valet, chauffeur, decoy, bag carrier, sounding board and whipping boy'.

A profile piece in the *Bulletin* noted he had 'innumerable opportunities for quarrelling with the press, but never has'.[5] Although he was tasked with 'presenting the man he serves in the best possible light in the circumstances' he had 'never dogmatically insisted that his man is incapable of error' and 'successfully given the appearance of being apolitical'. The *Bulletin* thought his effectiveness had been built on 'refusing to get on first-name terms' with any of the prime ministers he served, and declining invitations to drink with gallery journalists. It felt that Eggleton was ideally suited to his next post because, at the recent Singapore Commonwealth Prime Ministers Conference, the local *Eastern Sun* had complained about the 'racialism' of delegations that would only interact with journalists from their own country with the notable exception of Eggleton. It stressed that he had 'dealt with representatives of all news media with the same unflagging courtesy'.

Eggleton continued to be the soul of discretion until his last day, sending a note to McMahon on 6 April 1971: 'John Gorton has invited me to have a farewell lunch with him in the [Parliamentary] Members Dining Room tomorrow. You can rely on my discretion. I've never become involved in internal politics, and I don't intend to begin now'. Shortly before leaving for London, Eggleton also spoke with Fraser about his future. They were only two years apart in age. Eggelton was 38 and Fraser was 40. They both believed the ascendancy of McMahon would not arrest the Coalition's declining political fortunes and that a prolonged period on the Opposition benches would follow the next election. McMahon was not willing to let Fraser have the Foreign Affairs portfolio, suggesting 'he would do better to have some experience in an economic portfolio'. The Country Party were also opposed to Fraser's return to Cabinet, some of its members telling Eggleton they felt Fraser 'had been dishonest'.

> I met him in the corridor in Parliament House one day and he decided to have a chat. We sat down in one of the big leather benches that line the corridors. He was saying how depressed he was. He felt that his career had come to an end and he didn't know what to do. I remember saying to him, 'Look, I think you need to get this into perspective. I don't see anyone more likely to be the leader of the Liberal Party in the future.[6]

The retired Sir Robert Menzies shared Eggleton's opinion, believing that only Fraser had the personal strength and leadership potential to arrest the Party's long-term decline. Fraser returned to Cabinet in August 1971 as Minister for Education and Science, the portfolio he had held from February 1968 to November 1969. As for Eggleton, there were no undertakings that he would return to political life in any capacity or that he would become a servant of the Liberal Party. He certainly gave no hints to Fraser that he was interested in returning to Parliament House.

Eggleton started the next phase of his working life in late April 1971. He would fill a new position but it would rely on experience and expertise that he had only recently acquired. Towards the end of 1969, and following consultations between the Australian Government and Buckingham Palace, Gorton seconded Eggleton to the team organising the forthcoming royal visit to Australia. He became the media coordinator for the 35-day tour from April to early May 1970. Eggleton was assisted by the Department of Defence's director of public relations, Harry Raynor, and Bruce King from the Australian News and Information Bureau. The Queen's visit coincided with the bicentenary of HMS *Endeavour*'s passage along the east coast of Australia which preceded British settlement of the continent. Eggleton worked closely with Buckingham Palace and the Queen's press secretary, Bill (later Sir William) Heseltine, who had a similar career path. Heseltine was born in Fremantle. He joined the Prime Minister's Department in 1951 and was private secretary to Prime Minister Menzies (1955–59), Acting Official Secretary to the Governor General (1960–61) and then Assistant Federal Director of the Liberal Party (1962–64) before becoming Press Secretary to the Queen (and Assistant Private Secretary in 1972).

With guidance from Heseltine, Eggleton was responsible for the royal tour's media planning and venue arrangements. His duties began with a reception for the Queen at which the formally accredited media were introduced. Eggleton accompanied the royal party throughout the extensive tour. Every event was meticulously planned but there were several tense moments. At Cooktown in far north Queensland many of the journalists, especially the international correspondents, neglected to watch the time and missed their chartered RAAF flight to the next venue. The local pubs served as a temporary oasis while their plight was being considered. Eggleton was able to make some urgent calls to people in high places, persuading the RAAF to divert another Hercules transport plane to rescue those he referred to as 'the happy wanderers'.

One of the most memorable moments for Eggleton was escorting the Queen to Green Island on the Great Barrier Reef. The visit coincided with her birthday. As the boat arrived, the waiting media team spontaneously burst into a chorus of 'Happy Birthday Dear Queen'. In the big cities they perfected the new concept of royal walkabouts. Eggleton and Heseltine, accompanied by a security detachment, led the royal party through streets lined with well-wishers. Heseltine had experimented with the idea in Britain with the walkabouts proving a great success in Melbourne and Sydney. As was often the case, Prince Philip enjoyed little jokes with the press and making mischief for the photographers. The only hiccup was in Melbourne where Eggleton asked the local police not to obstruct journalists and photographers. The *Age* reported that 'British pressmen said the behaviour of the Victorian Police was the worst and most inconsiderate of the tour'.[7]

The 1970 tour was the last lengthy royal visit to Australia and there was general satisfaction with the outcome. The media coverage, both in Australia and Britain, was favourable and the journalists were content with the arrangements. The royal yacht HMY *Britannia* was deployed to Australia for the visit. On the last day of the tour, Eggleton was invited on board for an audience with the Queen and Prince Philip. The Queen conveyed her personal thanks for his contribution and presented him with the insignia of Commander of the Royal

Victorian Order (CVO). He received a swag of letters praising his handling of the media and the receipt of this honour. Janet Hawley of the *Australian* wrote:

> Never before have I seen such a superbly efficient human dynamo in action. Along with the entire Royal Tour press corps, I was just as completely fascinated seeing you in action, as studying the four Royals. Lord knows how you cope with the enormous amount of work and still manage to be so thoroughly likeable and unflappable throughout. I'd be a complete neurotic and have everyone hating me if I tried your lot.[8]

The Chief of Bureau of the London *Daily Express*, Ross Mark, had observed many royal visits. He remarked: 'In a long assignment like this one, it would have been easy for any of your team to blow their cool or lose efficiency. But never once. It really was an amazing performance of efficiency, helpfulness, and wonderful professionalism.'[9] Future federal Labor minister, Barry Jones, sent a telegram on the award of the CVO: 'Congratulations on joining the ranks of the aristocracy'.

Of all the virtues for which he was praised by correspondents, Eggleton's 'coolness' under pressure was mentioned most often. In a personal profile published by Sydney's *Telegraph* newspaper, he explained that 'one of the reasons I probably have survived for five years in this job is that I have the capacity for not getting tensed up. I do not know the secret of it. But generally I have the philosophy of doing the best I can at all times.'[10] He would analyse problems and then learn from any mistakes. As for his ability to work long hours, Eggleton explained that he had no difficulty sleeping, did not drink alcohol (because 'I just do not like it') and 'do not get caught up in late night parties'. He also commented that 'the work appeals to me tremendously. If you are happy in what you are doing, this is always the great secret'.

After the dramas of the previous few years, Tony, Mary and the two younger Eggleton children were relieved to be leaving Australia for a new adventure. The initial term of appointment was three years with provision for extensions. They departed on 18 April 1971 with their newly issued Australian diplomatic passports. Their eldest child, Stephen, remained in Australia and boarded at Bowral's Chevalier College. The Commonwealth Secretariat had arranged temporary accommodation in Kensington while they looked for a home. There was one strange moment on Eggleton's first full day in London. He noticed a cavalcade of approaching cars flying the Australian flag. The cars slowed and both John

Gorton and Ainsley Gotto waved excitedly. Gorton was visiting British military establishments as Australia's Defence minister. Not surprisingly, Gorton did not serve long in the portfolio.

McMahon demanded Gorton's resignation following the publication of the first in a series of six articles appearing under his name headed 'I did it my way' in response to the release of Alan Reid's book, *The Gorton Experiment*, in July 1971. Eggleton was contacted by a number of media organisations but refused to comment. There were rumours that Eggleton was intending to produce his own account of the Gorton years. Gotto telephoned Eggleton to ascertain the truth of these rumours because she was intending to write a series of articles for *Woman's Day*. She did not think Eggleton would approve of these articles 'but she felt that they would not do any harm'. He offered no judgement but warned Gotto that 'people would be looking for anything that confirmed her influence over the prime minister'. Eggleton was 'intrigued to find that she (and probably John Gorton) was still deluding herself ... I can just imagine [Gorton] thinking it's all rather funny ... Even now, he clearly still cannot appreciate the delicacy of the entire relationship'. Shortly after he arrived in London, Eggleton wrote to Gorton:

> I am content enough with the new job. I have to admit that I miss the excitement of the old days, but then I always knew that whatever I did after the PM's office would bound to be something of an anti-climax. But it is a very pleasant change, and Mary and the children are appreciating my more regular working hours.

The Commonwealth Secretariat had been located in stately Marlborough House since its establishment in 1965. The Secretariat was central to the transition of the British Empire to the Commonwealth of Nations. Its formation was proposed by several of the newly independent African nations. Its foremost advocate was Kwame Nkrumah, the first President of Ghana, who believed that small and isolated African countries, like the one he represented, could only develop by working together. The older nations of the Commonwealth – especially Canada, Australia and New Zealand – had a duty to the newer ones, particularly setting favourable terms of trade. A 'central clearing house' was needed to prepare and promote plans for economic development. Others thought a secretariat was needed to prepare for future meetings and to produce background papers on relevant topics. Several of the African leaders wanted an umpire to assist in the conciliation of disputes between Commonwealth nations.

The British Government had thought the Commonwealth was 'theirs' to manage. Civil servants employed in the Commonwealth Relations Office (CRO) within the British Foreign Office had little enthusiasm for the Secretariat. They believed an entity that was responsible to every member nation would undermine the cohesion of their own work and the stability of the Commonwealth itself. The Australian Government agreed in principle to the Secretariat's establishment but stressed that 'its functions and the nature and authority of its staff require a great deal of examination'. Menzies did not want the Secretariat's staff to have any executive authority. Noting these reservations, a representative group of diplomats was tasked with developing proposals for further consideration. The creation of the Secretariat was officially approved in January 1965 and the organisation formally established six months later.

Arnold Smith, a former Rhodes scholar and experienced Canadian diplomat, was elected its first Secretary-General. He would serve in the post from 1965 to 1975. Smith had strongly advocated the need for an information department within the organisation. He explained that:

> Such a large job needed to be done in bringing home to all sorts of people the benefits and the potential in the association that was the new Commonwealth, that every available ally was important. Many were extremely effective ... but there was still a gaping hole at the centre, in the Secretariat, where for some years we even had to pay our press officer from part of the administration division budget because there was no budget voted for her post.[11]

Despite an annual circulation of 200,000 copies, the British Government had withdrawn funding for the magazine *Commonwealth Today*.

After several years of agitation, the Heads of Government acknowledged the need for an information department in January 1971. The invitation to Eggleton to head the department had come just days later although he had become aware of the position in a letter from Bill Heseltine dated 24 June 1970. He replied: 'I am only too well aware that I cannot go on being the press secretary to the prime minister forever, and after five years in the post I could be tempted by the right opening. It sounds like the Commonwealth job could be challenging and interesting, and might be the kind of thing that would appeal'. He received a position description and advice on the likely salary and conditions. In October 1970 he met Donald Kerr, the architect of the new department's structure, when he came to Canberra for meetings. Kerr was an Australian economist and former journalist. He had been the Controller (Overseas) at the British Central Office of Information when seconded to the Secretariat in 1969. There were two candidates for the job – Eggleton and an unnamed New Zealander.

Before Eggleton was informally interviewed for the position (which was meant to happen during the Singapore conference in January 1971), he wrote to Gorton: 'This is the hardest note I've ever had to write to you but I think – if you will look at things from my point of view – you will understand'. He then explained the essence of the new position and that it is preferable to 'entering private industry'. He went on: 'It is not that I am in any way discontent or unhappy in the job. I have always enjoyed it immensely, and I feel our working relationship has never been better. But I must look to tomorrow and I don't believe this is an opportunity that I can afford to pass up'. He concluded by asking Gorton for 'your goodwill and understanding in undertaking this challenge'. The Prime Minister's response was low-key. He told Eggleton that Australia would not contribute any additional funds for his new work and that 'he would not touch the Secretariat job with a barge pole although he saw the advantages from my personal point of view'. Notably, his discussion with Gorton did not elicit 'any special warmth reflecting my years of devoted service' but Eggleton was told he could reply on the Prime Minister's goodwill and understanding. Eggleton was then asked to prepare a list of replacement candidates and mentioned that he favoured Reg McDonald.

The creation of the new position within the Secretariat was a matter of satisfaction for Smith and his senior colleagues. The first director was naturally under considerable pressure given the weight of expectation. Australian journalist Bruce Juddery noted that Eggleton, was 'expected, through the media, to do no less than put a new zip into the entire Commonwealth association – a thankless, futureless task in the eyes of a good many people for whom the Commonwealth is dying on its feet, or perhaps its bottom'. Taken at face value, 'for Mr Eggleton to succeed in this task would be little less than a miracle'. The 'Englishman who now proclaims himself almost belligerently to be an Australian', conceded 'there will not be overnight results. It's a long, hard haul. I'll be satisfied if after two or three years – we are beginning to get tangible results'. Geoffrey Tebbutt writing in the Melbourne *Herald* quipped that the 'Secretariat is getting a better man than it deserves in Tony Eggleton ... Of course, I wish Mr Eggleton well personally. Yet I don't want him to succeed too well. If he does, he may persuade us that the rancorous, decrepit and now essentially alien Commonwealth ought to be preserved at all costs'.[12] Eggleton stressed that he was 'a firm believer in the Commonwealth. Ever since I can remember it has been knocked and called obsolete and irrelevant. But how can it be irrelevant when it embraces 32 countries – a quarter of the world's population. It must be able to play a role for the good of the world'.[13]

Undaunted by the challenges, Eggleton was keen to 'run my own ship, have my own staff, still fulfil my wish to travel and not lose my interest in the media'. He also knew that after being a recognisable face in Australia, 'I had become a big fish in a relatively small Australian pond. It would be a very different story in England'. In a private note dated 11 April 1971 he reflected that his new job

> is something of a gamble, career-wise, family-wise and personally. But it's probably no bigger a risk than previous moves, such as coming to Australia in the first place or leaving the ABC to tackle the national capital. You've got to be in it to win it. I would like to have a try at the international scene, and see if I can make some impact there. I know I am giving up a great deal but I cannot afford to get into a rut. The London job could be a path to the 'big time'.

Smith said he preferred the Eggletons lived in central London and was prepared to increase the housing allowance to make that possible. The family moved into a particularly desirable part of the West End, not far from Oxford Street and Marble Arch. The main bedroom and a large sitting room overlooked the private garden of the fashionable Montagu Square for which they had a personal key. Selfridges, the second-largest retail premises in Britain and widely considered the best department store in the world, was within walking distance. Eggleton's daily stroll to Marlborough House took him through Grosvenor Square, Berkeley Square and St James Street.

His first task was establishing the new department. Some of the groundwork had been undertaken by Kerr whose recommendations for its structure and remit were prepared after 'individual consultations with some 700 senior people throughout Commonwealth countries'. Kerr did not think his scheme was a 'straightjacket ... Tony will have a lot of scope to develop it'. Eggleton inherited some staff and specially appointed others. He chose the Sri Lankan journalist and diplomat, Charles Gunawardena, as his assistant. [Gunawardena held the director's post from 1979–87]. New publications were launched and contacts were sought with diplomatic correspondents among the London press. Eggleton was also adamant that 'putting the modern Commonwealth into clearer perspective calls for something more than increased flow of information'.[14] He made exchange opportunities for journalists and media training in developing nations a leading priority. While the Secretariat could supply endless amounts of data, he thought the problem of public information 'is much more basic – the very shortage of trained and experienced communicators of any kind'. Eggleton was also concerned about journalistic standards and professional ethics, and the need for Commonwealth nations to become 'increasingly aware of the potential and relevance' of information. He was conscious that 'the media are not going to publish or broadcast material just for the sake of publicising the Commonwealth'. They were more likely to promote stories that fed 'disenchantment and cynicism' towards the organisation.

This awkward reality was immediately apparent after Eggleton observed an early press conference held by the Secretary-General. Eggleton had proposed a background briefing for Commonwealth newspaper correspondents but Smith 'favoured an open press conference'. The attendance was poor with the *Financial Times* the only London paper to send a representative. Eggleton lamented that Smith 'had to play a straight bat to so many questions that the press became bored and restive'. There was 'little, if any, news in what he had to say, and most of the correspondents must have felt it was a waste of time'. His advice to the Secretary-General when speaking with the media was to set an agenda and be 'free to speak openly on the topics concerned'.

In an interview with Cy Fox that was syndicated to a number of Canadian regional newpapers, Eggleton conceded that 'the old empire may have been a relatively short-lived chapter in history and that the international ties resulting from it constitute in many cases about the only characteristic the 30 Commonwealth countries of today have in common'.[15] And yet, he thought its present leaders 'have to build on this accident of history and try to talk over the world's problems among ourselves with a greater chance of success than we'd have in a larger world forum'. In an article published in Melbourne's *Age*, Eggleton claimed the 'world would feel the chill if the sun set on the Commonwealth' which was now a 'multi-racial association' in which Britain was an 'equal partner'. The Melbourne *Herald* suggested that 'if Tony Eggleton were not such a skilled, likeable and experienced propagandist, we should all be merrily laughing at his description of the 'special sort of way' in which the British Commonwealth conducts its business.'[16] The *Herald* was expressing its editorial incredulity that the Uganda ruled by the murderous despot, Idi Amin, had not been expelled from the association.

Eggleton was personally disappointed that Britain's recently launched New Statesman magazine had claimed the Secretariat's efforts to improve journalism included 'an appreciation of the advantages to the community of big corporations', noting that Rio Tinto Zinc had made a substantial contribution to the Information Department's budget. He explained that 'the idea of regular training courses for senior journalists specialising in finance is not designed to produce tame apologists for big business.'[17] Although various companies were approached to fund the department's proposed finance courses, the training would be 'run by professional newspaper organisations like the British National Union of Journalists and the Commonwealth Press Union'. These courses would be part of the only postgraduate program offered in Britain with Eggleton seeking an affiliation with the University of Cardiff. He countered the *New Statesman*'s claim with an insistence that 'such a scheme could produce journalists able to see through the propaganda that big business can put out'.

Having established modest objectives, Eggleton prepared for the Commonwealth Finance Ministers' Conference to be held in London in October 1971. Australia was represented by the Treasurer, Billy Snedden. The Secretary-General was looking for increased input to a special fund for technical assistance. The Australian officials, reflecting government policy at the time, were advising Snedden against this expenditure. In a private meeting, Eggleton was able to convince Snedden to announce an Australian contribution to the fund – much to the surprise and irritation of the Foreign Affairs officials. Needless to say, Eggleton's ability to raise funds enhanced his standing with Smith. It also helped his efforts to overcome the costs of copyright, contract and royalties associated with the sharing of television programs, and to assist with expenditures on cable news releases.

The Secretary-General appointed Eggleton to his 'inner cabinet', involving him in the development of the Secretariat's policy and strategic planning. He attended conferences in various parts of the Commonwealth as the organisation's chief 'salesman', making arrangements for the media and handling press briefings. Eggleton found it refreshingly different to his work as press secretary in Canberra. He missed some of the political action but it was a pleasant change not to have the media calling him around the clock. In London, unless there was a major issue, even the media seemed to respect 'diplomats' hours'. The Eggleton family also had a busy social program in London which included being on the invitation list for royal occasions at Buckingham Palace. They attended the summer garden parties and evening diplomatic receptions. They also went to dinner at St James' Palace where their friend Bill Heseltine lived in an apartment owned by the Royal family.

Not long after Eggleton started his new job in London there was an official visit to Britain from Prime Minister Bill McMahon and his wife Sonia. The Prime Minister was accompanied by a team of political correspondents from Canberra, most of whom wanted to speak with Eggleton at Marlborough House. To save time and avoid playing favourites, he hosted a luncheon in one of the ornate reception rooms. Eggleton realised the Prime Minister was in Britain because, almost immediately, he received a telephone call. The McMahons had arrived from Washington where Sonia had caused a sensation by wearing an evening gown with an eye-catching expanse of leg. 'That dress', as it became known, sparked international headlines. McMahon was calling from the Savoy Hotel where a media pack had gathered seeking more photos of his glamorous wife. Mrs McMahon felt trapped in the hotel and wanted help escaping. Eggleton's advice was to have a car waiting and leave through the main exit, in something less newsworthy than her Washington outfit. She should pose briefly for the photographers before departing for her London commitments. The photo opportunity satisfied the media and she was not bothered again. Eggleton's advice might have implied he was among the conservatives who were bothered by her choice of 'inappropriate' evening wear at the White House. This was untrue. Eggleton's only concern was her privacy and security. Never intending to make a statement, she was surprised by the response of fashion commentators and political observers. 'That dress' was, she told Eggleton, heavy and warm. On their return to Australia, both McMahons wrote letters of appreciation to Eggleton for his discreet assistance. But the tide of time was running out for the McMahon prime ministership.

Eggleton visited the Australian High Commission in London on election day (2 December 1972). He was unsurprised by the result. Indeed, like many others associated with the Coalition government, he believed the 1969 election victory would probably be its last for some time. The vulnerable McMahon was defeated by triumphant Whitlam but only narrowly. The swing to Labor was 2.5 per cent (on a two-party preferred basis) and the new government's majority was only nine seats. Whitlam had, of course, made up more ground during the 1969 election when the Labor Opposition took 18 seats from the Coalition Government. Shortly afterwards Eggleton visited Canberra 'for talks with the new administration'.

In a confidential report to the Secretary-General, Eggleton observed that 'Australia had abandoned its customary low profile in international relations, has changed its voting pattern in the United Nations, has rebuffed racist regimes, and is confronting France over nuclear tests in the Pacific'. He thought Australians had welcomed these initiatives and 'favour a more distinctive and independent Australian voice on the international scene'. After speaking with Prime Minister Whitlam 'and a large number of the new ministry', he left Canberra 'much encouraged that we can expect a more positive and constructive Australian approach to Commonwealth affairs in future'. Eggleton also offered an appraisal of the domestic political scene. He reported that 'the Opposition is in disarray and is feuding with its former Coalition partner, the Country Party'. The Labor Opposition had managed to conceal its internal divisions during the recent election campaign but 'its 'honeymoon' period has already started to wear thin'. Eggleton assessed Labor's foremost challenge as the 'maintenance of unity and harmony in its own ranks'.

On returning to London, Eggleton helped organise the Commonwealth Heads of Government Meeting (CHOGM) which was hosted by Canadian Prime Minister Pierre Trudeau in Ottawa in 1973. This was the first CHOGM to call on leaders to participate in genuine debate rather than deliver formal speeches crafted principally for domestic audiences. As chairman, Trudeau contributed to the success of this new format by cross-examining and questioning the prime ministers who had no choice but to abandon their prepared texts. The *Toronto Globe and Mail* thought 'the most important mouth at the conference belongs to Tony Eggleton, a competent little Australian who is press officer at the Commonwealth Secretariat in London'.[18] After each session, Eggleton briefed the international media contingent which included the Australians who had travelled with Gough Whitlam. There were odd moments during the meeting because Eggleton was occasionally asked to give advice to the Labor Prime Minister. Both were amused by this unlikely turn of events.

Of greatest personal interest to Eggleton was Whitlam's private statement to the Secretary-General that he proposed a rapid move towards independence for Papua New Guinea (PNG) because he was 'deeply ashamed to be the last imperialist power'. PNG would be granted self-government in December 1973 with the target date for independence set for late in 1974. To ensure PNG's local politicians appreciated the importance of the Commonwealth to their country's future, Smith and Eggleton visited Post Moresby in April 1974. Notably, Eggleton was the only member of the Secretariat with any experience of PNG.

On other occasions Eggleton represented the Secretariat at meetings of various Commonwealth organisations that were based in London, such as the Royal Commonwealth Society and the Commonwealth Institute. He had developed an impressive network of contacts with key people across the association. These contacts included Derek Ingram, the highly respected English journalist and doyen of Commonwealth affairs. He lived near the Eggleton home in Montagu Square and became a lifelong friend. Being based in London had other personal benefits. The family enjoyed regular holidays in Europe and were joined by son Stephen who came to England twice every year, usually coinciding with the British summer and the Christmas holidays, at the Secretariat's expense. After living in Australia for 21 years, Eggleton was also able to see his English family regularly, including his now aged parents Tom and Winnie. On 4 November 1972, Tom had a fatal heart attack while watching television. Sad as his death was for the family, Eggleton was pleased to have spent some time with his father during the previous year and to be on hand to support his grieving mother.

As Eggleton became better known across the Commonwealth, he started to receive a stream of visitors including London-based journalists, international correspondents and foreign diplomats seeking briefings on Commonwealth affairs. A French diplomat said his country was impressed with the workings of the modern Commonwealth and wondered whether the organisation might be expanded to include 'non-British' countries. Eggleton suggested that, from France's perspective, it would be more appropriate to expand further the Francophone network which had been established in March 1970. It was one of his European contacts who managed to create a potential problem.

A trade diplomat attached to the Romanian Embassy often visited the Secretariat and his interests began to extend beyond the Commonwealth. He asked searching questions about Australian politics, Australian political figures and government processes. Eggleton became uneasy when this frequent visitor extended lavish entertainment and expensive gifts. At Christmas he left an envelope on Eggleton's desk containing £100. Eggleton refused to accept the gifts and the money but thought it prudent to report these gestures to the security people at the Australian High Commission. They identified what appeared to be the standard tactics of a Romanian intelligence officer. The man was hard to shake off but eventually got the message that Eggleton was not for sale. In a private note, Eggleton revealed that he conferred with an Australian intelligence officer who suggested he continue to meet the diplomat but 'in view of my position with an international organisation, and my reputation in Australia, he would not favour involving me in a counter-espionage operation. This I fully endorsed. But said I would, of course, wish to cooperate in the national interest'.

During Eggleton's time with the Secretariat he made one small decision with long-term ramifications. Smith mentioned that high commissioners had national flags to fly on their official cars but he, as Secretary-General, had no equivalent identification. Eggleton suggested the Commonwealth should have its own distinctive logo. Knowing it would be near impossible to get more than 30 governments to agree on an appropriate design, Eggleton produced his own without bothering to consult any of the member nations. The logo featured a depiction of the globe surrounded by the letter 'C'. The C comprised a semi-circle of small strokes representing the Commonwealth's membership and diversity, as well as its lines of contact and communication. He began publishing the logo on every communication from the Secretariat's information division. There were no questions and no criticism – in fact, there was no reaction at all. Eggleton suggested to his colleagues that they be bold enough to go a step further and feature the logo on a pennant for the Secretary-General's car and for Commonwealth flags and bunting used during official events. It was not long before the governments of member nations assumed the design would be incorporated into all printed material.

Around the Secretariat the logo was dubbed the 'Eggleton hedgehog' because, at a glance, it resembled a round object with lots of spikes. More than 30 years later Eggleton was contacted by academics researching the evolution of the modern Commonwealth. They wanted to explore the collaborative process that had been used to design and approve the official logo. They sought Eggleton's advice because they could not find a paper trail in the Secretariat's archives.

After two years, and having achieved a number of major and minor successes, the introduction of the Commonwealth logo among them, Eggleton began to think of the future. His Secretariat appointment was initially for three years but now he wondered whether for the sake of his family and his career, he needed to be pondering a few options. In a private note he mused:

> Arnold Smith has been a delight to work for but apart from one or two instances, such as the Heads of Government meeting in Ottawa, and other overseas trips, the job has really been something of a bore. I have always been able to keep myself busy but it was rarely stimulating or exciting … In my own fields, results were slow to achieve, and despite lip service to the Information Program, it was only too apparent that most governments were not really interested. Lack of money meant there was little new scope for expansion.

He was merely 'jogging along in this sinecure' and found he was 'losing my joy of work and my self-respect'. Eggleton also found Britain to be a drab place with industrial unrest, average weather, poor food and people who were without 'courtesy or efficiency'. He missed being with his elder son and had tired of being a 'perpetual tourist'. Australia had become his home and its politics the mainstay of his professional life.

Endnotes

1   Reid, *The Gorton Experiment*, p. 402.
2   Tony Eggleton, 'John Gorton and the American Embassy Affair', private note, Canberra 4 April 1971.
3   https://pmtranscripts.pmc.gov.au/sites/default/files/original/00002373.pdf
4   Kenneth Randall, 'Man behind three prime ministers', *Australian*, 11 February 1971.
5   'Tony moves on', *The Bulletin*, 20 February 1967.
6   Quoted in Ayers, *Malcolm Fraser*, p. 192.
7   'Police told to leave press alone', *Age*, 7 April 1970.
8   Personal letter from Janet Hawley, 15 May 1970.
9   Personal letter from Ross Mark, 18 May 1970.
10   Ted Crofts, 'Just keep your cool, says Tony', *Telegraph*, 16 April 1970, p. 2.
11   Arnold Smith, *Stitches in Time: The Commonwealth in World Politics*, Andre Deutsch, London, 1981, p. 124.
12   Geoffrey Tebbutt, 'Side Lines', *Melbourne Herald*, 18 February 1971.
13   'Mr Unflappable Leaves', *Canberra News*, 15 April 1971, p. 1.
14   Tony Eggleton, 'Getting to know you', *Commonwealth Press Union Quarterly*, October 1972, p. 24.
15   Cy Fox, 'Eggleton – salesman for the Commonwealth', *Leader-Post*, Saskatoon, 4 April 1972, p. 5.
16   'Sine Lines', *Melbourne Herald*, 22 February 1972.
17   'Tony and the financial press ruckus', *Australian*, 21 July 1972.
18   Geoffrey Stevens, 'Why are they in Ottawa?', *Toronto Globe and Mail*, 9 August 1973.

The newly appointed Director of Navy Public Relations, April 1961.

Outside the United States Navy School of
Journalism, September 1961.

With a press party at the RAN College, HMAS *Creswell*, August 1962.

Flight deck of HMAS *Melbourne* off Brisbane, Exercise Carbine, August 1963

Address by the South Vietnamese Ambassador, Tran Van Lam, National Press Club, Canberra, September 1963.

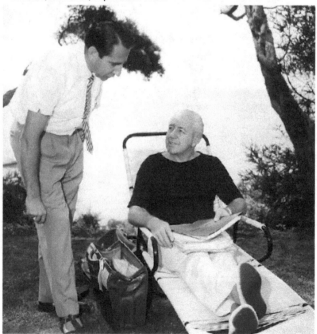

Prime Minister Holt at his Portsea beach house, March 1966.

Prime Minister Holt's visit to Bien Hoa, South Vietnam, April 1966. Eggleton is second from the left holding the prime ministerial briefcase.

Recording Prime Minister Holt's election policy speech, GTV 9 studios, Melbourne, November 1966.

The Eggleton Family photographed for the *Australian Women's Weekly*, February 1968.

Prime Minister Gorton and Mrs Betty Gorton (in gloves) with President Johnson and Mrs Ladybird Johnson at the White House north portico, Washington DC, May 1968. Eggleton is standing second from the left.

Prime Minister Gorton visits Emerald, Queensland, September 1968. Eggleton is holding the prime ministerial briefcase in the middle ground to the left.

Prime Minister Gorton preparing to deliver his election policy speech, GTV 9 studios, Melbourne, October 1969.

Prime Minister Gorton during a Parliament House news conference, June 1970.

l have (discussed with mr eggleton the terms
telephone
of a/conversation l had with him earlier in.apologising t(
the prime min̄ister for a remark l had made in the House
this afternoon.

l have told mr eggleton l did not use the word[
the prime minister read to the ⨯⨯⨯⨯⨯⨯ House in disclosi[
my apology.
That l had said to the prime minister mr
eggleton earlier was that l had made "made an ass of
myself", that l was sorry, that l wanted to apologise, ⨯⨯⨯
that l had not meant that the Prime Minister was a liar, i
been an "impulsive remark",
but that he had been "bloody unfair" to me.

mr eggleton in our discussion tonight said
emphasise TO   my Conc(
he had wanted to make an impact on the prime minister/and
that he had not known the words he (m ear h
had typed on the message passed to the Prime Minister
His message to the Prime Mi[
Was NOT INTENDED AS A DIRECT[

l have handed a letter to the speaker, sir Con[
william aston, unreservedly apologising to the House for my
⨯. l have assured him l
respect the House and that l deeply regret the incident.

l would say in explan̄ ition of my ⨯⨯⨯
outburst that it related solely to a single incident in which
the credibility of the Prime Minister and myself was
at stake.

l had thought he was being extremely unfair
in glossing over in generalised terms a remark he was suppose[
to have made to me in replying to a question on allegations
attributed to Sir thomas daly.

Yet he had used a direct quote in my reply to
this remark. l felt this had distorted our conversation and
given a completely wrong impression of what the Prime Ministe[
had said to me LAST WEDNESDAY Ⓡ

Allen Ramsey's draft apology letter to Prime Minister Gorton showing Eggleton's penscript
amendments, March 1971.

Eggleton stands between deposed Prime Minister Gorton (left) and the Prime Minister-Elect, William McMahon, on the front steps of Parliament House in Canberra, March 1971.

The Commonwealth of Nations Secretariat headquarters, Marlborough House, London, March 1972.

Prime Minister Whitlam (centre) and Commonwealth Secretary General, Arnold Smith (right), Canberra, April 1973.

Preparing for the Commonwealth Heads of Government Meeting (CHOGM), Ottawa, July 1973.

Election campaign staff breakfast, May 1974. Eggleton is third from the right.

(left to right) Senator John Carrick (Leader of the Government in the Senate), Prime Minister Malcolm Fraser, Eggleton and Sir John Atwill (Federal President of the Liberal Party) at the Liberal Party Secretariat, Canberra, April 1981.

Prime Minister Fraser during the unsuccessful March 1983 Federal election campaign.

(left to right) Eggleton, Senator Reg Withers (Secretary to the Shadow Cabinet) and Opposition Leader, Andrew Peacock, on board a RAAF VIP aircraft during the 1984 election campaign.

Launch of the Coalition's Tax Advertising Campaign by Opposition Leader, John Howard, Adelaide, July 1986.

Eggleton flanked by the Liberal Party leaders with whom he worked as Federal Director, (left to right) John Howard, Andrew Peacock, Malcolm Fraser and John Hewson, October 1990.

Mary and Tony Eggleton, Liberal Party Federal Council Farewell dinner, October 1990.

National Council for the Centenary of Federation, Old Parliament House, 1998.

CHAPTER 9

Political player   1974–75

By mid-1973, Eggleton believed the Commonwealth's standing had improved appreciably after the less than satisfactory outcomes of the 1971 Singapore Conference and the withdrawal of Pakistan in January 1972 after Commonwealth recognition (and later admission) of breakaway Bangladesh. He felt the association had new confidence and renewed vitality. Eggleton took advantage of accumulated leave and returned home to Australia with his family. They enjoyed a motoring holiday around the south-east coast of the continent from Melbourne to Sydney. As he went back to London, Eggleton realised he was missing Australia and its politics. The diplomatic life at the Secretariat, while comfortable and rewarding in its own way, lacked excitement and fulfilment. His family was being further fragmented as Andrew would remain in Australia and join Stephen at Chevalier College.

Having hinted that he would probably return to Australia after three years in London, Eggleton started to receive job offers. There had also been soundings from public relations firms and mining companies. Talbot (later Sir Talbot) Duckmanton, General Manager of the Australian Broadcasting Commission (ABC), was keen for Eggleton to rejoin the corporation in a senior post. In July 1973 he told Duckmanton that, although he was being offered an extension in London, 'my preference would be to return to Australia, provided there was the right opportunity. On the other hand, the Secretariat position is not the sort of attractive proposition to be casually relinquished'. The strongest offer came from the Liberal Party. It was conveyed by an unexpected visitor to Marlborough House: Billy Snedden. He had become leader of the Opposition following the election of the Labor Government in December 1972.

Snedden was in London on Liberal Party business and told Eggleton he 'just wanted to keep in touch'. He had, in fact, a clear agenda. Before leaving Britain,

Snedden raised the prospect of Eggleton returning to Australia and joining the Liberal Party organisation. This was not the first time his name had been associated with the Federal Secretariat. With the retirement of James Robert 'Jock' Willoughby, its long-serving Federal Director (1951–68), there was press speculation that Eggleton was a possible 'outside' candidate. Writing in the *Australian Financial Review* (AFR), Walsh observed that Eggleton was already experienced and 'had worked in close liaison with the various State officials of the Liberal Party and is well versed in the party machinery. The fact that he is not even a member of the Liberal Party would not debar him, though it could cause some comment.'[1] Walsh thought that Gorton needed Eggleton as his press secretary more than as federal director and his decision to remain in the prime minister's office was a wise one.

As Eggleton was very comfortable in his London position, he remained non-committal when approached in 1973. If he did work for the Liberals, he would have to leave the Commonwealth public service and the security of employment he had known for the past 15 years. Peter Golding, originally from the publicists engaged covertly by Gorton and Gotto in 1970, urged Eggleton to work with the Liberals as the party desperately needed his expertise. In his view, 'Snedden is not good on television, but more than that he doesn't seem to handle the press well. He tends to bicker with them and debate in interviews, and the result is that there is a tendency for journalists and interviewers to get their backs up.'[2] He was convinced Eggleton could improve Snedden's technique and differentiate Coalition policies from Labor's plans. In a private letter to Asher Joel, a Country Party member of the New South Wales Legislative Council, who had offered him a job with his public relations company, Eggleton explained that 'my next step after the Commonwealth Secretariat is a crossroads decision for me. It may well shape the course of the rest of my working life.'

Meanwhile, Arnold Smith was planning to extend Eggleton's contract at the Commonwealth Secretariat in the hope he would remain. In a letter dated 27 November 1973, Eggleton told Smith that he 'envisaged staying on for at least a full five-year term.'[3] Smith's plan was to give him a 'trouble shooter' role for the Commonwealth, operating as the Secretary-General's personal representative, which would make him a competitive candidate for the position of Assistant Secretary-General and ultimately the top job. Smith was convinced that Eggleton would be well-suited for the post and would attract wide support. It was another tempting prospect. It was, in a way, a happy dilemma for Eggleton. He was standing at a career crossroads and was in demand from prospective employers. He was attracted to the special role with the Commonwealth but wondered whether this was best for his family. If he accepted promotion within the Secretariat and stayed in London, it might be many years before he and wife Mary could return to Australia permanently.

The Liberals were intensifying their efforts to attract him. Eggleton received a series of phone calls from Snedden outlining several employment possibilities. Liberal Party Federal President, Bob (later Sir Robert) Southey, followed these soundings with a detailed offer. He would initially serve as Special Adviser to the leader of the Opposition and Director of Communications within the Liberal Party's Federal Secretariat. After a period of transition, depending upon when elections were held and when the incumbent (Bede Hartcher) could be moved on, he would become the Liberal Party's Federal Director in mid-1975. There were follow-up phone calls from businessman and future Liberal Party Federal President, John Elliot, and members of Snedden's own staff eager to draw on his experience and expertise. What Eggleton did not know was that his salary would be underwritten by three Melbourne businessmen that included Elliott. He was yet to become aware that the incumbent, Bede Hartcher, was anxious about Eggleton's return and what it would mean for him. Malcolm Fraser, Andrew Peacock and another senior Victorian parliamentarian, Don Chipp, were also opposed to providing more organisational support for the Party leader.

Eggleton changed his mind several times. He was concerned that state divisions of the Liberal Party would continue to restrain federal priorities and feared the long-term ability of the Party to pay his salary. In mid-November, Eggleton wrote to Southey declining the offer. He felt the prospective responsibilities were simply too limited. He would be little more than 'chief press secretary' to the parliamentary Leader. Southey then travelled to London to persuade Eggleton to reconsider the Liberal Party's offer. He made a strong bid over lunch. Eggleton decided to resolve the impasse by setting a high benchmark for salary and conditions (including a minimum 12-month 'golden handshake' if the Party no longer wanted him), stating he would accept the offer if they accepted his terms. Southey returned to Australia and consulted with Snedden and Elliott. Eggleton was advised that the Party had agreed to a salary package that exceeded what he had asked.

Eggleton wrote to Smith on 20 February 1974.

> You will remember that when we last talked about the pressures on me to
> return to Australia, we acknowledged that some of my old colleagues may not
> accept 'no' for an answer … it is still with some mixed feelings, and no little
> sadness, that I have to tell you that I feel obliged to take on the task that my old
> colleagues have wished upon me. They want me to play a central coordinating
> role in rebuilding the Party, serving in a bridging capacity between the Party
> organisation and the Parliamentary party.

In a private note, Eggleton recorded that 'Smith took my resignation in good
spirit. He was obviously disappointed … but with his strong instincts for politics,
he could see the obvious attraction of the Liberal job'. Shortly afterwards, Eggleton
was replaced by the former BBC presenter and producer, Nick Harman. Smith
later remarked of Eggleton's contribution:

> He managed to produce good information material on a miserably small budget,
> help run the Ottawa Heads of Government Meeting with aplomb and gave me
> invaluable political advice, not only about Australia and Papua New Guinea,
> but in many other spheres.[4]

On 24 February 1974, the Liberal Party formally announced Eggleton's new
role. His return was widely reported and even made the papers in Papua New
Guinea.[5] Max Walsh had earlier revealed that Eggleton 'is expected to return
to Australia soon to become what might be called 'the Liberal Party's Mick
Young'.[6] Mick Young was the Labor Party's National Secretary. Walsh accepted
there were contrasts between the two men and 'nobody would be quicker to
reject the description … than Tony Eggleton. He is no carbon copy of anybody'.
Walsh suggested, however, that 'you cannot buy or create Mick Youngs, but you
can, the Liberal Party believes, emulate what he did' after 1969 – making Labor
attractive to the voters. Eggleton's task was giving the Liberal Party a 'facelift'.

The Eggleton's plans for an orderly departure from London were thrown into
disarray by an unexpected late night telephone call from Snedden. The Whitlam
Government had called a snap double dissolution election for 18 May 1974 and
the Liberal Party wanted Eggleton back in Australia as soon as possible. The
Secretary-General generously cooperated with the accelerated timetable. Having
made plans for an Easter holiday in the Netherlands, Mary and the children
decided to go ahead with the trip. Eggleton flew out almost three years to the

day of his arrival in London. Was this to be a new chapter in their lives or the continuation of the one they thought had ended in 1971? It was hard to tell but there were several viable escape routes. In a private note he mused that 'if and when we win government, there's a gentleman's understanding that I can get almost anything I want, including a diplomatic appointment. If we stay in opposition, and I tire of it, there may even be prospects of getting back into international civil service'. He made a pledge to himself: 'the dice have been rolled, and the gamble is on. I shall have to play hard and with no regrets'.

Eggleton responded to dozens of letters offering congratulations with the same words: 'I don't have any illusions about the job I've taken on. But despite the inevitable difficulties, I am sure it is something that will give me a lot of personal and professional satisfaction'. He was greeted at Sydney airport by a waiting throng of reporters, photographers and cameramen. One newspaper headline read: 'Liberals' Secret Weapon Flies In'. Eggleton stressed that he 'did not have a magic wand to help them win', although he added: 'you win some and you lose some, but I expect to win this one'.[7] He told the ABC's John Highfield that 'I believe in pragmatic rather than dogmatic politics – on flexibility to meet contemporary needs rather than preconceived ideology. For my money, a Liberal government stands for responsible, reliable and ethical government'. He told Alan Ramsey that 'my whole way of life steered me towards Liberal politics'.

When Eggleton started work at Liberal Headquarters on Blackall Street in the Canberra suburb of Barton, the Party, the Federal Secretariat and the parliamentary leader, Billy Snedden, were still learning and applying lessons from the December 1972 election loss. It would not take a great deal of probing to conclude that after 23 years of unbroken Coalition rule, the Australian people had simply voted for change. Discerning the electorate's dissatisfaction with the Gorton and McMahon governments, Labor's 1972 election slogan summed up the prevailing mood: 'It's time'. The Liberal Party could not avoid the soul-searching that followed defeat at the polls. There was an assumption based on Australian electoral history that Labor would govern for at least two terms before the Coalition stood a chance of returning to the Treasury benches. The previous one-term government, led by James Scullin, was voted from office in 1931. Whitlam and his ministers were likely to enjoy the goodwill of voters until at least the next election. Labor was likely to be in power until 1978. This interregnum gave the Liberals a chance to identify attractive candidates, refresh its philosophy and renew the party organisation. The latter task was associated with considerable urgency.

The Liberal Party's Federal Secretariat did not have a prominent advisory role prior to 1972 although Jock Willoughby was regularly consulted by Menzies about public opinion and election strategy. Snedden had sought the Secretariat's assistance in revising the Liberal's policy platform which had not been reviewed since Robert Menzies had established the Party in 1944. Snedden also formed a Policy Support Unit outside extra-parliamentary administrative structures to operate as a 'think tank', undertaking research and assessing competing policy alternatives. In March 1974, the Secretariat published a 138-page amalgam of Liberal Party positions and policies under the heading *The Way Ahead*. It was essentially an expanded version of the draft party platform that had yet to be formally approved. Snedden hoped to end the master-servant relationship between the parliamentary party and the party organisation which could be maintained while the Liberals were in government but not in Opposition when neither the shadow cabinet nor backbench parliamentarians could rely on support from the public service.

Learning from what he perceived were the weaknesses of the Holt and Gorton campaigns in 1966, 1967 (half Senate), 1969 and 1970 (half Senate), Eggleton was keen to surround the Party leader with an experienced and effective team. Snedden's personal staff was enlarged with every member knowing what was required of them. Eggleton was met with a universally positive response. The team met early each morning to reflect, anticipate and plan, ensuring the Party leader was well briefed before he embarked on the day's commitments. Snedden agreed to set a precedent for Liberal leaders by holding daily press conferences. This enabled the campaign team to 'get on the front foot and set the day's agenda'. Eggleton believed in seizing and holding the initiative. Snedden exuded full confidence in his team and wanted Eggleton beside him at all times. The media noted a growing confidence in Snedden's handling of campaign engagements. The Liberals were fighting on ground they had chosen.

Things seemed to be going well until the final few days when disaster struck. Snedden unfairly blamed Eggleton for the campaign ending in virtual capitulation.

> The election was very stressful for my voice. I fell into a serious trap by accepting advice from Eggleton ... that I should go to Newcastle, as although we could

not win any seats there it was important for the Senate vote. At Newcastle I went into a little hall which was surrounded by Labor supporters who also packed the place and got into the balconies above where they cut the wires to the loudspeaker system. I was foolish enough to stay and try to be heard – obstinacy on my part – I wasn't going to be shouted down by this mob. My voice was destroyed and for five days I could not talk. The treatment was silence. The momentum of the campaign was lost and, although it was regained, we needed another week and we would have won.[8]

Eggleton was hardly to blame for the sabotage while the purported consequences of Snedden losing his voice just before the poll overstated the power and persuasiveness of his oratory.

The election result was close and several days passed before the final outcome was known. There was a swing of 1 per cent to the Coalition in two-party preferred votes resulting in a net gain of 3 seats. There was a swing against the Labor Government of 1 per cent with the loss of one seat. Whitlam's majority was reduced from nine seats to five in the House of Representatives although Labor gained five seats in the Senate at the expense of the Democratic Labor Party which was now without any parliamentary representation. It took 11 days for Snedden to acknowledge that he had not won the election before unwisely commenting: 'we were not defeated. We did not win enough seats to form government'.

Snedden believed he had done well enough to continue as Party leader and pursue reforms of the Party organisation. Eggleton thought so too. Not expecting Whitlam to call an election in the first half of 1974 after only 16 months in office, the Liberal Party was still preparing to face the people. In the circumstances, the Liberals were remarkably effective and could have secured victory if a small number of votes and a few preferences had been distributed differently. The main criticism of the strategy was the uneven and, in places, unproductive investment of resources. The Liberal's election campaign reflected national intent but lacked national coordination. There was also a lack of corporate commitment to what the Party was offering the people. Despite the extensive consultation that preceded its release, *The Way Ahead* was not personally embraced by most members of the shadow cabinet. The Party's policies on economic management and reformed federalism were still evolving and lacked detail. Snedden could not be chided for the Party not being ready for an election that no-one within Coalition ranks had predicted. The Leader of the Opposition had fought a credible campaign and was considered the logical leader to take the Liberals to their next electoral contest.

While Snedden tried to counter the political force of nature that was Prime Minister Gough Whitlam, the head of the Party's policy unit and the Acting Federal Director, Dr Tim Pascoe, supervised changes to the structure and staffing of the Federal Secretariat and made the difficult decisions. Pascoe had previously worked for the American-based consultancy firm, McKinsey. Until the Secretariat was revamped to include oversight of all policy and communication units, Eggleton would continue to oversee media activity and serve as Snedden's Special Adviser.

Behind the scenes as Eggleton was busy scouting for suitable staff, a former acquaintance arrived at an opportune time. As Eggelton was preparing to depart for London in February 1971, his assistant Mary Newport mentioned 'there was this nice young man outside' his office that Eggleton might remember. The 'nice young man' had sold him a car in 1970. Eggleton did remember Vince Woolcock, noting that unlike other car salesmen he 'wasn't a spiv'. In a break from his own tradition, Eggleton bought a Ford instead of a Holden. Woolcock read in the *Canberra Times* that Eggleton was leaving for London and indicated he was willing to re-sell the car. After saying he also wanted a job, Eggleton introduced him to a parliamentary colleague who was reorganising office space. Woolcock made himself useful and was immediately hired. After Eggleton returned from London in April 1974 he was again approached by Woolcock wanting a job. Having acquired a reputation for being willing to 'do anything', Eggleton thought 'a good Man Friday around a political party would be useful. I was right. Employing Vince was one of my best decisions ever'. The former car salesman was adept at organising meetings, planning conferences and creating networks. Woolcock became universally known as 'Mr Fixit'.

Renewing the Federal Secretariat was intended to revive the Liberal Party across Australia. When drafting its foundation documents, Menzies had insisted that the new Liberal Party of Australia should be an integrated federal organisation with a division in each state, a Federal Council and Federal Executive with equal state representation and a Joint Standing Committee on Federal Policy. The Federal Council would include leaders of the federal and state parliamentary parties but would not be dominated by elected politicians. The majority of state delegates could not be members of parliament. The Council's remit was to 'express the views of Liberals on current political questions as they arise'; raise, invest and administer party funds; coordinate the activities of state divisions when they involved federal matters; and, alter and amend the party's platform and constitution. There would be a permanent Federal Secretariat located in Canberra. Appointed by the Federal Executive and subject to its direction, the Secretariat was initially responsible for coordinating the activities of the state divisions on a federal basis; implementing the decisions of the Federal Council and Federal Executive; research and publicity; and, liaison between the party organisation, the parliamentary party and the public.

The upheaval associated with Snedden's commitment to organisational renewal was not one of the factors that led to disaffection with his leadership. Some of his parliamentary colleagues and key figures in the party organisation did not think he could defeat Whitlam despite the narrow loss in May 1974. A move gained momentum to replace Snedden with Malcolm Fraser. After the 1972 election, Fraser had responsibility for the primary industries portfolio in the shadow cabinet. After a shadow cabinet reshuffle in 1973, Fraser was given industrial relations and Andrew Peacock the shadow foreign affairs portfolio. Fraser felt snubbed. By the end of 1974, Fraser was disillusioned with Snedden but denied any personal involvement in moves to replace him. Snedden asked Eggleton to meet privately with Fraser to prepare a public statement reaffirming his support for the leader. It was a delicate task but Eggleton and Fraser managed to devise a statement that was acceptable to Snedden. There were echoes of Fraser's confrontation with Gorton in Eggleton's advice to Snedden that he not 'try to score points off Fraser and cut him down to size'.

Far from being the end of the matter, disenchantment with Snedden continued to grow as his standing in the polls further declined. Some of Snedden's supporters were increasingly uneasy about the management of his office. They felt their leader was being poorly served by his personal staff. Snedden bristled at these criticisms and resisted taking any action. The demand for change intensified among members of the Liberal Party executive committee. The Party organisation insisted that, on a temporary basis, Snedden should install Eggleton as his chief of staff to reorganise his office and supervise his staff.

As Snedden had maintained a warm relationship with Eggleton, he accepted the advice of his Party colleagues. According to Eggleton, the timing of his arrival in the leader's office could not have been worse. There were persistent rumours of an imminent spill with most of Snedden's personal staff engaged in canvassing support for their boss. Snedden recognised that it would be inappropriate for Eggleton to be 'working the phones' on his behalf given he was on a short-term secondment from the Federal Secretariat. Others would rally support for the embattled Leader of the Opposition. In his memoirs, Snedden mistakenly concluded that Eggleton was among those working against his leadership.

> When the Morgan Gallup polls came out on 6 March [1975] I was disappointed in the results, but did not worry about them because the Opposition were getting 48 percent and I had a 28 percent approval rate. However, certain influential people in the party were saying 'This is terrible! Terrible!' Amongst them were Eggleton and Dr Tim Pascoe, from the Staff Planning Committee, where the latter was taking a role of saying that 'something ought to be done about Snedden'.

At a meeting of the Federal Campaign Committee held at the YMCA in Melbourne on 13 March 1975, it was Pascoe not Eggleton who declared that the Party could not win the next election with Snedden as its leader. Eggleton made no comment and played no part in generating support for either Snedden or Fraser in the subsequent leadership spill. In a private record of the meeting, Eggleton described Snedden's demeanour as 'aggressive and somewhat petulant'. Snedden was 'totally fed up with the bucketing' he was receiving from colleagues and the media. He was demanding loyalty from those around him including within the Party organisation. Eggleton found it 'a rather embarrassing confrontation. I knew that many of the people around the table had, in fact, written Snedden off. I felt some sympathy for Snedden but it seemed to me slightly melodramatic and a rather desperate outburst'. Eggleton was to become his new principal private secretary in all but title. Snedden seemed to accept some blame but was less than ready to take corrective action.

The influential member for Chisholm in Victoria, Tony Staley, and the Federal President, Bob Southey, decided together to move against Snedden. They believed the Opposition leader had run out of 'plausibility'. They were also concerned in the midst of this intrigue to preserve Eggleton's personal and professional standing as the incoming Federal Director. Southey later explained:

> I rang Timothy Pascoe who was still [Acting] Federal Director and we discussed it. Timothy and I both foresaw that Bill Snedden would be wanting to use Tony Eggleton as part of his defence, to get Tony to make announcements and help

with press conferences and so on, which would mean nailing Tony's flag to the mast. I worked out with Pascoe that we would send Tony somewhere else – I can't remember what we thought up, but we found something important for Tony to do outside Canberra, so when he was called on by Bill Snedden, he just wasn't available. Now if you like, that was disloyalty. However, I believed that Tony Eggleton himself was important enough to be kept out of this kind of thing. I have little doubt that if we hadn't taken that action Tony would have had to work for Snedden at that time. Tony would have been damaged goods as far as Malcolm Fraser was concerned, and Malcolm's term in office would have been a great deal more difficult than it was.

Eggleton had been in the leader's office in Melbourne for a couple of days when the leadership challenge was announced. A special party meeting was called for 21 March 1975. Eggleton flew back to Canberra with Snedden on the evening prior the critical party room vote. During the flight Snedden reminisced about his childhood, his ambitions and his life in politics. He told Eggleton he was bitterly disappointed that his colleagues were turning against him. On arrival at Canberra airport, Snedden was welcomed with applause and supportive banners. Although he was never asked to express a view, Eggleton felt that Snedden had diligently served the Liberal Party and the Coalition. He kept a 'steady hand on the tiller' in the difficult and demoralising days that followed the 1972 election loss. Snedden led an effective campaign in 1974 and directed the revitalisation of the party's organisational wing. While most of Snedden's colleagues were prepared to acknowledge his achievements, many were simply not convinced he could defeat Whitlam at the next election despite the Labor Government's erratic performance and poor polling.

Eggleton drafted some draft remarks for use with the media in anticipation of Fraser's election. He advised him to adopt a 'strong, no nonsense approach' that would 'leave no doubt about who's running the show and who is the next prime minister' He counselled Fraser to 'be relaxed, patient and affable but no need to be too friendly, we are looking for respect not mateship'. He suggested the new leader have answers to questions about his loyalty, his conservative brand of liberalism, his attitude to Whitlam and views on an early election.

Fraser defeated Snedden by a margin of 37–27 and became Leader of the Opposition on 21 March 1975. Some of those who voted for Snedden, such as Jim Killen and Andrew Peacock, were not convinced their present leader could win the next election but were more committed to seeing Fraser defeated. Eggleton announced the result of the party room ballot to the assembled press in King's Hall – just as he had done in 1969 and 1971 when Gorton had been challenged by Fairbairn and then McMahon. Before Eggleton could return to the party room he was taken in hand by Vic Garland, one of the Liberals backing Malcolm Fraser. Garland said it would be imprudent for Eggleton to make any further public comment. Eggleton was steered towards an office on the Senate side of Parliament House where, he recalled: 'I walked in and there were all the conspirators. I was quite surprised to see Bob Southey there, I have to say. That surprised me. I hadn't realised how deeply he'd been involved. Malcolm was there, with his feet up on the desk.'

Southey told Eggleton they hoped he would temporarily run the new leader's office. He agreed to do so until mid-year when he was to become the Party's Federal Director. In the course of one week, Eggleton found himself in the odd position of being chief of staff to two parliamentary leaders of the Liberal Party. Eggleton excused himself and returned to Snedden. He had not spoken with the defeated former leader since the party room vote. Snedden was distressed but magnanimous about the idea of Eggleton helping Fraser establish himself as the new leader and continue the Party's rejuvenation. Eggleton felt for Snedden, who had striven hard to renew and revive the Liberal organisation.

Fraser immediately made use of Eggleton's assistance. There were a host of media interviews to manage. Eggleton felt that Fraser performed with conviction and looked every inch a leader. The immediate impression was that the Coalition was now in firm hands and would be highly competitive at the new poll. Liberal morale was on the rise. Among Eggleton's priorities was the recruitment of staff. The most significant arrival was Dr David Kemp, later a senior minister in the Howard Government, who was appointed Fraser's senior advisor on 16 April 1975. Fraser reshuffled the shadow ministry and commented on his colleagues' suitability for their new roles. The second last was John Howard whom he described as 'an able and talented young man who would make an effective contribution in the field of consumer affairs and commerce'. Eggleton had suggested that Fraser replace the words 'young man' with 'lawyer' but was ignored.

Ahead of his first appearance on the ABC's 'Monday Conference' in late April 1975, Eggleton told Fraser to think about how he would respond to suggestions he was 'aloof, arrogant, etc', that he had a 'privileged upbringing' and was sustained financially by 'private means', and whether he would be scrapping any of Whitlam's reforms. When approached for comment by the *Sydney Morning Herald's* 'Column 8', Eggleton stressed the Liberal Party would be united before the election and 'if I were Gough, I'd be worried. In just two days, Mr Fraser has overcome much of the sectional disappointment on the leadership issue'.[9] When asked whether he needed to 'polish' Fraser's image, he replied: 'It's not necessary, I think he's doing nicely, thanks'. In a feature article in the *Nation Review*, Mungo MacCallum, claimed that Eggleton's 'usefulness must now be questionable. One Labor man said last week that if by some mischance Eggleton was working for him, he would insist that Eggleton wrote all his ideas on some colour of distinctive paper so that he could pick them out easily and toss them away without having to read them first'.[10] MacCallum also contended that Fraser's deficiencies would become apparent to the public soon enough. He would not last long as Liberal leader.

In June, Eggleton returned to the Party's Federal Secretariat to begin work as Federal Director. Pascoe had assembled a competent staff and Eggleton looked forward to exercising his new responsibilities, principally preparing for the next election. Fraser asked Eggleton to serve as secretary to the shadow cabinet, ensuring a close rapport with the parliamentary party. The second half of 1975, which coincided with Eggleton's first six months in the Secretariat, was domi-nated by crises and controversies.

The key issue was the Senate's decision to block the Whitlam Government's appropriation bills. These bills, also known as 'supply', authorised government spending for several months until the annual budget was approved. Under the Australian Constitution, the Senate cannot originate or amend such legislation but has an unlimited ability to defer or defeat it. Although the Senate had not previously blocked the Government's supply of money, Whitlam stated that Labor's opposition to the Gorton Government's budget in 1970 was 'no mere formality. We intend to press our opposition by all available means on all related measures in both houses. If the motion is defeated, we will vote against the bills here and in the Senate. Our purpose is to destroy this budget and destroy the government which has sponsored it'.

In 1974, Snedden had threatened the same action. The Senate voted to defer action on supply before Whitlam called a double dissolution in the hope that Labor might gain control of the Senate. At the press conference that followed his elevation to the Liberal leadership, Fraser said he believed that governments were entitled to govern for three years 'unless quite extraordinary and reprehensible circumstances' intervened. These words were widely interpreted to mean the Opposition would not block supply and that Fraser wanted talk of an election 'out of the air'. But if the Opposition were to block supply, Fraser added, he would proceed in such a way that 'Mr Whitlam would wake up one morning and find that he had been caught with his trousers well and truly down'.

The Senate elected in May 1974 consisted of 29 Labor Senators and 29 Coalition Senators. The remaining two seats were held by Michael Townley, a Tasmanian independent who joined the Liberal Party in February 1975, and Steele Hall, a former Liberal Premier of South Australia and member of the breakaway Liberal Movement. The Government's best prospect was a tied Senate vote. In 1975, the resignation of a Labor senator (Lionel Murphy) and the death of another (Bert Milliner) led to their replacement with an Independent (the non-party affiliated Mayor of Albury, Cleaver Bunton) and a rank-and-file Labor Party member (Albert Field) who had vowed never to vote for the Whitlam Government. The Coalition effectively controlled the Senate, assuming its own members adhered to party discipline.

On 15 October 1975, and with the full support of shadow cabinet, Fraser announced that the Coalition would

> use the power vested in us by the Constitution and delay the passage of the Government's money bills through the Senate, until the Parliament goes to the people. In accordance with long established constitutional practice which the Prime Minister has himself acknowledged in the past, the Government must resign.

Fraser claimed that the parlous state of the Australian economy and a succession of scandals had left him with no choice but to force the Government to hold an election. Tensions were high among parliamentary Liberal Party members with a divergence of opinions about the confrontational tactics being adopted by Fraser and the leadership team. Early in November the media was reporting concern among senior Liberals that Fraser might not be able to sustain a united party room. There were fears about a few 'waverers' among the Liberal senators who might cross the floor and vote with the Government to pass supply. It was critical the issue be resolved before the possible fracture of Coalition solidarity.

Eggleton attended and made notes of the weekly shadow cabinet meetings that followed the decision to block supply. His own views on the looming crisis were not recorded. His remarks were restricted to the Party's readiness for an election campaign although Pascoe had strong contrary views and shared them with Fraser. After speaking with the Victorian state director, Peter Hardie, Pascoe told Fraser: 'If you attempt to take power now and, in the process, break your principles, then I question whether you will have the moral force and credibility to solve Australia's long-term problems'.[11] In a memo dated 12 October 1975 (whose contents were not revealed publicly until 2015), Pascoe argued that 'Australia's long-term problems (including resolution of the Labor [sic] relations confrontation) will need new deals in the broadest sense and must be generated through consultation and not through confrontation. The challenges will require the highest political and moral leadership'. Unlike Pascoe, Eggleton was concerned about the broader consequences of blocking supply and was preparing a paper on alternative courses of action but ultimately believed 'it was the right thing to do'.

Eggleton spent much of 10 November at Parliament House with a meeting of the entire shadow ministry. He made a personal note of the discussion:

> Pressures on government as banks declined to cooperate. Two major banks have already told Hayden that they cannot be in his scheme … Believe we are close to crunch point … with money running out and grave doubts about the legality and practicality of alternative financing schemes, it cannot be long before the Governor-General will feel compelled to intervene. Meanwhile we must remain resolute and united. Federal fundraising [for the Liberal Party's election campaign] ahead of target.

Early on the morning of Remembrance Day (11 November), there was a meeting between Fraser, Phillip Lynch (Deputy Leader of the Liberal Party), Doug Anthony (Leader of the Country Party), Whitlam, and two senior Labor ministers, Frank Crean (Deputy Prime Minister) and Fred Daly (Leader of the House). It failed to resolve the crisis. Whitlam said that 'if the appropriation bills are not passed today, he would go to Government House to recommend a half Senate election'.[12] Fraser told Eggleton he would be calling on the Governor-General, Sir John Kerr, at lunchtime. The Leader of the Opposition was hoping for a favourable outcome but was far from certain about Kerr's intentions. Fraser suggested to Eggleton that he remain in Parliament House until he returned from Yarralumla.

Fraser was meant to see Kerr after the Governor-General had spoken with the Prime Minister. As Whitlam had gone back to his office after addressing the Parliament rather than proceeding immediately to Government House as expected, Fraser left for Yarralumla first. When Fraser's Principal Private Secretary, Dale Budd, noticed that Whitlam's car had not departed, he tried to contact the driver of Fraser's car, without success. Budd later took a call from the Governor-General's Official Secretary, David Smith, explaining that 'you are now working for the Prime Minister. He is on his way back. He wants to see Senator Withers, Mr Menadue [head of the Department of the Prime Minister and Cabinet (PM&C)] and Mr Yeend [deputy head of PM&C] as soon as possible'. Budd then advised the two senior members of Fraser's staff, David Kemp and David Barnett, that Fraser was now the Prime Minister. At some point Eggleton was also told and decided he would greet Fraser at the curb on his return from Government House. As he walked through King's Hall, Eggleton encountered a group of journalists who told him 'it's all falling apart', believing that Whitlam had been to Yarralumla to call a half Senate election and Fraser's strategy of blocking supply had failed. Eggleton 'kept a straight face' and gave nothing away. The young member for Bennelong, John Howard, encountered Eggleton on his return from a lunch time walk. He 'appeared to be waiting for someone ... Tony gave nothing away, and I did not then know what had happened'.[13]

Eggleton quietly greeted Fraser as Prime Minister. Fraser smiled and, as the two men walked across King's Hall to his office, Eggleton was asked to summon an urgent meeting of the shadow cabinet in Fraser's office. Fraser then walked past Howard and offered no more than a polite greeting. Howard noticed that Fraser was carrying something in his right hand and 'realised later it was the Bible on which he had just been sworn in'. The anxious shadow cabinet members were quickly assembled. Fraser walked solemnly into the room, giving no indication of the nature of the news he was about to share. He raised the tension by continuing to look sombre as he took his seat. An age seemed to go by. Eggleton recalls:

> Malcolm said to Withers, 'Reg, how long would it take you to get Supply?' [The Senate leader responded] 'Hell, Malcolm, are we crumbling at this stage? We ought not to, you know. Are you serious?' [Fraser then said] 'Yes, Reg, how long would it take for you to get Supply?' [Withers replied] 'Ten minutes'. [Fraser retorted] 'You've got five' ... In a crisp and matter of fact tone, Fraser

then said to the leader of the Country Party, Doug Anthony: 'Doug, you are deputy prime minister'.[14]

Fraser could barely bring himself to say the words but the incredulity of his colleagues made it necessary, 'I'm the prime minister'.

With a general election looming, Eggleton's priority was to ready the campaign headquarters in Melbourne. The Party had identified a suitable building but some of the fit-out needed to be completed. A staffer was sent quickly to Melbourne to arrange for telephones and teleprinters to be installed. There were fears the unions would go on strike and refuse to work on the Liberals' headquarters given the depth of feeling prompted by Whitlam's dismissal. These fears were unfounded and the facilities were set up within a couple of days.

With Fraser's personal backing the party organisation agreed that this would be the Liberals' first coordinated national effort. A campaign committee represented all elements of the party but the Federal Director was the clearly designated official in charge. Fraser wanted Eggleton to travel with him throughout the election so they could handle emerging challenges and seize fresh opportunities. Eggleton never doubted Fraser's support or his ability to draw on Fraser's organisational authority. Tim Pascoe served as the deputy campaign director at the Melbourne headquarters and telephoned Eggleton every day for updates and briefings. At regular intervals Eggleton would slip away from Fraser's entourage to participate directly in the development and approval of campaign advertising.

Although the union movement was incensed at the sacking of Whitlam and bitterly resented Fraser's part in the Labor Government's downfall, the business community and employer groups – the natural constituency of the Liberal Party – were eager for a change of government. The media moguls Kerry Packer and Rupert Murdoch offered their advice. Eggleton gave them the code names 'Mr Smith' and 'Mr Jones'. He received their calls on most days of the campaign and was pleased to know they were on the Coalition's side. Murdoch wanted to see aspects of the campaign at close hand and Eggleton arranged for him to attend some of the public meetings. While in Melbourne, Eggleton occasionally met Packer in his suite at the old Hotel Australia. Both were given a preview of the advertising material.

As Fraser was no longer the Leader of the Opposition, the Party decided that he should be referred to as the 'Liberal leader' rather than the 'caretaker prime minister' throughout the campaign. The Party's officials did not want to add fuel to the fire of the dismissal controversy. Fraser took a personal interest in the campaign theme and advertising from day one. The Liberals' agency, Masius, proposed the slogan 'Turn on the Lights'. It was an allusion to the 'dark' days of Labor. Fraser was dubious about the slogan at first but accepted the advice of Eggleton and others who wanted to distance the Liberal campaign as much as possible from the events of Remembrance Day. Labor opted for 'Shame Fraser, Shame' with Whitlam arguing that 'a great wrong must be put right', and that 'parliamentary democracy as we know it must be saved'. Labor made the constitutional crisis the centrepiece of its pitch for re-election as Whitlam encouraged the public to 'maintain the rage' over Kerr's actions and Fraser's complicity.

During the first week of the campaign some of the state divisions expressed dissatisfaction with 'Turn on the Lights' and asked Eggleton to reconsider. But the Liberal slogan had developed a momentum of its own with the accompanying 'jingle' sung by popstar Renee Geyer. Cartoonists had a field day with the theme. Eggleton found the staff at Masius to be both skilful and imaginative. They approached the production of the television, radio and press material like a round-the-clock news agency. New material would be created whenever they saw opportunities to improve the impact of the messages. This flexibility proved highly effective as early polling showed the voters were more interested in the party that could govern the country efficiently than the circumstances of Whitlam's dismissal.

Eggleton had also allowed scope for flexibility within the campaign strategy. This proved to be prudent when Fraser developed a minor ailment that forced him to spend a couple of days in bed on the eve of the official launch. This was not the disaster that it might have been. It generated some timely human interest coverage with the newspapers carrying sympathetic pictures of Fraser in pyjamas being cared for by wife Tamie. The Liberal leader was soon back on his feet. Fraser performed strongly throughout the campaign. Leadership, integrity and the economy were the dominant issues. Successive polls suggested that the Government was heading for a landslide defeat. The people might have differed on whether the Governor-General had acted correctly; they were less divided on whether they wanted another three years of Labor rule. Eggleton was confident the Coalition would win but refused to speculate on the likely extent of its majority and maintained a full schedule of campaign events until polling day. There was no room for complacency and nothing would be left to chance.

On 13 December 1975, Malcolm Fraser achieved the largest Parliamentary majority in Australian electoral history. Labor suffered a 7.4 per cent two-party preferred swing and the loss of 30 seats. The Liberals could have ruled without the National Country Party but the Coalition was preserved. All of the electoral gains that Labor had made since Holt's landslide victory against Arthur Calwell in 1966 were wiped out. The new Opposition had just 36 members in the House of Representatives. Fraser had led the Coalition to a very substantial victory. The caretaker prime minister was now the elected prime minister.

On election night at the Southern Cross Hotel in Melbourne, Eggleton was showered with praise from ecstatic Liberals. The party presented him with a handsome new desk as well as sending him and Mary on an overseas holiday. The new Federal Director struggled to absorb the rapid turn of events that had enveloped him. It was less than two years since he had agreed to become a servant of the Liberal Party. They were back in government and he was firmly ensconced as the head of the Party's organisational wing. There had been no better time for him to become Federal Director. Indeed, it would never get any better.

Endnotes

1   Max Walsh, 'Top Liberal Party post open: fund-raising frictions', AFR, 31 July 1968.

2   Golding to Eggleton, personal letter, 11 February 1974.

3   Smith to Eggleton, personal letter, 10 December 1973.

4   Arnold Smith, *Stitches in Time*, p. 289.

5   *Post-Courier* (Port Moresby), 25 February 1974, p. 6.

6   Max Walsh, AFR, 10 August 1973.

7   *Canberra Times*, 19 April 1974, p. 3.

8   Billy Mackie Snedden and M Bernie Schedvin, *Billy Snedden: An Unlikely Liberal*, Macmillan, Melbourne, 1990, p. 151.

9   Column 8, SMH, 25 March 1975.

10   Mungo MacCallum, 'The Resurrection', *Nation Review*, 28 March-3 April 1975, p. 629.

11   https://www.afr.com/politics/afr10featuresgraphic--20151110-gkvd2c

12   http://gallery.its.unimelb.edu.au/umblumaic/imu.php?request=multimedia& irn=11885.

13   John Howard, *Lazarus Rising: A Personal and Political Autobiography*, Harper Collins, Sydney, 2010, p. 87.

14   Quoted in Philip Ayers, *Malcolm Fraser: A Biography*, Mandarin, Melbourne, 1989, p. 296.

CHAPTER 10

A force of nature   1976–83

A ustralia's twenty-second prime minister was a force of nature, not unlike the man he succeeded – Gough Whitlam. Malcolm Fraser was a big man in every respect. He was physically imposing at 193 centimetres in height and mentally tough. Much of the contemporary commentary and subsequent analysis of his leadership style, including his dealings with the Liberal Party's Federal Director, Tony Eggleton, focussed on the small group of individuals from whom he often took regular advice rather than on the much wider range of people he consulted on an occasional basis.

The political journalist Michelle Grattan credits Fraser with building 'an impressive power structure' that served to magnify his influence and extend his control.

> He was dominant in Cabinet, the Parliament and the Liberal Party in a fashion that demanded parallels with Menzies. He relied upon his own department, headed by Alan Carmody and then Geoffrey Yeend, for 'across the board' advice; upon his strong private office under David Kemp [for the first half of 1981]; and he spoke daily with Liberal director, Tony Eggleton, his political touchstone. Fraser refined the technique of prime ministerial government.[1]

Brian Buckley, who was very close to the deputy Liberal leader, Phillip Lynch, claimed the locus of power was much smaller and narrower. He asserted that 'the government at one time was run by a triumvirate consisting of Fraser, the head of the prime minister's department, Sir Alan Carmody, and Tony Eggleton, who worked in harmony with a cabal of rural interventionists who dominated the ministry.[2] A similar view was offered by Charles Richardson, a ministerial adviser to the Kennett Liberal Government in Victoria during the 1980s. He noted that centralism was a

> ruling principle within the government; decision-making was heavily concentrated in the Prime Minister's office and a small number of senior ministers. In what has become a pattern under Coalition governments, ministerial staff were cut back and the role of the public service (although not its independence) was strengthened .... Central control was also extended to the Liberal Party federal secretariat, where Tony Eggleton was a loyal agent of Fraser.[3]

The accounts offered by Buckley and Richardson are intended to be critical but overlook the reality of the Fraser years. Only a handful of commentators noted that Fraser actually had a large number of advisers. Consistent with his earlier approach to ministerial deliberation, Fraser consulted widely and on matters spanning the entire scope of public administration before making up his mind and taking a decision. In addition to holding very frequent Cabinet meetings (often at short notice), Fraser consulted an eclectic group of political 'outsiders' from industry, commerce and the universities, such as Sir James Balderstone, a prominent public company director, and Professor John Rose, an economist at the University of Melbourne, who could be trusted to keep their counsel confidential. He also spoke regularly with Keith Sinclair, a former editor of the *Age* newspaper and one-time speechwriter to Harold Holt. Fraser knew from two decades in federal parliament that the possession of good ideas and the provision of sound advice were not restricted to his party room colleagues, the public service, his private office or the organisational wing of the Liberal Party.

Within the Federal Secretariat, Eggleton was a loyal agent of the Liberal Party and its leader rather than Fraser's vassal or his office's emissary. The Federal Director did not seek or expect to find himself at the epicentre of Fraser's decision-making processes. He wanted to know sufficient about what the leader was thinking and planning to ensure the Party organisation generated the political support he needed to succeed and warned of public opposition that might imperil the Party's hold on power. From the outset, Fraser esteemed Eggleton's judgement and trusted his discretion. The Federal Director seemed to be without personal or professional agendas that might distort the advice he was giving or the priorities his staff would pursue. There was never any hint that Eggleton had his eye on entering parliament or securing public office at home or a diplomatic post abroad. Nor was he among the 'faceless men' who wielded patronage behind closed doors or a puppeteer who quietly but assiduously settled scores or pulled strings.

When Fraser sought external assistance with several staff reorganisations, Eggleton's contribution was usually restricted to recruitment processes or suggesting suitable individuals with the right aptitude, ability and temperament. As a former press secretary, Eggleton was used to smoothing the sometimes fractious relationship between Fraser, his senior press officer, David Barnett, and the head of the Government Information Unit, Vincent Matthews. Michelle Grattan reported that Barnett's departure was 'not prompted by any particular difference. Rather he is tired and somewhat disillusioned, after what is an eternity in an incredibly high-pressure job working for a man who would not win any prize as boss of the year'.[4]

Eggleton assiduously preserved harmonious working relationships between the parliamentary and organisational wings of the Liberal Party. He worked well with every public servant in the prime minister's office, drawing on his knowledge of the challenges and complexities he experienced from 1965 to 1971. He also formed effective partnerships with Fraser's principal policy advisers and speechwriters, including two men with very different outlooks – David Kemp (later Liberal member for Goldstein, 1990–2004) and Petro Georgiou (later Liberal member for Kooyong, 1994–2010). The most sensitive relationship he was asked to massage involved Alan Jones – future coach of Australia's national rugby union team and prominent broadcaster – who was hired as a speechwriter 'mainly because of his reputation as a wordsmith, a reputation enhanced by his own political speeches'.[5]

Jones had been an unsuccessful Liberal candidate for New South Wales State Parliament before joining Fraser's office in 1979. Within months of his arrival, Fraser was dissatisfied with Jones' contribution and asked Eggleton to speak with him. Jones revealed his disenchantment with Fraser's office and felt the Prime Minister lacked confidence in his work. He gave Eggleton a list of concerns about how Fraser's office was managed which partly explained why he was not more effective. In reply, Eggleton counselled Jones to refrain from being openly critical of members of the Liberal Parliamentary Party and professional staff as these comments may have been seen 'as an extension of the Prime Minister's own opinions'. The conversation ended with Eggleton recording that Jones was 'seriously considering his future … and mentioned the possibility of putting his hat in the ring once more for pre-selections.'[6] Over lunch at the end of 1980, Jones told Eggleton that he was considering alternative opportunities and was exploring a chief executive's position with an industry organisation in Sydney. Although he resisted 'any impression or perception that he is being eased out …. he has accepted the fact that it would be better if he moved on'. He left Fraser's office in early 1981.

Fraser looked to the Federal Director as his day-to-day link with the organisational wing of the Party. A dedicated telephone line was installed between his desk and Eggleton's office. They were in regular contact and had developed a positive rapport while in Opposition. At Fraser's request, all of Eggleton's written communications were on distinctive blue paper and given priority. Eggleton served on parliamentary strategy committees and took part in the pre-Question Time briefings at Parliament House. Fraser expected him to anticipate and identify politically sensitive issues. When Fraser went into the debating chamber for Question Time, Eggleton remained behind in the prime minister's office to listen to proceedings. Afterwards, they would review the outcomes and compare notes, usually over a cup of tea.

It was clear to everyone who dealt with Fraser that he made no secret of wanting Eggleton's opinions and often accepting his counsel. Eggleton was neither a king maker nor a deal broker. He was a servant of the Liberal Party and, foremost, its elected leader who happened to be Malcolm Fraser after March 1975. Eggleton did not seek the political limelight nor avoid taking responsibility for his actions. Although he was in one sense a functionary, he brought ideas and insights that Fraser and his government might not have considered in the development or delivery of public policy. He also tried to see, and to have others see, the best in people even as he appealed to his colleagues' sense of the greater good. In a world of personal intrigue and private vendettas, Eggleton stood apart in representing values and virtues that were often overlooked or ignored. He did not see people as being expendable resources whose emotions played no part in how they performed nor in how they deserved to be treated. It was for these reasons that Eggleton's counsel was sought by minor and major political figures on matters ranging from the wellbeing of their families to their future ministerial prospects. It was partly Eggleton's urging that had persuaded Fraser to remain in parliament after the turmoil of Gorton's demise in 1971.

Eggleton was not without his critics in either the parliamentary or organisational wings of the Party although few were prepared to be named. This was in part because the extent of his remit was not always clear and there were different views on when he might have overstepped its limits. There would always be considerable difficulty separating questions of administrative efficiency from issues of public policy and matters of political expediency. Was Eggleton an institutional bureaucrat or a party activist? Solutions to the kind of problems that crossed his desk involved personal opinions and philosophical positions, however lightly held his opinions and positions might have been. Eggleton was not without an agenda of his own that transcended matters of professional efficiency and organisational effectiveness. He could not avoid having his own thoughts about the decisions that he was (or would be) obliged to implement but they were (and remain) difficult to detect. There were certainly times when the medium was the message and instances when explaining how a government deliberated on a matter was more important than the outcome of its decision-making.

Eggelton's political outlook appeared to be that of a centrist, representing the Liberal mainstream and reflecting the nation's aspirational middle class. Because he could see divergent points of view, he considered himself temperamentally unsuited to parliamentary life, lacking the commitment and passion needed to pursue issues in the face of opposition.

> I don't go around pushing barrows or having bright ideas about personal policy that I'd like to see achieved and go dashing around doing those sorts of things. I give advice when it's sought and when it's appropriate that I should do so in the context of the job that I do.

When asked by journalist Michelle Grattan about the stresses and satisfactions of his work, Eggleton explained:

> This was always a job I wanted. I remember when I was a press secretary, I often thought I wouldn't mind going on to be Federal Director. Because of the fact that I'm interested in politics, but not particularly keen to be a member of parliament, the job that seemed to most be me was Federal Director.[7]

Eggleton knew that Fraser looked to him for 'party political input, for political reactions' and was grateful that the prime minister was 'very proper' about maintaining boundaries:

> he never involves me with departments or in putting forward advice that
> should come from the bureaucracy. He uses me as a party political person to
> give another line of advice and another viewpoint where he thinks it's relevant.
> But it's never in a way where it's the principal or the dominating line of advice.

Fraser never felt bound to accept Eggleton's advice, or anyone's advice for that matter, even when the advice was offered strenuously and with conviction. When Fraser decided to establish a royal commission to examine allegations made by the Liberal backbencher, Don Cameron, that the Finance Minister, Eric Robinson, had been complicit in electoral boundary-rigging in Queensland, Eggleton was equivocal. Warren Beeby of the *Weekend Australian* mistakenly claimed that Eggleton encouraged the inquiry and was damned by some Party members for doing so. Throughout the avoidable controversy, Eggleton remained in close contact with Robinson and conducted several candid conversations about public reactions to the inquiry and whether he had become a political liability for the Fraser Government. Eggleton thought the inquiry was unnecessary and unwise but made two of his staff available to review the evidence and study the transcript. Eggleton also thought Fraser erred in dismissing Senator Reg Withers from the ministry after the royal commissioner was critical of his involvement in preserving the name Macpherson for an electoral division in Queensland – in line with the Australian Electoral Commission's own guidelines. Eggleton did not believe that Withers had acted wrongly or deserve to be sacked. He feared a disgruntled Withers would encourage unrest among backbenchers (which he did). The judgement of history has vindicated Eggleton with most commentators believing the senator was sacrificed to justify the holding of an inquiry that ultimately found no evidence of unlawful conduct.

In assessing Eggleton's relationship with Fraser and the Cabinet, many observers confused power with influence. Eggleton had little of the former but a great deal of the latter. A *Sydney Morning Herald* profile headed 'Eggleton, the never missing link', illustrated this confusion. After claiming he had considerable power, the profile actually described the basis of his influence which was in being 'the two-way bridge, between top party officials and the prime minister. When the party wants to know what the prime minister is thinking it asks Mr Eggleton; when the prime minister wants to know what the party is thinking he asks Mr Eggleton'.[8] The journalist clearly mistook authority for agency. More astute commentators observed that Eggleton might have had too much influence as an unelected party official.

Laurie Oakes reported that 'there are many who believe Mr Eggleton is far closer to the prime minister than is healthy. This makes it difficult, according to the critics, for Mr Eggleton to provide the sort of detached political advice a person in his position should give. It would compromise him, they say, in any move for a leadership change because he is so totally identified as in the incumbent's camp'.[9] In a separate news story, Oakes suggested that the 'interests of the prime minister may not always coincide with the interests of the party'.[10] He repeated something he had heard from a disgruntled Liberal parliamentarian: 'he is not so much the Federal Director of the Liberal Party as Malcolm Fraser's chief press secretary'. Oakes offered some advice: 'Mr Eggleton might be wise to put just a little distance between himself and the prime minister, though this may be easier said than done in view of Mr Fraser's reliance upon him'. This was advice that others repeated when Eggleton's assistant, Darcy Tronson, was appointed Fraser's principal private secretary in November 1978, replacing Dale Budd who was departing for the private sector. Budd was credited with creating an 'island of tranquility' in Fraser's office that his successors were unable to replicate.

Citing unnamed parliamentary sources, gallery journalist Neil O'Reilly reported: 'they say Eggleton's job is to tell Fraser what the party machine is thinking. But they say Eggleton tells the party machine what Fraser is thinking, and why the machine should come into line'.[11] O'Reilly concluded his article on 'The men who help the PM make up his mind' with the observation: 'the unflappable Eggleton never seems to be fussed by these criticisms'. Most importantly, as the Federal Director retained Fraser's trust and confidence there was no chance anyone would move against Eggleton. Andrew Clark was probably closest to the mark when he noted that Eggleton 'projects an image of sympathy for all, and people like talking to him'.[12]

Unlike Holt and Gorton, Fraser was prime minister for every minute of every day. His staff were expected to take phone calls at any hour, especially when Fraser was travelling overseas and felt out of touch. The Prime Minister appeared to assume the time in Canberra was the same as wherever he happened to be in the world. When Eggleton chided him about time zone differences late at night and the need to be 'reasonable' in requiring that certain things be done, the Prime Minister's response was inevitably the same: 'Well, it's a reasonable time of day here'. Fraser would sometimes go to inordinate lengths to contact his staff and was usually indifferent to the inconvenience he might cause. On one occasion Eggleton was driving to Sydney in his distinctive blue Rover when he was pulled over by a police highway patrol car. Convinced he had not committed any traffic offence, the officer informed Eggleton that the Prime Minister was on the phone at the nearby police station and he would provide an escort.

Even in practical matters, Fraser's determination to have his way would not concede hurdles or obstacles although they could have humbling consequences. On returning to the Savoy Hotel in London where he was staying with Eggleton during a Commonwealth meeting in London, the foyer was packed and the lifts were crowded. Fraser charged off through the ballroom with Eggleton behind him, convinced he knew another way of getting to their rooms. Undeterred by a hotel staffer who insisted 'you can't go that way, sir', Fraser opened an unmarked door and strode confidently into the room, accompanied by the sound of crashing mops and buckets. His shortcut was, in fact, a hotel broom cupboard. Without conceding error, Eggleton noticed the hint of a smile on Fraser's face. The Prime Minister was not without the ability to recognise that his impatience could land him in difficulty.

In other circumstances, Fraser could be blunt to the point of rudeness. Eggleton remembers being part of a meeting with a group of businessmen in the Prime Minister's suite at Parliament House. The atmosphere had become tense and the conversation terse, and Fraser was not in the best of moods. When Eggleton told Fraser he had been unnecessarily aggressive towards his visitors, the Prime Minister seemed surprised, even shocked. It was not that Eggleton had dared to criticise his behaviour but the conduct he had deigned to chide. Fraser replied: 'Rubbish Tony, I speak to Tamie like that all the time'. In Eggleton's view, Tamara Margaret Fraser (nee Beggs) possessed many more social graces than her husband and provided the charm needed to soften some of his hardness. She was an indispensable foil to her husband. Eggelton realised that the Prime Minister was often reserved in his dealings with other people and was far from his best in large social gatherings. He was inclined to remain in the company of someone with whom he was comfortable while Tamie worked the room with graceful ease and ready conversation.

Eggleton was well acquainted with Fraser's personal preferences. 'Advancing' was the name given to preparations for the Prime Minister's engagements. Fraser wanted to be assured, and then reassured, that everything had been thoroughly checked before his arrival at a public function. There had to be an appropriate lectern, adjusted to the right height, while the microphone and dual 'fail-safe' public address system had to be tested. In case of emergencies, there needed to be a designated office or room for urgent phone calls. He never wanted to be in a position where he could not communicate with others or be contacted by his staff. Fraser was often impatient and always exacting, driving himself and everyone around him for reasons that were not always apparent. He expected his staff to respond quickly and energetically irrespective of how urgent they believed the task happened to be. Those who avoided hard work or had a propensity to make mistakes (particularly if they tried to cover them up) would not last long in his service. Fraser recognised that he often raised the temperature in difficult discussions, and appreciated having people around him who could exert a calming influence. Eggleton was one of these people.

For Eggleton, serving the Fraser Government was both demanding and rewarding. He received opportunities and responsibilities that were rarely, if ever, available to any other party official – Labor or Liberal. He was, in some respects, a member of the extended Fraser family. Occasionally, Eggleton would meet Fraser at the Lodge for an early morning chat, then they would walk over the hill to Parliament House. There were also plenty of crises to manage. Eggleton was a close confidant to a succession of Party presidents during the Fraser years – Sir Robert Southey (1970–75), Sir John Atwill (1975–82) and Dr Jim Forbes (1982–85). Fraser acknowledged and respected the part played by the Party organisation in sustaining the Parliamentary Party. Fraser wanted an active and dependable party machine, with a Secretariat that remained strong and relevant even while the party was in government. He also required that the Secretariat be ready to deal with opposition when political fortunes turned full circle. Fraser attended the Liberal Party state conferences and rarely missed a meeting of the Party's Federal Executive. With Fraser's encouragement, new organisational committees were established to assist policy development. Party members appreciated increasing opportunities to register their opinions and access to the Prime Minister's thinking.

Within the Secretariat, Eggleton insisted that paid staff (he also managed volunteers) should be objective, dependable and responsive. They were to provide skilled and professional assistance whenever required but were not to engage in personality politics or political gamesmanship. This was the foundation upon which Eggleton intended to build the Secretariat's reputation and to preserve his independence as Federal Director. The Secretariat would serve the Party's interests at all levels and in every aspect of its corporate life, including its renewal.

In 1976 the Federal Executive established a Philosophy Sub-Committee to address the political philosophy that undergirded the party's policy platform. In some respects this Committee continued the work Billy Snedden had initiated as Party leader in 1973. The two most influential contributors were Sir Robert Southey and Chris Puplick. In a published compendium of perspectives on classical liberalism and its contemporary interpretation, they contended that

> the largely empirical nature of Liberal thinking, and the fact that hitherto the Liberal Party of Australia has not found occasion to set out its beliefs at length and support them with argument, have led to assumptions that it has no firm philosophy; that its guiding motives are merely pragmatic, opportunistic, reactive, even mercenary, its Platform and policies reflecting the expediency of the moment.[13]

The Secretariat provided Ian Marsh, Martin Rawlinson and Nicholas Wright to assist its activities.

This was not work for which Eggleton believed himself well-suited. He was not a student of political philosophy or theories of government, and never pretended to be. Eggleton would give practical expression to the Party's ideology while giving the Secretariat a sense of its own identity. Having achieved some success with the Commonwealth Secretariat logo, Eggleton decided to devise a new logo for the Party. He told the *Age* that it was 'in response to requirements of the day and age' rather than an attempt to copy American political parties.[14] His first attempt was a stylised 'L' incorporating the Australian flag. Tony Ferguson, Labor's communications director, referred to the logo as 'Tony Eggleton's coat of arms' and dismissed the Liberal's corporate branding as 'nonsense'. The logo was accepted by the Party and the press without objection, and continues in use.

Although Eggleton was employed to manage the Liberal Party's domestic affairs, Fraser invited Eggleton to serve as a special advisor on Commonwealth issues. A New Zealand journalist, John Monks, judged Fraser to be the foremost advocate of Commonwealth affairs during the 1970s and remarked that he and Eggleton had views on 'South Africa, Namibia, Zimbabwe and apartheid [that] coincide exactly'. Monk credited Eggleton with being 'the constant driving force behind Malcolm Fraser's determined bid to become a noted Commonwealth – if not world – statesman'.[15] Eggleton was able to use his extensive Commonwealth contacts to prepare the ground for Australian initiatives and for Fraser's distinctive involvement. Prior to his first Commonwealth Heads of Government meeting (CHOGM) in London in June 1977, linked to the Queen's Silver Jubilee celebrations, Fraser sent Eggleton ahead to hold preliminary talks with diplomatic representatives and the media. The Commonwealth Secretariat welcomed the Australian momentum, as did key Commonwealth institutions and figures.

The *Australian* referred to the early despatch of Eggleton as a 'political master stroke' because 'no-one else in Australia has Mr Eggleton's close Commonwealth contacts or insight into the way its officials and leaders act and think at these meetings'. He would facilitate 'coffee break diplomacy' during the meeting, allowing Fraser to deal with delicate issues that would otherwise have been too complicated to negotiate during plenary sessions. The newspaper reported that Eggleton was crucial to fostering the close and enduring friendship that would develop between the Commonwealth Secretary General, Shridath Ramphal, and the Australian Prime Minister. To avoid any domestic political fallout, the Federal Secretariat rather than the Department of Foreign Affairs covered Eggleton's travel expenses.

Fraser saw the Commonwealth as a valuable means of focussing ideas and initiatives as well as a body in which Australia could exercise global influence. It did not take long for Fraser to make an impact. He won the support and respect of most Commonwealth prime ministers, particularly those from developing nations. His elevated standing was visibly apparent on the ornate staircase in Lancaster House in London during the 1977 meeting. Fraser had made an early speech of relevance to developing nations and, as he descended the stairs, was surrounded by an enthusiastic group of African and Caribbean leaders. A beaming Michael Manley from Jamaica had his arm around Fraser's shoulder. It was evident Australia was well placed to make a contribution. Fraser recognised that smaller nations were often eclipsed more prosperous ones, and worked to make CHOGM more inclusive. This led to his initiative for regional meetings, at which smaller countries would have a louder voice. The first of these meetings, held at Sydney's Hilton Hotel during February 1978, was the target of Australia's first and only domestic terrorist attack.

Fraser also took a prominent role in responding to contemporary Commonwealth problems, including apartheid in South Africa and the resolution of the 'Rhodesian impasse'. The latter involved a complicated dispute. The leaders of the former British colony of Southern Rhodesia announced a Unilateral Declaration of Independence (UDI) in 1965 after refusing to accede to the British Government's direction that black majority rule precede independence from Britain. Rhodesia gradually severed all remaining ties with the United Kingdom and became a republic in 1970. The Australian Government had never accepted Rhodesia's independence and considered it a rogue state. The Australian Trade Commission in the Rhodesian capital, Salisbury, was closed and diplomatic messages from the Rhodesian Government were ignored.

Refusing to permit black majority rule, Rhodesia was subjected to economic and diplomatic sanctions while a number of nationalist movements participated in a guerrilla struggle against the regime in Salisbury led by Ian Smith. By the late 1970s, the end of white minority rule seemed inevitable but tensions between rival nationalist parties threatened to descend into civil war. The relationship between the new Zimbabwean Government and the British Government, and the fate of the 250,000 members of the white minority after the introduction of majority rule, were areas of acute disagreement. Fraser believed the Rhodesian regime was racist and immoral. He wanted to see the full participation of 'all groups of Rhodesians' in the future of their country. Fraser also tried to have the Rhodesian Information Centre in Sydney, which was acting as a de facto consulate, closed but backed down when he discovered that a third to a half of his Liberal parliamentary colleagues opposed such action and a significant number of Australians were fighting with the Rhodesian security forces. Fraser's position was considered too progressive and troubled the more conservative members of the Coalition who felt Rhodesia was better remaining a non-Communist ally than a potentially Marxist adversary. Fraser thought otherwise, believing that minority rule was more likely to provoke Cuban or Soviet intervention. Fraser nonetheless refused to be diverted from his beliefs which Eggleton shared without qualification. Minority rule had to end.

Working alongside the Prime Minister and having a larger public profile than the four Australian public service chiefs who were part of the official Australian delegation, Eggleton drew on his existing Commonwealth links to advance Fraser's agenda. The Secretariat in London asked him to undertake special projects, such as a review of non-governmental organisations across the Commonwealth. With Fraser's encouragement, he accepted an invitation for a comprehensive tour of Canada and meetings with national and provincial leaders. Fraser hosted a full-scale CHOGM in Melbourne in 1981 and asked Eggleton to play a central role in the meeting. Eggleton accepted a government consultancy while continuing to juggle his Liberal Party duties. Eggleton had access to all sessions and took responsibility for the twice-daily media briefings. In the planning stages, he was also given the job of personally assessing – and testing – the accommodation to be assigned to visiting dignitaries, including the suites in new hotels.

Having assumed an important role in Commonwealth affairs and recognising the continuing centrality of Britain to its activities, Eggleton suggested to Fraser that he invite the newly elected leader of the British Conservative Party, Margaret Thatcher, to address the Liberal Party's Federal Council meeting in September 1976. Fraser had no objection to the invitation but thought Eggleton was being unduly optimistic about Thatcher ever becoming prime minister. Eggleton was closely involved with Thatcher and her staff during the visit. Watching her in action, particularly her personal style and deft handling of the media, left Eggleton in little doubt she would one day occupy No. 10 Downing Street – the British prime minister's London residence. Thatcher used her Canberra speech to launch a significant political initiative. She reflected on the operations of the Socialist International (which was formed by like-minded left wing parties in 1951) and called for centre and centre-right parties to establish their own international association. In subsequent private talks, she spoke of setting up a European Democrat Union and encouraged Eggleton to take the lead in forming a Pacific Democrat Union. With these regional bodies in place, there could then be a world-wide umbrella association: the International Democrat Union. Eggleton agreed to talk to the Prime Minister and the Liberal Party about the proposal.

Thatcher and her staff were impressed with the Liberals' electoral success and were delighted with coverage of her Australian program. There had been positive reporting in the British media as well. Thatcher's advisers asked Eggleton whether he would be willing to manage the Conservative Party. He thanked them for their confidence in his abilities but was adamant that he wanted to remain in Australia for his family's sake. After returning to London, Thatcher invited Eggleton to make campaign presentations to her Party's senior people. She was particularly taken with how the Liberals had employed television advertising which she felt was much more effective than the Conservative's own bland approach. He went to London with a tape of their productions, giving campaign briefings to staff and parliamentarians. Some of those with whom he spoke were destined to be ministers in the future Thatcher government.

On the eve of the British general election in May 1979, Fraser received a phone call from Peter Carrington, the Conservatives' leader in the House of Lords. He wanted to visit Australia to discuss election planning. Fraser pledged to do all he could. Carrington spoke with the Prime Minister and several members of Cabinet, and spent time at the Federal Secretariat. Thatcher and Carrington then flagged the possibility of Eggleton being in London for the election. This was agreed. Eggleton became a member of the Conservative Party's campaign team, headed by Party Chairman, Lord Peter Thorneycroft. Thatcher asked Eggleton to be present when she recorded her television messages. This was the same day he arrived in London somewhat jet-lagged. Although attending a number of campaign events with Thatcher, it was deemed prudent for Eggleton to keep a low profile. He was in touch with her throughout the election and contributed to the twice-daily strategic planning meetings with Thorneycroft. A feature story on his role in the British campaign and his guidance on effective exploitation of the media by political parties was published in the *Australian Women's Weekly*.[16] The author was a young journalist who was still making his name: Malcolm Turnbull.

On election night (3 May), Eggleton was monitoring and assessing ballot results with senior members of Thatcher's staff. She was given a rousing reception on arrival in her electorate. She invited Eggleton to her office as the counting of votes continued. Although Thatcher was not completely confident she had won, Eggleton assured her that she had before passing her the telephone. Fraser was on the line from Canberra. Eggleton had arranged for him to be the first person to congratulate Thatcher on her victory. Although the two leaders were on good terms personally, Fraser was worried about Thatcher's attitude to southern African issues, especially the legal and diplomatic standing of Rhodesia. Fraser asked Eggleton to ring Carrington the morning after the election to propose that senior Australian officials travel urgently to London to present Australian thinking about these matters. Fraser thought they should build on the strength of personal relationships cemented by the successful election. Carrington consulted Thatcher and was told the Australians, including Eggleton, would be most welcome. In a spirit of mutual friendship and political solidarity, Thatcher made an official visit to Canberra within weeks of becoming Britain's Prime Minister.

In addition to brief family reunions, Eggleton used his frequent trips to the United Kingdom to console the former Governor-General, Sir John Kerr, who was then living in London. Their association began while Kerr, a friend of the Liberal Federal President, Sir John Atwill, was still at Yarralumla and Eggleton was at the Federal Secretariat. With Atwill's encouragement, Kerr would ring Eggleton's office and suggest he come over to the official residence for a chat. They had afternoon tea in the study where Kerr had changed the course of Australian politics. With deep-seated and smouldering resentment over the dismissal of Gough Whitlam, Kerr stood down from vice-regal duties at the end of 1977 and went to live in self-imposed 'exile' in London.

During one of his visits to the former Viceroy, Kerr offered Eggleton afternoon tea at his recently acquired office in Pall Mall. Somewhat to Eggleton's embarrassment, the former Governor-General slipped out to a little kitchen where he boiled the kettle and made the tea. Kerr was very much alone. On another visit Kerr handed Eggleton a draft manuscript for his autobiography and asked for an opinion. Over lunch at the historic Stone's Chop House, Eggleton remarked that it offered a reasonable and rational exposition of the drama of 1975. He added that constitutional experts would no doubt still find plenty to debate and dispute. Eggleton's judgement was correct. Kerr remained a divisive figure long after the publication of *Matters for Judgement* in 1978.

Eggleton began to sense that the warm relationship between Fraser and Thatcher would be tested by disagreements over foreign policy at the CHOGM held in Lusaka, the capital of Zambia, in August 1979. Fraser made an official visit to Nigeria on his way to Zambia. As he wanted some preliminary work done before the Lusaka meeting, Fraser asked Eggleton to accompany Andrew Peacock, the Minister for Foreign Affairs, on his advance mission. They were the only passengers on the trans-Africa flight with Peacock making the most of the empty RAAF aircraft to engage in his physical fitness routine. On arrival in Zambia, the two men worked closely, holding constructive ministerial-level talks on the future of Rhodesia. The Australian Financial Review thought the decision to send Eggleton ahead of the official party 'was an expensive luxury' on Fraser's part, implying that 'his presence in Lusaka was more important than his position in Australia'.[17] The newspaper observed it was 'somewhat unorthodox to use a party official for such a role' but acknowledged nonetheless that as a former member of the Commonwealth Secretariat, Eggleton was 'probably better informed than most about the personalities and backgrounds of the various leaders at Lusaka.'

The conference was personally important to Fraser who had been at the forefront of Rhodesia's transition to majority rule and international recognition. The sensitive negotiations were made more difficult by Thatcher's tendency to be awkward and unpredictable on some issues. CHOGM eventually agreed on a positive way forward with the Commonwealth Zimbabwe-Rhodesia Peace Plan. The British would resume responsibility for Rhodesia, negotiate with all parties to produce a draft constitution which would be put to the people, before the holding of elections that would be supervised by officials from London. The situation in Rhodesia was desperate and a resolution was needed. Around 500 blacks were being killed every week in the long-running 'bush war' and more than 1000 whites were fleeing the country every month. The Commonwealth solution was far from perfect. Thatcher had limited the concessions she was prepared to make given the depth of domestic sympathy in Britain and the strong kindred ties that still linked the United Kingdom and Rhodesia. Difficulties then arose.

There was a large Australian media contingent in Lusaka with fast approaching editorial deadlines. If the journalists were forced to wait until official announcements the next day, the time zone difference meant they would be left without a story for their editors. The plan would be old news when their reports eventually appeared in print. Fraser and Eggleton decided to brief them prior to the official announcement.[18] A couple of British journalists infiltrated the briefing and immediately sought confirmation of the proposed peace plan from Thatcher's press secretary. Thatcher was furious, believing the Australians had deliberately sought to lock her into the plan before she had consulted with sceptics and critics in London. She assumed Fraser and his accomplice, Eggleton, were trying to present her with a *fait accompli*. The first inkling of approaching trouble was when the Commonwealth Secretary-General sought out Fraser and Eggleton at the prime ministerial village. Ramphal was concerned that Thatcher might renege on the understandings that had already been negotiated. Eggleton then received a call from the British High Commission in Zambia informing him that a car was on its way to convey him to the British residence where he was to meet with the British Foreign Secretary, Lord Carrington.

Eggleton was greeted by a dismayed and perplexed Carrington who said 'The Lady' was convinced the Australians had 'set her up'. Eggleton explained the reason for the impromptu briefing of the Australian media. The British Prime Minister was unimpressed and unpersuaded. The needs of Australian journalists were unimportant given the gravity of what was at stake. There were rumours that Thatcher would boycott a reception that evening for visiting prime ministers that was to be hosted by the Australian High Commissioner. She eventually appeared with her husband Denis although both did little to hide their anger. Denis spoke harshly with Eggleton making clear his belief that Eggleton was either dumb or duplicitous in speaking with untrustworthy journalists in advance of final decisions. During the reception, the heads of government adjourned informally to an adjoining room to endorse the communiqué that had already been released by the Australians. To add insult to Thatcher's injury, most of the Commonwealth leaders were elated by the turn of events. They had feared she might change her mind at the last minute and welcomed what they considered Fraser's 'master stroke'.

As Fraser and Eggleton walked into the conference centre the following morning, many of the African, Asian and Caribbean leaders were lining the walkway to the meeting room when they greeted Fraser with a long, spontaneous round of applause. Unsurprisingly, Fraser's relations with Thatcher were permanently tarnished. The decision to brief the Australian media was sincere but mistaken. Thatcher accepted Eggleton's explanation but remained unconvinced of Fraser's motives. Putting aside this incident, Thatcher was always appreciative of Eggleton's efforts to advance her concept of a worldwide organisation for centre and centre-right parties. Thatcher and Eggleton had many productive meetings as the International Democrat Union (IDU) evolved and grew in standing. Australia led in the formation of the Pacific Democrat Union (PDU), later renamed the Asia Pacific Democrat Union (APDU). The PDU was launched in Tokyo in June 1982, with Sir Phillip Lynch, the Deputy Leader of the Liberal Party, representing the Australian Government. Eggleton also helped with the evolution of the European Union and, subsequently, the establishment of the IDU which was inaugurated in London in June 1983. Thatcher and the Vice President of the United States, George H W Bush, were the keynote speakers at its first conference.

During a visit to Washington, Eggleton was asked to visit the White House to speak with Republican Party politicians and staffers about supporting IDU initiatives. He presented a series of ideas and initiatives to James Baker, the White House Chief of Staff to President Ronald Reagan. Baker was wary of suggestions that Republicans should be associated with a 'democrat' organisation. Enlightened Republicans were nonetheless able to look beyond the organisation's title and saw the value of like-minded parties cooperating more closely. In time many centre and centre-right parties around the world sought to participate in its deliberations and programs. An increasing number of regional organisations flourished under the IDU banner. Eggleton was involved with these organisations for many years, first as Executive Secretary of the PDU, then as Chairman of the APDU from 1998 to 2005. He was also a member of the IDU Executive with responsibilities that took him around the world.

Less politically problematic for the Americans was an idea from the Australian Consul-General in New York, Sir Robert Cotton, who suggested the introduction of a program to facilitate exchange visits between people involved in politics. Eggleton took the idea to Fraser, who endorsed it, and they launched the Australian Political Exchange Program. It was initially for political up-and-comers in the United States and Australia but was later extended to many other countries. The successful scheme was available to all political parties, their parliamentarians and organisational staff. Eggleton served for an extended period on the Program's selection committee.

In addition to his Commonwealth contacts, Fraser relied upon Eggleton's media connections which included the owner of Consolidated Press Holdings, Kerry Packer. The links forged with Packer in the 1975 campaign were maintained while the Coalition was in office. Packer contacted Eggleton from time to time offering his opinions, especially around election time. Eggleton did not consider it a close relationship although he experienced firsthand Packer's well-known capacity for spontaneous kindness. In 1977, Eggleton fell ill after returning from an overseas trip and was confined to bed for three weeks. It was the only significant illness of his entire working life and was the subject of media reporting. A Channel 9 van arrived outside the Eggleton family home in Canberra. The political reporter Peter Harvey told Mary Eggleton he was delivering a gift on behalf of Kerry Packer. The crew installed a top-of-the-range home entertainment system with a message from Packer who hoped it might hasten Eggleton's recovery.

In August 1981 the Federal Secretariat building in Canberra was invaded by 60 young unemployed people, demanding a meeting with the Minister for

Employment and the Minister for Social Security. Eggleton was out of his office at the time. Fraser suggested to Eggleton that he call the police and have the protesters ejected. Instead, Eggleton returned to the Secretariat and tried to negotiate a peaceful settlement by telling protestors outside the building that he was best placed to arrange a meeting once he had a sense of their demands. He asked whether he might enter the building but the request was refused. Soon afterwards the police forced their way in, cleared the building and made 19 arrests. There was only minor damage and no-one was hurt.

Members of the Labor Opposition, including the Shadow Industrial Relations spokesman, Bob Hawke, were furious about the level of force used to remove the protesters. At the end of what was a tumultuous afternoon, the Secretariat staff assembled in the Menzies' Room for a drink to settle their nerves. There was a loud banging on the front door. When Eggleton went to investigate he was met by the imposing figure of Kerry Packer. He had heard about the Federal Secretariat 'siege' and wanted to make sure its staff were recovering from the drama. He then joined them for a drink. Packer headed into the Canberra night with a word of warning to Eggleton: he was planning his own 'takeover' if Fraser and the government failed to 'improve their act'. Packer was not alone in thinking the Fraser Government had seen better days. While Eggleton was not responsible for the performance of the Parliamentary wing of the Party, he had to sell the Party's policy program to the electorate. His ability to have the Australian people accept what the Liberal Party was offering was the chief marker of his success.

Endnotes

1   Paul Kelly, 'John Malcolm Fraser', in Michelle Grattan (ed), *Australian Prime Ministers*, New Holland, Sydney, 2000, p. 363.

2   Patrick O'Brien, *The Liberals: Factions, Feuds and Fancies*, Viking, Melbourne, 1985, p. 28.

3   Charles Richardson, 'The Fraser Years', in JR Nethercote, *Liberalism and the Australian Federation*, Federation Press, Sydney, 2001, p. 218.

4   Michelle Grattan, 'The man in the hot seat calls it a day', *Age*, 20 March 1982.

5   Michelle Grattan, 'Bureaucratic wordsmith takes top office job', *Age*, 3 November 1979.

6   Aide memoire, 'Alan Jones', 22 April 1980.

7   Michelle Grattan, 'Machine men – Tony Eggleton: top cog', *Age*, 25 April 1977.

8   Special Correspondent, 'Eggleton, the never missing link', SMH, 22 May 1981.

9   Laurie Oakes, 'Cleaners tarnish the image of Mr Clean', *Age*, 13 December 1979.

10 Laurie Oakes, 'On the right hand of Malcolm', *Laurie Oakes Report*, 30 August 1978.

11 Neil O'Reilly, 'The men who help make up the PM's mind', *Sun-Herald*, 18 October 1981.

12 Andrew Clark, 'The men behind Malcolm Fraser', *Playboy*, October 1979, pp. 142–48.

13 CJ Puplick and RJ Southey, *Liberal Thinking*, Macmillan, Melbourne, 1980, pp. viii-ix.

14 'Liberals go for the big 'L'', *Age*, 26 February 1980.

15 John Monks, 'Malcolm Fraser: Tory leader with a conscience', *Dominion* (New Zealand), 23 October 1981.

16 Malcolm Turnbull, 'The Australian guiding hand', *Australian Women's Weekly*, 23 May 1979, p. 5.

17 Editorial, 'Post-Lusaka blues', AFR, 10 August 1979.

18 MEK Neuhaus, 'A Useful CHOGM: Lusaka 1979', *Australian Outlook*, vol. 42, no. 3, December 1988, p-p. 161–66.

CHAPTER 11

Coalition campaigning 1975–83

The Liberal Party's Federal Secretariat fulfilled a number of functions but one far outweighed the others in importance: winning elections. Having secured office with an unprecedented victory in December 1975, Eggleton was under unreasonable pressure to replicate his initial success as Federal Director. Believing they had a winning formula, the Liberal Party planned and implemented subsequent campaigns with a similar national structure. There was a central campaign headquarters and Eggleton travelled with the prime minister as overall campaign director. They made increasing use of their specially commissioned opinion polling and refined their advertising techniques.

Although the Liberals had achieved a record majority in 1975, Eggleton presented Fraser with some 'fairly gloomy' polling figures in the third-quarter of 1977 as the government pondered holding an election later in the year, ostensibly to bring elections for the House of Representatives and the Senate back into alignment. The Federal Secretariat was well prepared but suggested that May 1978 might have been preferable because opinions of incumbent governments rarely improved during election campaigns. In a detailed table of arguments for and against holding an election in December 1977, Eggleton placed 'Credibility' at the head of the arguments against an election and noted that the 'government has a record majority and should honour its election pledge of three years of good economic management'. He thought there was no real 'justification for an early poll' and thought it would prompt 'charges of political expediency, desperation and panic'. Arguments for an early election were headed by the 'electoral climate being less predictable in 1978' because of 'uncertainty about the pace of economic growth'. On reflection, Fraser believed the mood in the electorate was more favourable and eventually opted for December.

Once the decision was made, and it was purely Fraser's to make, Eggleton and his team hastened efforts that had been underway since September when a campaign headquarters was rented in Melbourne. Writing in the *National Times*, Paul Kelly observed that Eggleton's 'great talent is as a political organiser covering every conceivable option. He tries to put into practice the axiom that the party should always be ready for a campaign'. Further, he doubted that 'any Australian prime minister has ever established such a close and formalised working relationship with the head of his party organisation as Malcolm Fraser has with Tony Eggleton'. Kelly believed that Eggleton was 'essentially an administrator not innovator; this has been fundamental in his success with successive leaders, all of whom have interpreted Liberal ideology in very different ways, none more so than Malcolm Fraser'. There was also a personal dimension: Eggleton 'knows his place, has a good appreciation of his own capacities, never tries to overreach himself with the parliamentary leader, but builds through his own efficiency and manner a leadership dependent on himself'.[1]

For the Liberals it was largely a positive campaign with tax cuts as a key pledge. To highlight and promote this policy the Federal Secretariat designed advertisements that directly involved the electorate. The public was invited to 'dial a tax cut' and listen to a telephone voice summarising the proposed tax savings. This proved highly effective. Balanced attack advertising kept the heat on negative memories of Gough Whitlam, who was still leading the Australian Labor Party (ALP) despite its record loss in 1975. The anti-Whitlam 'Memories' television commercial was a classic example of attack advertising. When asked to identify the Party's campaign donors given the substantial cost of the advertisements, Eggleton declined. He was concerned that naming its supporters would lead to 'pressure from trade unions and their employees' and result in victimisation.[2]

The *Sunday Telegraph* thought the campaign

> brought home the contrasting styles of the Liberal's federal director, Mr Eggleton, and the ALP's national secretary, David Combe. Mr Eggleton spent most of his time with the prime minister keeping up a steady stream of personal and direct advice. He is a veteran of nine campaigns and five prime ministers, and regarded by the Liberal Party as the master tactician. David Combe paid less attention to giving personal advice to his leader and more to orchestrating the overall Labor campaign.[3]

The differences between the two men were the subject of a major review article in the *Weekend Australian*. Malcolm Colless' profile was headed 'King Penguin' and began with a physical description of its subject: 'he is small, dapper, with chiselled features and a unique 'yuk yuk' laugh. He is also one of the most powerful political figures in the country'. Eggleton explained that, unlike Combe who was a spokesman for his party, 'the Liberals like to have the party organisations and the professional officers play a low profile and I go along with that'. When asked about his Labor counterpart, Eggleton replied: 'I respect David as a professional doing his job. I quite like David. We have worked a bit together, particularly over the [May 1977] referendum campaign, where we were both seeking the same ends. I think that even if we wanted to have a better relationship it would be difficult because it would be misunderstood'.[4]

The Melbourne *Herald's*, Peter Costigan, remarked that Eggleton's 'election strategies and political judgements mean more to [Fraser] than anybody else's'.[5] This may have been, according to John Lombard of the *Daily Express*, because the 'non-smoking, non-drinking, non-socialising Eggleton keeps himself to himself'. Whereas Fraser 'is a man attracted to confrontation, drama and crisis', Eggleton is 'cool and confident'. Michelle Grattan suggested to readers of the *Age* that Eggleton 'knows when to admit political mistakes' and is 'treated with a respect often lacking when Mr Fraser is dealing with his own personal staff'. She also observed that Eggleton 'epitomises order and organisation [and] admits to being unhappy when things are untidy and disordered'. Grattan thought Eggleton was 'very much the political bureaucrat – and he once likened the federal secretariat to the party's public service'.[6]

Sentiment towards Fraser and the government was not as favourable as Eggleton had hoped. There was an element of enduring bitterness towards Fraser for bringing down Whitlam in 1975 and the spectre of an alleged corruption scandal involving Federal Treasurer, Phillip Lynch (see below). In the Sunday newspapers before polling day, political correspondents were speculating on the possible return of a Whitlam Government. The election, however, delivered another convincing win to the Coalition. The Coalition lost only five seats and Labor gained two with the Government enjoying a 35-seat majority in the House of Representatives – the second biggest in Australian parliamentary history to that time. It was Whitlam's fourth and final election as Leader of the Opposition. He bowed to the inevitable and resigned. In both the 1975 and 1977 election campaigns the Liberals were able to harness anti-Labor and enduring anti-Whitlam feeling. There were key differences in what the parties were offering and, although Fraser remained a divisive figure, he enjoyed strong support among voters for whom the events of November 1975 had no lasting significance. The Liberal campaigns were effectively conducted and free from major mistakes. But neither Eggleton nor the Federal Secretariat had faced an electable Opposition. As the Coalition Government was obliged to make unpopular decisions and was blamed for policy failures, the electorate's attention would shift from the Opposition's past to the Government's future.

The October 1980 election proved particularly heavygoing for the Liberals. It seemed that Bill Hayden might lead Labor to victory. The Federal Secretariat had begun preparing in July 1979 for the next poll when Eggleton thought the government was 'regarded as politically vulnerable by some sections of the community'. He told Fraser that 'the Labor Party cannot win the next election but we could lose it'. Eggleton thought 'all our actions and decisions must contribute to the rebuilding of an electorate climate of trust and confidence'. There should not be any 'further commitments that we may not be able to meet' while the Party needed to 'restore as many 'broken promises' as we reasonably can'. In sum, Eggleton said the Liberals needed to 'put performance before promise'.

Eggleton was not helped when a draft election strategy document dated 18 October 1979 was leaked to the *Australian Financial Review*. In an interview with Mike Willesee on Channel 9's *A Current Affair* on 12 November 1979, Laurie Oakes remarked that 'by identifying where the government is weak and setting it on paper, Mr Eggleton certainly hurt the government'. After Willesee described Eggleton as 'one of the cleverest politicians in Australia', and assuming he was 'terribly upset' by the leaking of the document, Oakes said that 'Eggleton has played it down. He has been very clever. He is an expert at putting out fires'. The Federal Director told the media it was a 'preliminary discussion paper' that had received more attention than it deserved although the document was marked 'Strictly Confidential' and sent to the Prime Minister as a statement of 'proposed tactics for election year'. After canvassing Eggleton's years as a press secretary, Oakes contended that he was 'an expert in taking the heat out of any issue that is likely to embarrass whoever he works for'. The controversy created by the leaked strategy document was partly remediated by the Federal Secretariat claiming it had a document headed 'ALP Campaign Planning' when it was nothing more than a series of discussion papers produced by Labor's advertising agency.

Former editor of the *Bulletin*, Donald Horne, turned on Eggleton for blatantly distorting facts. It was a highly personal attack in which Horne claimed that Eggleton symbolised all that was wrong about the Coalition government and the Federal Secretariat. Horne described Eggleton as a 'backroom party appa-ratchik' and a 'key influencer of public policy in Australia'. Worse, Eggleton was 'one of the great masters of political illusion – and illusionism is, I think, above all, the key to Fraser's style (and has to be)'. Horne was angered that Fraser had increased the prominence of the Secretariat 'as a spellbinders' workshop with Eggleton as managing wizard'. Although the Secretariat was 'entirely a political apparatus set up in a private building of its own, it may be of more importance in the week-to-week political processes of Australian government than much of what happens in Parliament House'.

Former Liberal staffer, Russell Schneider, thought 'the closeness of [Eggleton's] relationship with Fraser has not always worked in Eggleton's favour' although, he noted, Eggleton was one of the few men pre-dating Fraser's ascension to the leadership to remain 'a major yet friendly influence on the prime minister'.[7] According to Schneider, Eggleton was 'regarded with suspicion by many senior ministers – and some organisation figures – who resent his influence or distrust his closeness to the prime minister'. Apparently, unnamed others were 'more concerned with low-key, long-term self-promotion than remaining totally concealed in the backroom'. Schneider claimed that Eggleton was a 'nuts and bolts man' who created a myth of his own influence on the prime minister. These assessments were unfair to Eggleton. He had not sought prominence and most of his many communications with Fraser did little more than canvas options. Further, Eggleton had not sought elected office and showed no signs of wanting personal favours or private privileges as a consequence of his employment.

When the election campaign finally began in September 1980, the Liberal Party strayed considerably from the strategy outlined in the leaked document of 18 October 1979. Laurie Oakes remarked: 'the mystery is why the party switched its strategy so completely when the public opinion research it was conducting showed Eggleton's original blueprint was sound'.[8] Eggleton told Fraser that Labor was 'now credible' as an alternate government and Opposition leader Bill Hayden, supported by the popular New South Wales Premier, Neville

Wran, and Australian Council of Trade Unions (ACTU) President, Bob Hawke, was 'increasingly acceptable because he's offering something'. He felt that 'most issues are moving against us – except inflation and management of the economy'. Polling suggested the Coalition's standing with voters was continuing to decline with swinging voters 'tired of the 'tightening the belt' approach'. Voters believed 'the ALP is prepared to put money back in his or her pocket'. A week before the campaign, Fraser and a group of senior ministers meeting in Sydney asked Eggleton for his assessment of the likely result. He told them:

> If an election had been held this weekend, it would have been very tight indeed. However, it was likely we would have just scraped in because a large number of those planning protest votes would probably change their minds in the polling booth.

He also thought that Hayden's campaign had peaked and was 'clearly running into credibility trouble in respect of inflation and new taxes'. The consensus was that the Coalition would achieve 'an adequate majority' on election day. Two days later, the Liberal Party's advertising agency became convinced (on the basis of weekend phone polls) that the government was headed for defeat. Eggleton was largely unmoved because he had 'a degree of scepticism about the accuracy of phone polls'. The campaign strategy committee called for a major campaign initiative, particular in the area of family allowances. Eggleton's views were again sought and, after questioning the accuracy of polling, he was more concerned that 'a new initiative at this stage would present major political problems'. In sum, it would look like an attempt to buy votes. Eggleton said he was 'inclined to stay the course' and not make any new announcements. The campaign needed to remain negative in tone, asserting that Labor's policies were detrimental to Australia and the nation's families.

With almost all the polls predicting a government defeat, Michelle Grattan observed that the 'unflappable' Eggleton is 'putting a pukka face on it all'. As he had been 'responsible for much of the campaign strategy, [he] will bear a good deal of blame for a bad electoral reverse'. She quoted him as saying: 'we'll still be in Government on Saturday. The polls show the tide is moving towards us. I wouldn't predict the margin'.[9] Demonstrating that campaigns do influence election outcomes, one of Labor's spokesmen inadvertently tossed the Coalition a lifeline by tentatively raising the prospect of a capital gains tax on the family home. It cost the Opposition dearly. The unpalatable proposal – which Labor had not endorsed – was made the dominant issue for the last week of the campaign. Television, radio and full-page print advertisements warned of Labor's threat to the family home. The day before the election, the Liberal's pollster Gary Morgan was able to report that, for the first time in the campaign, the Liberals were drawing marginally ahead of Labor. He predicted they had probably gained enough last-minute momentum to get over the line. On the day before the election, Fraser spoke with Eggleton and thanked him for his efforts. Eggleton made a private note that Fraser was 'somewhat philosophical and had clearly prepared himself for whatever the outcome may be. However, he had by no means given up hope and was still talking about the future and the actions to be taken by his government'. Eggleton believed 'we still had a good chance of winning'.

The Coalition won the election with a reduced majority that only the Morgan Gallup poll had predicted.[10] Although 0.8 per cent behind the Government in two party preferred voting, the uneven spread of the 4 per cent swing against the Coalition meant that Labor fell 12 seats short of being returned to office. While Eggleton was pleased to have achieved a third consecutive election victory, it was a much tougher contest against the under-rated but solidly performing Hayden. British election analyst David Butler thought the Liberal campaign was too driven by polling and Eggleton had erred in making Fraser the focus of the Government's message.[11] Butler believed Eggleton and Fraser were 'over-influenced by the experience of 1977, when exploiting a 'fair go' approach, coupled with a Whitlam knocking trip down memory lane, they walked to an unexpectedly easy victory'. The strong emphasis on negative campaigning was controversial, even among Liberals. The member for Perth, Ross McLean, attributed the loss of his seat to the Liberal's insistence on 'belting the daylights out of our opponents. We should have been standing on our policies'.[12] The political hardheads believed the end justified the means. There were certainly no complaints from Fraser who could point to a 23-seat parliamentary majority although the Coalition had lost control of the Senate majority it had earlier gained at the 1977 election. The Government now had to deal with the Australian Democrats led by former Liberal minister, Don Chipp, which had secured the balance of power in the Senate.

Eggleton lamented that 'it was no easy task to keep the campaign in the context of pragmatism and reality when the media was focussing almost exclusively on the 'shadow boxing' of the opinion polls'. Although there was fear 'among well-meaning supporters', Eggleton believed the campaign 'adhered to pre-determined strategies, avoiding fragmentation of the national campaign and minimising the scope for charges of 'crisis' and 'panic'. The focus remained on 'winning the votes of the 'swingers' – the uncommitted and undecided'. But Max Walsh thought 'the whole campaign is quite the worst campaign that has ever been run by a government that I've ever seen. I just find it unbelievable'. He nominated the focus on Fraser's leadership as a 'disaster'. The latter criticism was justified. Eggleton was perhaps too close personally to Fraser to point out the electorate's growing dissatisfaction with Fraser's demeanour and persistent echoes of his now infamous quip: 'life wasn't meant to be easy'. The Prime Minister continued to appear imperious and arrogant, unattractive traits that commentators had identified when he became party leader in 1975.

Even after five years in office, Fraser remained a hard task master. His ministers had to meet high benchmarks while, in Eggleton's judgement, he could be unsympathetic and over-zealous in applying these standards – even if he applied them just as mercilessly to himself. Eggleton was drawn into a number of squabbles between Fraser and his ministers, the most significant involving Phillip Lynch and later Andrew Peacock.

On the eve of the 1977 election, the Treasurer and Deputy Liberal leader Phillip Lynch became embroiled in an alleged investment scandal involving land deals and the purchase of a Gold Coast residential unit. On 17 November 1977, Eggleton drafted a memo headed 'Lynch options' for the prime minister. The 'positive option' involved stressing the absence of any evidence of impropriety and claiming the Opposition was engaged in 'dirty politics'. The 'negative option' was two pronged: Lynch protests his innocence but decides to stand aside because he is too sick to defend himself or he is removed as Treasurer which 'the Opposition would present as the sacking for impropriety of the man who had been at the forefront of the government's economic policy'. Eggleton told Fraser that 'either of the two negative options will be damaging politically. Acknowledgement (and confirmation) of impropriety will cause the present Victorian malaise to spread to other states'.

The Cabinet met in Sydney the following day without Lynch being present. The Treasurer was in hospital receiving treatment for a kidney complaint. It was obvious that Lynch's personal financial affairs would detract from the Liberal campaign, if not derail it given the extent of media and political interest in what looked like corrupt conduct. Given it was impossible to separate right from wrong in a matter of days, the Cabinet came to the view that Lynch needed to step down. Lynch had already produced statements from his accountant and solicitor that discounted any possibility of corrupt conduct. Fraser asked Eggleton to speak with Lynch (by telephone) and raise the possibility of resignation. Lynch had a close relationship with the Federal Director and would often share with Eggleton his anger and disappointment with Fraser's attitudes and actions. Journalist Brian Buckley claimed that Eggleton blurred the line 'between courtesy and artificiality'. It was an unworthy slur. Eggleton had never leaked against Lynch or been anything other than sincere in what he had said and done. Lynch knew this which is why he continued to trust Eggleton.

Lynch told Eggleton he was 'bitterly disappointed at his treatment after all that he had done for the Party. He was being submitted to trial without consultation'. Lynch thought those 'pressuring him should get off the scent'. He told Eggleton that Fraser should 'get the dogs off because it was making it impossible for him to make a calm judgement. He would not act under this pressure'. The conversation ended with Lynch informing Eggleton he 'could make it clear to the Cabinet that he had never heard Phillip Lynch so angry and those pressuring him should be aware of how he felt'. One of those present at the Cabinet meeting, Jim Killen, recalled 'it was not long before everybody in the room knew that Lynch had no intention of stepping down and was determined to stay'. Killen described an 'ashen-faced' Eggleton reading from the notes he had taken of his phone conversation with the Treasurer:

> 'he is very put out', said Eggleton. He is very angry. He has said: 'I, too, have bits of paper. I will hold a daily press conference. I will bucket you all. You needn't think you are getting rid of me so easily. It's that Victorian crowd that is trying to get rid of me'.[13]

Lynch half suspected that Fraser wanted to replace him with the Minister for Industrial Relations, Tony Street, who would be more amenable to the Prime Minister's will. Fraser then spoke to Lynch. According to Killen, 'he put the phone down and turned to us thoroughly apprehensive and bewildered'. Lynch was apparently willing to consider certain proposals for his future – including standing aside as Treasurer. Killen recorded that 'Eggleton and officials were sent away to work on a draft letter'. It was a painful process but a resolution was reached. Lynch's resignation neutralised the matter as an election issue. Before the subsequent press conference, Eggleton advised Fraser to 'be firm but patient.

Continually make it clear that you are not prepared to cooperate with them in raking over the Lynch question'. If journalists persisted with questioning, Eggleton counselled Fraser to 'express disappointment that they did not want to discuss the real issues of the campaign'. He stressed that the Prime Minister should not 'walk out' of the press conference as he had earlier when the Lynch matters were raised. Walking out again would be depicted as the 'PM showing signs of tension after only a couple of days of campaigning'.

After the election, the allegations against Lynch were examined in detail. He was cleared of any wrongdoing and restored to Cabinet although by then John Howard, whom Fraser had appointed Acting Treasurer, kept the portfolio. Lynch became Minister for Industry and Commerce. He was also challenged for the deputy leadership of the Parliamentary Liberal Party by Killen who was appalled at what he considered Lynch's demanding behaviour. Killen told Fraser: 'I do not know what those 'bits of paper' were of which Eggleton spoke. I will not be threatened by anybody'. Killen never asked Eggleton to reveal what might have been written on the 'bits of paper' and Eggleton never spoke of it publicly or privately. The 'bits of paper' referred to by Eggleton were, in fact, the 1977 budget figures which Lynch believed Fraser had 'fiddled' for his own ends.[14] Lynch defeated Killen 71–20 in the subsequent ballot.

After losing the Treasury portfolio in 1977, Lynch's political career never recovered. By 1981 he had become increasingly tired and disenchanted. He was not in good health and his family wanted him to leave Parliament. Lynch asked Eggleton to handle negotiations with the Prime Minister on his behalf. He felt he was being unduly pressured by Fraser and was worried about the strength of guarantees for his post-retirement appointments. Fraser's only interest was that Lynch would resign from Cabinet. Eggleton suggested to Fraser that if Lynch were briefly Minister for Foreign Affairs and then was sent to Washington as Australia's next ambassador to the United States, the Party would be 'forced to turn to John Howard' as Lynch would be out of the country and unable to fulfil the deputy's duties. When the Washington option was ruled out by Fraser, Eggleton was asked to canvas his willingness to become ambassador to France or West Germany. Lynch replied that the 'European positions were a consider-able 'downgrading' on Washington … not nearly as significant and prestigious'. Lynch actually preferred domestic corporate appointments, such as the Qantas Board or the Reserve Bank Board. Reflecting his regard for Eggleton, Lynch mentioned that on retirement he 'would hope to maintain very close contact' with the Liberal Party organisation and 'intimated that he would be very interested in running for Federal President – as and when convenient and appropriate'. Eggleton encouraged him to nominate for pre-selection in his seat of Flinders to avoid becoming 'a lame duck minister' although Lynch and Eggleton both knew he had no intention of standing again.

When Lynch's health further deteriorated later in the year, Fraser asked Eggleton to negotiate the terms and the timing of his resignation and retirement. Eggleton visited Lynch's Melbourne home to settle these matters with him and his wife, Leah O'Toole. Both Lynch and his wife expressed their trust in Eggleton's integrity and truthfulness as he helped in the drafting of an acceptable letter and wanted him present during meetings with Fraser. Conversely, Fraser welcomed Eggleton's presence as a witness to what was said and done. Eggleton found ways to relieve the tension or reduce the embarrassment, depending upon the need. Eggleton was keen to secure a date for the by-election that would follow Lynch's resignation with the hope that it could happen before the November unemployment figures were released.

Finally, there was an exchange of letters that were signed in Fraser's Melbourne office. It was an emotional occasion for Lynch and an upsetting formality for him, Fraser and Eggleton. Refreshments had been ordered but Eggleton stopped staff from entering the room. They did not need to see Lynch's anguish. Eggleton regarded Lynch as a loyal and hard-working deputy leader, as well as a cohesive influence on the ministry. Although Lynch knew it was time for him to go, signing the irrevocable letter of resignation was a deeply painful moment and he was grateful for Eggleton's solidarity. It had been a personally draining experience for Eggleton but it was much less professionally demanding than managing Andrew Peacock.

As both the leader and deputy leader of the Liberal Party were members of the Victorian Division, Andrew Peacock's leadership ambitions would not be fulfilled while Fraser and Lynch remained in parliament. Fraser had known Peacock for two decades but they had little in common. In Victoria, Fraser represented the landowning 'establishment' and Peacock its urban 'society'. They were ambitious and, when required, ruthless. The Member for Kooyong was not close to either Fraser or Lynch and accused the Federal Secretariat of supporting his Victorian colleagues by 'bad mouthing' him. This was untrue. Eggleton took the initiative and met Peacock on 23 August 1978 to clear the air. He denied the Secretariat was the source of derogatory remarks and 'certainly not in any 'orchestrated' fashion'. With his long experience of journalists, Eggleton said it was 'not unknown for the gallery to spread stories designed to create dissension and distrust'. Further, he told Peacock that Secretariat policy was not to engage in politicking, 'the PM has never suggested that we should – and I would decline. Our role is to protect the future of the party regardless of the parliamentary scene'. Eggleton suggested to Peacock that it was only ministers who had little to do with the Secretariat, such as he and Killen, that were suspicious of its staff and critical of its activities. In reply, Peacock said he wanted to repair his relationship with Fraser and the Party, and asked to be used more frequently as a speaker at party events. Peacock was naturally concerned about his public profile.

Twelve months later the relationship between Peacock and Eggleton soured again. Peacock was incensed by a Laurie Oakes' story claiming that Eggleton had been invited to the United States to serve as a 'consultant' to the Republican Party during the 1980 presidential election.[15] Eggleton noted that Peacock was 'ill-tempered and aggressive, expressing his anger and his disapproval of any plans for discussions with an individual US party'. In his defence, Eggleton said the suggestion had come from the Liberal's Federal Present, Sir John Atwill, and that the contact would be 'low key and informal' and with members of the Republican Party's organisational wing. Peacock fanned the interest of journalists with several terse media releases.[16] Eggleton explained the whole matter to Fraser in a hand-written note dated 26 October 1979: 'I hope Andrew is satisfied now he has inflamed an issue that had already gone away. The publicity makes him look rather petty'.

Sensing the ill-will, Laurie Oakes remarked that 'there is clearly no love lost between the two men – and we are reliably informed it has nothing to do with Mr Peacock's name being left out of the glossy booklet on the Liberal Party that was handed out at the Federal Council meeting in Perth earlier this year'. In another hand-written note to Fraser, Eggleton commented: 'Political petulance and generating the suggestion of conflict with the professional wing – I should hardly have thought this would have helped an aspiring leader'. The same day Eggleton penned a personal letter to Peacock: 'I think it would be a pity if the media convinced themselves that there was 'bad blood' between us as, from my point of view, there is not'. Eggleton realised that Peacock would be a contender for the deputy leadership when Phillip Lynch decided to retire or relinquish the post and needed to maintain a healthy working relationship with him.

Fraser's interactions with Menzies' successor as the Member for Kooyong had been fraught for a number of years. From the late 1960s, both men saw themselves as future Liberal prime ministers. Peacock served in Fraser's first Cabinet as Minister for Foreign Affairs. There were frequent difficulties and disagreements over policies and procedures. Through these trials and tribulations, Eggleton continued to act as mediator. Fraser did not discourage his efforts whereas Peacock saw Eggleton as leader of the 'Secretariat Mafia' and wrongly assumed the Federal Director was in the 'enemy camp'. Eggleton's contacts with Peacock were hot and cold, although both saw the value of keeping in touch. Eggleton rightly sensed that the obvious rivalry between Fraser and Peacock was playing into Labor's hands.

Shortly before the 1980 election, Peacock threatened to resign over the likely poll date and his dispute with Fraser over Australia's attitude to the murderous Khmer Rouge regime in Cambodia. Eggleton told Fraser that while there were strong reasons for dropping Peacock from Cabinet, there were equally strong reasons for retaining him in the ministry. Dumping Peacock would harm the Government and its re-election campaign. Senator John Carrick, John Howard, Phillip Lynch and Ian Viner all wanted Peacock disciplined for making public his differences of opinion with Fraser. They thought Peacock was emotionally unstable and lacked perspective. Journalist Malcolm Colless reported that 'Eggleton took the party machine line that despite the intense feelings over the resignation issue the party could not afford to allow this to become a campaign issue because any sign of disunity in a traditionally conservative electorate [Kooyong] would be very damaging'.[17]

Shortly after the 1980 election, there had been a move among some backbench Liberals to replace Phillip Lynch as deputy Party leader with the Treasurer, John Howard, in order to thwart Peacock's leadership aspirations. Howard did not nominate but Peacock did. At the subsequent ballot, Lynch prevailed 47–35 but Peacock had cemented his place as Fraser's likely successor with the entitlement to nominate his preferred portfolio. Peacock voluntarily relinquished Foreign Affairs and took Industrial Relations to gain experience in a domestic portfolio. Unexpectedly, Peacock resigned from Cabinet in April 1981 after complaining that Fraser was interfering constantly in his portfolio and allowing the Cabinet

'Coordinating Committee' to dominate decision-making – a similar charge to the one Fraser had brought against Prime Minister John Gorton in 1971. Howard thought Peacock did not receive 'any rougher treatment than other senior ministers ... as a consequence, his resignation lacked justification, hurt the Government and was resented by many colleagues'.[18]

Eggleton 'bumped into' Peacock at Canberra airport on 7 May 1981. The former minister suggested he and Eggleton have a talk to which the Federal Director replied: 'I would be happy to talk with you at any time'. When he asked Peacock whether some rapprochement was possible, Eggleton was told: 'it was unlikely but to some extent it would depend on Malcolm Fraser. It was certainly too soon to think of restoring relations'. He neither 'hated nor disliked' Fraser, he 'disagreed with him and that was that'. Eggleton shared his angst over Peacock's belief that the Secretariat was leaking against him, insisting that it had not. The two men parted amicably with Eggleton mentioning that some in the Liberal Party were disappointed he was not in the Cabinet.

Several months later (8 October 1981), Eggleton had 'a long discussion with the Prime Minister about his leadership and the future of the Liberal Party. I suspect it was something of a watershed discussion'. Fraser told Eggleton he was 'happy to continue to serve as parliamentary leader but was only interested in leading a united party'. He would not endure being 'constantly undermined ... and a stage could come when he would not be prepared to put up with a constant guerrilla war'. Fraser did not think the Party could win the next election 'if it continued to be disunited over leadership'. As he has been prime minister 'for some years, he would find it no hardship to step down from the job [because] ... he was not going to get involved in head-counting and fighting desperately to hang on to office'. Fraser thought that if he was succeeded by anyone but Peacock, then 'Peacock would immediately begin another guerrilla war to undermine the new leader'. He presumed that Eggleton shared his feelings but 'very much hoped I would stay as long as he was prime minister'. By this time, there had been rumours that Eggleton would be knighted and become the next Secretary-General of the Commonwealth.[19] As he had not stayed for extended periods in any of his former positions, there was speculation he would soon depart. Eggleton wasn't going anywhere. Any possible job offer depended on Shridath Ramphal, the then Commonwealth Secretary-General, being appointed the successor to

Kurt Waldheim, the Secretary-General of the United Nations. Ramphal was shortlisted but not appointed.

Fraser asked Eggleton for the assistance of the Federal Secretariat in promoting party discipline and unity. Eggleton was privately relived that 'the PM was not pressing for draconian measures in relation to Peacock – he did not mention expulsion or other punitive actions'. Although Peacock's undermining had made Fraser's life 'miserable', Eggleton was in 'no doubt that [Fraser] is serious in saying that he would not put up indefinitely with leadership tensions'. Fraser floated the idea of a ministerial reshuffle but thought 'there seemed to be no likelihood of any vacancies and he was not prepared to force resignations'.

By November 1981, Peacock feared the Prime Minister had 'closed the door' on his ministerial future. Fraser asked Eggleton to speak with the Victorian state director, Richard Alston, about his dealings with party donors and the need for additional office staff. He also prepared an *aide memoire* for Fraser on the likelihood of a leadership challenge after the 3 April 1982 Victorian state election at which the Labor Party, headed by John Cain, was returned to power after 27 years of Liberal rule. Eggleton thought the outcome would precipitate another Peacock challenge. He advised Fraser to take swift and decisive action if he thought events and party sentiment were heading in Peacock's direction.

The tension increased dramatically on 5 April 1982 when Fraser announced there would be a spill of leadership positions to 'end the speculation once and for all'. Peacock declared that he would stand against Fraser because 'the results of recent elections have shown that the Liberal Party has lost the broad community support which it requires to govern effectively'. The next day Lynch indicated his desire to stand aside as Deputy Leader of the Liberal Party and 'to do this irrespective of whether there is a contest for the position'. A few weeks earlier, and knowing Lynch was hinting at retiring from politics before the next election, Eggleton had drafted a note for file on the 'Leadership Challenge'. The problem with Lynch's decision was the opportunity it presented to Andrew Peacock. If he failed to become Party leader, he might become the deputy leader without being a member of Cabinet.

Fraser told Eggleton that 'he would make it very clear to the Party that it would be an impossible situation to have Peacock as deputy leader. He would say point-blank that he just could not and would not work with Peacock. He might also arrange for Doug Anthony to come out with a statement that the Coalition could not work under Peacock'. It would, therefore, be 'necessary for John Howard to make a run'. Aged 42, Howard was nine years younger than Fraser (who had become Party leader just after his 44th birthday) but only five months younger than Peacock. Eggleton was much nearer in age to Fraser than Peacock and had a more natural affinity with him.

At the Party meeting held on 8 April 1982, Fraser defeated Peacock 54 votes to 27 and Howard was elevated to the deputy's position after defeating Michael MacKellar 45 votes to 27 on the second round of voting. Eggleton recorded in a private note that Peacock 'approached me in Kings Hall ... shook me by the hand and, in front of the media, made the following points: he still had leadership aspirations, however, he would not make another challenge before the next general election'. Eggleton thought he 'made the approach to me in the presence of the media as a deliberate tactic. We could certainly use it against him if he changed his mind'. Peacock eventually returned to Cabinet in October 1982 as Minister for Industry and Commerce. Two months later, Bob Hawke challenged Bill Hayden for the leadership of the Labor Party. Hawke's narrow defeat by 42–37 votes suggested time was running out for the Opposition leader. It was likely the highly popular Hawke would prevail next time around and present a much greater threat to Fraser's prime ministership.

An election was due to be held in 1983 and the odds of the Government retaining office were lengthening by the day. Everything appeared to be conspiring against the Coalition although Richard Carlton remarked on ABC television's *Nationwide* program on 10 December 1982 that 'the Fraser-Anthony team backed by Mr Tony Eggleton and his supremely efficient secretariat have never lost an election and they are still odds on to survive next year'. A few months earlier the *Sydney Morning Herald*'s Paul Kelly declared that Fraser and Eggleton were the 'only stars left as the Liberal lights dim'.[20] Kelly still regarded Eggleton as 'without peer as political adviser and strategist in Australia'. He also thought that deputy Party leader, John Howard, was 'starting to wear and sound a little thin. Yet it seems just yesterday that he was the 'wonder boy'. Where will he be in another ten years?'

Within the Party, the unpredictability and volatility of the political landscape resulted in some controversy about the timing of the election. The pressures on Fraser included intensive lobbying by business leaders who wanted an end to early election speculation. Eggleton attended a meeting with Fraser, Howard and the National Party Cabinet minister, Peter Nixon, on 2 February 1983. Fraser wanted to call an early election to exploit internal tensions between Hayden and Hawke, and fears the prevailing drought would further worsen economic conditions. The preferred date was 5 March. There would be a short election campaign with Fraser expecting he would be facing Hayden as the Labor leader. Howard recalls that 'Eggleton said to both Nixon and me, 'I think we should win''.[21]

The morning of the following day (3 February), Fraser arranged to see the Governor-General at short notice to request an early election. Fraser suspected that Hawke would move against Hayden sooner or later and preferred his electoral contest be with Hayden. As the Governor-General's official secretary, David Smith, later explained: 'Fraser hoped to use the one-hour time difference [between the Australian Capital Territory and Queensland where the Labor caucus was meeting] to pre-empt Hayden's announcement [that he would resign in favour of Hawke] with his own announcement of an early election. He had reasoned that the Labor Party would be unlikely to change leader after an election had been called'.[22] The Governor-General, Sir Ninian Stephen, told Fraser he would need to read carefully his letter and the attachments (which ran to a total of 39 pages) and could not give him an immediate decision. Fraser would have his answer by 3.30pm. The Labor Party proceeded with its bloodless leadership transition, not knowing that Fraser had just sought an early election. Eggleton was at the Liberal Party's advertising agency in Melbourne with members of the campaign team when they heard that Hawke was the new Opposition leader. He was already a formidable adversary and would be enjoying the usual political honeymoon during the election campaign. These were the worst possible confluence of circumstances working against the government's re-election.

The campaign team suggested to Eggleton that he telephone Fraser and recommend he withdraw his request for an early election. Eggelton spoke with Fraser but it was too late for the Prime Minister to credibly change his mind. Meanwhile, the Governor-General asked for some 'additional advice' which was not tendered until 4.45pm. Fraser was granted an early election and made the announcement in the knowledge that he would be fighting the Bob Hawke-led Labor Party. A disappointed Hayden remarked that 'a drover's dog' could lead the Labor Party to victory, such was the unpopularity of Fraser and his government. Smith contended that 'Fraser's decision not to withdraw his request was one of the most stupid political decisions that he ever made … he had at least four hours in which to rethink his failed strategy, but lacked the wit to change course'.

Eggleton was aware that Hawke, a popular and well-known figure, embodied a very different challenge to Hayden but believed the Coalition could still win. He told John Hamilton of the *West Australian* that he was 'quietly confident' because 'the question mark over Mr Hawke has always been there. It is gradually growing'.[23] Privately, Eggleton shared the view of Western Australian premier, Sir Charles Court, that the Government needed six months or so to devise and deliver a strategy that would diminish Hawke's electoral appeal.[24] They now had one month. Eggleton would, as he had in 1977 and 1980, rely on his knowledge of the electorate and its mood. According to journalist Peter Bowers,

> Eggleton has set up such an elaborate monitoring and intelligence gathering operation that he has been able to speed the velocity of politics to the point where he, Fraser and the entire advertising campaign can change course at 24 hours' notice. Such tactical mobility gave the Liberals a tremendous advantage. By the time the Opposition – and the media – had caught up the issue had taken off.[25]

Several weeks later Bowers observed that Eggleton's operation 'failed to pick up Hawke's mistakes simply because he made none, or none that mattered'.[26]

Almost as soon as the campaign started, the disastrous Ash Wednesday bushfires cut a swath through South Australia and Victoria. Seventy-five lives were lost and more than 3,000 homes destroyed. Eggleton was in Sydney with Fraser, who summoned the military and emergency service chiefs to a conference at Kirribilli House. Fraser felt this national tragedy demanded his undivided attention and decided not to campaign further until the end of the emergency. Labor, understandably, saw no reason to stop campaigning. Eggleton told senior ministers and Party officials that the campaign would have two phases. The honeymoon phase would last until the policy launches. The reality phase would start when Australians seriously contemplated the possibility of 'voting for Labor under the new, untried and untested leadership of Bob Hawke or voting for the strong, stable and durable leadership of Malcolm Fraser'. Then, he suggested, the polls would be turned around and Labor's lead would diminish. Eggleton believed he could achieve, as he had in 1977 and 1980, a four per cent swing back to the Coalition in the final two weeks of campaigning.

Laurie Oakes described the Liberal campaign as a shambles and a 'blueprint for defeat'.

> First, you make sure your opponent is the most popular politician in the country. Then you carefully craft the election campaign so it occurs at the beginning of his honeymoon period with the electorate. The third step is to allow yourself only three weeks to erode your opponent's popularity and credibility, when you could have had eight months.[27]

Oakes was incredulous that the Liberal Party would campaign on its record which was characterised by 'soaring unemployment, economic downturn, high interest and inflation'. It was for these reasons that he could not fathom why Fraser, after consultation with Eggleton, would call an early election. After a few weeks of campaigning, Oakes thought Fraser's 'campaign form has been so bad and Mr Hawke's so good that, if the Liberals do win the election, a steward's inquiry would be called for'. Former campaign staffer, Jonathon Gaul, criticised the Secretariat for becoming 'too professional, with not enough people who are hungry and dedicated. The same agency produced the ads year in, year out, so there is no need to be seen to be competing for business'.[28]

The loss of five campaign days during the bushfire crisis cost the Coalition dearly. Facing a reinvigorated Labor under Hawke's leadership, the Liberals were on the back foot but Eggleton refused to panic. He told the *Age* that

> campaigns are like races now. They are fast-moving, changing every day, with issues rising and then sinking into oblivion at a hectic pace. This is a relatively modern phenomenon. It means the campaign has to be measured and continually monitored and reassessed.

Max Walsh disagreed. He did not think the 'last man standing' would win the race.

> It's as if Mr Eggleton is saying that the years preceding the election campaign don't count at all. I don't believe that. I think there are times when people can be swayed by intense campaigning, by saturation advertising. But those are the exceptions rather than the rule.

As the electorate was being asked to reject the past (Fraser) and embrace the future (Hawke), there was a dinner in Sydney to celebrate Fraser becoming Australia's second-longest serving prime minister and one of its youngest. [Fraser was a year younger than Hawke]. During the meal, concern about a potential election loss gave rise to proposals that they commit even more public money to policy initiatives during the final stage of the campaign. Fraser readily endorsed this idea because he still felt the Coalition could be returned to office. Eggleton doubted whether more money was the answer but considered it unwise to pour cold water on an offer of extra funds for advertising. Sitting alongside him was the Party Treasurer, Sir Robert Crichton-Brown, who promised within days to find an additional $500,000. He quipped it was the 'most expensive dinner he had ever attended'.

Eggleton's foremost challenge was to make Fraser look better on television. He explained to the *Age*'s Michael Gawenda that

> campaigns are now planned and designed to take advantage of the electronic media. You plan a function and ask yourself 'will it look good on television? How can we maximise television coverage?' Public meetings aren't good enough. The audience you are trying to reach is sitting out there in front of television sets.[29]

More people than ever before were watching television and Liberal Party research had shown that 'television is the most trusted part of the media. It has the highest level of believability. Any politician who wants to succeed has to come to terms with television and learn to use it well'.

The man Fraser replaced as Liberal leader, Billy Snedden, had visited the electorate of Fadden in Queensland and concluded that no-one was listening to Fraser. Snedden contacted Fraser with a series of suggestions about what he might do, including Hawke's challenge of a public debate. The prime minister was 'totally antagonistic and I realised he was immune to my views because he did not want to hear them. I spoke to Eggleton and he too was immune. They were too distant from the electorate to understand'.[30] In a subsequent conversation, Snedden pleaded with Fraser: 'Don't talk to your own people. They haven't advised you well up till now'. But Fraser was unwilling to 'give a platform to Hawke' and ignored Snedden's prompting.

The Coalition was unable to regain traction with its message during the campaign and remained well behind in the polls. There was no major economic initiative as the Treasurer, John Howard, had insisted the country could not afford additional spending. By the last weekend of the campaign it was obvious the Liberals were highly vulnerable in a number of seats. In a rare interview with Patrick Tennyson on Radio 3UZ in Melbourne four days out from the election, Eggleton defended the tenor of the Liberal campaign, explaining that all campaigns must have 'a mixture of both positive and negative' messaging. He resisted the charge that the Liberals were scaremongering on interest rates. He thought that 'Mr Hawke probably peaked last week' which suited the Liberal campaign because Eggleton believed it was 'the last week, the countdown week, where people really concentrate their minds'. Eggleton suggested that Hawke was putting on 'a tremendous performance' and hoped that Australians would not 'put showmanship before leadership'. Conversely, he told Tennyson that Fraser was 'very often misunderstood'. He added that 'respect is certainly more important than popularity'. Writing in the *Daily Mirror*, Laurie Oakes thought the 'overwhelming likelihood is that Labor will win'.

Eggleton met privately with Fraser to tell him the polling gave little hope of making up enough ground in the last week to retain office. Fraser showed no surprise but gave an assurance: 'Tony, you can be sure that for every hour and every day that's left, I will campaign as though I am a winner'. He was true to his word. There was universal recognition that Fraser left his best effort to the end: an address at the National Press Club three days before the election. The *Australian* thought that 'if he had made the same speech two weeks ago, the current debate would have been conducted on a higher level and been more instructive to voters'.[31] It suggested that 'every Australian who wishes to cast his vote responsibly on March 5' needed to consider his speech carefully. The *Age* was unmoved, telling its readers that 'Labor deserves its chance to get the country going again'.[32]

Election night at the Southern Cross Hotel in Melbourne proved to be a dismal affair for the Liberals. It was soon apparent that there was a substantial 3.6 percent swing to Labor which had gained 24 seats. This was the biggest defeat of a federal government since 1949 and the worst swing against a non-Labor government in Australian political history. In his brief, tearful concession speech, Fraser accepted responsibility for the timing of the election, the conduct of the campaign and the outcome of the vote. Fraser would not re-contest the leadership of his party. With Bob Hawke the new prime minister, an emotional Fraser privately conveyed his personal thanks to ministers and campaign workers. They stood around awkwardly. To raise the flagging spirits of those who had gathered in the hotel ballroom, someone broke into a spontaneous rendition of the campaign song, 'We're not waiting for the world'. The assembled group tried hard, especially for the sake of the Frasers, to join the singing with a brave face. It was futile. They all knew the Fraser chapter in Australian political history had closed. They also knew the Coalition was heading for the Opposition benches, probably for an extended period.

Fraser took Eggleton aside to tell him he would not continue in parliament and would resign his seat of Wannon. Early the next morning there was a knock on Eggleton's door at the Hotel Windsor in Melbourne. It was Andrew Peacock. He had Fraser's blessing to seek the party leadership. He was prepared to stand but wanted to be sure that Eggleton would remain as Federal Director. He received that assurance and was elected leader on 11 March 1983.

Were Eggleton and the Federal Secretariat partly to blame for the election loss? Journalist David Marr reported that:

> Eggleton's job is now on the line. The party is shell-shocked, not merely by defeat but by the size and uniformity of the swing against it. And the secretariat is blamed not only for the conduct of the campaign (Eggleton is personally identified with the decision to retain the advertising agency Masius despite party criticism) but for not keeping Fraser's Government in touch with the Party and its Platform. Instead it allegedly became an echo of the prime minister.[33]

Eggleton told Marr that 'the critics don't see beyond the close rapport between Tony Eggleton and Fraser. My relationship with the prime minister was not palsy-walsy. It was very frank'. When asked whether he wanted to serve a new Party leader, he replied instantly: 'I have no intention of walking away from the job'. He continued to believe after nearly four decades, the Liberals are 'professional, resilient and indeed, Australia's most successful political party'.

Brian Buckley contended that the Liberal Party organisation, and Eggleton in particular, 'ought to have been telling the government unpleasant truths rather than acting as an extension of Fraser's personal staff'. According to Buckley,

> Eggleton, for all intents and purposes, was paid by the Party, [but was] effec-tively a member of Fraser's staff and quite an influential one at that. The state divisions did not like this, but Fraser was in a very powerful position and it was very difficult for them to stop it. Eggleton was a very good wheeler and dealer and very smooth on the surface. He always had a very attentive ear ... there was always the temptation for a federal party functionary to try and attach himself to the prime minister because that is where the real power lies. This

is especially so in the Liberal Party, unlike the Labor Party, where the machine has greater power over Labor governments.[34]

In contrast to Labor figures like Bob McMullan and David Combe who were 'quite prepared to go in and tell the prime minister what he doesn't want to hear ... Eggleton wasn't doing it'.

Future Liberal Party Federal President, John Elliott, thought it was 'a fact of life' that the Federal Secretariat became the 'voice of the prime minister and not that of the Party'. Once elected to government, it was difficult for the Federal Secretariat to influence policy. In Opposition, however, Elliott thought the Secretariat offered parliamentarians a source of support as they were 'looking for a way to get back' into office. As for the criticism of Eggleton, Elliott remarked:

> [He] is a master tactician when it comes to running elections ... I was chairman of the federal strategy committee for every one of Fraser's elections and I think he is a great organiser, but Fraser is such a dominant man. Eggleton helped him a lot during the course of the campaigns; but I don't think you will ever get a strong federal secretariat when you are in government [when] the head of the secretariat has to work well with the prime minister.[35]

Eggleton agreed to be interviewed by Fairfax journalist, Peter Bowers, after the election.[36] He conceded that the Party was 'wrong-footed' by the replacement of Hayden with Hawke, and was obliged to abandon most of the campaign work it had undertaken in 1982. The subsequent campaign was planned and implemented 'in probably the shortest time frame I had ever experienced'. Hawke's ascendancy dominated the first week of the campaign and the bushfires the second week. The 'loss of four days was very significant in terms of momentum'. The third week was marred by the Coalition's loss in the Western Australian state election. Eggleton found it was 'difficult to keep the kind of consistent line running that we wanted'. As Labor was pursuing a presidential-style campaign around Hawke, the Liberals were forced to promote the much less popular Fraser. In any event, 'all the research showed that the electorate had become fairly sour, was clearly in the mood for change and really was not listening to talk about achievement, past record or even to a large extent about what we saw for the future'. One more week of campaigning might have lessened the Coalition's loss but not the outcome. Bowers compared the Liberal's position in 1983 with that of Labor in 1975 before asking: 'how does the Liberal Party start to rebuild?' Eggleton played it safe: 'after more than 30 years we have a very strong party organisation. We are a pragmatic party and we have a great deal of resilience.'

While Eggleton might have cited the competing and contrary views that were offered during the campaign by people like Snedden in an attempt to change the Liberal's campaign message, the electorate had tired of Fraser and the nation was wearied by prolonged drought, economic recession, industrial confrontation and high unemployment. Voters were drawn to the charismatic Bob Hawke and Labor's slogan of 'Bringing Australia Together'. There was little that either the Federal Secretariat or the campaign committee could realistically have done that would have been sufficient to prevent the Hawke ascendancy. The Liberal Party accepted the near inevitability of defeat and did not blame the Federal Director or the Secretariat for the result. Eggleton would return to work the following Monday morning without the substantial presence of Malcolm Fraser who had given routine and regularity to his life over the previous eight years.

Eggleton had appreciated Fraser's self-discipline and the orderly manner in which he approached the tasks before him. They were, in these senses, very similar individuals. As a person of habit and custom, Eggleton had processes and procedures for doing most things at home and at work. He sought stability and preferred to avoid surprises which he would struggle to control. Of all those with whom he would work, Eggleton was most suited to Fraser. Of the many people upon whom he relied as Prime Minister, Eggleton was the one with whom he felt most at ease. The question for Eggleton was whether he could establish a sufficiently harmonious relationship with Andrew Peacock for the Liberal Party to have any chance of defeating the Hawke Government at the next election. Given the electorate's tendency to give winning parties two terms of office, it was conceivable that Eggleton would not taste Federal electoral success again until 1989. The Liberal Party was potentially facing six years in the political wilderness.

Endnotes

1   Paul Kelly, 'The coming campaign', *National Times*, 24–29 October 1977, p. 14.
2   'Libs fear pressure on their backers', *Daily Telegraph*, 14 November 1977.
3   '$13 million gamble on the campaign trail', *Sunday Telegraph*, 11 December 1977.
4   Malcolm Colless, 'The Pros', *Weekend Australian*, 19–20 November 1977.
5   Peter Costigan, 'Decisions made at high level', *Herald* (Melbourne), 26 November 1977.
6   Michelle Grattan, 'Eggleton no campaign Charlie ...', *Age*, 3 December 1977.
7   Russell Schneider, 'Maltese Falcon', *Weekend Australian*, 22–23 March 1980.
8   Laurie Oakes, 'Liberal campaign contradicts its own strategy', *National Reporter*, vol. 1, no. 27, 15 October 1980.
9   Michelle Grattan, 'Polls don't darken Fraser's mood', *Age*, 16 October 1980.
10 Leonard Radic, 'The year the polls were a bad guide', *Age*, 20 October 1980.
11 David Butler, 'Move over, Whitlam – Fraser now Aunt Sally', *Age*, 18 October 1980.
12 'McLean critical of Lib. campaign', *West Australian*, 20 October 1980.
13 James Killen, *Killen: Inside Australian Politics*, Methuen Hayes, Sydney, 1985, p. 272.
14 Brian Buckley, *Lynched*, Salzburg Publishing, Melbourne, 1991, p. 223.
15 *Oakes Report*, 24 October 1979.
16 Nikki Savva, 'Eggleton is 'warned off'', *Sun*, Melbourne, 26 October 1979.
17 Malcolm Colless, 'Liberal machine keeps pumping for its leader', *Australian*, 21 April 1980.
18 John Howard, *Lazarus Rising: A Personal and Political Biography*, Harper Collins, Sydney, 2010, p. 120–21.
19 Laurie Oakes, 'London job for top Lib tipped', Melbourne *Sun*, 26 January 1978; 'London job is tipped for Lib', *Courier Mail*, 26 January 1978.
20 Paul Kelly, 'Fraser and Eggleton: the only stars left as the Liberal lights dim', SMH, 14 May 1982.
21 Howard, *Lazarus Rising*, p. 132.
22 David Smith, 'Fraser knew about Hawke but failed to pre-empt his ascension', *Australian*, 4 January 2012.
23 John Hamilton, 'A quiet confidence pervades Liberal bunker', *West Australian*, 17 February 1983.
24 Geoff Kitney, 'The two fatal errors that left the door open to Labor', *National Times*, 6–12 March 1983.
25 Peter Bowers, 'Hawke: no mates, so Chipp is hardest hit', SMH, 26 February 1983.
26 Peter Bowers, 'Whoever wins, keep praying for a US recovery', SMH, 5 March 1983.
27 Laurie Oakes, 'Blueprint for defeat', *Daily Mirror*, 2 March 1983.
28 Anne Summers, 'Fraser faces defeat', AFR, 4 March 1983.
29 Michael Gawenda, 'The making of a media circus', *Age*, 5 March 1983.
30 Snedden and Schedvin, *Billy Snedden*, p. 212.
31 'A forceful stand on liberal principles', *Australian*, 2 March 1983.

32   'A choice to test one's nerve', *Age*, 4 March 1983.

33   David Marr, 'The sour taste of defeat', *National Times*, 13–19 March 1983.

34   O'Brien, *The Liberals*, p. 27.

35   O'Brien, *The Liberals*, pp. 101–2.

36   Peter Bowers, 'The Liberal blitzkrieg was stopped dead', *Courier Mail*, 11 March 1983.

CHAPTER 12

Division and disunity   1983–90

In Australian politics the conventional wisdom is that oppositions do not win elections, governments lose them. The defeat of the Fraser Government in March 1983 seemed almost inevitable. Fraser was much less popular than Bob Hawke whose electoral appeal was unprecedented. The Liberals had been plagued by disunity whereas Labor leader Bill Hayden had made way for Hawke, albeit with considerable personal bitterness. The Coalition had been in office for more than seven years and Australian voters were willing to give a renewed Labor another chance after the tumultuous Whitlam era.

As was the custom after every election, Eggleton completed a preliminary assessment of the result and the lessons that had been learned on 11 March 1983. The assessment mentioned widening the Party's membership base and anticipating the new Labor Government's likely amendments to the *Electorate Act* and public funding of election campaigns. He did not believe the Secretariat contributed to the defeat although the weekly bulletin *Inside Canberra* claimed that 'the Eggleton team ran an appalling campaign, totally out of tune with the mood of the electorate … it is no secret that Mr Peacock and a number of other former ministers in the Fraser Government are not great fans of Mr Eggleton because he was so close to Mr Fraser'.[1] Eggleton did not accept this criticism. In a personal briefing note for Federal Secretariat staff, he stressed that 'it's always possible to find someone to be critical of anything' but the 'only messages I've received have been of support urging me to stay'. He noted that the Liberals were 11 per cent behind at the start of the campaign and closed to be within 4 per cent of winning. Eggleton believed the Party had a good leadership team in Peacock and Howard, and Senators Chaney and Durack, and would soon be seen as 'an alternative government'. He also took from the safe in his office a worse-case contingency plan that included a check-list to aid smooth transition to Opposition.

As ever, the Secretariat was ready to provide a range of professional support services to the Parliamentary party. Eggleton outlined three main priorities for the following 12 months. First, the Secretariat had a 'central role in the initiatives and programs designed to rejuvenate the Party and to restore its electoral fortunes'. Second, it would make a 'major contribution to the redefinition of Liberal principles and objectives, to the articulation of themes and directions, and to the development of policy'. Third, it would offer 'general support to both wings of the Party, especially in relation to political tactics and strategy, opinion polling and research, marketing and public relations'. The only new staff appointments would be in the Policy Development Unit.

Given the Liberal Party had lost government and suffered a substantial defeat, a more extensive review was ordered by the new leader and the Federal Executive. Eggleton released the detailed postmortem in September 1983. Entitled *Facing the Facts: Report of the Liberal Party Committee of Review*, it was widely known as the 'Valder Report' after the committee's chair and president of the New South Wales division, John Valder. Eggleton was a member of the committee and his deputy, the future Howard government senior minister, Nick Minchin, was its secretary. The report was candid and critical. It noted that 'in the last year [the Liberal Party] has suffered a series of reverses to an extent not experienced in the previous 40 years'. A consequence of its electoral success was that 'the Party has been allowed to run down'. It had lost credibility; was inconsistent and wedded to pragmatism and expediency; had identified with large companies rather than small businesses; and, was indifferent to the disadvantaged. In sum, it had lost the 'middle ground' or the 'forgotten people' that Menzies had in mind when he formed the Liberal Party in 1944.

The report also recommended a review of Party membership and recruitment, the establishment of specialist membership groups and renewal of local branches, many of which had been operating as 'closed shops' for the purpose of advancing the aspirations of prospective candidates for public office. The Federal Secretariat could be further 'professionalised' with an increase in paid staff over volunteers and play a leading role 'in coordinating national political activities and initiatives'. The responsiveness of the party organisation to parliamentarians was a constant complaint and needed to be improved. The Secretariat was performing well in the conduct of centralised campaigning but there was too much reliance on advertising agencies. The report's main thrust was the need for the Liberal Party to be much clearer about the things for which it stood. But as Gerard Henderson later observed, the Valder Report 'suffered the fate of many such reports. It was launched with some publicity and then all but forgotten.'[2] While he accepted that some of its insights were 'overcome by the demands of day-to-day politics', there was 'no central structure by which the recommendations in the Valder Report – in whole or in part – could have been imposed on the party'.

For its part, the Federal Secretariat encouraged closer cooperation between Liberals at both the state and federal levels. It would convene and service regular planning and coordination meetings, bringing together the respective parliamentary leaders under the chairmanship of the federal leader. These consultations would be held at different venues around Australia. Apart from contributing to policy and planning, they would result in useful media coverage and strengthen personal relationships. A case in point was a meeting of Liberal leaders in Alice Springs, when the business sessions were followed by an expedition to Uluru. Eggleton managed to reach the summit with future New South Wales premier, Nick Greiner. On a Coalition level, consultation and teamwork were enhanced by regular leaders' dinners at Parliament House. These informal gatherings brought together leaders from both chambers with the Liberal and National Party federal directors.

Eggleton had no doubts about the immense challenge the Coalition faced in defeating the Hawke Government at the next election. There had not been a one-term federal government in 50 years and Hawke continued to enjoy improving economic conditions and substantial personal popularity. Eggleton also opposed 'the view that we need to look for a new constituency because Labor has the middle ground. That is still our natural constituency and it would be imprudent and unsuccessful for the Liberal Party to conclude otherwise.'[3] The Party might regard some policy options as a 'bit radical' but needed to present them in a 'pragmatic way' that demonstrated 'a clear philosophy and choice'.

His advice was timely. The Liberals were beginning to be fractured by tensions between the so-called 'wet' and 'dry' wings of the Party as a tussle began for possession of the Party's 'soul'. Was it a liberal party or a conservative one? Writing in the *Sydney Morning Herald* on 18 October 1984, Max Walsh thought the Liberals were facing an 'ideological takeover' by neo-conservatives that included the businessmen, John Elliott, chief executive of Western Mining, Hugh Morgan, and the former Treasury Secretary, John Stone.[4] Walsh thought that each 'in his own way can save the non-Labor forces from becoming a rudderless vessel propelled hither and yon by each piece of puffery from the market researchers'. Walsh claimed the Party's dependency on flawed poll-driven policy development was largely the work of Eggleton and Peacock.[5]

Peacock remained cautious of the Federal Secretariat after his clashes with Fraser but maintained a sound working relationship with Eggleton. The new leader acknowledged the Secretariat's extensive input and endorsed its priorities ahead of the next election – whenever that might occur. In fact, Hawke decided to call an early poll in December 1984, less than two years after taking office for reasons that were neither clear nor compelling as far as the electorate could discern. The Liberals had structured a long and spirited campaign to take the fight to the Government with the slogan 'Stand up for your family'. The Labor Party and the media assumed the Coalition would suffer a few damaging setbacks but Eggleton was alert to potential problems from day one. Eggleton explained to Robert Thompson of the *Sydney Morning Herald* that 'when you have been in politics as long as I have, you don't even trust your own watch'.[6] He carefully orchestrated the movement of his 'four heavies' – Peacock, John Howard, Fred Chaney and Peter Durack – because 'they are your best news generators'.

Peacock proved to be an especially effective communicator, increasing his approval rating from 19 per cent to 54 per cent by the end of the campaign. Most commentators believed that Peacock had prevailed over Hawke in the first televised leaders debate in part, according to journalist Robert Haupt, because Eggleton was there 'making all sorts of detailed inquiries about camera angles, lighting, make up and all that sort of thing'. Haupt thought Hawke's advisors were 'far more confident and weren't going into that detail'. Eggleton had great respect for his Labor 'opposite number', Bob McMullan, and the need to capitalise on the other side's mistakes: 'I am subconsciously thinking 'now what is Bob McMullan thinking today', and I am sure he is doing the same, saying 'what is Eggleton doing in his bunker today'.[7] After a month of campaigning, Eggleton thought 'the result will be close. There would be no landslide either way and if things went well in this last week of the campaign, a victory for the Coalition could be on the cards'.[8]

Most commentators noted that Hawke lost control of the agenda and mishandled the campaign. Eggleton told Bill Hitchings of the Melbourne *Herald* that the length of the campaign worked against Labor because the Coalition was 'able to home in on the issues, such as assets tests, superannuation and the planned new taxes. They are the issues of this election and we have been given the time to make them the issues'.[9] Eggleton and the Federal Secretariat were praised for their overall strategy and nuanced tactics despite planning for a traditional three-week campaign sometime in late 1985 or early 1986. He also took the risk of dispensing with a major set-piece campaign launch with a long speech – which Eggleton considered a 'relic' – in favour of releasing a detailed policy manifesto.[10] Party workers were certainly buoyed by the momentum the Liberals had gained over just a few weeks and eventually believed the Hawke Government could be defeated. As he stressed to the *Age*'s Russell Barton, 'there is no second prize in politics and there is no point in thinking of campaign strategies which are aimed at anything else but winning'.[11]

During the campaign, Peacock was critical of Eggleton's staff for talking to the media about the Opposition's tactics. Some of these comments were untimely and perhaps injudicious. Conversely, the Secretariat was obliged to deal with Peacock's own campaigning style and the leader's firm views on engaging with the electorate. There was also resentment within the Secretariat that Peacock's office changed his itinerary for 'questionable' reasons without informing them. Eggleton's assessment was echoed by radio broadcaster John Laws who said Peacock's staff 'let him down ... through inexperience and lack of know-how'.[12] Unlike campaigns with Fraser, Eggleton remained at the headquarters and had a 'political liaison officer' travel with Peacock to maintain close communication. More inclined to engage in unscripted activities and unconventional arrangements, Eggleton feared 'it is not impossible that Andrew Peacock is accepting money personally and has a personal slush fund'. If Peacock was unhappy with Eggleton's approach, he failed to identify an alternative overseer. Eggleton privately lamented: 'I didn't get knocked down by the stampede of people wanting to be campaign manager'.

Although the media had initially predicted a massive Labor victory, the Hawke Government received a fright with the Coalition achieving a swing of 1.93 per cent, capturing nine seats. It was not enough to win back government but given a recent electoral distribution appeared to favour Labor, the Liberals were credited with winning the campaign. Labor's foremost authority on polling, Rod Cameron, thought the decision to hold an early election was 'ridiculous' because it 'completely destroyed Bob Hawke's 'above politics' reputation'. The *Australian Financial Review* was highly critical of the Prime Minister: 'having presided over an ill-conceived campaign which was designed to guarantee two more terms but resulted in its becoming extremely vulnerable to the short-term exigencies of politics, the authority of the Prime Minister carried through his first term has been delivered a severe blow'. Eggleton had not expected the Coalition to reduce the Government's parliamentary majority by very much. In the Secretariat's post campaign report he announced: 'against the odds, the outcome was a rebuff for Labor'. As the need for an early election was never made clear, Eggleton observed 'there was resentment in Labor ranks, with most criticism directed at Mr Hawke personally'. Eggleton gleefully repeated the remark of one journalist, 'The messiah is dead'.

This result was a major fillip for the Party and for Peacock. It also vastly improved relations between the Party leader and Eggleton with the Federal Director again becoming secretary of the shadow cabinet. Andrew McCathie reported in the *Australian Financial Review* that 'Eggleton will play a role similar to the one he occupied during the Fraser years when he made an almost daily input into the Government's tactics'. But there the good news ended as protracted in-fighting allowed the Labor Government to divert attention from its own difficulties to Liberal disunity. A party that could not manage its own members could hardly be trusted to manage the nation's affairs. With the Labor Government praised for its economic reforms and willingness to overhaul the tax system, Peacock struggled to make much headway against the supremely confident Labor Treasurer, Paul Keating. Howard believed Peacock was under-performing and had little prospect of defeating Hawke in 1987. The media were talking up Howard's electoral prospects and leadership potential. The deputy Liberal leader shared the Government's passion for ideas and initiatives and looked, and usually sounded, more credible than Peacock when criticising the Government's handling of the nation's finances.

Eggleton sent a confidential memo to Peacock on 13 May 1985 about escalating leadership tensions within the Liberal Party: 'I don't need to tell you that we should put this sort of reporting and speculation to rest as quickly as possible. There's no doubt Labor would try to exploit it ... To the best of my knowledge, the whole thing has been grossly exaggerated. Still, as we know, it's the perceptions that count and will be reflected in the opinion polls'. Over the next few months

Howard declined to pledge unconditional support to Peacock while Peacock would not accept any ambiguity from Howard. He wanted public assurances that Howard would not challenge him for the leadership – the very assurances he declined to give Fraser a few years earlier. Apart from the lack of trust between the leader and his deputy, their respective personal offices generated some of the antagonism.

Adding to the perception of Liberal disarray was the evolving role of the Party's Federal President. Previous leaders of the Party's organisational wing were largely inconspicuous and usually uncontroversial. They included retired parliamentarians and company directors. By the 1980s, they had been replaced in several states and federally by high profile and often outspoken public figures whose media statements, especially on policy issues, sometimes put them on a collision course with the parliamentary party. The first of the 'new' style of Federal President was John Valder.

Eggleton had been intimately involved in a plan to have Valder, a Sydney stockbroker with a reputation for straight-talking, replace the incumbent, Jim Forbes, as Federal President in mid-1985. Forbes was a long retired, former Liberal federal parliamentarian (1956–75) who had held the position since May 1982. Eggleton detected a mood for change but told Valder and his supporters that he needed to be neutral and would not work against Forbes in the interests of Party unity. He also wanted to avoid the perception that the Federal Presidency was the latest front in the continuing battle between Peacock (the Party leader) and Howard (the deputy leader) and the New South Wales and Victorian divisions of the Party.

Before the matter was settled, the *Australian* wrongly claimed that Peacock 'appears to have succeeded against a move by the party's federal director and the federal secretariat to install the president of the NSW branch, John Valder, as the Federal president this year'. Eggleton wanted to avoid a contest for the position and hoped that Valder might wait another year when he would probably be elected unopposed. He tried to manage what he described as an 'impasse' and offered to draft a media release, explaining why the position was being contested, to limit the political damage. Both Forbes and Valder confided in Eggleton about their thinking and eventually spoke with each other. Forbes told Eggleton on 9 June 1985 that Valder had 'frequently referred to his admiration for the very proper role I had played in all of this'. Eggleton was, of course, conscious that he would need to work closely with whoever was elected given the Federal Director was directly responsible to the Federal President.

Shortly after Forbes withdrew, Eggleton spoke with Valder about what he might include in his acceptance speech when he was elected Federal President in July 1985. The *Sydney Morning Herald*'s Mike Steketee gave a candid account of what followed during a meeting of the Party's Federal Executive.

> Eggleton has an aversion to political confrontation, unless it involves his opponents. Imagine, then, the mortification he felt as he sat, very uncomfortably, next to John Valder who was spending the first hour of his presidency chatting away in his inimitable style on who might be the Liberal leader at the next election … Imagine poor Mr Eggleton's feeling of shock when Mr Peacock exploded like a volcano in front of Mr Valder in a room off the conference floor.[13]

Steketee also reported that Eggleton invited Peacock to a small dinner with Valder and the tension was eased.

Suggesting three 'rebel' Liberal parliamentarians ought to resign, Valder was interviewed by Michelle Grattan while Eggleton looked on. At the end of the conversation, Valder told Grattan that 'he supposed Tony would put me over his knee and spank me for outspokenness'. Grattan remarked: 'A mind reader might have found the urbane Eggleton thinking: 'If only I could''. Eggleton was certainly troubled by Valder's bravado and lack of discretion but he recognised his organisational capacities after he rebuilt the New South Wales Division in the early 1980s when it was on the verge of implosion.

The Peacock–Howard rivalry was implicated in the Government overtaking the Opposition in the Morgan opinion poll published in the *Bulletin* on 28 August 1985. The Government's approval rating was up 3 points to 47 per cent while the Coalition slipped 1 point to 46 per cent. Hawke's approval rating was 52 per cent compared with Peacock at 48 per cent. Eggleton told Valder that 'Andrew intends to brush off the media follow-up by simply saying that he fully expects the polls to continue to fluctuate'. Eggleton was being told by the Party's state pollsters that electoral support for Howard was substantially lower than for Peacock and that Howard would turn the Liberals into a 'New Right' political party. He felt that both Peacock and Howard had placed the Party in an untenable and unsustainable position. The Party was 'bleeding' and the implications were highly damaging.

In a private note drafted in early September 1985, Eggleton detailed Peacock's recent lament that Howard was not 'making a full contribution and that his ambitions were getting the better of his loyalty. I said that I felt every effort should be made to overcome the difficulty and try to bridge the gap'. Eggleton feared that 'some of Peacock's staffers, together with people like Reg Withers, contributed substantially to Andrew's growing resentment about Howard'. Conversely, the *Age*'s Michelle Grattan commented after hearing the deputy leader's budget reply speech at the National Press Club on 28 August 1985 that 'John Howard is not your conventional Brutus. But his defence of Mr Peacock, in response to a question about business's lack of enthusiasm about the leader, was a study in unconvincing sincerity'.[14]

Eggleton was the preferred go-between and was in regular contact with both Peacock and Howard. In the overall interests of the Party, Eggleton had tried to resolve the tensions but could only express surprise when Peacock confided that 'it would be possible to get John Moore up as Deputy ... The whole issue was dynamite – so I just filed it away in the back of my mind and did not mention it to anyone'. Alister Drysdale, a senior staffer in Peacock's office, then revealed to Eggleton the beginnings of a plan to oust Howard. 'I told Alister that I did not want to get involved with this kind of strategy but I was glad to be kept informed of thinking'.

Howard kept in touch with Eggleton believing him to be an honourable man who did not take sides. On 2 September, Peacock asked his deputy to return to Canberra the next day for a discussion about the leadership. Howard then telephoned Eggleton and appealed for his support. Eggleton made a note of Howard's insistence that 'he had done nothing to undermine the leadership (nothing overt, that is) ... but sounded a bit worried and unnerved'. He wanted Eggleton 'to have the above background in case I was backgrounding the Monday press'. At a shadow cabinet meeting on 3 September, Eggleton 'tried to persuade [Howard] to act in the best interests of the Party – and to remove the ambiguity that led to our current problems. Howard said he would consider the matter further and was working on a form of words'. Although Peacock said he wanted a 'non-confrontationalist solution', Eggleton believed he wanted to be rid of Howard permanently, suspecting Howard was planning a leadership spill within weeks. This was not true but Peacock could not be persuaded otherwise.

An attempt was made to craft a mutually acceptable public statement in which Howard would declare loyalty to Peacock. A succession of drafts had not produced a text that both men could sign. Such was Howard's regard for Eggleton's integrity and impartiality that he asked the Federal Director to supervise the drafting. After lengthy consultation, Eggleton believed they had finally achieved a solution. Howard seemed on the verge of agreeing and shook hands with Peacock. Howard returned to his office and consulted his staff, including his mentor, Senator Sir John Carrick, and then telephoned his wife, Janette. Neither believed he should agree to the words he had just endorsed. He returned immediately to Peacock's office and told him: 'I can't go along with this'. The wording was now unacceptable. Howard's response implied the belief that his integrity was being questioned:

> I am not plotting. I have not been plotting. I have not drawn up lists of shadow ministers. I have not made any approaches to people ... The response I have given on the possibility of a leadership challenge is fair and reasonable. This response does not represent any disloyalty or treachery to Mr Peacock. I have spent my life serving the Liberal Party and I am willing to match my record of loyalty to its leaders, present and past, with that of anybody else in the party.

As Errington and Van Onselen observe, 'it was Peacock's paranoia more than anything said, or not said, that caused him problems'.

In the face of this apparent stalemate and Howard's refusal 'to rule out a challenge to my leadership', Peacock decided on a party room spill to remove Howard as deputy leader on 5 September 1985. Peacock told Eggleton, but apparently none of his colleagues, that if Howard defeated John Moore in a ballot for the deputy leadership, Peacock would resign. Ever discreet and committed to keeping confidences, Eggleton told no-one. As Henderson noted: 'In other words many of those who took part in the Howard/Moore ballot did not understand that they were voting, in fact, for the leadership. It was a complete stuff up'.[15] Howard defeated Moore by 38 votes to 32. Peacock then asked Howard, Durack and Chaney to his office (which adjoined the party room) where he announced his intention to resign. On returning to the party meeting, Peacock called for nominations for the now vacant Party leadership. Howard then defeated Jim Carlton 59 votes to six.

The Liberal Party's Federal Executive was meeting at the same time as the Parliamentary party and Eggleton arranged for his assistant (Jackie Jurd) to inform him of the outcome. They were stunned by her message: 'John Howard is the new leader of the party'. Peacock had miscalculated the Party room mood. The majority of the Parliamentary party were content with the leadership team of Peacock and Howard. In voting for the retention of Howard as deputy, they assumed they would be maintaining the status quo. However, Peacock interpreted the re-election of Howard as a vote of no confidence in his leadership. Hence, dramatically and unexpectedly to everyone but Eggleton, Howard emerged as leader. Shortly afterwards, Peacock visited the Secretariat where the Federal Executive meeting had concluded. Eggleton looked on as Peacock

> made a very emotional appearance (accompanied by [his second wife] Marg St George). He was very controlled and gracious. He thanked the Party for their cooperation and assistance, and was particularly generous in his praise for me. It was very stylish exit. A remarkable day in Liberal politics ... a half day is a long time in politics.

The emergence of Howard as Liberal leader was favourably received in many quarters. The unanticipated outcome did, however, plunge the Party deeper into the political wilderness as the Hawke Government eagerly exploited the Liberal's disunity. The price of this disunity would be many more years in opposition. To all intents and purposes, there were now two Liberal parties in Canberra: the Howard Party and the Peacock Party. Labor had a cutting battle cry: 'If the Liberals can't govern themselves, they can't govern the country'. It was hard to disagree.

After gaining the Party leadership in unexpected circumstances, Howard proved to be a hard-working and determined Opposition leader, with strong policy credentials. He was an able parliamentary performer and an articulate media contributor. But he was not an inspiring public personality and, at this stage of his career, he struggled to gain political traction and electoral credibility. He was poorly regarded by Victorian Liberals and the business community in Melbourne. They spoke disparagingly about him and had no confidence he could lead the Party to electoral success. It was ironic that many of these people, who were so ready to ridicule him in the 1980s, later became his most energetic supporters. Howard was soon concerned about deteriorating perceptions of his performance among journalists and in the business community, his inconsistent ratings in the opinion polls, and the general fragility of his position. The party was disunited and dispirited, while Peacock was once again casting a long shadow.

By March 1986, 'a very worried Howard' was sharing with Eggleton his angst about National Party dissatisfaction with his leadership and the Coalition's overall health. He was also 'distressed by this week's polls and felt that he would be 'dead meat' if he didn't improve his ratings. He felt that, sooner or later, the 'boys' would reject him if it did not appear he could win'. Howard also felt that Nationals' leader, Ian Sinclair, preferred Peacock and might have been quietly working against him. Eggleton was alarmed by Howard's 'paranoia about the media' and counselled him to take a broader view. He needed to heed his own advice in December 1986 when the *Daily Telegraph* reported under the heading 'Tony Talk':

> We understand that some senior Federal Liberals concerned about Opposition leader John Howard's performance are looking at the person who's selling the 'product' – Tony Eggleton, the Party's Federal Director – and could soon be asking him to lift his performance if he wants to hold his niche in Canberra.[16]

The contrary view was put by the journalist Paul Lyneham: 'He's the man who's made survival such an art form you could dump him in Iran wearing a Salman Rushdie mask and he's still be back at his desk at 6.40am sharp the next morning'.

At the close of 1986, Eggleton told the Party's Federal Executive that the Hawke Government 'is scared that it is going to lose the election; while, at the same time, the Coalition is displaying symptoms of a lack of confidence in winning'. The Party's 'own supporters have been demoralised' although the public 'no longer have confidence in Hawke [and] Keating is no longer trusted'. The Coalition should have been seen as the alternative government but as a result of ill-discipline and bickering, 'we were left looking divided and irresolute'.

The Coalition was searching for strong and decisive leadership when the National Party premier of Queensland, Joh Bjelke-Petersen, threw political caution to the wind. The Premier saw himself as the slayer of a resurgent socialist menace. He set his sights on becoming prime minister, in lieu of an inept federal Coalition and its weak leadership. The 'Joh for PM' push was never realistic or credible. Nonetheless, some reporters took it seriously and the whole saga further debilitated the Coalition. Eggleton remarked in February 1987 that 'in my two decades with the Party, I don't think I can recall such a disconcerting period for our side of politics'. Apart from the Joh campaign, he thought 'we should be confidently looking forward to a good win at the next election (and this is still within our grasp)'. In March 1987, the *Sunday Telegraph*'s political reporter Warwick Costin predicted that within the next three months, Howard, Valder and Eggleton would all be gone because they 'have little support in the Peacock camp'.[17] After this story appeared Peacock rang Eggleton to apologise because references to the Federal Director 'were totally unfounded'. But by May 1987, Eggleton was telling the Party's executive that 'we have slipped back into political 'no man's land' where we are very exposed to pitfalls and sniping from all sides' although the Liberals only needed a 2 per cent swing to deliver the nine seats that would allow them to form government.

In the immediate lead-up to the 1987 election campaign Eggleton was pre-occupied with negotiations and strategies to neutralise the damage of disunity. He accompanied Howard to Brisbane for 'peace talks' with Bjelke-Petersen and key figures in the National Party. This was followed by a discussion that Howard referred to as 'one of the more remarkable political meetings of my entire life'. It took place late in the evening at Howard's Wollstonecraft home.[18] Howard, his chief of staff, Grahame Morris, and Eggleton met three representatives from the 'Joh for PM' campaign including Sir Robert Sparkes, the president of the Queensland Nationals. Howard was incredulous: 'the 'Joh for PM' campaign was finished, but they thought it had all been rather unfair, because if the rest of the National Party had come on board it might have been successful'. What they could not concede was their campaign effectively shattered the Federal Coalition which took a decade to recover. They had to fight the federal election as separate Liberal and National parties rather than as a united Coalition. Fraser had told Eggleton that 'the disunity and divisiveness caused by Joh-Bjelke-Petersen would cost the Liberals the election'. He was right.

Policy drafting and other Opposition campaign preparations were severely hampered by the Queensland farce. Despite the unfavourable political landscape, Howard fought a vigorous and laudable campaign. Eggleton travelled extensively with him, conscious that his other travelling companion, wife Janette, was also an influential adviser. Howard was also trying to overcome a substantial dis-advantage entirely of his own making. Treasury analysis of the Coalition's tax package revealed a 'double counting error' of $1.63 billion – which was a very substantial amount in 1987. Consequently, the Coalition could not deliver its tax cuts. When Howard tried to suggest the error was only $540 million, he only worsened the damage. Keating seized on what was an elementary mistake and persisted with an attack on the Coalition's inability to manage the nation's affairs. Polling suggested that Howard had minimal appeal with voters and the public were thoroughly unimpressed with Coalition disunity. Eggleton showed Howard a private poll conducted by Gary Morgan for the Liberal Party not long after the tax error was revealed to show the Coalition was trailing Labor by 18 points.[19] The Hawke-Keating combination was inspiring much more confidence than Howard and his treasury spokesman, Jim Carlton.

Eggleton acknowledged that the campaign started badly and struggled to recover. He also believed the media were highly partisan. It was, he contended, 'one of the most jaundiced periods of reporting of campaigns I have seen in my 25 years in Australian politics'. He went on: 'There's a feeling of [media] hostility to the Coalition coming through. So is the friendship of the Prime Minister [Bob Hawke] with the media barons. I'm not paranoid about it. But I believe the question of political commentary and reporting is spontaneously emerging as an issue in its own right.'[20]

On election night, 11 July 1987, the early counting favoured the Liberals. Eggleton and Howard were watching television at their Sydney hotel when a commentator forecast a Liberal win. They were both realistic enough not to get too excited. It was, however, a close result despite the difficult campaign. Labor won on preferences, 50.8 per cent to 49.2 per cent. The Liberals and Nationals achieved a one per cent swing but disunity and distractions had clearly taken their toll. The electorate was not convinced the Liberals had the capacity or cohesion to form a credible government, or to deliver on their policies. The Liberals, under Howard's leadership, had done reasonably well in debilitating circumstances. Howard had boosted his personal approval rating to a record 54 per cent although it would not last. The Opposition Leader resolutely pressed on and the Secretariat supported him with new initiatives but it was often a case of one step forward and two steps back.

Within 24 hours of the election loss, there was a meeting of Howard, Chaney, Elliott, Valder, and Eggleton. Howard attributed the Party's defeat to the 'Joh for PM' campaign. Others, such as Malcolm Fraser, were far from convinced. The former prime minister was critical of Howard's presentation and leadership style. There was, however, consensus that Howard should remain leader. He had only fought one election and dumping him would look like desperation. Peacock ran for the Party leadership in the wake of the election loss and was defeated by Howard 41–28 votes. Peacock nominated for the deputy leadership and was successful against a field of 11 candidates. He was offered and accepted the Treasury portfolio despite his earlier discomfort with economic issues. Howard chose Nationals senator and former Treasury Secretary, John Stone, as the Coalition's finance spokesman. Howard's position was still far from secure and most of the shadow cabinet felt a sense of uncertainty as they faced a third term Labor Government.

Within the Federal Secretariat, Eggleton sought more authority to direct campaigns,

> not just its Federal elements such as advertising and campaign headquarters, but actual operational responsibility for everything, including the leader's staff ... If you have that authority and things go wrong, then you put up with the kicks. But it's a bit irritating if you get the blame for matters you have no control over.[21]

He told Alan Ramsey that 'you never fight an ideal election campaign, you fight it on the landscape you're given. You're the bunny. Perhaps the last thing you want is an election, but suddenly that's where you are, you're the campaign director, and it's all uphill'.

With the election lost, Eggleton's immediate focus was preparing for John Elliott's term as head of the Party's organisational wing and looking forward to exploiting further his considerable fundraising abilities. Both Howard and Peacock had several serious confrontations with Elliott after he succeeded John Valder as Federal President on 30 October 1987. As Party Treasurer, Elliott managed to double the Federal Secretariat's budget with staff numbers increasing from 10 to 24 after the 1984 election. He was pledging to double the budget again as Federal President. Eggleton told Alan Ramsey that Elliott's 'whole philosophy is to win. And, despite his personality, he is a team player'. These carefully chosen words were more diplomatic than accurate. Peacock was aggrieved that Elliott was ignoring the usual protocols and commenting critically on policy within his area of responsibility. On the day Elliot became Federal President, Howard stressed that 'he would continue to support Elliott if he agreed to abide by the traditional division of organisational/parliamentary responsibilities ... and would not continue making public statements on policy'. Howard proposed a set of ground rules. They would be drafted by Eggleton who was adamant they not be released to the media because 'such a document would generate a major news story based on a lack of confidence between the Organisational and Parliamentary leaders. It would be seen as an act of weakness not strength. Further, the document would be used as a check list to measure all Elliott's future statements'. The ground rules were drafted and the only copy was held by Eggleton in the Secretariat.

Not unexpectedly, Elliott frequently ignored the ground rules. On 23 March 1988 he publicly proposed the introduction of a consumption tax – the GST. Howard was livid. He proposed cancelling an overseas trip to Tokyo and Manila in order to confront Elliott. Eggleton persuaded Howard to ask Valder to confer with Elliott as the previous Federal President. While overseas, Howard decided that Elliott had to be removed from office. On his return, Howard asked Eggleton to arrange a meeting between the Parliamentary leadership group and the organisational leaders. Howard insisted that Elliott abide by the ground rules. Elliott 'rejected out of hand making any further statement' about the ground rules and 'we found ourselves at an impasse. Howard was highly agitated and Elliott simply stared across the table and held his ground. I intervened and said that it might be a good idea if, as Chief Executive, I took John Elliott into my office for a private chat'. Eggleton persuaded him to include some suitably contrite words in his opening speech at the Party's Federal Council meeting in three days time. Howard emphasised that Elliott was on his last chance and 'any further breaches would have to result in a change of presidency'. The details of this confidential meeting were reported in the next day's newspapers. Elliott, who had flown overnight to Japan, regarded the media coverage as a breach of faith by Howard's staff (whom he thought were duplicitous). Elliot told Eggleton he would not honour the undertaking he had given the previous evening. Eggleton then drafted a statement that Elliot might read to waiting media on his return to Australia and offered some paragraphs that he might include in his opening address at the Federal Council meeting that Eggleton thought would satisfy Howard's demands.

Before the Federal Council meeting began at the Hyatt Hotel in Melbourne, Howard was adamant that a statement issued in Elliott's name earlier in the day 'did not go nearly far enough'. Howard called an impromptu meeting of Liberal shadow ministers and secured their backing for 'his uncompromising stand about Elliott and the words to be included in the Council speech'. Both Eggleton and Valder thought Howard was taking an excessively hard line with Elliott who seemed prepared to offer an apology. Eggleton thought Howard was 'in a very emotional and explosive state'. There was a further stand off as some of Elliott's supporters recognised the impossible situation in which Howard was being placed. There was agreement that Howard and Elliott would be left alone with Eggleton to draft a suitable statement.

After further discussions, Eggleton

> finally hammered out some agreed words. Every word was fought over but finally I had a draft of a kind that seemed acceptable to them both. However, it was the basic minimum as far as John Howard was concerned. More bitterness broke out when Elliott demanded that Howard's office should do no further briefing prior to his making his speech. As tempers began to flare again, I said I was getting sick and tired of the way they were behaving. I had not given 20 years of my life to see this happening to the Party ... Before we left the room there was a somewhat stilted reunion. I stood over them as they both shook hands, and we agreed that we would put on the best possible face as we crossed the foyer back to the Executive [meeting].

Howard was ready to acknowledge that his fraught relationship with Elliott 'was making life very difficult' for Eggleton. Eggleton had enormous respect for Howard and did not believe he would give in. He told Alan Ramsey:

> John Howard is not a quitter. I've worked with every leader of the Liberal Party and he is by far the most resilient and toughest of them all. He's certainly had the roughest road. Yet he has an absolute determination to become prime minister. I don't believe there is the slightest chance in the world of Howard quitting. People still under-estimate him.[22]

Although the state presidents had more power, Elliott had a substantial personal profile and extensive influence with ordinary Party members who, he believed, ought to have a more prominent role in Liberal affairs. Things needed to change. Rather than the autonomous state divisions assuming responsibility for campaigning in marginals seats, Elliott and Eggleton 'wanted a measure of federal coordination and a campaigning presence with the state people in these critical seats'. They also recognised the need for generational change and approached Andrew Robb, the Executive Director of the National Farmers Federation, to see if I would move to the Liberal Party as Tony's deputy, with a view to taking over after the 1990 election, subject to performance. There were no guarantees but I had the inside running for the top job if they liked what I did for the next campaign.[23]

Robb agreed and started at the Federal Secretariat. His first task was 'to set up a campaign unit within the Federal Secretariat to work with the states and coordinate the marginal seats'.[24]

As Peacock had been wary of Valder, Howard was suspicious of Robb who had a close relationship with Elliott. Howard soon felt that Robb was 'white-anting' him and 'objected strongly to Robb being privy to all the Party activity (research, etc ... actions in the Leader's office) and then feeding it all back to Elliott'. Consequently, Howard told Eggleton that Robb was 'not welcome' in his office. In a private note, Eggleton described Howard's mood as 'very hostile' and mentioned his 'white hot anger, frustration and desperation'. Worst of all, he was finding it 'difficult to trust the Secretariat'.

Nonetheless, Eggleton and the Secretariat, particularly a staffer he recruited from the British Conservative Party named Graham Wynn, worked closely with Howard to produce a comprehensive policy manifesto, *Future Directions*, which was launched in December 1988. Eggleton explained that *Future Directions* drew on the model of British political manifestos but 'it doesn't mirror their strategy exactly, it has been tailored to our own views and political climate'.[25] Rejecting the charge of populism, Eggleton insisted it was not research *driven* but research *tested*. In what Eggleton called the 'Age of Anxiety for middle Australia',[26] *Future Directions* marked a crucial step forward in Eggleton's theory that opposition parties move through three phases: they are initially irrelevant and then become credible before they turn into an alternative government. Eggleton felt the Liberals failed to 'sell themselves' as the alternative government in 1987.

The cover featured a traditional family, a typical middle-class home and a white picket fence. Remarkably, the conservative and conventional theme of the graphic design attracted nearly as much media attention as the manifesto. This initiative was a successful policy exercise although the 1950s 'white picket fence' strategy remained a critical point of reference for some years. The Party was trying to capitalise on positive responses to *Future Directions* at a time when many senior Liberals, especially in Melbourne, were becoming increasingly despondent about Howard's prospects of becoming prime minister. The

Bulletin had famously dubbed him 'Mr 18 per cent' for his low approval rating before asking: 'Why does this man bother?'

Influential Australian Liberals with British connections decided to take advantage of a visit to Australia by the famous English novelist Jeffrey Archer, who also held high office in the Conservative Party. They invited him to Canberra for a 'pep talk' with Howard. It was a fleeting and strange encounter. Eggleton collected Archer from Canberra airport and took him to Parliament House late in the afternoon. He met with Howard and a small number of people, then Eggleton returned him to the airport for an evening flight to Sydney. Archer was not impressed with Howard, feeling he needed to exude greater strength and confidence. Archer also thought he should smarten himself up and suggested the party invest in an updated wardrobe for the alternative prime minister. In other words, an image makeover. Eggleton was underwhelmed by the advice. Archer had overlooked Howard's substance.

Coincidentally, Federal President John Elliott was emerging as a potential Parliamentary leader. Over the previous two years he had displayed drive, ambition and charisma with some parliamentarians thinking he could be the circuit-breaker for the Peacock-Howard rivalry and might be the Liberal Party's electoral saviour. There was a great deal of scheming behind the scenes to promote his prospects. Eggleton was aware that 'Elliott gave very serious consideration to entering Parliament with an eye to getting the leadership before the next election'. Believing that Howard's hold on the leadership was tenuous at best, Eggleton suggested to Elliott that he appoint Peacock staffer, Alister Drysdale, to his personal staff. Drysdale started working for Elliott in mid-1988.

When the Liberal Member for Higgins, Roger Shipton, could not be induced to stand aside, there was no other safe federal seat into which Elliott could be 'parachuted'. With his own business commitments demanding priority, the 'Elliott for Parliament' campaign soon lost momentum. Elliot and his supporters still regarded Howard as a lost cause and continued to look for another way forward. As the focus turned back to the Member for Kooyong and Elliott had 'mended fences' with Peacock, the faltering Elliott bandwagon decided to swing behind the former Party leader. Howard was further hampered by unrelenting media derision and poor opinion polling. Elliott was now convinced he had to go.

Eggleton was conscious of the personal intrigue but did not want to get involved. Elliott and his friends understood that Eggleton was in an invidious position. He was an employee of the Party organisation and reported to Elliott as Federal President. He also had responsibilities to the parliamentary leader. As a courtesy, Elliott and his office kept Eggleton advised to the extent that was prudent. On the eve of the move against Howard, Eggleton was aware but not privy to the full extent of the strategy (which involved the simultaneous replacement of the Nationals' leader, Ian Sinclair) or the identity of the key players. Because of the veiled nature of the communications, Eggleton was never quite sure how much was simply gamesmanship.

On 9 May 1989, there was a Coalition leaders' dinner in Howard's suite at Parliament House. There were several apologies, including Peacock and Fred Chaney. Howard, Sinclair, Bruce Lloyd (Deputy Leader of the National Party), Paul Davey (the Nationals' Federal Director) and Eggleton were present. Although the mood was cordial, with such significant absentees Eggleton sensed they may have been participating in something akin to the final meal of a condemned man. He later reflected: 'I did not enjoy my dinner. It was an unreal atmosphere, and I wondered why John Howard and Ian Sinclair did not read more into the absence of the other Liberal leaders'. Eggleton knew a challenge was being mounted but remained silent. He was in a quandary,

> caught between loyalty to the leader and concern about our election prospects ... I was in an impossible position over all of this. I knew of the Federal President's [Elliott's] role, and the growing concern over the Howard leadership ... I could not ignore the awful research findings. The research pointed to a political dead end for John. Although I had a general awareness of the movement against John Howard, I kept well away from the plotting. Apart from my own sensitivities, those planning the move realised that it would be inappropriate and imprudent to involve me.

Shortly after the dinner, Howard received a visit from Peacock and Chaney to inform him that they proposed to move a spill of leadership positions the following day. Eggleton received early morning calls advising of the unfolding situation with Peacock saying he wanted Eggleton to continue as Federal Director.

At the Party room meeting, there were 43 votes in favour of the spill motion and 28 against. At the ensuing ballot, Peacock received 44 votes and Howard

27. After two rounds of voting for the deputy's position, Fred Chaney defeated Peter Reith by the same margin. Eggleton called on Howard after the vote. He was devastated and distraught. He had made an immense effort over more than three years as leader and was looking forward to a second chance at becoming prime minister. Howard's political prospects, indeed his entire political future, appeared to have collapsed in a matter of hours. It was hardly surprising that he was emotional given those he considered friends had abandoned him without any apparent regret. Not unlike Menzies who lost the prime ministership in 1941 after his own party deserted him, Howard looked to be finished politically. Eggleton tried to lift his spirits and encourage him to think positively about the future. He had offered similar advice to Malcolm Fraser in 1971 when he was bereft of hope.

Eggleton urged Peacock to find a senior position for Howard in the shadow cabinet. Peacock was receptive but ultimately more obligated to those colleagues who had made him leader. Eggleton pressed Peacock to consider Howard for the Defence portfolio but was unsuccessful. A week later, those who had plotted to remove Howard, the so-called 'Cardinals', agreed to appear on ABC television's *Four Corners* to boast about how they managed to execute their coup. Eggleton described it as a 'fit of self-indulgence'. The gloating interviews infuriated Howard and his supporters, largely destroying any advantages that might have been gained by the change of leadership.

Eggleton 'advised Peacock to get rid of [John] Moore and [Wilson] Tuckey and use the Moore position to put Howard back in the team. Andrew could not make up his mind. He was receiving a diversity of advice. Also, he felt very obligated to Moore and Tuckey for their roles in the coup'. A few more days passed and Peacock told Eggleton he was 'considering demoting them rather than sacking … giving them second rate portfolios in the outer Ministry'. By the time of the 30 May Party room meeting, however, 'Peacock changed his mind and decided to tough it out. I have little doubt that Chaney was against restoring Howard to the shadow ministry'. Howard was offered the shadow education portfolio which, Peacock suspected, he would decline.

Howard told Eggleton on 17 May that the *Four Corners* program had totally changed the landscape and 'had a major impact on public perceptions of the Liberal Party'. He would not 'share a table with dishonourable men of this kind' and felt that Eggleton was the only man he could trust because even the Federal

President (Elliott) had turned against him. After his conversation with Howard, Eggleton

> did not see any prospect of getting cooperation from John Howard. He is now determined to present himself as a man of principle in marked contrast to the 'gang of four' [Moore, Tuckey, Peter Shack and Chris Puplick]. His staff confirmed to me that he is now engaged in a crusade. As I left the room John Howard said to me that these events could lead anywhere and things were not over by any means.

Eggleton wrote to Howard on 1 June 1989 wishing him well and offering him some consolation: 'After some 30 years in Canberra and involvement with politics, I'm only too well aware of the unpredictable twists and turns. One thing is certain ... you never say never in politics'. Eggleton concluded in a private note that 'I expect Andrew will pay a high price for not acting firmly against Moore and Tuckey. Many people saw this as weak leadership. There was widespread demand for them both to be removed from the front bench'.

There was to be no political honeymoon for Peacock. Eggleton was inundated with letters of protest, especially from Liberals in Howard's home state of New South Wales. He had never had such an avalanche of negative correspondence. It was pretty clear that, come the next election, Liberal support would be seriously depleted in Sydney. Eggleton had further meetings with Howard in the hope of some rapprochement. Howard was so incensed at the attitude of his former colleagues that he refused to serve in the shadow cabinet. Eggleton continued to talk with Peacock about the virtue of restoring Howard to the front bench and looked for opportunities. It took months to create the right circumstances for Howard's return to the inner team as Shadow Minister for Industry, Technology and Commerce. Eggleton was delighted, telling Howard on 30 October 1989: 'I'm sure we can win and will well ... as you quite rightly said [when rejoining the shadow cabinet], it's time for putting Party first and concentrating on the job of getting rid of the Hawke/Keating Government'. Howard replied a few weeks later: 'I shall be doing all I humanly can to secure a win at the next election. The omens look very good but there is still a lot to be done'.

Howard's return was attributed to Eggleton's influence. The *Sunday Herald*'s Gervase Greene asserted this was not the first time Tony Eggleton has found himself up to his ears in political chicanery ... Mr Eggleton dismisses his role as nothing more than intermediary but it is significant that he emerged from the latest Coalition ruction with scrupulously clean hands. He always has. Despite being involved in some of the most spectacular political upheavals in the history of the Liberal Party, Mr Eggleton has emerged with both a spotless reputation for integrity and very few enemies.[27]

After the dumping of Howard, Eggleton resumed his previously close relationship with Peacock. Eggleton tried to move beyond the leadership traumas and continue planning for the next election. Peacock looked to Eggleton for help in sorting out office problems. Eggleton made his deputy, Andrew Robb, available to serve as Peacock's chief of staff for the last six months before the election. Peacock also encouraged Eggleton's increasing involvement with members of the Parliamentary party and his participation in leadership retreats at Thredbo. In terms of policy, Peacock was uneasy about the pressure being exerted by some of his colleagues to put a consumption tax on the policy table. He knew that Eggleton doubted the wisdom of trying to sell such a policy in the context of an election campaign. Peacock invited Eggleton to a Coalition leaders meeting with the goal of dissuading them. On the surface, Peacock gave the impression he was prepared to support the tax but was grateful that Eggleton succeeded in steering the meeting away from this controversial proposal. It was not a topic on which he could have campaigned with credibility or conviction.

Eggleton had long decided that, whatever the outcome of the 1990 election, he would not continue as Federal Director beyond that year. Loyalty had kept him in the role for 15 years at the wishes of the organisational and parliamentary leadership. Each time he raised the prospect of moving on, he received appeals and incentives to stay. Many people saw the Federal Director and the Secretariat as the Party's one consistent, stable and reliable entity. By 1990, however, he would have done it all and was ready for change.

The decision was made easier by the demanding routine he had set himself. Throughout his tenure the day started no later than 5am. Following his early morning run, he was at the office by 6.30am. His long-serving and loyal 'Mr Fix It', Vince Woolcock, arrived ahead of him to raise the secretariat's flag and assess the morning papers. When Howard was leader he was often on the telephone before 7am to compare notes about the morning papers and prepare for radio interviews. The media started calling soon after then. With an eye to teamwork, Eggleton chaired the daily staff meeting at 8.45am. They reviewed the contemporary political scene as well as progress with programs and priorities.

On parliamentary sitting days Eggleton attended the morning meeting of the Coalition strategy group at Parliament House. When in Canberra, he didn't stop for lunch. He would usually consume an apple and a biscuit. Most weeks found him on a couple of interstate trips, while there were overseas commitments from time to time. For interstate appointments during John Elliott's term as Liberal Party Federal Treasurer and Federal President, he sometimes travelled in Elliot's private jet. Elliott would drop into the Canberra office and raise tens of thousands of dollars within an hour. He had private line access to all the nation's business leaders and, whatever figure they offered, he would shame them into adding an extra zero or two. If there were no unexpected dramas during the day, Eggleton tried to get home by 6.30 or 7pm. Dinner was often eaten while watching the television news before he spent the remainder of the evening sifting documents for the next day. At weekends, all the newspapers were delivered to his home. On Saturday mornings it took a couple of hours to scan them all and be ready for calls from the media and the leader.

Eggleton's final challenge as Federal Director was the 1990 election which was held on 24 March. The Secretariat staff built on their collective experience, creating a nationally directed campaign with input from all levels of the Party. Research suggested to the campaign committee that Peacock should fight a positive campaign by convincing the electorate that the Liberals' policies had appeal. Voters knew they wanted to be rid of the Labor Government but were still to be persuaded to vote for the Coalition. The committee opted for a campaign highlighting what Peacock and the Liberals had to offer as a credible alternative government.

As the campaign progressed there was lobbying from within the party for more negative advertising. This view was not shared by the parliamentary leadership or the advertising agency and, based on the research that had shaped the party's fundamental strategy, Eggleton was reluctant to change course mid-campaign.

This was the first time the campaign director had oversight of the leader's personal team. Peacock gave his all. His cooperation and commitment added to the friendship and mutual respect that had grown between him and Eggleton.

The Coalition won more votes than Labor, some 400,000 more votes, but they were not distributed in the right places. The outcome was a cliffhanger. The result was so close that it was almost a week before the result was known. The Liberals had taken 10 seats from Labor. An additional 3500 votes across six seats would have won them the election. As expected, Peacock's strong support in his home state of Victoria was not matched by voting trends in Howard's home state of New South Wales. Despite Labor's vote falling by more than six per cent the Government managed to retain office. This was the first time that Labor had won three consecutive elections in its 100 year history.

In his brief to the Federal Executive, Eggleton commented that 'of my 13 Federal campaigns, this was the most unpredictable and most frustrating. We had a country that wanted a change of government but right up until election day, couldn't quite accept us as the alternative'. Ultimately, he observed, 'people held off to the end to make up their mind' and most voted for the Australian Democrats, a minor party, which preferenced Labor over Liberal candidates. The Nationals vote also detracted from the Coalition's overall position. Nevertheless, Eggleton noted, 'Labor was pushed to the wire and the Peacock/Blunt team came tantalisingly close to victory ... we did a lot better than might have been expected in an unforgiving political atmosphere soured by perceptions of Liberal instability and unreliability'. This led him to have 'no doubt we will see the return of Liberal government in Australia no later than 1993 ... which will be a nice touch on the eve of the Party's 50th anniversary'.

He took pride in an independent assessment concluding that the 'campaign ran smoothly, and there were few if any criticisms of the campaign management'. He concluded his final campaign report by stressing the importance of planning: 'don't leave winning until the election campaign ... it is not realistic to expect to deliver in four to five weeks that which has not been set in train in the previous weeks, months and even years'. According to Eggleton, since the defeat of the Fraser Government in March 1983 the Liberal Party had lacked what he considered the essential the four Cs: 'credibility, consistency, confidence and cohesion'.

Former Federal President, John Valder, suggested Eggleton succeed Elliott as the incoming Federal President. After dismissing suggestions that 'any of the blame' could be laid at the door of Eggleton and his team, Valder was adamant 'they were let down by the parliamentary leadership'. Valder contended that 'throughout the whole of the past decade, Tony Eggleton was a pillar of calm and good sense! After 15 years as an 'excellent federal director … his experience and wide respect would make him an equally good federal president! Eggleton had no real interest in the position although he received telephone calls urging him to nominate and 'would need an awful lot of persuasion to change my mind! He thought it would 'set a bad precedent if someone from the organisation decided to nominate.'[28] The position was filled by Ashley Goldsworthy, the Victorian managing director of AV Jennings homes.

With seven federal elections and five leadership changes since 1975, Eggleton's journey as Federal Director had been a mixture of achievement and anxiety. Following the 1990 election campaign, which most commentators agreed had been highly successful given the Liberals had been plagued by disunity for five years, Eggleton announced his decision to stand down and was pleased to be succeeded by his able deputy, Andrew Robb. The transition took place at a meeting of the Federal Executive at the Wentworth Hotel in Sydney on 11 May 1990. It was a fitting moment: this was Eggleton's 100th Executive meeting and it was almost 15 years to the day since his appointment.

Eggleton remained temporarily in the Secretariat. He was appointed special adviser with a range of elder statesman responsibilities that included revision of party structures and oversight of the Liberals' international relationships. He was given a suite in the National Press Club not far from the Secretariat building. A testimonial dinner, coinciding with a meeting of the Federal Council, was held in the ballroom of the Sheraton Hotel in Brisbane on 24 October 1990. The 400 guests included four of the nine parliamentary leaders that Eggleton had served – Malcolm Fraser, Andrew Peacock, John Howard and John Hewson – and all of the living Federal Presidents: Bob Southey, John Atwill, Jim Forbes, John Valder, John Elliott and Ashley Goldsworthy.

A slide presentation captured moments of his career and speakers included Fraser, Hewson, Brisbane Lord Mayor Sallyanne Atkinson, Valder and Atwill. Elliott chaired the event and presented him with the party's Outstanding Service Award, only the second recipient after Dame Pattie Menzies. John Gorton was not well enough to attend but Ainsley Gotto was present. A tribute was read from Gorton, along with others from Margaret Thatcher, Doug Anthony, the United States Republicans, Sir William Heseltine, Sir David Smith, Sir Robert Crichton-Brown and the Canberra Press Gallery. His wife Mary was also warmly acknowledged.

During his years as Federal Director, Eggleton had won three elections and lost four. The first election victory was the most significant; the last was the nearest to victory and possibly the most demanding. The Liberals were predicted to win in 1975 and expected to lose in 1990. Although the Coalition was not returned to office under Peacock, Eggleton could leave the Federal Secretariat in good spirits at a time of his own choosing with his reputation in tact. He later described the previous seven years as 'by far the saddest period ... you could take one step forward and two steps back'.[29] Despite the recent defeats, Eggleton's deputy, Andrew Robb, referred to him as 'deeply respected' and 'highly distinguished'. A number of political campaigners who later achieved national prominence had acquired experience and gained expertise under his mentorship. He had worked with all nine leaders of the Liberal Parliamentary party and, as federal director, with five federal presidents, 46 state presidents and 35 state directors.

Eggleton contributed to the transformation of Australian political campaigning. The conduct of elections that once were 'oddly amateur and instinctive, have become increasingly technical and self-conscious operations'.[30] His name was mentioned among those considered the best operators in recent Australian political history, a list that included Labor's Mick Young, David Combe, Bob McMullan and Bob Hogg. Eggleton was credited with the introduction of comprehensive media monitoring arrangements. As the political scientist Scott Bennett has noted, they became 'part and parcel of the campaign effort by the parties, who see them as means of keeping their campaigns under a tight control while offering a means of picking up on the mistakes made by their opponents'.[31]

Appraisals of his time as Federal Director were consistently favourable. Michelle Grattan described him as 'the great survivor, and the great realist'.[32] Eggleton had critics and enemies but 'more remarkably, he commanded great trust ... he was not seen as an intriguer – although intrigue was afoot all around him – and this was the key to his political longevity. In party crises, you would find most of the protagonists talking frankly to Tony Eggleton'. He was 'pragmatic, non-ideological and all about winning; finding solutions; an excellent crisis manager; an astute judge of media reaction; better at handling the here-and-now than mapping out the distant future'. In a private note read at his Secretariat farewell, Grattan conveyed the best wishes of the Press Gallery and noted that, at heart, he remained a journalist and that 'none of us would see him as the party propagandist selling a line'. Writing in the *Daily Telegraph Mirror*, David Evans remarked that he was 'an impressive television performer – better than some of the party leaders he worked for – and at the last election performed so credibly that some viewers wanted to know where they could vote for him.'[33]

He told his Party colleagues that they did 'squander some opportunities and paid a high price for disunity'. He was 'disappointed that Andrew Peacock and John Howard did not become prime minister ... both deserved better and came tantalizingly close to the prime ministership'. He thought that 'barring disunity, complacency or stupidity – all of which are possible in politics – the government benches are within reach' and he expected John Hewson, the new Liberal leader, to be victorious in 1993. Unlike his decision to leave parliamentary life in 1971, he had not settled on a new position before he left the Secretariat at the end of 1990. He would shortly turn 59 and believed he had at least one more challenging job of ahead of him.

Endnotes

1   'Doubts on Liberals' back room', *Inside Canberra*, Vol. 36, no. 9, 18 March 1983.

2   Gerard Henderson, *Menzies Child*, p. 283.

3   Geoffrey Barker, 'How right is right?', *Examiner*, 21 January 1986.

4   Max Walsh, 'Issues and ideas', SMH, 18 October 1984.

5   Quoted in O'Brien, *The Liberals*, p. 107.

6   Robert Thompson, 'Inside the bunker, the Liberals are on top', SMH, 16 November 1984.

7   Robert Thompson, 'Inside the bunker, the Liberals are on top', SMH, 16 November 1984.

8   Michael Gwenda, 'At last, the Liberal bear is stirring', *Age*, 28 November 1984.

9   Bill Hitchings, 'Eggleton, a force behind Lib men', *Herald* (Melbourne), 9 November 1984.

10   Mike Steketee, 'Andrew gets every chance: free kick and a free plane', SMH, 12 October 1984.

11   Russell Barton, 'A giant gap, no matter how quickly you say it', *Age*, 15 October 1984.

12   John Laws, 'The party's over, fellas', *Sunday Telegraph*, 27 January 1985.

13   Mike Steketee, 'Peacock: a matter of authority', SMH, 19 July 1985.

14   Michelle Grattan, 'Defender of Liberal faith delivers his manifesto', *Age*, 29 August 1985.

15   Henderson, *Menzies Child*, p. 287.

16   *Daily Telegraph*, 6 December 1986.

17   Warwick Costin, 'Bid to dump 2 top Libs!', *Sunday Telegraph*, 22 March 1987.

18   Howard, *Lazarus Rising*, pp.165–66.

19   Howard, *Lazarus Rising*, p. 169.

20   Alan Ramsey, 'Rupert and Genteman John', *The Way We Were: The View from the Hill of the 25 Years that Remade Australia*, New South Press, Sydney, 2011, p. 359.

21   Alan Ramsey, 'Liberal phoenix arises from the electoral ashes', SMH, 14 November 1987.

22   Alan Ramsey, 'Why Howard must pull off the big sell', SMH, 12 November 1988.

23   Andrew Robb, *Black Dog Daze: Public Life, Private Demons*, Melbourne University Press, Melbourne, 2011, p. 82.

24   Robb, *Black Dog Daze*, p. 85.

25   'And now … here's the John and Maggie Show', *Herald* (Melbourne), 14 December 1988.

26   Nikki Savva, 'Howard to seek the Age of Contentment', *Sun*, 19 November 1988. See also Geoff Kitney, 'Libs seek disaffected ALP voters', AFR, 28 October 1988.

27   Gervase Greene, 'Mr Cool in the Liberal's kitchen', *Sunday Herald*, 12 November 1989.

28   Adrian Bradley, 'Eggleton may run for Lib president, *Herald* (Melbourne), 9 April 1990.

29   Helen Trinca, 'Former federal party director laments disloyalty', *Weekend Australian*, 8–9 October 1994, p. 8.

30   David Butler and Austin Ranney, 'Introduction', in Butler and Ranney (eds), *Electioneering*, Clarendon Press, Oxford, 1992, p. 4.

31   Scott Bennett, *Winning and Losing: Australian National Elections*, Melbourne University Press, Melbourne, 1996, p. 148.

32   Michelle Grattan, 'The end of a career at the heart of Liberal politics', *Age*, 25 March 1991.

33   David Evans, 'Eggleton takes CARE after leaving Liberals', *Daily Telegraph Mirror*, 25 March 1991.

CHAPTER 13

CARE and compassion   1990–96

S oon after the Coalition's federal election defeat on 24 March 1990, Eggleton received a phone call from Malcolm Fraser in Copenhagen where he was attending a meeting of CARE International. CARE is an acronym for 'Cooperative for American Remittances to Europe' which was later changed to 'Cooperative for American Remittances to Everywhere'.[1] It was founded in 1945 as a non-sectarian, apolitical, non-government organisation that would distribute food aid to those starving at the end of the Second World War. Americans could pay $10 to send a CARE package, initially surplus Army ration packs, to Europe for a family member, if they could be located.

After 1948, CARE moved into general relief projects and, after 1953, to countries beyond Europe with greater emphasis on broader development work. In 1979, the continued expansion and increasing popularity of CARE's work necessitated the formation of an umbrella organisation to coordinate a number of national offices beyond the United States. CARE International was established in January 1982. In addition to its more traditional work in reforestation and soil conservation, CARE responded to a series of humanitarian crises in Africa, principally Ethiopia and Somalia. By the 1990s, CARE was a very substantial global organisation that was refining, consolidating and expanding its work over more than four decades. Malcolm Fraser played a central role founding CARE Australia in 1987 with his daughter, Phoebe, becoming a CARE aid worker.

Fraser asked Eggleton if he would be interested in becoming Secretary-General of CARE International. Eggleton didn't know much about the organisation and had no idea what the job entailed but said he would be pleased to talk about it further when Fraser was back in Australia. He heard nothing for most of the year. Fraser was eventually back in touch in November 1990 to tell Eggleton he would soon become the chair of CARE International's board. Fraser did not have confidence in the incumbent Secretary-General and thought Eggleton would be ideal in the role. Eggleton needed to fly to Paris early in 1991 to be interviewed by CARE's Executive Committee. Fraser suggested it would be helpful for Eggleton to have a British passport and to 'present myself as an Englishman rather than as an Australian … to avoid the appearance of stacking the central organisation with Australians'.

In his formal application for the position, Eggleton mentioned 'a long career encompassing management; strategic, tactical and administrative planning; political 'damage control'; cooperative federalism; and international relations'. Through the Commonwealth Secretariat and the International Democrat Union he had gained 'considerable experience in fostering contacts between diverse people and in promoting cooperative relationships'. His principal referee was Alois Mock, chair of the European Democrat Union.

Eggleton thought there would be no harm in the interview although Fraser had not told him there would be other candidates. In fact, there were several international applicants who all appeared more suitably qualified. Eggleton was made aware that 'the French had raised some complaints over Malcolm's 'high-handed' attitude on the selection panel'. The interview committee was suspicious of Fraser's manoeuvring and vetoed his participation in the interview process. Eggleton expressed his frustration in a private note dated 18 December 1990:

> I get the feeling that Malcolm is not feeling quite as confident about influenc-ing the appointment … and he's afraid that some (perhaps Americans and Europeans) will try to roll out a candidate to derail the Fraser strategy. I'm not too happy about all of this. It was one thing to be invited to do a job. I could even live with the need to submit a formal application. But I am uneasy about having to seek 'references' and to get caught up in some internal CARE politics.

Later that day Fraser rang to say the committee had chosen him as the best appointee but were uneasy about his lack of first-hand experience in the aid sector. Fraser explained that it was 'virtually a unanimous decision. He did not speak and did not need to'.

Just short of his 60th birthday, Eggleton was about to tackle an entirely new challenge in a new industry in a new country. It was also a lot to ask of wife Mary who would leave behind their home and family. They agreed to share the challenge and Eggleton's appointment was announced on 14 March 1991. At the press conference at which his appointment was announced, Eggleton cited the phrase for which Fraser had become infamous, 'life wasn't meant to be easy', before emphasising that the 'Fraser/Eggleton team' will be 'doing our best to make it easier and better for a lot of the struggling people of the world'. Liberal Party Federal President Ashley Goldsworthy offered the Party's congratulations and observed

> this brings a formal end to Tony Eggleton's 30 years of professional associa-
> tion with the Liberal Party. His dedicated service will long be respected and
> remembered. He is one of Australia's greatest Liberals and a great Australian.

With the prospect of a Coalition election victory in 1993 in mind, a number of Liberal party notables, including Andrew Peacock and John Howard, contacted Eggleton before his departure in the hope that he might consider returning to an Australian Government appointment in two years time. Peacock said he would personally find a suitable position for Eggleton, believing 'it would be much easier for me to be appointed to a government job after a stint in Europe with CARE'. At that moment, Eggleton was focused entirely on his next challenge rather than the one after.

Key to Eggleton's effectiveness was George Radcliffe, a senior officer with CARE United States with a lifetime of experience inside the organisation. Radcliffe was born in Eastern Europe and had fond childhood memories of receiving one of the first CARE packages at the close of the Second World War. Radcliffe also aspired to the Secretary-General's position but the selection committee suggested he should be invited to serve as Eggleton's deputy. Radcliffe offered to meet Eggleton over breakfast the day following his interview. They established an immediate rapport and Radcliffe advised the committee he would be prepared to serve as Eggleton's deputy. It was the start of a warm and constructive relationship.

The first issue they needed to consider was the physical location of the Secretariat. CARE International's headquarters was in central Paris but, with escalating rents, Fraser and the Executive proposed the exploration of other options. As a first step, Eggleton and Radcliffe were asked to visit Paris, Geneva and Brussels to determine the most appropriate base for their headquarters, both operationally and financially. Early in 1991 they made an extensive tour of the major European countries, making contact with leading figures in the European CARE organisations. There were visits to France, Germany, Switzerland, Belgium,

Norway, Austria, Denmark and Britain. Taking into account geographic, political and economic factors, they concluded Brussels was the best option. The choice was confirmed as they sat together in a café in Brussels' historic Grand Place. Brussels became CARE International's new headquarters.

In a note to Fraser on 12 March 1991, Eggleton mentioned that during their tour he and Radcliffe 'generally got a positive response'. Only then did Eggleton become aware that there was 'still some residue of resentment about the handling' of his appointment and that 'the International Secretariat does not enjoy a good reputation among most CAREs, and there are doubts about roles and cost effectiveness in the future'. CARE Germany was keen to see 'a more active CARE International Secretariat that would 'break the mould' and recommend new projects'. CARE Britain hoped the Secretariat would 'improve the effectiveness of CARE directors meetings, develop longer-term strategy; improve the quality of CARE International board meetings; and, try to help the 'fallen' CAREs'. CARE Denmark wanted the 'Secretariat's results and performance monitored against objectives' and was 'concerned about the secretive nature of CARE Australia'. CARE Norway was positive about the need for enhanced cooperation and collaboration, and looked forward to more regular and closer consultation between member nations. CARE Austria had preferred Geneva – the 'NGO capital of the world' – to Brussels and were concerned about the 'Anglo-Saxon nature of the leadership of CARE International [and] urged that any further staff appointments to the Secretariat be European'. CARE France was concerned about the Secretariat's tight budget. They also had reservations about five year appointments but were 'looking forward to a better relationship with the new CARE International Secretariat'.

A few weeks later (7 May 1991), Eggleton and his wife flew into Brussels to embark on this new stage of their lives. The CARE office was at 58 Boulevard du Regent, a convenient, central business address adjoining one of Brussels' busy intersections. They had temporary living accommodation in the 'Residence Hanovre' (*Chaussee De Vleurgat*). The location was satisfactory, near the impressive Avenue Louise, but the cramped nature of the apartment meant there was every incentive to begin searching for a more permanent home.

Eggleton and Radcliffe timed their arrival in Brussels to coincide. They were able to stare together in trepidation at the total disarray of their new office. All of the fittings, files and equipment from the Paris headquarters had simply been dumped in the new location. Eggleton felt there was an urgent need for an office manager to take the staff in hand and administer the organisation's operations. Within a couple of weeks they were able to recruit Vicky de Proost, a highly efficient Belgian, who was to become a mainstay of the CARE office. She spoke fluent English, French and Flemish, was tough and resilient, and knew her way through the many bureaucratic minefields facing an international aid agency based in Belgium. Eggleton soon found that he led a happy and hard-working team. They all started early with the daily meeting of the half-dozen staff occurring at 8am. Eggleton continued his custom of rising at 5am to complete his morning jog before starting the hour-long walk to the office at 6:30am. It was a pleasant stroll although it did come with some hazards in the winter with a couple of nasty falls on icy paths.

Almost immediately after assuming their new roles, Eggleton and Radcliffe faced a meeting of the CARE International board. Fraser had been unhappy with the past management of these events and looked to Eggleton to improve their quality, content and conduct. He said, 'I want you to run them like you ran the Liberal Party'. An agenda and papers were assembled within a couple of weeks. In June they set off for the meeting in Norway. All the delegates seemed pleased with the new arrangements, not least Fraser. His accommodation was something of a challenge. The venue was the picturesque Holmenkollen Park Hotel, among the ski jumps on the hills overlooking Oslo. The bedrooms were not particularly spacious and the Frasers had masses of luggage, having been on a fishing expedition beforehand. The very tall Fraser and his wife Tamie ended up sharing their modest-sized room with photographic gear, wading boots, fishing rods and an assortment of tackle.

Eggleton told the board that he 'never expected this to be an easy role' and accepted there would be 'differing views' about the structure of CARE International and how its Secretariat could best support field operations. He stressed that 'under my leadership the Secretariat will not engage in intrigue and gamesmanship' and that he hoped to make 'a modest contribution'. The CARE International board thereafter met at least twice a year, interspersed with meetings of the executive committee. Meeting venues alternated between developed and developing countries. Eggleton chaired the national directors committee, comprising the chief executives of the national CAREs. These meetings brought together the senior staff of all 12 founding member nations. Their recommendations were essential input for the deliberations of the board and executive. Policies and priorities flowed from this governance structure, guiding and monitoring CARE's humanitarian work that was now reaching 30 million people in 70 countries. There was an annual CARE budget of nearly a billion dollars. It was clear why Fraser was determined to make sure these gatherings were thoroughly prepared and effectively managed.

The combination of an international president and secretary-general from Australia represented a ground-breaking realignment in the leadership. CARE United States, as the foundation member, had traditionally held the key positions and exerted the most influence. Presidents had usually come from North America and the Secretary-General from the United States. Each of the members saw the merit of a president who had been a prime minister with the capacity to attract public attention and the ability to open doors. Fraser's dominant style was not always welcome but, initially at least, the board members considered it a price worth paying in return for his drive and leadership. He was deeply committed to humanitarian causes and was respected in the developing world. He got things done, raising the stature and profile of CARE. Fraser's energy was critical to the momentum being developed within the Secretariat. A meeting of the CARE United States board on 11 December 1991 said it was 'impressed by the professional manner in which Messrs Eggleton and Radcliffe have undertaken the responsibilities of the secretariat' and acknowledged the 'leadership of Mr Fraser'.

With the help of locally-engaged support staff, the Secretariat was soon functioning smoothly. As a non-government organisation there was much red tape and countless bureaucratic hurdles which called for all the skills and experience of the multilingual staff. One of the perplexities was the French-Flemish language divide. Streets and boulevards had dual names which could be a navigational disaster. This also applied in the countryside, where towns and cities had different names, depending on the cultural division and whether it was a French or Flemish map. There were language implications and duplication at all levels. Depending on the suburb, there was either French or Flemish television but not both.

Gaining approval to reside in Belgium also involved a convoluted bureaucratic process. The Eggletons were eventually registered in the French-speaking commune of Uccle, where they had found a permanent place to live. Their new home was a modern apartment on the fourth level of 'Residence Val Longchamp' at 221 Avenue Winston Churchill. Many family and friends visited the Eggletons during their time in Brussels, as well as Australian politicians transiting through Europe. Waterloo was only a few kilometres from their home and they became proficient guides to the famous battlefield. They often explored surrounding countries and kept a series of purses in the car glovebox so they had local currency for refreshments wherever their travels took them.

At the newly established CARE Secretariat Eggleton had a roomy and well-equipped office overlooking the bustling Place Madou. Fortunately, his third-floor windows were double-glazed, shielding him from the frequent bursts of road rage. A computer had appeared alongside his desk at which he looked askance. He had spent his life working on a portable typewriter but the no-nonsense office staff refused to accept drafts from such an outdated piece of equipment. They were determined to convert Eggleton to the new technology and before long he realised they had done him a favour.

At Fraser's urging, one of Eggleton's early tasks was developing relations with the European Union (EU) and seeking financial support for CARE. Fraser's name opened many doors and, remarkably, Eggleton was able to obtain a partnership arrangement for CARE Australia which gave them access to funding for emergency projects. It was one of the EU's first such partnership agreements, with Fraser travelling to Brussels to participate in the official signing ceremony. It was only in retrospect that the EU realised that the Australian organisation probably should not have qualified because it was not part of the European community. Eggleton further advanced links with the EU by appointing a full-time staff member to liaise with the Community's officials in Brussels. Fraser also encouraged Eggleton to adjust the operational priorities of CARE. There was an increasing focus on emergency response, while not diminishing the traditional emphasis on longer-term development work. New policies were devised in a diverse range of areas, while CARE sought to strengthen its advocacy.

Bookending his time with the Liberal Party's Federal Secretariat was inclusion in the Queen's Birthday Honours List in June 1991. Eggleton was made an Officer of the Order of Australia (AO) for 'service to politics and government as Federal Director of the Liberal Party of Australia'. As he was unable to attend the investiture in Canberra, his honour was presented by the Australian Ambassador in Brussels, David Sadleir. The Ambassador hosted a special reception at his residence, inviting Eggleton's CARE team and senior staff from the embassy in lieu of his absent family. The formal presentation was conducted with great dignity before a celebratory lunch. Eggleton had frequent contact with the Australian Ambassador during his time in Brussels. On Anzac Day 1992 he and Mary were invited to participate in commemorative events at Ieper (Ypres). There was a ceremony at the monumental Menin Gate where they joined the group march to the town hall.

Eggleton travelled extensively as Secretary-General. He spent time in South Africa preparing the ground for the establishment of a local CARE office. There were several trips to Taiwan to encourage and support the local staff there. He was in Tokyo when he received news of his mother's death. Winnie was aged 95. He arrived back in England in time for her funeral. Eggleton's travels with CARE included many memorable episodes, both amusing and hair-raising. He accompanied Fraser to Somalia at the height of the conflict between opposing warlords. As fighting had closed the Mogadishu airport, their light aircraft from Nairobi was diverted to a distant and inhospitable strip normally used by drug-runners. It had been a long flight in a small aircraft with no toilet, which Fraser needed. The air strip was similarly devoid of any such convenience. There was not even a tree to provide some privacy. Fraser tried his best to hold on but as they began the journey in a convoy of jeeps he soon reached his physical limit and asked for the vehicles to stop. As there were female aid workers in the convoy, Eggleton was assigned the task of acting as a tree to afford the very tall prime minister a little dignity. The Somalian machine-gunner on the roof of the jeep was highly amused.

As they approached Mogadishu the party encountered roadblocks manned by heavily-armed youths. They respected the CARE logo and waved them through without demanding payment. In Mogadishu they were given accommodation at the CARE compound. The evening hours were punctuated by gunfire. The next day Fraser and Eggleton, accompanied by armed guards, inspected CARE's warehouses and food distribution centres. They received word that CARE Australia workers at a regional centre had been captured by a warlord's fighters. Fraser was not going to stand for such interference and insisted on meeting the warlord and negotiating their release. In an armed convoy they travelled to the centre of Mogadishu, where the Australians were handed over to another convoy controlled by the opposing forces. On arrival at the warlord's heavily fortified headquarters, Fraser and Eggleton were ushered into a room where a group of fighters were sitting with weapons at their feet. Fraser's imposing figure made an impact and, in a tense exchange with the warlord, he secured the release of the CARE staff.

Despite security warnings, Fraser decided they should fly into the Somalian hinterland to inspect the CARE operations at Baidoa, not far from another CARE compound that had been invaded. His daughter Phoebe was in charge of the humanitarian work in Baidoa, having established the compound some months earlier. She was a familiar and much-respected figure in her CARE vehicle which was adorned with a gunman on the roof. Her staff included a number of other young women. With the various rival armies on the march around Baidoa, Fraser directed that all the women should be evacuated. They protested strongly, not least his daughter, but Fraser refused to leave until arrangements had been made for their departure. The group managed to fly back to Mogadishu airport which was then under mortar attack. Fraser's contingent wanted to take off for Nairobi as quickly as possible. A local official intervened and explained a fee was required before they could depart. The CARE staff were familiar with this routine and were carrying large sums of American cash. With gunfire in the background, a deal was struck and dollars were exchanged. Finally, Fraser and Eggleton were on their way to the relative safety of Kenya. Fraser was convinced that increased military assistance was required for aid agencies working in Somalia. Within a couple of weeks they were in New York meeting with the United Nations Secretary-General. Fraser put his case and more forces were made available.

Fraser also made a point of seeing the humanitarian crisis in Rwanda first-hand. Travelling in a small chartered aircraft, a contingent from CARE hopped from one isolated landing strip to another where the plane's fuel tank was topped up by hand-operated pumps. On arrival at the landing area closest to the emergency operations, the plane carrying Fraser and Eggleton manoeuvred for a spot among a throng of military transport aircraft. The strip was in bad shape after coping with numerous humanitarian flights. Their little plane rattled and shuddered over the pot holes as they touched down. The area was swarming with youthful aid workers proudly wearing their respective aid agency t-shirts. Young men and women, some still in their teens, were driving large trucks and unloading the urgently needed supplies. The CARE vehicle, with dodgy brakes, bumped its way along the corrugated dirt roads to the refugee camp. Within days a few dozen refugees had become a torrent of 300,000. CARE assessed the traumatic scene, met with the local United Nations representative and made plans for the expansion of the humanitarian response.

On another assignment, Eggleton had a lucky escape from a difficult situation in Kenya. After attending a CARE conference at a coastal resort some distance from Mombasa, a car was provided to convey him to the airport. With dusk falling, and still some miles from Mombasa, the car broke down. The driver spoke no English. He simply shrugged his shoulders, implying there was nothing he could do, and disappeared into the dark. The vehicle was near a desolate, shabby village. The men were shuffling home at the end of the day, past Eggleton who was stranded on the roadside with his suitcase. The looks, body language and atmospherics were unfriendly. This was not a place for a hapless aid agency official to spend the night. There had been little or no traffic when suddenly headlights illuminated the deserted road. Eggleton had no idea what sort of vehicle it might be approaching but he stood in the middle of the road and waved it down. Luckily, it was an English couple returning from safari. They were on their way to the airport and booked on the same flight to London. Eggleton narrowly averted another serious security incident.

Most of Eggleton's CARE travels were not as dramatic. Mary accompanied him on more predictable journeys to London, New York, Paris, Rome, other major European cities and a CARE International meeting in Ecuador. As one of the world's highest cities (at 2850 metres or 9350 feet above sea level), many delegates were afflicted by altitude sickness in Quito. In the hotel at breakfast time the helpful staff surreptitiously slipped drugs into the tea, a recommended but illegal antidote. After the Quito meeting, the Eggletons had the opportunity to cruise in the Galapagos Islands. This was a deeply memorable experience despite Mary being pecked on the ankle by a blue-footed booby and requiring treatment by the ship's doctor. Another conference to which Secretariat officials were accompanied by their spouses was held in Zimbabwe. The conference occurred before the worst years of the Magabe regime when the capital, Harare, and the surrounding countryside were considered relatively safe. The spouses were taken on scenic tours and, at the end of the conference, there was a group visit to Victoria Falls. They had breakfast on the Zambezi River and encountered hippopotamuses as they drifted towards the falls.

Eggleton and Radcliffe were an effective team and enjoyed the respect of the CARE International family. Good progress was made coordinating and supporting

CARE's work around the globe and overcoming internal disputes. Ironically, CARE Australia was Eggleton's biggest challenge. He felt the entrepreneurial chief executive in Canberra was inclined to ignore operational codes and procedures which infuriated his international colleagues. CARE Australia was often doing outstanding work, especially in rapidly responding to emergencies. Other CARE member nations were concerned that Australia was aggressive and did not play by the rules, especially in Somalia which was a CARE United States area of primary responsibility. Across the Pacific, CARE United States was manoeuvring to reduce the size and scope of CARE International, conducting its own bilateral consultations with member nations, and drafting its own clauses for 'sanction and suspension' of member nations in evolving CARE International statutes.

Part of the challenge was Fraser serving as chair of CARE Australia while simultaneously being the organisation's international president. Invariably, he supported his Australian chief executive and, when disputes arose, leaned towards the interests of his fellow Australians. During Eggleton's time in Brussels there was an ugly confrontation between a senior staff member of CARE United States and the Australian national director with enduring ramifications. It was not only the Americans who felt the Australian's combative style was harming the entire organisation and believed Fraser was intentionally avoiding the problem. These tensions made life difficult for Eggleton and the Secretariat. As Secretary-General he had to act in the interests of CARE International while trying to maintain a positive relationship with Fraser and CARE Australia. After the June 1994 CARE International board meeting, Fraser met the national director of CARE United States to address American concerns. Eggleton noted that 'it was a terrible gathering. Malcolm was laying down the law and being somewhat hectoring in his tone. [The American national director] sprang from the table, reached for his jacket, and said he had no intention of putting up with all of this. I managed to hose things down'. The damage had, however, been done. Relations deteriorated to the extent that CARE Australia was close to being expelled from CARE International. Fortunately, Eggleton had established a solid rapport with all the member nations and eventually the Australian crisis was resolved. The experience clearly demonstrated that it was unwise to have a CARE International president concurrently chairing the board of a CARE member nation.

Eggleton subsequently took steps to change the statutes so this conflict of interest could not arise again but, in the meantime, had to deal with the Americans 'questioning the value and viability of CARE International in its existing form' with certain American officials arguing that being part of an international organisation was 'an albatross on the back of CARE United States'. The Americans resented having to 'prop up' financially a number of national organisations (such as Norway, Denmark, France and Britain) and were dismayed by the 'ambivalence' of CARE Japan and the 'belligerence, indiscipline and intransigence' of CARE Germany. There were also the 'constant frictions with CARE Australia'. The need to address problems elsewhere within the organisation was 'distracting and debilitating'. Unsurprisingly, these concerns diverted the CARE staff in Atlanta 'from their primary tasks'. Eggleton's strategy was to overhaul the governance arrangements and allow for the expression of 'national aspirations' within an overall international outlook that was conscious of the requirements imposed on aid agencies by domestic governments.

At a meeting of the CARE International board in November 1994, Fraser expressed his sorrow at the inability of the organisation to work effectively as a confederation of agencies committed to the same objectives. He believed 'the pattern of behaviour in recent times ... has done grave damage to CARE International' involving what he 'regarded as deliberate deception, based on a clear lack of trust' and 'corruption of due process'. By March 1995, Eggleton told Fraser that the CARE 'family is not very enthusiastic about its Australian cousins. But, unless CARE Australia seeks conflict, then the rest of the family is not looking for a divorce. It would prefer a united family'. The Australians were seen as

> disruptive and uncooperative; they look for confrontation instead of consul-
> tation; they want to bend the rules to suit themselves; it's a pain trying to do
> business with them; their actions and attitudes do little to stimulate confidence
> or mutual trust.

Eggleton did not believe these 'sweeping perceptions' were accurate or fair but, he told Fraser, 'that's the terrain that we face'. He also conveyed the organisa-
tion's growing personal antipathy to Fraser, while recognising the enormous amount of good work he had done, and the fear that CARE Australia would withdraw formally but continue to operate as an independent agency. Eggleton recognised that the key issue for CARE Australia was one of principle: CARE's global operations had to be based on cooperation and not integration. Although Eggleton believed the Americans also wanted cooperation undergirded by

effective coordination, use of the word 'integration' in earlier drafts of revised governance documents was not meant to imply 'total uniformity and central dominance'. He realised that some of the smaller members of the confederation were 'disenchanted by the way in which competition is replacing collective action'. He conceded the development of a 'Lead Membership' system was 'flawed and increasingly restrictive, with inherent instability resulting from the competition for 'territory' and the 'carving up' of the world by the Lead Members'.

By April 1995 there were strains in the relationship between Eggleton and Fraser that revealed the complications of mixing personal friendships and professional responsibilities. Eggleton was conscious that the European members were concerned about Australian financial processes and administrative transparency, and wanted a change of local management. CARE Britain insisted it would have nothing to do with CARE Australia until it received certain assurances and there were changes in key personnel. Eggleton told Fraser in May 1995 that 'there are enough restrained and reasonable people ready and willing to keep Australia in the fold; but there are those who would be quick to support termination of membership and a mid-year change in the CARE International presidency'. Radcliffe didn't relish dealing with Fraser as he was uncomfortable with the president's style and tone. He always tried to avoid taking the calls from Australia and was happy for Eggleton to receive them.

Fraser finally resigned as international president in 1995 after several earlier threats to do so. This signalled to Eggleton that his time in Brussels was also coming to an end. CARE wanted Eggleton to stay on but he felt four years away from Australia was enough. The organisation was expanding on a solid foundation while governance and operational structures had been reviewed and improved. CARE was evolving as a significant emergency response organisation in parallel with its traditional development role. Codes and statutes had been enhanced, committee systems streamlined, and European fundraising was growing. The International Secretariat was well-regarded and acknowledged by the membership to be professional, effective and dependable. He was satisfied with what he had achieved.

> At an age when many people would have been retiring, the CARE appointment had given me a new career and a fresh perspective. It had been a timely and welcome opportunity after a lifetime in politics. The work was rewarding in every respect. There were fine people around me, whether the volunteer

board members or the devoted professional staff at headquarters and in the field. And then there was the satisfaction of contributing to humanitarian and development projects around the world.

As Eggleton approached the end of his term, the one remaining shadow was the periodic intransigence of CARE Australia, as well as confrontational actions by a couple of other CARE members. CARE United States, as the oldest and biggest member, was still disillusioned by the behaviour of petulant and unco-operative members. It raised doubts about retaining them in the confederation. These concerns were top of the agenda at a meeting of the CARE International board in Atlanta in June 1995. CARE Australia made conciliatory noises but there were question marks about Australia's continued membership. Eggleton had no inkling that CARE Australia's problems would soon become his problems.

He had just returned to Brussels when history repeated itself with another fateful Sunday afternoon telephone call from Malcolm Fraser. The entrepreneurial national director of CARE Australia had run into trouble with the Australian media and the Federal Government. His management had been the subject of a Channel 9 television *Sunday* 'expose' in February 1995 and his handling of government contracts was under formal investigation. It was not a question of personal dishonesty but organisational propriety. CARE Australia had been adding an administrative 'margin' to some of its activities, charges that were obscured in specimen budgets and funding applications. It had also apparently overstated its expenses on the delivery of aid projects. Channel 9 accused CARE Australia of using rice bound for Rwanda to bribe the Kenyan president, Daniel Arap Moi, and diverting money donated for trucks in Bosnia 'to other purposes'.

An internal report headed 'CARE Australia Re-structuring' concluded that 'the huge sums of money that have been generated from emergency projects have produced a 'cargo cult' mentality within CARE Australia'. It claimed there had been 'an extravagance of expenditure not seen before in an Australian NGO' leaving non-executive staff with low morale and 'an organisation that lacks any moral or ethical base'.[2] According to Eggleton, the trouble was the national direc-tor's style and his creative reallocation of Federal Government funding, without necessarily obtaining official approval. Fraser had backed the national director until the growing storm left the board with little choice but to act decisively. The media were portraying CARE Australia as an embattled organisation facing accusations of fraudulent behaviour, financial misrepresentation and professional negligence. After the CEO stood down and CARE offices in Perth and Melbourne were closed with the retrenchment of 25 administrative staff, Eggleton received the surprise call from Fraser.

Fraser wanted Eggleton to cut short his remaining months with CARE International and return immediately to Canberra to become the national director of CARE Australia. It was a disturbing and daunting proposition. He played for time by offering to fly to Australia the following week so he could assess the situation and have personal discussions with the major players. Eggleton felt he owed it to Fraser and CARE to respond to this urgent appeal but he insisted on certain conditions. There needed to be an agreement that recognised and respected the distinction between the responsibilities of the national director and the chair of the board. Eggleton did not relish dealing with an intrusive, 'hands-on' chairman with the stature of Malcolm Fraser. Eggleton's other conditions included seeking 'full cooperation and mutual goodwill with all members of the CARE International Confederation' while 'all financial, fundraising, contractual and accounting practices will be strictly in accordance with Australian standards and donor expectations and requirements'. Fraser agreed. CARE Australia issued a public statement on 21 June 1995 that Eggleton was returning to Canberra and would become the national director on 1 September 1995: 'The Board is confident that CARE Australia is now positioned to overcome its recent problems, and to resume its role as Australia's foremost agency in the on-the-ground delivery of developmental and emergency aid'.

Writing in the *Age*, Karen Middleton reported that Eggleton's appointment would restore CARE Australia's 'tarnished image'.[3] Speaking from Brussels, Eggleton said the Australian organisation had 'run into these rough seas and it's been clearly damaged. But I think the Australian people will rally around and see that significant steps are being taken to remedy the problems'. After declining to comment on recent controversy, Eggleton emphasised that 'one has to be very conventional, very orthodox, very proper in meeting all the codes and expectations in the way you handle funds ... we need now to be able to demonstrate that lessons from the past have been learnt'. Domestic donations to CARE Australia had more than halved. Eggleton conceded that 'people were very sad, very disappointed. They wanted to believe in us, and I am here to tell them that they still have very good reason to'.[4] The *Australian Financial Review*'s Geoffrey Barker reported that the 'Director of Public Prosecutions had not yet reported on the findings of last month's report by independent auditor BDO Nelson Parkhill, which revealed that CARE Australia had intentionally overstated budgets in its presentation to AusAID for project funds'.[5] Media coverage of Eggleton's return was universally positive. His 'name' would restore faith in CARE.

The assessment mission to Canberra had left Eggleton with no illusions about the magnitude of the task at hand. CARE Australia was in deep financial trouble, public donations were diminishing, staff morale was at rock bottom, and they had lost the confidence of AusAID and the aid industry more generally. Meanwhile, the organisation was subject to official investigations and faced a hostile media. A timetable was agreed to allow Eggleton to hand over his international duties to his deputy in Brussels. He was pleased that the loyal George Radcliffe would be succeeding him as Secretary-General. CARE International members welcomed Eggleton's willingness to take on the Australian predicament and hoped it might again become a constructive member of the confederation.

The day after his return to Australia in September 1995, Eggleton was straight to work. The staff in Canberra were apprehensive. He held a series of meetings and, helped by the senior managers, focused on the most urgent steps to be taken. Fraser asked him to prepare a survival strategy as quickly as possible. Eggleton put an inventory of recommendations to the board's finance committee within the first fortnight. CARE Australia was not short of funds for field work. Despite domestic problems, it still enjoyed the confidence of international donors and had many millions in project money available. This was, however, tied to the projects for which it was provided. What CARE Australia lacked was the unrestricted funding needed to run the organisation, such as administration and accounting. If CARE Australia could not raise sufficient operating funds by November 1995, Eggleton told the board it 'might be more responsible to accept the inevitable and set in train the orderly liquidation of CARE Australia' to avoid insolvency. He was adamant that 'CARE Australia must not be allowed to collapse in reprehensible circumstances, ie., unable to meet its debts and commitments, and in owing money to designated humanitarian fund accounts'.

Eggleton outlined a series of steps to significantly reduce budget expenditure and reintroduce active fundraising. He argued that, considering he had returned from Brussels early in the hope of saving CARE Australia, they should persevere with the survival strategy. With an element of understandable reservation, the board agreed although Eggleton conceded that 'revenue estimates can only be 'guesstimates'. He embarked on a 'concerted public relations and marketing program', and secured short-term assistance and guarantees from CARE United States.

Fraser, Eggleton and former Labor minister, Barry Jones, sought help from the Hawke Labor Government, which had responded favourably to Eggleton's return and was willing to assist. The Minister for Foreign Affairs, Gareth Evans, and the Minister for Overseas Development, Gordon Bilney, made public statements of support, as did other ministers. AusAID dropped its ban on working with CARE Australia. The Government took a positive approach to easing the organisation's cash flow problem. Both the Government and Opposition respected the quality of CARE Australia's humanitarian operations and appreciated its strong Australian identity in the field. They certainly did not want it to fail. By November 1995, Eggleton reported to the board that political support had been revived but public support had not. Donations that were not tagged to emergency operations were still lagging behind administrative needs because the organisation 'has not yet been forgiven by former, disappointed donors'.

Meanwhile, Eggleton's good relations with CARE United States meant the Americans were prepared to stand guarantor for the recovery plans. Eggleton also spoke to Kerry Packer and visited Channel 9 in Sydney to negotiate a no-cost withdrawal of the legal action that CARE Australia had, in despair and anger, launched against the network. He wanted to minimise any further and pointless legal costs while rebuilding relations with the media. There was also a new approach to fundraising. Since its formation in 1987 CARE Australia had relied too much on monies raised in emergency situations. It needed to generate a solid, reliable funding base, not dependent on generous responses to humanitarian crises.

These steps and strategies slowly began to stabilise the organisation and board members started to breathe a little more easily. In an atmosphere of fresh confidence, the public once again rallied in support of CARE Australia's fundraising campaigns. Its standing within the local aid community generally improved and it survived audits and investigations. There was still a long recovery road ahead but the organisation was out of intensive care. CARE International was heartened by the collegial and cooperative spirit of the Australians under Eggleton's leadership, making meetings far more harmonious. Eggleton travelled to Paris to mark CARE's 50th anniversary in May 1996. In addition to formal meetings there were celebratory events hosted by the French President and CARE France. A special train took a group of representative officials to Le Havre for the unveiling of a monument where the first CARE parcels were unloaded in 1946. On returning home, Eggleton discussed a succession plan with Fraser. He had only agreed to fill the position in the context of crisis management and had no wish to be a long-term incumbent. In any event, the role was better suited to an experienced CARE official with personal experience of field operations. Fraser was reluctant but appreciated his point of view. Eggleton had delivered on his commitment to get CARE Australia back on track and was entitled to take an extended break.

Despite the poor publicity that enveloped CARE Australia in 1995, there were 170 Australian and international applicants for the position of national director when it was advertised in mid-1996. The successful candidate was Charles Tapp who had previously worked with CARE in several operational and management roles. Most recently he had been national director of CARE United Kingdom, helping to steer it out of financial difficulties. Tapp took the reins on 1 September 1996, meaning Eggleton had served for exactly 12 months. CARE Australia expressed its appreciation to Eggleton with farewell functions, gifts and acknowledgements. CARE United States president Peter Bell, one of the most significant figures in the international organisation, sent a personal message:

> During your five and a half years in the employment of CARE, you have won the admiration, respect and affection of colleagues around the world. Throughout our ups and downs together within CARE International (CI), your professionalism and integrity served to steady the CI movement and to steer it in the right direction. And now, at a critical juncture, you have successfully brought CARE Australia through a difficult and challenging year of transition.

The CARE Overseas Association (COA) offered its own tribute:

> COA wishes to put on record its appreciation to Tony Eggleton for the fine work he has done in restructuring CARE Australia. Under his astute leadership, CARE Australia has overcome enormous problems over the last few months and is now positioned to become once again one of the most dynamic and important members of CARE International. We welcome CARE Australia back to centre stage.

In a private note, Eggleton confided that 'when I was persuaded by Malcolm Fraser to devise a survival strategy for CARE Australia I had no idea how long I would be in the job. There was real doubt about how long CARE Australia could survive. In the event, it was a close run thing'. But the rescue effort had come at a price.

Eggleton's relations with Fraser were severely strained in the second half of 1996. It seemed to Eggleton that Fraser had expected regular discussions whereas Eggleton only contacted Fraser 'when I felt it was truly necessary'. Fraser then tried to thwart the appointment of his successor and 'this resulted in a heated exchange of views'. Fraser also accused Eggleton of trying to 'slip an issue through' the CARE Australia board without adequate consultation although the issue had been canvassed in agenda papers circulated a week before its meeting. Fraser also suggested Eggleton was missing strategic opportunities when he declined to pursue involvement in an emergency operation in Burundi that Eggleton judged 'might jeopardise the financial viability' of the organisation. Fraser even compared Eggleton unfavourably with his predecessor in Canberra. Eggleton realised the 'trouble with ringing Malcolm is that you have to cope with a degree of paranoia … I [also] made it clear from the time that I took on the CARE Australia 'rescue' mission that, as CEO, I would not brook operational interference'.

After resigning as national director, Eggleton accepted an appointment to the board of CARE Australia. He was now 65 and had decided to retire from the full-time workforce. He mused privately:

> after working for 50 years, I sometimes see some attraction in a more relaxed lifestyle. On the other hand, I've never really thought much about retiring, and don't feel I've really reached retirement stage … I don't intend to look for any further employment. I suppose if someone came to me with a suggestion, I might consider it. I'm not sure what the future will bring, especially as I intend to 'leave it to fate' … I made it clear to the PM's office (Grahame Morris) that I don't have a 'wish list'.

He and Mary marked the occasion of his departure from CARE with a 4000-kilometre driving tour of Western Australia to take in the spring wild flowers. It was an enjoyable start to what they expected to be a more relaxed way of life after a half-century of paid employment.

Not surprisingly, it was not long before the Liberal Party reached out to its longest serving Federal Director. After losing the apparently 'unlosable' election in 1993 with John Hewson as leader, and then replacing Hewson with Alexander Downer, the Liberals turned again to John Howard in January 1995. Howard invited Eggleton to join his personal team on election night in March 1996. Having been present when the Party lost office 13 years earlier, it was an evening to savour. After numerous trials and tribulations, Howard had led the Party back into government with a resounding victory against the Labor Government which had been led by Paul Keating since late in 1991.

Once Howard had acknowledged his victory at the Party's formal election night reception at the Wentworth Hotel, his personal team went to a private suite at the Inter-Continental. A small group of family, friends and supporters shared the moment. After the *Bulletin* magazine had disparaged him as 'Mr 18 per cent' when his popularity fell to a record low in 1989, they naturally relished the 'Howard victory' headlines as the first editions of the morning papers were delivered. As they chatted about the life and times of past prime ministers, Howard mentioned to Eggleton that he would like to do something for Malcolm Fraser. Howard conceded that the Liberals were not in the same league as Labor in honouring their former leaders. Fraser was not attracted to offers of diplomatic postings, not even the High Commissionership in South Africa. When asked about his own aspirations, Eggleton said he was content to remain a private citizen and enjoy his retirement. Howard was not so easily diverted and Eggleton's sense of public duty was undiminished.

Endnotes

1   See Wallace J Campbell, *The History of CARE: A Personal Account*, Praeger, New York, 1990.

2   This document was undated and unattributed. It was sent to Eggleton by the acting national director, Dr June Kane, on 30 October 1995. In a separate document, the CARE Regional Manager in Nairobi, Tony McGee, suggests the restructuring document was drafted by Joanne Hall.

3   Karen Middleton, 'Eggleton new CARE Australia director, *Age*, 22 June 1995.

4   Marion Frith, 'Taking care of business', *Age*, 2 December 1995.

5   Geoffrey Barker, 'Eggleton takes up CARE challenge', AFR, 22 June 1995.

CHAPTER 14

Active retirement   1997–2007

Different people have different attitudes towards their employment. Some people work in order to live. For others, work is the essence of life. Tony Eggleton saw his work as a means of providing for his needs and those of his extended family, and as a way to advance social organisation and enhance human flourishing. To him, the value of work was a function of the salary that was on offer and the satisfaction to be derived. As he approached his 65th birthday, a milestone that usually signified for those of his generation the likely end of full-time employment, Eggleton could not quite accept he had arrived at the conclusion of his working life. He was, he told an interviewer, 'not the retiring kind'. He felt his experience and expertise continued to suit him for public service, albeit something less demanding than a five-day a week job that obliged him to sit in an office. In addition to his continuing membership of the CARE Australia board, he agreed to assist the National Stroke Foundation and the Old Parliament House 70th Anniversary Celebration committee.

Prime Minister John Howard had already raised the prospect of a government position. With the Coalition back in power federally he was being considered for several posts including chairmanship of the National Capital Authority. In May 1997, Howard asked Eggleton directly if he would consider an overseas appointment. Having been away for more than four years in Brussels, he told the Prime Minister that another international job would not be well received by his family. They discussed several options but focused primarily on the possibility that he might become the Chief Executive of the Centenary of Federation Council. The Council was to prepare the nation to

> commemorate a defining moment in Australia's history – the creation of the Commonwealth of Australia and hence the nation on 1 January 1901. The centenary is a truly national event which provides a focus for recognising the

nation's achievements since Federation, strengthening national confidence and identity, and enhancing our sense of unity, purpose and direction for the next century.

The Chief Executive's position had been in existence for less than 12 months but already attracted considerable controversy. It certainly required significant reserves of emotional intelligence and a good grasp of organisational management.

Planning for the commemoration was commenced by the Keating Labor Government. An advisory committee headed by former Victorian Premier, Joan Kirner, produced 'A Report from Australia' in 1994. Many important lessons about the conduct of previous national commemorations had been learned by public administrators, particularly from the bicentenary of European settlement on Australia Day 1988. The Australian Bicentennial Authority was incorporated in the Australian Capital Territory in 1980 but established its main office in Sydney to the irritation of the other states. The anniversary's proposed theme then attracted criticism from all shades of political opinion. The Authority's chair and chief executive were both replaced in 1985 as its planning became more sensitive to actual and potential objections, especially from the Indigenous community. Governance problems aside, there was a very substantial program of events and activities that were organised, funded and promoted by a Federal government agency.

After wide-ranging consultation and a Federal election delaying the appointment of its members, the Centenary of Federation Council was established in 1996. The Council's inaugural chair was businesswoman, Janet Holmes à Court. The first executive member was a retired senior Army officer, Major General Ken Taylor. The Commonwealth nominated eight members to serve alongside the eight members selected by the States and Territories (one from each jurisdiction) with one member representing the Australian Local Government Association. After Holmes à Court commented on the 1996 election outcome in a manner that might have been interpreted as a criticism of the incoming Coalition government, she submitted her resignation. Nearly nine months later, the Government announced that prominent businessman and adventurer, Dick Smith, had been appointed to the position. A member of the Council's executive, former New South Wales Education Minister, Rodney Cavalier, was surprised by the Government's lack of urgency given the Centenary was less than four years away.

We duly discovered the reason: the Prime Minister was trying to persuade Dick Smith to accept appointment to a position in which he had no interest. By persistence unending and for other reasons about which one does not speculate, John Howard prevailed over Dick's reluctance to accept the post. He did not prevail over Dick's lack of interest. From the first day to the last, Dick did not muster a scintilla of enthusiasm for the cause of the Centenary.[1]

There were also problems within the Council's secretariat. General Taylor lived in Perth and recruited a staff that consisted largely of former military personnel who were determined to be based in Western Australia from where they would liaise with the Council's small staff at Old Parliament House in Canberra and the Commonwealth Department of Communications and the Arts. After the Council's first meeting, which was held in Hobart in March 1997, it became apparent to Smith, Cavalier and others that the governance arrangements and the key personnel were ill-suited to the task. Preparation for the initial meeting was poor. There was nothing resembling an agenda and crucial information, such as financial delegations, were missing. The members had little confidence in the capacity of the executive leadership to fulfil the Council's charter. At an impromptu meeting of several Council members at the Melbourne airport departure lounge, they agreed there could not be a repeat of what had happened in Hobart. Cavalier offered to act on their behalf.

He met privately with Smith who was also distressed by the Hobart meeting. He told Cavalier he was contemplating resignation unless Cavalier assumed the practical responsibilities of chairing the Council's meetings. Wanting to avoid the controversy of losing two Council chairs within 12 months, the Prime Minister agreed to Cavalier's appointment as deputy chair. He was offered the position by the Minister for Communications, Richard Alston, who was surprised by Howard's personal support for the former Labor minister. There was also the matter of the executive member. Smith believed 'the CEO who had been initially appointed was simply not the right person for the job.'[2] Taylor was persuaded to resign. Smith was relieved that 'the prime minister gave me immediate support and replaced the incumbent with the highly experienced veteran Tony Eggleton'. Cavalier, who was simultaneously appointed deputy chair of the Council, observed that

Mr Eggleton brought with him the immense advantage for a celebration of the quintessentially political event: an intimate association with the mainstream of Australian politics. In addition to 15 years with the national office of the

Liberal Party, Tony enjoyed a public standing for competence earned in the aftermath of the drowning of Harold Holt, service to a succession of Liberal leaders, service to the Commonwealth in London, a career as a working journalist who knew well the foibles of the working press.[3]

Eggleton was holidaying in the Northern Territory with wife Mary when the announcement was made. On returning to Canberra, Eggleton invited Cavalier to dinner at the Commonwealth Club where he heard Cavalier's account of the Hobart meeting and the conditions that Smith had placed on his continuing membership of the Council. Eggleton had not realised the extent of the difficulties he had inherited. As Smith had no interest in governance, Eggleton and Cavalier agreed on revised structures, a new approach and parameters spanning their respective roles.

It was the start of a productive and rewarding five-year journey for Eggleton. Many years earlier his thoughts had focused on how the nation might mark the Centenary of Federation and wondered whether he might be involved. The Council was a diverse group, representing a broad range of political opinion, but from the outset they agreed to approach the Centenary as a national project that deserved to be commemorated without political point scoring. The members consistently adhered to this commitment despite state election results leading to increasingly strong Labor representation. The Labor and Liberal members represented their states and not their parties with the close relationship between the New South Wales and Victorian members being crucial to the Council's effectiveness.

With Smith playing next to no role in the Council's affairs, Eggleton worked closely with Cavalier. They were an unlikely duo with complementary temperaments. Although from different sides of party politics, Eggleton shared Cavalier's infectious enthusiasm for history and commitment to the long-term civic benefits of the Council's work. He especially appreciated Cavalier's political knowledge and respect for democratic institutions and parliamentary processes. The President of the Australian Historical Association, Professor Stuart Macintyre, suggested the Council was well served by Eggleton and Cavalier having 'a concern for history'.

> I discussed with Eggleton and Cavalier the advantages of a scheme that would provide relatively small subventions to enable the publication of important and accomplished history theses, and the Council funded such a scheme that will result in a score of such contributions to historical scholarship.[4]

Smith acknowledged important distinctions between the roles of the Council chair and the Chief Executive. He understood the need for formal deliberations and accurate recordkeeping but was not keen on what he perceived as dreary meetings. Eggleton and Cavalier found ways to lighten Smith's burden. As the Council's Chair, Smith would formally open the meetings before Cavalier addressed the agenda and managed the proceedings as Deputy Chair. To keep the claustrophobic Smith content throughout longer meetings, Eggleton and Cavalier arranged for the Council to meet in the brightly lit dining rooms at the rear of Old Parliament House that looked out on Permanent Parliament House. The infamous Hobart meeting had been held in a windowless room.

After establishing the Council on a firm administrative foundation, the Council noted the challenge it would face generating public interest in the Centenary which would follow the Sydney Olympic Games. The Council was also conscious of the widespread ignorance of Australian history. A survey conducted by the Council found that less than 27 per cent of Australians were familiar with the broad outline of the Federation story and only 18 per cent knew the name of the first prime minister (Edmund Barton). That the Australian nation came into being through a vote rather than a war was apparently considered 'boring' while Australia's democratic foundations were assumed rather than esteemed by those who took the orderly transfer of power between political parties for granted. According to the survey data, more interesting were public debates about Indigenous reconciliation and the prospect of an Australian republic. Clearly, the Council needed to devise and deliver a major public education program to undergird its other activities.

The Council met at different venues around Australia but most frequently at Old Parliament House in Canberra. When plans were being made for office space, Eggleton was asked if he preferred the Council to work out of a new building in Canberra or at Old Parliament House. He leapt at the chance to return to his old workplace and was delighted to be working from the downstairs corner suite once occupied by the Treasurer. Eggleton led a talented team of 30 staff. The Canberra secretariat worked in unison with on-the-ground organisations set up by the states and territories, coordinating their efforts and assisting with fundraising and publicity. The detailed planning and preparation required for the hundreds of endorsed activities necessitated extensive travel throughout Australia and discussions with premiers and chief ministers. Most were supportive of the Council's priorities and proposals although the temptation to lament the dominance of the Federal government was too great to resist among those who thought Eggleton was the Prime Minister's personal emissary.

The Western Australian Premier, Richard Court, expressed his doubts about the value of his state remaining in the Federation with Eggleton and Cavalier. They refused to take the bait. Court certainly left Eggleton, and Howard too, in no doubt that the relocation of the Council's secretariat from Perth to Canberra with Taylor's resignation was deeply resented in Western Australia. For good measure, the Premier shared with Eggleton his frustration at the lack of attention that Prime Minister Howard was showing to his state and its interests. The Commonwealth of Australia had been in existence for nearly a century but some of the states had not entirely lost the separatist mentality that had taken the former colonies more than a decade to overcome prior to Federation.

Notwithstanding the official indifference of Western Australia, South Australia and Tasmania to the centenary and the reluctance of their governments to contribute, the Council's strategy was deliberately expansive and national: to reflect on the past, create pride in the present and build confidence in the future. Interest in the Federation story was generated through media coverage, public projects and activities, and celebrations that were scheduled throughout 2001. The Council encouraged education authorities to expand the teaching of Australian history in their schools, funding a wide range of books, exhibitions, seminars and documentaries dealing with Australian nationhood since Federation. There were also infrastructure projects that would leave a lasting legacy. Everything authorised by the Council was branded with the highly successful Centenary symbol. The stylised logo, based on an outline of the Australian continent and Tasmania, captured the spirit of the occasion. It became a popular symbol not only for the anniversary in 2001 but as a decorative badge to denote national identity in years to come. Notwithstanding the complexity of the planning process, and the large sums of money involved (and who would fund state and local activities), the Council managed to avoid conflicts, leaks and scandals. Cavalier remarked that

> The signature comment on the success of Tony Eggleton was the affection in which he was held by all National Council members and Council staff. More than once we were privy to private information about ministerial or governmental behaviour. Not once did a word leak, not once from a body which consisted of about half-a-dozen card-carrying members of the Labor Party and several

others committed to our Party. Nor from a staff, resident in Canberra, which I would estimate voted Labor at a ratio of about 10–1. It just did not matter.[5]

As the Centenary year approached, Smith flagged his desire to resign from the Council. He had never been keen on public speaking, formal events, reception lines and glad-handing. Eggleton tried to persuade him to remain. Smith's main focus at this time was chairing the Civil Aviation Safety Authority and the implementation of a reform plan that was being opposed by the major airlines. When he was unable to secure the political backing he needed for changes to air safety regimes, Smith resigned from CASA and the Centenary Council. His successor was Peter Hollingworth, the Anglican Archbishop of Brisbane, who was a founding member of the Council and a Commonwealth appointee. Hollingworth was not deterred by the prospect of formalities. He was, in fact, energised by social events.

Formal public duties were high on the agenda when Eggleton went to London in 2000 for 'Australia Week', an international celebration marking the passage of the *Commonwealth of Australia Constitution Act* through the British Parliament on 9 July 1900. It was an opportunity to further raise Australia's profile in Britain and Europe. John Howard led a delegation of former Australian prime ministers and premiers. They attended Question Time in the House of Commons, where they were amused by British Prime Minister Tony Blair's embarrassing slip of the tongue when he referred to America instead of Australia. One of the week's many highlights was a special church service in Westminster Abbey, also attended by the Queen. The Australian flag flew above the Abbey and the didgeridoo was played by Richard Walley, the indigenous member of the National Council. At the end of the service, the political dignitaries were presented to the Queen before other members of the Council. The Queen immediately recognised Eggleton and was visibly pleased to see him. The London initiative attracted some media criticism among local commentators who complained that Australia was still subservient and rendering obeisance to Britain. These events also coincided with the introduction of the Goods and Services Tax (GST) which had prompted the Leader of the Opposition, Kim Beazley, to remain in Australia. It was nevertheless a valuable curtain raiser for the Centenary and generated interest at home and abroad.

The Centenary year was launched with commemorations and ceremonies on 1 January 2001. There was a parade through the streets of Sydney to Centennial

Park and an evening ceremony. A game of test match cricket the next day was badged the Centenary of Federation Test. Not unlike a Sheffield Shield game in January 1901, all the state governors attended and several premiers. Eggleton and wife Mary were among a small group of guests invited to join the Prime Minister for New Years Eve dinner at Kirribilli House. They then watched the Sydney Harbour fireworks from the adjoining Governor-General's residence, Admiralty House. There were distinctive events across Australia throughout the year, including at the Royal Exhibition Building in Melbourne which hosted the inaugural meeting of Australia's new Commonwealth Parliament on 9 May 1901. There was also a formal sitting of the two houses of Federal parliament in Melbourne's Parliament House, the first such sitting outside the Federal Capital Territory since 1927.

A unique Indigenous gathering held in Alice Springs, the Yeperenye Federation Festival, was attended by people from throughout Australia. It was the biggest ever corroboree and gave Aboriginal people a distinctive stake in the anniversary year. The prime minister's office had been nervous about the event, fearing that it might be used to stage an anti-government demonstration. Eggleton made a point of consulting with Indigenous leaders and the event remained non-political. There was a similar outcome with other events that might have been used to push a partisan agenda.

During the Centenary (2001), Peter Hollingworth was appointed Governor-General and was succeeded by the distinguished historian, Geoffrey Blainey, who had been a member of the Council since its inception. The final months of the commemorations and celebrations were overshadowed by the September 11 terrorist attacks in the United States and the subsequent multi-national invasion of Afghanistan that included Australian forces. The morning after returning from the Yeperenye Festival, Eggleton was listening to early morning radio as he prepared for work. At first, he thought it was a tasteless and over-dramatised promotion for an upcoming television or radio program. It was a few minutes before he registered the reality of commercial aircraft being flown into public buildings in New York and Washington. Despite the tragedy and with celebrations seeming out of place, the Council persisted with most planned events although the scheduled Commonwealth Heads of Government Meeting was postponed and the Centenary Naval Review on Sydney Harbour was cancelled.

Final assessments of the Centenary activities and the Council's achievements were uniformly positive. The Council had fulfilled its charter without significant political problems or fractures in social cohesion. The Centenary had given Australians a fresh and expanded insight into their history and the nation's evolution. The anniversary had spawned specially commissioned publications and research materials, as well as tangible and practical infrastructure projects, that were funded by the Centenary budget. Blainey's judgement was insightful and illuminating: 'It was, without doubt, the most decentralised celebration ever staged in Australia. Australians everywhere had been given the opportunity to share in the Centenary'.

While the Council was Eggleton's principal preoccupation from 1997 until early 2002, there were other demands on his time. Prime Minister Howard asked Eggleton to accept the chairmanship of the Pacific Democrat Union, a position he would hold from 1998 to 2005. During the Fraser era, Eggleton had played a key role in the establishment of this centre-right political organisation. Reflecting the Union's steady growth, one of Eggleton's first acts as chair was to change its name from PDU to APDU (Asia Pacific Democrat Union). Among his duties was an invitation from the Kuomintang Party to study electioneering in Taiwan. While in Taipei he visited the Chiang Kai-Shek memorial, which stirred memories of his meeting with the former Chinese (later Taiwanese) president while press secretary to Harold Holt.

Within CARE, Fraser instigated his election as vice-chair of the Australian board and used Eggleton to short-circuit CARE International proposals that the former prime minister feared might weaken the confederation. At a CARE International board meeting in Cambodia, Fraser convinced the president, Sir Harold Walker, to appoint Eggleton chair of the newly formed strategy committee. It would review future plans, priorities and operations and was made up of representatives from most CARE member nations. Over a number of years the committee met at various international locations and continued to enlarge the organisation's global reach.

In November 2001, the CARE International board met in Melbourne, marking the start of yet another phase in Eggleton's continuing relationship with the organisation. Shortly before the meeting Sir William Deane, the former Australian Governor-General, had been selected to succeed Fraser as chairman of CARE Australia. As a highly regarded 'Living National Treasure', Deane's willingness to accept the appointment was a major coup for CARE Australia. He had been a patron of CARE throughout his term as Governor-General and championed the cause of two Australian aid workers, Steve Pratt and Peter Wallace, and their Yugoslav colleague, Branko Jelen, who were falsely convicted of spying for NATO and wrongfully imprisoned during the Balkans war in 1999. They were later pardoned and released by Yugoslav president, Slobodan Milosevic.

Deane decided his priority should be strengthening the Australian organisation. He asked Eggleton, as vice-chair, to handle international commitments. Eggleton became the regular Australian delegate to the CARE International board and to the principal governing body, the General Assembly. Three or more times a year he travelled to meetings in Brussels and other overseas locations. Eggleton spent several years overseeing all aspects of CARE's governance, including appraisal of board structures and the selection of office-bearers. The international chair, Lydia Marshall, looked to him for drafting of strategy and policy papers, as well as regular tactical advice.

Eggleton was now well beyond the official retirement age but showed little interest in slowing down until December 2001 when Red Hill in Canberra was ravaged by bushfires. Eggleton observed the midsummer 'snowflakes' fluttering down as people anxiously watched flames race across the treetops. The nearby Eggleton home was safe but there was another more personal threat at hand. A few days after the fires were extinguished, Eggleton was running up Red Hill when he felt a pain in his chest. He shrugged it off as a symptom of the lingering smoke although the pain persisted during his morning runs. After a couple of weeks he consulted a physician who promptly put him in the care of a cardiac specialist. Tests revealed the need for open-heart surgery and a double bypass. It was not an immediate crisis – medication could temporarily relieve the discomfort – but it was nonetheless a serious warning. In the weeks prior to the operation, his chest pains were limited to morning exercise. Eggleton's only concession to the pain was choosing a level path around Parliament House and The Lodge in lieu of Red Hill. During the operation the surgeon decided he needed a third bypass to prolong his daily exercise routine. Eggleton was nonetheless told his running days were over and that he should switch to brisk walking. He was out of hospital in five days and, careful to avoid the 'invalid trap', soon resumed his regular pattern of activity. He often stopped and spoke with parliamentarians who shared the walking and running tracks around Red Hill. It was a way to stay informed and offer a few insights to those on his side of politics. Future prime minister, Tony Abbott, was a beneficiary of his wisdom on many occasions. Eggleton was back to driving a motor vehicle within a month of his operation and just six weeks later was chairing a CARE International meeting in Brussels.

Thanks to Eggleton's sustained efforts, CARE Australia had been welcomed back into the international CARE family without reservation or qualification. On 29 July 2002, Deane asked Eggleton whether he was interested in the chairmanship of CARE Australia. Eggleton was surprised by Deane's description of himself as an 'interim' chair before the former Governor-General explained that he preferred not to have an active media profile. Just as surprising to Eggleton was Deane's suggestion that John Howard might be a potential chair when he retired from politics. At a board meeting 15 months later (October 2003), Deane raised the prospect of succession and, Eggleton recalled, 'indicated that he wanted to canvas this matter in a more substantive way'. Deane suggested that Eggleton withdraw from the meeting along with the board's three staff observers, Robert Yallop, Grant Thomas and Phoebe Fraser. Although Eggleton's strong preference was for Deane to continue, the board had decided unanimously that Eggleton should succeed Deane in October 2004. Eggleton was only the third incumbent after Fraser and Deane. Eggleton assumed the position just as CARE Australia was facing its most daunting and distressing operational crisis. A formal announcement and a 'transitional lunch' were immediately cancelled. The only public acknowledgement of Eggleton's new role was on the CARE Australia website.

On 19 October 2004, the CARE country director in Iraq, the much admired and respected aid worker, Margaret Hassan, was abducted by gunmen in Baghdad. Hassan was married to an Iraqi, had lived in Iraq for 30 years and had become an Iraqi citizen. She was Irish by birth and had a British passport but had been employed by CARE Australia for a number of years to manage the agency's operations in Iraq. She was universally well-regarded for her humanitarian work and was previously untroubled about her safety and security. Hassan was critical of United Nations sanctions after the first Gulf War (1990–91) and had publicly opposed the invasion of Iraq in March 2003. Her abduction not only appalled those within CARE, the kidnapping sent shockwaves around the world. Australian and British diplomats did not initially think Hassan's Muslim kidnappers would cause her physical harm. It was more likely they would use Hassan as a political pawn and the source of a ransom payment. Her captors initially demanded the withdrawal of British troops from Iraq and the cessation of CARE's operations in the country. CARE readily announced that its Baghdad office would close but the British Government was not prepared to meet the abductors' political demands nor were they willing to contemplate paying ransom.

The drama was unfolding as the CARE Australia leadership gathered in Melbourne for the annual general meeting and the election of office bearers. Eggleton was confirmed as the new chair of the Australian board. As Deane did not want to walk away from CARE at such a critical time, Eggleton proposed the former Governor-General take responsibility for a specially-convened crisis coordination committee. Its members would be Robert Glasser and Robert Yallop (CARE Australia staff members), Philip Flood (a retired diplomat and former head of the Department of Foreign Affairs and Trade) and Peter Smedley (businessman and company director). The Australians felt responsible for Hassan and made it clear to CARE International they were prepared to play a central role in negotiating her release. The Canberra secretariat was manned 24 hours a day and CARE staff were sent to Baghdad to cooperate with British and Iraqi security forces. CARE also engaged its own expert advisers, Corporate Risk International. Eggleton and Deane gave serious consideration to packing their bags and heading for Baghdad but were dissuaded by the Australian and British governments.

CARE staff and aid workers throughout the region were deeply unsettled by Hassan's distressed appearance in a series of video messages which were recorded by her captors and screened on the Al Jazeera television network. The first four videos were different to those circulated after similar kidnappings at that time. There was no identification of the group responsible and, until the fourth video, Hassan appeared against a neutral backdrop. It was plain that Hassan's health and wellbeing were steadily deteriorating. In one video a bucket of water was thrown over her after she fainted.

CARE knew it was unacceptable to comply with ransom demands but the agency was desperate to save her life. They agonised over how they could legally and responsibly deal with her captor's demands. Fraser advocated doing whatever was necessary to secure her release. He had known Hassan for many years and admired her work. He did little to hide his lack of confidence in CARE International and the British Government. For most of the time that Hassan was being held, Eggleton expected to receive a ransom demand. Fraser wanted

Eggleton and Deane, as chair of the crisis coordination committee, to gather $2 million to be available when the demand was eventually received. Fraser felt that neither man was doing enough to ensure they were adequately prepared for such a scenario. Fraser was mistaken. It was high on their agenda but Eggleton and Deane were aware that CARE's policy was not to pay any ransom money as it increased the latent risk faced by all CARE staff, not only aid workers, in countries like Iraq. There was agreement that a group of 'friends' rather than CARE itself might wish to provide money for Hassan's release. Eggleton contacted a small number of known wealthy donors to canvas the possibility. He was then advised that paying a ransom might be contrary to Australian law. Such payments could be interpreted as funding terrorist activity. There might have been mitigating factors and possible loopholes in the legislation but Eggleton remained opposed in principle to paying ransom. Fraser was undeterred by the possibility of prosecution. He thought the Howard Government would be unlikely to take legal action against a group of high-profile Australians if they managed to secure Hassan's release.

Eggleton angered Fraser when, as chair of the CARE Australia board, he continued to press CARE's no ransom position. Eggleton thought soliciting money would be wrong given his formal position in the organisation and duty to uphold its statutes. In any event, a demand for ransom had still not been received. Hassan's abductors continued to focus on their political demands: withdrawal of British troops from Iraq; the release of female Iraqi prisoners; and, the cessation of aid operations in Iraq. Eggleton's mood drifted between optimism and pessimism although he did not believe Hassan's abductors would kill her. Her reputation for apolitical compassion and demonstrable personal commitment to Iraq led to public protests in Baghdad and calls for her release.

Fraser was much angrier with British Prime Minister, Tony Blair, who made a series of unhelpful public statements that he thought imperiled Hassan's release. He argued that the Australian and British governments, and the 'USA dominated CARE International', had been compromised by their involvement in the 'Coalition of the Willing' that had invaded Iraq in March 2003. Fraser offered to speak personally with Prince Hassan of Jordan and Yasser Arafat of Palestine. He had dealt with them before and believed they would respond to his urging. But CARE was unwilling to accept Fraser's offers of assistance. Out of frustration he resigned from the CARE Australia Advisory Council. Eggleton told Deane:

'Obviously, Malcolm didn't feel we gave sufficient weight to his opinions in the context of the Margaret crisis. I think he is only comfortable with 'control and direction' and not simply 'advice''. Over the previous four weeks, Fraser had sought his own legal advice, dealt directly with the British High Commissioner in Australia, contacted Hassan's husband in Baghdad, by-passed the national director and consulted directly with CARE Australia staff, and approached several prospective donors. In a private note, Eggleton listed his grievances with Fraser and ended the inventory with his 'demanding and dictatorial attitude'.

Within CARE, spirits plunged when the British ambassador in Dohar advised that Al Jazeera had a received a tape showing a European woman of Hassan's build with her back to the camera being shot through the head at close range by an assassin with a small calibre handgun. Expert examination of the video suggested the woman was probably Hassan. Although identification could not be confirmed, everything pointed to her murder on 16 November 2004. Her body was never found. Months later, some of her personal belongings were discovered in a house in Baghdad and an Iraqi national was sentenced to life imprisonment. Despite all the assurances during the agonising weeks that preceded her death, Eggleton wondered whether the British authorities were as engaged and active as they claimed to be. Her family in Britain were highly critical of the British Government's handling of the abduction.

Many CARE Australia staff were among Hassan's close friends. Her murder was devastating and she was mourned throughout the world. Deane was mortified by her death. He had met her several times while chair of CARE Australia and was full of admiration for her compassion and commitment. In the hours after the news of her murder was received, Deane invited Eggleton to his Canberra home and together shared their grief and disbelief. As news of the tape was highly confidential (Al Jazeera had decided not to report its existence), Eggleton and Deane undertook to speak personally with John Howard who was 'visibly shaken by the account of her killing'. When the news became public, Eggleton and Deane arranged for CARE staff to be briefed and a memorial service to be held. As the crisis coordination committee was no longer needed, Deane asked Eggleton to assume full responsibility for oversight of CARE Australia. Eggleton issued a public statement:

> the callous and senseless killing of Margaret Hassan was one of the bleakest episodes in the 60-year history of CARE. A lifetime of humanitarian service

was no guarantee of personal safety. The tragedy was a reminder of the increasing dangers facing aid workers, and resulted in CARE further developing and strengthening its security and safety procedures.

Despite their personal differences, Eggleton still believed that Fraser was 'undoubtedly the most influential president ever to lead the CARE International board'. Fraser moved CARE from 'being primarily a development agency to an organisation that could also respond effectively and promptly to emergencies around the globe'. He also raised CARE International's role as an advocate for humanitarian causes, leaving the 'world body with wider horizons and a stronger voice'. At the CARE General Assembly held in India in November 2006, Eggleton formally ended his long association with CARE International. At a farewell ceremony in Chennai's Hilton Hotel he was presented with a plaque engraved with a board resolution:

> Recognising his deep commitment to CARE International's vision of a world where poverty has been overcome, and his tireless service to the governance and operations of the CARE International Confederation … We the undermentioned on this day acknowledge and applaud the vital contribution of Tony Eggleton during 16 years of service to CARE International.

A final note from the chair of CARE International, Lydia Marshall, read: 'You have probably served CARE in more capacities than any other single individual; staff, board, national CARE, CARE International, and secretariat. As such, you embody an enormous amount of institutional memory and dedication'. He had attended 36 CARE International board meetings.

In October 2007, his direct involvement with CARE Australia's operations also ended when he retired as vice-chair although a tangible link remained when he was appointed to the CARE Australia Advisory Council. Eggleton was standing down at a time when the organisation had never been in a stronger position, financially, professionally and operationally. CARE was highly respected by AusAID and the aid industry generally. Staff morale was high. When reflecting on his years with CARE, Eggleton offered a brief summation: 'Politics was exciting; CARE was fulfilling'.

Alongside his oversight roles with CARE, Eggleton had served on the Australian Aid Advisory Council and the *Foreign Affairs* Editorial Advisory Board. He was also chair of the CEW Bean (War Correspondents) Foundation (with personal support from the deputy chair, Rodney Cavalier, and former Federal minister and Labor Senator, John Faulkner) and continued to chair the Asia Pacific Democrat Union. In 2006 the Howard Government asked him to chair the Centre for Democratic Institutions, a role previously performed by a minister or parliamentary secretary. The Centre's objective was to strengthen democracy and political governance in South East Asia and Melanesia. He was surprised by the invitation given he was then in his mid-70s. Announcing the appointment, the Minister for Foreign Affairs, Alexander Downer, said:

> Mr Eggleton's extensive high-level experience in working with political parties, electoral and parliamentary institutions and processes will be extremely valuable as the Centre seeks to become the premier democracy advancement centre in the Asia-Pacific region.

With the defeat of the Howard Government in November 2007, it was unlikely Eggleton would again be asked to render public service. Having seen the end of the Fraser era, he knew that governments had life cycles and it was time for the Coalition to reconfigure itself in Opposition. Eggleton's private belief was that John Howard should have retired in 2006 after a decade as prime minister. By then he had already become the second longest serving, after Sir Robert Menzies. Howard could have 'gone out on his own terms and at the top of his game'. Eggleton considered his defeat a grim end to a remarkable career. In an exchange of letters following the election loss, Howard observed:

> We have had a long association stretching back to the time that I entered parliament 33 years ago. In that time, I have had some great years of political success and achievement as well as more difficult, frustrating years in opposition where nothing seemed to go right. During that latter period your calm, steady and patient counsel was something that I will always recall with affection. Our party has held government for 42 out of the 63 years of its existence. That is not a bad record. You, personally, can take special pride in knowing that you are the only person to have been a close personal and political adviser to the three Liberal Party leaders who accounted for the great bulk of those 42 years.

Since arriving in Australia in 1950, Eggleton had known all 11 Australian prime ministers and had worked with each one of the Liberal leaders. His association with Malcolm Fraser was the most significant and enduring.

Fraser had never encouraged Eggleton to move to 'the front line' of Australian politics because he needed him too much in the Secretariat. Fraser increasingly relied on Eggleton's candour and ability to remain calm in times of crisis. Despite complaints that Eggleton failed, or perhaps refused, to convey hard truths to Fraser because he preferred not to be the bearer of bad news, Eggleton was always prepared to tell Fraser things he did not want to hear about his political fortunes and his personal behaviour. Eggleton challenged Fraser's domineering personality and belligerence when he faced censorious colleagues and critical journalists. While Fraser never felt the need for Eggleton's approval, he nonetheless disliked disappointing the man who was usually his strongest supporter. Eggleton appealed to the 'better angels' of Fraser's nature. When necessary, Eggleton pointed, and sometimes pushed, Fraser towards the nobility of which he was capable.

After the 1983 election, close colleagues became even closer friends. Their enduring friendship made disagreements and disputes difficult for the more sensitive Eggleton to bear. Fortunately for Fraser, Eggleton did not maintain grudges and was willing to overlook insults and injuries. Although they were less than two years apart in age, the ever-prepared Eggleton quietly drafted a tribute-obituary for Fraser in April 2004. It pre-dated their disagreement over CARE's response to the kidnapping of Margaret Hassan. Eggleton began by stressing that Fraser was 'much more' than a successful politician; he was a 'champion of the oppressed, disadvantaged and under-privileged' and 'placed frankness above discretion, often to the discomfort of old Party colleagues' being 'far more liberal and progressive than his contemporaries'. Eggleton remarked that Fraser 'did not dodge controversy and didn't place great store on personal popularity'. In another document, headed 'Some personal memories', which was dated after Hassan's murder, Eggleton conceded that Fraser was 'not everyone's cup of tea. He could be demanding, infuriating and sometimes too strong-willed for his own good'. He was essentially a 'reserved and private man, and this often contributed to the false perception of an aloof and brusque personality'. Eggleton judged that Fraser's 'determination sometimes translated into bloody-mindedness' but felt deeply privileged to have had him as a boss and a colleague.

The rift between them that began late in 2004 did not last long. After a few years they were again in regular contact. On 12 December 2009, Fraser telephoned Eggleton to say he was 'distressed at the emergence of the strong right wing and the eclipse of the moderates [within the Liberal Party]'. He feared that 'extreme conservative elements could have control of the Party for a long time'. As it was no longer a 'liberal' party, he told Eggleton that he would be resigning his life membership. Fraser remarked that his best days with the Liberal Party were during his prime ministership when he and Eggleton were working closely together. Eggleton noted privately that after trying to persuade Fraser to remain a member, he 'was disappointed but not surprised'. Eggleton did not 'foresee significant electoral implications' flowing from his resignation before adding, 'I don't think that would have been Malcolm's wish'. When Fraser died in March 2015, Eggleton continued to speak warmly of his departed friend, and made no mention of any difficulties in their long relationship. His gratitude to Fraser was undiminished.

It is unlikely that anyone will ever rival Eggleton's service to the Liberal Party or his broad experience of Australia's evolving political culture. Given the rapidity with which political careers start and often end, and the high turnover of party officials both Liberal and Labor, Eggleton stood alone in surviving a succession of leadership changes, electoral defeats and staff purges. He could walk away with the abiding esteem of both his colleagues and the enduring respect of his adversaries. That he was, to quote veteran journalist Alan Reid, a 'very proper man', played a very great part in his effectiveness and longevity.

Endnotes

1   Rodney Cavalier, Text of an after-dinner speech delivered at the Commonwealth Club, Canberra, 20 March 2002, 'Final reflections on the Centenary year and the National Council', later published in the *New Federalist*, no. 8, December 2001.

2   Dick Smith, *My Adventurous Life*, Allen & Unwin, Sydney, p. 251.

3   Cavalier, 'Final reflections on the Centenary year and the National Council'.

4   Stuart Macintyre, 'Bicentennial blurs, Centennial serendipity', address to the Nation/States Conference, University of Adelaide, 16 December 2001.

5   Cavalier, 'Final reflections on the Centenary year and the National Council'.

CHAPTER 15

Character and conviction

A good biography does more than present an account of the subject's principal achievements or assemble their public accolades. It conveys insights into character and conviction, revealing the preferences and prejudices, strengths and weaknesses, fears and anxieties that influenced the subject's attitudes and actions. The foremost challenge for the political biographer is including some reference to the inner life of their subject. What were they like? Who mattered to them? How did they deal with setbacks? Were they personally content? The answers to these questions point to the 'measure' of a man or woman and if they attained goodness or, perhaps, even acquired greatness.

The ancient Greek philosopher Plato thought 'the measure of a man is what he does with power'. Plato was concerned with whether a man enriched himself or preferred to encourage others. Centuries later, when honour was a prominent theme in essays exploring nobility, the Anglican cleric Robert South suggested that 'if there be any truer measure of a man than by what he does, it must be by what he gives'. This sentiment was echoed by the great English writer, Samuel Johnson, who remarked that 'the true measure of a man is how he treats someone who can do him absolutely no good'. More recently, and in the context of overcoming private prejudice and public disadvantage, the American civil rights leader, Martin Luther King, contended that 'the ultimate measure of a man is not where he stands in moments of comfort and convenience, but where he stands at times of challenge and controversy'. Not dissimilar was the advice given to the 46th President of the United States, Joe Biden, when a young man: 'My dad always said, 'Champ, the measure of a man is not how often he is knocked down, but how quickly he gets up''.

The common element in each of these aphorisms is the centrality of character: the sum of the qualities that define an individual. Character includes his or her motives, intentions, temperament and, ultimately, their behaviour. These components of character shape, and give substance, to someone's resolve, habits and discipline, as well as providing the overall moral structure within which he or she makes decisions. Character helps a person to transcend the appeal of passing preferences and petty prejudices. It determines the tone and tenor of an individual's attitudes to other people and his or her approach to life's problems and possibilities. Strength of character is revealed in how an individual responds to adversity. Character offers a vantage point from which to gauge the measure of a man or woman.

Tony Eggleton unintentionally disclosed much of his character in private 'notes for file'. They were initially intended as source material for a book he might one day write. As he did not think they would be seen by others, these notes are candid and critical. When something important occurred, his aim was to record the facts – as he saw them – before offering a personal reflection. As an immediate observer of events with wide-ranging consequences, Eggleton was fulfilling one of the journalist's primary duties: producing the first draft of history. He also described his reactions to what he had seen and heard. Two frequent reactions are disappointment and despair with attitudes and actions he thought were unproductive or undignified. These reactions were focussed primarily on those with whom he worked, such as a succession of prime ministers, but they revealed much about Eggleton as well. Implicit in his reactions were statements about what he thought and, occasionally, what he should have done. While empathetic to others, Eggleton expected something approaching perfection of himself.

The previous chapters have portrayed a man of considerable character who was respected by allies and adversaries, superiors and subordinates, friends and acquaintances. Eggleton was highly principled and known for truthfulness and integrity. Those who did not share his beliefs and convictions, objectives and priorities, nevertheless considered him sincere and honest. Eggleton's public life drew him daily into conflict and controversy with forceful men and women who did not see the world as he did but he made a point of conducting himself with civility and dignity. There was never adequate reason to dispense with good manners or common courtesy. Despite differences over issues of principle and points of procedure, Eggleton never descended into abuse or acrimony. No policy, no program, no position was ever advanced by resorts to rancour or malice.

Whatever the objective, it never justified actions or attitudes that demeaned people or diminished the position they held. Ends did not justify means.

Unlike so many others around him in political life, Eggleton always managed to remain calm. He was revered for his temperament and admired for his consistency. These characteristics, crucial to his effectiveness and longevity as a political 'operator' for more than 40 years, were instilled in him from a young age and were at the core of his being. The Eggleton family home in Swindon was a model of stability. His mother was the contented homemaker and his father the loyal long-term employee of the Great Western Railway. They did not speak harshly to their children as they helped them become confident adults. At home and at school, good manners symbolised respectability while personal civility was the foundation of sound relationships.

Alan Reid's description of Eggleton in 1971 as 'a very proper man' aptly sums up his persona. Eggleton believed there was conduct proper to each and every situation in life. A clear distinction needed to be made between family and friends, superiors and subordinates, and the behaviour deemed acceptable when dealing with each. There was also the private man and the public man. Eggleton believed it was important to separate work and leisure. Hence, his discomfort with socialising at work and having colleagues as friends. The proper boundaries between personal desires and professional obligations could be blurred and the outcome was never favourable.

Eggleton's attentiveness to form and formality made him something of an oddity among his fellow journalists at Parliament House in Canberra. They variously thought of him as a traditionalist, a conservative or perhaps old-fashioned because he would always adhere to what he considered were the dictates of protocol and the demands of etiquette. This meant arriving at work on time, being well-dressed and showing appropriate respect to those in authority. Eggleton did not take liberties and deferred to the dignity of an individual's office when he had doubts about their personal behaviour. While others resorted to profanities and caricatures, Eggleton never swore and refused to engage in name-calling. A self-contained man, invariably self-effacing and humble, Eggleton felt no need for vindication or vengeance. What others thought of him was always a secondary concern.

In an ABC television interview screened on 12 August 1970, Anne Deveson described him as 'untiring, always courteous and unflappable ... he is tremendously approachable, friendly and reliable'. She referred to him as 'a very well-ordered man, both in his dress and undoubtedly in his work'. Two decades later, the political scientist, Norman Abjorensen, labelled Eggleton as the 'affable patrician'.[1] Newspaper columnist, Helen Trinca, observed that he was always 'discreet, controlled, courteous'. She thought he was 'one of the most consistently important figures in the party, yet he goes out of his way to minimise his role'.[2] Harold Mitchell, formerly of the advertising firm, Masius Wynn Williams, told aspiring politicians that 'you need someone who can remain calm in the eye of a storm ... in Tony Eggleton I saw the great strength that you can have in any situation in life if you calmly keep your feet on the ground'.[3] Mitchell remarked during election speculation and discussion of compelling political slogans in July 2017 that 'as the high flying political operators attempt to take off, I'd advise them to do two things. Find a Tony Eggleton to guide them and tell a true story in three words – maybe four'.

The former Official Secretary to the Governor-General, Malcolm Hazel, thought that Eggleton's ability

> to stay part of the A Team for so long was due to two factors: his respectfulness and his authoritative manner. But he was never authoritarian or arrogant. Tony was renowned for being well prepared. He always listened to arguments and would then calmly say 'there might be another option'. And he was listened to because of his calm and thoughtful style. He was always discreet, a characteristic valued by leaders especially in the political context.[4]

Nick Minchin, at one time the youngest member of the Liberal's Federal Secretariat, recalled the gracious and polite way in which Eggleton spoke with other people, irrespective of their status or standing. Minchin appreciated his willingness to include staff members when he needed to talk through a problem; personal transparency in dealing with opposing factions; refusal to promote his own views or the private opinions of colleagues; readiness to accept responsibility for his decisions and actions; and, commitment to the nurture of rising organisational staffers. He was the 'foremost professional' on the Liberal side of Australian politics in the 1970s and 1980s.

Eggleton's CARE colleague, Robert Glasser, was struck by similar attributes. He projected an internationalist image that precluded any sense that he favoured Australians; was never accused of having partisan motives or an interest in self-promotion; readily drew on his range of professional experiences to broaden the context in which an organisational problem needed to be considered; was thoroughly committed to building relationships; and, made himself an expert on proper processes as the basis for discerning consensus and delivering change. Eggleton was effective at CARE because he had enormous political nous; could devise strategy; identify personal strengths; make compliant behaviours attractive; and anticipate the forces and factors that might derail his plans and preparations.

Eggleton's media peers attributed his effectiveness to the same traits. According to long-serving Press Gallery journalist, Rob Chalmers:

> You did not have to be his mate, take him to lunch, flatter him or listen to political propaganda. For busy journalists, most importantly, he was rarely away from his desk, one floor below the gallery in his tiny office; not for him the non-members bar. I could go directly to him in his office to put a query. If it was a Cabinet matter, Eggleton would reach into a drawer and produce a large volume, which he would briefly study. He then would give me a run down on where a particular issue stood: the interdepartmental committee has reported to the appropriate minister; the minister will draw up a submission to Cabinet; this will be considered next week; the cost of the project is $X million; and room will have to be found for it in what is expected to be a tight budget. In short, you had something with a factual basis for your story.[5]

Max Walsh offered a similarly warm tribute to Eggleton after the Liberal's 1990 election loss and his decision to stand down as Federal Director:

> Tony has taken a bit of stick from his political opponents in the wake of the Liberal failure to win the election. While they have criticised his marketing skills, nobody has attacked him personally and that is something of a rarity in Australian politics. I've had professional dealings with Tony for 25 years now and if I could put in my two pennies, he has always been the consummate professional in his dealings with the media. Accessible, always courteous and helpful, and totally straight. Let me tell you, there aren't too many people in Canberra who answer that description.[6]

His political longevity was a function of his firm grasp of organisational dynamics and obvious lack of institutional ambition. After reciting his contributions to the Party and its leadership during the second half of the 1970s, Sir Robert Southey, the Liberal's former Federal President, told Eggleton that 'I possibly better than anyone else know what you have done for the Secretariat. After the unhappy – but necessary – surgery over which I had to preside, its personnel resources were strained and its morale was low. You rebuilt it. That achievement will have my lasting admiration'.[7] His successor as Federal President, Sir John Atwill, told Eggleton that he considered 'the last seven years which I have worked with you and your team at the secretariat to be as happy as any I can remember. I do not believe there has been one jarring note in all that time and that must be most unusual for those in the world of politics'. Alan Ramsey declared that 'nobody in politics has Eggleton's remarkable continuity' and referred to him as the Liberals' 'faithful family retainer' and 'unique' in Australian political history.[8]

As Eggleton did not personally threaten either the position of those in elected office or antagonise the 'wet' and 'dry' factions of the Liberal Party, members of the House of Representatives and the Senate from every state shared their secrets and sought his counsel. They knew he did not want their jobs. Eggleton explained many times that he was more interested in government than politics. He had been associated with rumours of preselection for the House of Representatives in September 1968 and again in March 1970. He showed no interest in these overtures and did not encourage them. In June 1977, the *Australian's* Warren Beeby asked Eggleton to comment on rumours he was being offered a place on a Liberal Party's ticket for the Senate.[9] He replied: 'What for? I like what I'm doing'. Beeby noted that he was 'not your everyday concept of a backroom boy, pulling strings and making politics work. There's no cigarette smoke or poker player's eyeshade image about the Federal Director. But he is content and intends to keep on doing it'.

Writing ahead of the likely 1983 election loss, Michelle Grattan observed that '[Eggleton] lacks parliamentary ambitions or observable political passions: he is the true professional rather than the true believer. The party's pollsters, more than its platform, set Eggleton's political compass'.[10] The year after he concluded his term as Federal Director, Gerard Henderson interviewed Eggleton for his book, *Menzies' Child*, which was published on the 50th anniversary of the Liberal Party's formation. Henderson asked 'why, in view of his considerable influence within the party, he had never tried for Liberal preselection'. Eggleton replied in a manner of fact way, 'that the real reason he had declined to enter the 'front line' of politics was that he often used to feel that he 'could get up in the House and debate either side of an issue''. By way of contrast, his Labor counterparts, Bob McMullan and Gary Gray, both entered parliament and served in Labor ministries. Eggleton's protégé at the Liberal Secretariat, Nick Minchin, was elected to the Senate in 1993 and became a senior minister in the Howard Government. Eggleton's successor as Federal Director, Andrew Robb, was elected to the House of Representatives in 2004 and was a junior minister in the Howard Government and a senior minister in the Abbott Government.

Eggleton wisely avoided the allure of elected office. Lacking the right temperament and sufficient ambition, he would not have excelled as a politician. Had he accepted nomination, he would probably have languished in the Senate and devoted most of his energies to formal committee work rather than attacking Labor's policies. He was not a combative or confrontational person and tried to avoid conflict where possible. Eggleton did not shy away from difficult conversations but he rarely initiated them. He knew his limitations and was ever conscious of the temptation to advance his interests at the expense of principle. As a man of principle – a proper man – he knew that short-term gain would likely lead to long-term pain. He refused to act out of character because consistency of character was crucial to his performance and, sometimes, his survival. It would also oblige him to be someone other than Tony Eggleton – something he would not contemplate.

Away from the office and the pressures of public life, Eggleton enjoyed the simple pleasures of a stable home and a loving family. He was never a great fan of team sport nor a devotee of the arts. He and Mary preferred to travel throughout Australia and abroad, and were content with each other's company. They also conferred over each of his career moves and considered the impact of competing job offers on their three children: Stephen, Andrew and Judith. The national capital became their permanent base after relocating from Melbourne to Canberra in 1960. Fortunately, only the first of two extended absences – London (1971–74) and Brussels (1991–95) – disrupted their family life. After a long and debilitating illness, Mary died in May 2015. She was 87. They had been an inseparable team for more than half a century. He was consoled by the universally high regard in which she was held and the continuing companionship of his many colleagues and friends.

Eggleton continued to enjoy good health and a consistent daily routine through his long retirement. He would rise early for his morning walk – usually around 3am – and then read the newspapers and watch the television news before most people had sat down for breakfast. He kept in touch with the Liberal Party organisation and continued to be consulted for political counsel and personal advice. It was hardly surprising that he was approached for comment on significant historical events. Few Australians had his range of experiences. Eggleton was intimately involved in the advent of television in 1956; the sinking of HMAS *Voyager* in 1964; the accidental drowning death of Harold Holt in December 1967; the hugely successful Royal Tour of 1970; the end of John Gorton's tumultuous prime ministership in 1971; the reconfiguration of the British Commonwealth in the early 1970s; the dismissal of the Whitlam Government in November 1975; the re-election of the Fraser Government in 1977 and 1980; Coalition disunity and election losses in 1984, 1987 and 1990; the devastating humanitarian crises of the mid-1990s; the revival of CARE Australia in 1995; the commemoration of the Centenary of Federation in 2001; the nurture of Asia-Pacific democratic institutions; and, the murder of aid worker, Margaret Hassan, in 2004.

Over 50 years, Eggleton did much to shape national conversations and facilitate international dialogue with his intuitive understanding of public opinion and intimate knowledge of information management. He rejected the charge that he ever traded in misinformation or resorted to manipulation as the Liberal's Federal Director and was offended by suggestions from journalists that he was either a conjuror or magician whose task was deception or distortion. Facts could not be altered but how they were interpreted was never fixed. Few ideas were completely right or utterly wrong but they could be shown to have advantages and disadvantages that would help or hinder those who were subject to their implementation if they became public policy.

There were moments, however, when Eggleton might have downplayed often ill-informed public opinion and urged the pursuit of principle. For instance, he consistently counselled his Liberal Party colleagues against embracing a consumption tax because it would be difficult, if not impossible in his judgement, to persuade voters that such a measure would be in the national interest and, by extension, in their interest. Was he too attentive to the electorate's mood given how fickle it could be? Sometimes. His job was, of course, to 'road test' ideas and initiatives with sample groups of voters but there were moments when he, and others, arguably attributed too much weight to the self-interested reactions of undecided voters in marginal constituencies when good public policy involved the investment, and possible loss, of political capital and parliamentary majorities. It was not until the Howard Government won office with a substantial majority in 1996 that the Coalition found the courage to commit itself to introducing the Goods and Services Tax (GST). Although the Howard Government nearly lost office at the October 1998 election, the nation was ultimately the beneficiary of the Prime Minister, the Treasurer and the Cabinet pursuing a principle.

Having informed the Liberal Party of likely public reactions to policy decisions, Eggleton left the Ministry to explain its decisions to the Coalition party room, the parliament, the press and the people. He had ideas and suggestions on timing and strategic communications but he avoided becoming the prototype 'spin doctor'. As expected, Eggleton tried to draw public attention away from the Liberal Party's internal stresses and strains at a time when division and disunity were being depicted as the precursors to parliamentary schism and organisational eclipse. The Liberal Party's demise was being openly discussed between 1985 and 1990 when, ironically, the Labor Government was dealing with its own brand of factionalism. Eggleton's objectives were countering exaggeration and promoting a sense of proportion while trying forlornly to promote a party that was preoccupied with personal disputes rather than policy development. He disliked doing deals because his conduct was bound by lines of principle that he would not cross. On several occasions he was dragged towards the limits of what he considered acceptable behaviour. He accepted the possibility of dismissal in refusing to act contrary to conscience, conviction and character.

Throughout his long career in public administration, Eggleton remained a journalist at heart. His principal concern was keeping the public informed. He believed a well-informed electorate was more likely to acknowledge difficult policies and accept tough decisions. Journalists were an important conduit between governments and citizens, and organisations and their stakeholders. He never forgot what he had read in *You Want to be a Journalist?* in 1944. Journalism was more than a job. It was a vocation requiring a particular kind of commitment. Cecil Hunt's had stressed that journalists needed to be transparently energetic, with vast reserves of energy, mental and physical, to meet the emergency rush. They are quick to assimilate details and assess their relative significance. They have a flair for arriving at a conclusion that others would reach by a logical but laboured progression. They have a knowledge of human nature much above the average. They have graduated from the University of Life.[11]

Eggleton knew he was intellectually curious and had a facility with words, spoken as well as written. He also knew a few things about human nature having encountered all kinds of people during his time with the *Swindon Evening Standard*, the *Bendigo Advertiser* and the ABC in Melbourne and Adelaide. Over the years he improved his ability to find the right words and, ultimately, the best words for each audience and every occasion. Eggleton was never a passive observer of human affairs. He explored the ability of words to capture wisdom and convey insights. He recognised the capacity of prose to communicate sublime truths that could easily be concealed by poor choice of words.

Eggleton strived to be an effective communicator of thought, word and deed, especially in times of conflict and controversy. In preparing press releases and drafting meeting communiques, he tried to discover consensus and detect agreement in the hope of finding common interests and shared goals. As politics was essentially a contest of ideas, Eggleton wanted the contest to be fair, informed and balanced. He was not wedded to a detailed ideology or committed to fixed positions other than believing in the importance of liberty to pursue the course of one's own life free from the intrusions of government. Eggleton recognised the inherent worth of opposing viewpoints and resisted gainsaying and argument merely for the sake of argument.

Assured of his self-discipline and recognising he was unlikely to be either the smartest or strongest person in the room, Eggleton nonetheless tried to be the most informed and the best prepared. His contributions to discussions and debates would be cogent and compelling because he had assessed options and weighed merits. The constant struggle for him was becoming more proficient in the tasks at hand. He might not become the best but he would strive to be better. Progress was measured looking back rather than looking ahead. Eggleton's approach to life was captured in a poem entitled 'Youth's ambition' which he typed out on a solitary sheet of paper in 1948.

> Burning fire n're distinct
> Burning all my life
> That ambition for perfection
> Fighting every strife
> Onward 'till the goal is reached
> Never looking back
> 'Till dreams become reality,
> Imagination, fact.

Many of the lessons that can be drawn from the life and times of Tony Eggleton are self-evident in the preceding chapters. One is less obvious. In addition to commending initiative and industry, discipline and discretion, in all walks of life, he demonstrated the importance of self-knowledge when making vocational choices and self-awareness when negotiating career challenges. From the age of 12, Eggleton became increasingly conscious of his aptitudes and abilities which he considered alongside his interests and ambitions. From the age of 16 he started to take notice of his strengths and weakness, and where he could exploit the first and eradicate the latter. Identifying the most productive challenges were crucial to personal advancement and professional development. He wanted to learn and be extended but in a gradual way that did not leave him dispirited. Discerning the suitable job was more important than finding the perfect job which, in any event, did not exist. Eggleton also placed a premium on work that was worth doing for its own sake. He took this approach to every position he considered after joining the ABC in 1951.

His character rested on his convictions and was expressed in his conduct. His identity would determine his destiny. At a time when the incivility of parliamentary processes and the vacuity of election campaigning has alienated many voters from political parties and political debate, the nation's leaders might look to the example of Tony Eggleton and ponder the lasting legacies of his contribution to Australian life. They begin and end in character.

Endnotes

1   Norman Abjorensen, *John Hewson: A Biography*, Lothian, Melbourne, 1993, p. 150.

2   Helen Trinca, 'Former federal party director laments disloyalty', *Weekend Australian*, 8–9 October 1994, p. 8.

3   https://www.smh.com.au/opinion/it-is-possible-to-win-an-election-with-only-three-words--maybe-four-20160505-gona8k.html

4   Email to the author dated 21 October 2020.

5   Rob Chalmers, *Inside the Canberra Press Gallery*, ANU Press, Canberra, 2011, pp. 126–131.

6   Walsh Report, 'Retiring Federal Director of the Liberal Party discusses the election campaign', ABC Television, 8 April 1990.

7   Personal letter from Southey to Eggleton dated 18 May 1982.

8   Ramsey, *The Way We Were*, p. 314.

9   Warren Beeby, 'PM's master stroke pays off', *Australian*, 9 June 1977, pp. 1–2.

10 Michelle Grattan and Russell Barton, 'Backroom manoeuvres', *Age*, 26 February 1983.

11 Cecil Hunt, *You Want to be a Journalist?*, Michael Joseph, London, 1938, p. 22.

Acknowledgements

The publication of every book leaves the author with a considerable debt of thanks to those who have provided information, contributed insights or read drafts. My principal debt is to Tony Eggleton for his encouragement, generosity and patience. There was considerable risk allowing me to see personal papers that had not been sifted to remove damaging material or sorted to guarantee a favourable perspective. Without Tony's goodwill and active participation I would not have commenced this book and would certainly not have finished it. I am also grateful to his children for clarifying aspects of Eggleton family affairs. In my explorations of Tony's working life I was helped by distinguished former public servants Dale Budd, Malcolm Hazel and Philip Flood; former Liberal Federal parliamentarians John Howard, Philip Ruddock and Nick Minchin; former New South Wales Education Minister and Deputy Chair of the National Council for the Centenary of Federation, Rodney Cavalier; Tony's CARE colleagues Robert Glasser and Robert Yallop; former Deputy Chief of the Naval Staff, Rear Admiral David Campbell; former Private Secretary to the Queen, Sir William Heseltine; Professor William Maley of the Australian National University (whose late father, Ray, was Tony's predecessor as press secretary to Prime Minister Menzies). As ever, my UNSW Canberra colleagues at the John Howard Prime Ministerial Library, Professor David Lovell, Andrew Blyth, Annette Carter and Trish Burgess (who read the manuscript and alerted me to errors and inconsistences), were supportive and forbearing.